Austin Maxi Owners Workshop Manual

Alec J Jones

BSc Eng, C Eng

Models covered

Austin Maxi 1500, 1750, 1750 HL, 1750 HLS, 1.7L,
1.7 HL and 1.7 HLS

ISBN 0 85696 892 7

ABCDE
FGHIJ
K

Printed in England   *(052-6H1)*

HAYNES PUBLISHING GROUP
SPARKFORD YEOVIL SOMERSET BA22 7JJ ENGLAND
distributed in the USA by
HAYNES PUBLICATIONS INC
861 LAWRENCE DRIVE
NEWBURY PARK
CALIFORNIA 91320
USA

Acknowledgements

Thanks are due to BL Cars Limited for the assistance with technical information, to Castrol Limited for lubrication details and to the Champion Sparking Plug Company who supplied the illustrations showing the various spark plug conditions. The bodywork repair photographs used in this manual were supplied by Holt Lloyd Ltd who supply 'Turtle Wax', 'Dupli-color Holts', and other Holts range products. The Section in Chapter 10 dealing with the suppression of electrical interference was originated by Mr I. P. Davey and was first published in *Motor* magazine.

Thanks are also due to Gearchange Limited of Burtle, Nr Bridgwater, Somerset for the loan of a cable operated gearbox which was used in this manual.

Lastly special thanks are due to all those people at Sparkford and Yeovil who helped in the production of this manual. Particularly Brian Horsfall who carried out the mechanical work, Stanley Randolph who planned the layout of each page and David Neilson who edited the text.

About this manual

Its aim

The aim of this manual is to help you get the best value from your car. It can do so in several ways. It can help you decide what work must be done (even should you choose to get it done by a garage), provide information on routine maintenance and servicing, and give a logical course of action and diagnose when random faults occur. However, it is hoped that you will use the manual by tackling the work yourself. On simpler jobs it may even be quicker than booking the car into a garage, and going there twice to leave and collect it. Perhaps most important, a lot of money can be saved by avoiding the costs the garage must charge to cover its labour and overheads.

The manual has drawings and descriptions to show the function of the various components so that their layout can be understood. Then the tasks are described and photographed in a step-by-step sequence so that even a novice can do the work.

Its arrangement

The manual is divided into thirteen Chapters each covering a logical sub-division of the vehicle. The Chapter are each divided into Sections, numbered with single figures, eg 5; and the Sections into paragraphs (or sub-sections), with decimal numbers following on from the Section they are in, eg 5.1, 5.2, 5.3 etc.

It is freely illustrated, especially in those parts where there is a detailed sequence of operations to be carried out. There are two forms of illustration; figures and photographs. The figures are numbered in sequence with decimal numbers, according to their position in the Chapter; eg Fig. 6.4 is the 4th drawing illustration in Chapter 6. Photographs are numbered (either individually or in related groups) the same as the Section or sub-section of the text where the operation they show is described.

There is an alphabetical index at the back of the manual as well as a contents list at the front.

References to the 'left' or 'right' of the vehicles are in the sense of a person in the driver's seat facing forwards.

Unless otherwise stated, nuts and bolts are removed by turning anti-clockwise, and tightening by turning clockwise.

Whilst every care is taken to ensure that the information in the manual is correct, no liability can be accepted by the authors or publishers for loss, damage or injury caused by any errors in, or omissions from, the information given.

Introduction to the Austin Maxi

The Maxi was first introduced in April 1969 with a 1500 cc engine of new design integral with the transmission.

In October 1970 a 1750 cc version became available and the gear selector mechanism, which on the original models was cable operated, was changed to rod change.

In October 1972 the 1750 HL and Automatic models became available, the HL having an uprated engine delivering 95 bhp compared with the 84 bhp of earlier 1750 models, the improvement being the result of fitting twin carburettors. The 1750 HL has an improved standard of finish and distinctive trim.

The 1750 HLS was introduced in April 1979 and was similar to the previous HL having twin carburettors. However the new HL introduced at the same time was fitted with a single carburettor.

In August 1980 the Series 2 models were introduced. Improvements on these models were largely confined to trim changes, although a new type of lighting switch and additional warning lights (for handbrake and choke) were also included.

The Maxi range ceased production in July 1981.

Contents

The Austin Maxi HL

The Austin Maxi 1750

General dimensions, weights and capacities

General dimensions

Wheelbase:
Up to 1980 .... 104 in (2.642 m)
1980 on (Series 2) .... 104.1 in (2.644 m)
Track (unladen):
Front .... 53.8 in (1.367 m)
Rear (up to 1980) .... 53.2 in (1.351 m)
Rear (1980 on – Series 2) .... 53.8 in (1.367 m)
Turning circle (between kerbs) .... 33 ft 9 in (10.3 m)
Overall length:
Up to 1980 .... 158.4 in (4.02 m)
1980 on (Series 2) .... 159.8 in (4.06 m)
Overall width .... 64.1 in (1.629 m)
Overall height (unladen) .... 55.3 in (1.40 m)
Ground clearance (static laden) .... 5.5 in (139 mm)

Weights

	Manual transmission	Automatic transmission
Kerb weight (with full fuel tank):		
1500 and 1750 models (up to 1980)	2204 lb (1000 kg)	2213 lb (1004 kg)
HL and HLS models (up to 1980)	2216 lb (1005 kg)	2225 lb (1009 kg)
1.7 L models (1980 on)	2171 lb (985 kg)	2180 lb (989 kg)
1.7 HL and HLS models (1980 on)	2182 lb (990 kg)	2191 lb (994 kg)
Maximum towing weight (1 in 8 gradient)	1904 lb (864 kg)	
Maximum vehicle loading (5 people plus luggage)	875 lb (397 kg)	

Capacities

Fuel tank:
Early models .... 9 Imp gal (41 litres)
Later models .... 10.5 Imp gal (48 litres)
Cooling system (with heater) .... 9 Imp pints (5.1 litres)
Engine oil:
Manual gearbox models, including filter .... 9 Imp pints (5.1 litres)
Automatic transmission models, drain and refill, without filter:
Dipstick marked 'COLD-HOT' .... 13 Imp pints (7.4 litres)
Dipstick marked 'HIGH-LOW' .... 10 Imp pints (5.7 litres)
For filter add .... 1 Imp pint (0.6 litre)
For torque converter add .... 3 Imp pints (1.7 litres)

Buying spare parts
and vehicle identification numbers

Buying spare parts

Spare parts are available from many sources, for example: Leyland garages, other garages and accessory shops, and motor factors. Our advice regarding spare parts is as follows:

Officially appointed Leyland garages – This is the best source of parts which are peculiar to your car and otherwise not generally available (eg complete cylinder heads, internal gearbox components, badges, interior trim etc). It is also the only place at which you should buy parts if your car is still under warranty; non-Leyland components may invalidate the warranty. To be sure of obtaining the correct parts it will always be necessary to give the storeman your car's engine and chassis number, and if possible to take the old part along for positive identification. Remember that many parts are available on a factory exchange scheme – any parts returned should always be clean! It obviously makes good sense to go straight to the specialists on your car for this type of part for they are best equipped to supply you.

Other garages and accessory shops – These are often very good places to buy material and components needed for the maintenance of your car (eg oil filters, spark plugs, bulbs, fan belts, oils and grease, touch-up paint, filler paste etc). They also sell general accessories, usually have convenient opening hours, charge lower prices and can often be found not far from home.

Motor factors – Good factors will stock all of the more important components, (eg. pistons, valves, exhaust systems, brake cylinder-pipes/hoses/seals/shoes and pads etc). Motor factors will often provide new or reconditioned components on a part exchange basis – this can save a considerable amount of money.

Vehicle identification numbers

Modifications are a continuing and unpublished process in vehicle manufacture quite apart from major model changes. Spare parts manuals and lists are compiled upon a numerical basis, the individual vehicle numbers being essential to correct identification of the component required.

Commission number: Located on a plate mounted on the right-hand side of the bonnet lock platform.

Car number: Located on a plate mounted on the right-hand wing valance.

Engine number: Stamped on the cylinder block or on a metal plate secured to the cylinder block between the ignition coil and distributor.

Body number: Stamped on a plate fixed to the left-hand side of the bonnet lock platform.

Tools and working facilities

Introduction

A selection of good tools is a fundamental requirement for anyone contemplating the maintenance and repair of a motor vehicle. For the owner who does not possess any, their purchase will prove a considerable expense, offsetting some of the savings made by doing-it-yourself. However, provided that the tools purchased are of good quality, they will last for many years and prove an extremely worthwhile investment.

To help the average owner to decide which tools are needed to carry out the various tasks detailed in this manual, we have compiled three lists of tools under the following headings: *Maintenance and minor repair*, *Repair and overhaul*, and *Special*. The newcomer .to practical mechanics should start off with the *Maintenance and minor repair* tool kit and confine himself to the simpler jobs around the vehicle. Then, as his confidence and experience grows, he can undertake more difficult tasks, buying extra tools as, and when, they are needed. In this way, a *Maintenance and minor repair* tool kit can be built-up into a *Repair and overhaul* tool kit over a considerable period of time without any major cash outlays. The experienced do-it-yourselfer will have a tool kit good enough for most repair and overhaul procedures and will add tools from the *Special* category when he feels the expense is justified by the amount of use to which these tools will be put.

It is obviously not possible to cover the subject of tools fully here. For those who wish to learn more about tools and their use there is a book entitled *How to Choose and Use Car Tools* available from the publishers of this manual.

Maintenance and minor repair tool kit

The tools given in this list should be considered as a minimum requirement if routine maintenance, servicing and minor repair operations are to be undertaken. We recommend the purchase of combination spanners (ring one end, open-ended the other); although more expensive than open-ended ones, they do give the advantages of both types of spanner.

Combination spanners - $\frac{7}{16}$, $\frac{1}{2}$, $\frac{9}{16}$, $\frac{5}{8}$, $\frac{3}{4}$, $\frac{13}{16}$, $\frac{7}{8}$ and $\frac{15}{16}$ in AF
Adjustable spanner – 9 inch
Spark plug spanner (with rubber insert)
Spark plug gap adjustment tool
Set of feeler gauges
Brake adjuster spanner (where applicable)
Brake bleed nipple spanner
Screwdriver - 4 in long x $\frac{1}{4}$ in dia (flat blade)
Screwdriver - 4 in long x $\frac{1}{4}$ in dia (cross blade)
Combination pliers - 6 inch
Hacksaw, junior
Tyre pump
Tyre pressure gauge
Grease gun (where applicable)
Oil can
Fine emery cloth (1 sheet)
Wire brush (small)
Funnel (medium size)

Repair and overhaul tool kit

These tools are virtually essential for anyone undertaking any major repairs to a motor vehicle, and are additional to those given in the *Maintenance and minor repair* list. Included in this list is a comprehensive set of sockets. Although these are expensive they will be found invaluable as they are so versatile - particularly if various drives are included in the set. We recommend the $\frac{1}{2}$ in square-drive type, as this can be used with most proprietary torque wrenches. If you cannot afford a socket set, even bought piecemeal, then inexpensive tubular box spanners are a useful alternative.

The tools in this list will occasionally need to be supplemented by tools from the *Special* list.

Sockets (or box spanners) to cover range in previous list
Reversible ratchet drive (for use with sockets)
Extension piece, 10 inch (for use with sockets)
Universal joint (for use with sockets)
Torque wrench (for use with sockets)
'Mole' wrench - 8 inch
Ball pein hammer
Soft-faced hammer, plastic or rubber
Screwdriver - 6 in long x $\frac{5}{16}$ in dia (flat blade)
Screwdriver - 2 in long x $\frac{5}{16}$ in square (flat blade)
Screwdriver - $1\frac{1}{2}$ in long x $\frac{1}{4}$ in dia (cross blade)
Screwdriver - 3 in long x $\frac{1}{8}$ in dia (electricians)
Pliers - electricians side cutters
Pliers - needle nosed
Pliers - circlip (internal and external)
Cold chisel - $\frac{1}{2}$ inch
Scriber (this can be made by grinding the end of a broken hacksaw blade)
Scraper (this can be made by flattening and sharpening one end of a piece of copper pipe)
Centre punch
Pin punch
Hacksaw
Valve grinding tool
Steel rule/straight edge
Allen keys
Selection of files
Wire brush (large)
Axle-stands
Jack (strong scissor or hydraulic type)

Special tools

The tools in this list are those which are not used regularly, are expensive to buy, or which need to be used in accordance with their manufacturers' instructions. Unless relatively difficult mechanical jobs are undertaken frequently, it will not be economic to buy many of these tools. Where this is the case, you could consider clubbing together with friends (or a motorists' club) to make a joint purchase, or borrowing the tools against a deposit from a local garage or tool hire specialist.

The following list contains only those tools and instruments freely available to the public, and not those special tools produced by the vehicle manufacturer specifically for its dealer network. You will find occasional references to these manufacturers' special tools in the text of this manual. Generally, an alternative method of doing the job without the vehicle manufacturer's special tool is given. However, sometimes, there is no alternative to using them. Where this is the case and the relevant tool cannot be bought or borrowed you will have to entrust the work to a franchised garage.

Valve spring compressor
Piston ring compressor
Balljoint separator
Universal hub/bearing puller
Impact screwdriver
Micrometer and/or vernier gauge
Dial gauge
Stroboscopic timing light
Dwell angle meter/tachometer
Universal electrical multi-meter
Cylinder compression gauge
Lifting tackle (photo)
Trolley jack
Light with extension lead

Buying tools

For practically all tools, a tool factor is the best source since he will have a very comprehensive range compared with the average garage or accessory shop. Having said that, accessory shops often offer excellent quality tools at discount prices, so it pays to shop around.

Remember, you don't have to buy the most expensive items on the shelf, but it is always advisable to steer clear of the very cheap tools. There are plenty of good tools around at reasonable prices, so ask the proprietor or manager of the shop for advice before making a purchase.

Care and maintenance of tools

Having purchased a reasonable tool kit, it is necessary to keep the tools in a clean serviceable condition. After use, always wipe off any dirt, grease and metal particles using a clean, dry cloth, before putting the tools away. Never leave them lying around after they have been used. A simple tool rack on the garage or workshop wall, for items such as screwdrivers and pliers is a good idea. Store all normal spanners and sockets in a metal box. Any measuring instruments, gauges, meters, etc, must be carefully stored where they cannot be damaged or become rusty.

Take a little care when tools are used. Hammer heads inevitably become marked and screwdrivers lose the keen edge on their blades from time to time. A little timely attention with emery cloth or a file will soon restore items like this to a good serviceable finish.

Working facilities

Not to be forgotten when discussing tools, is the workshop itself. If anything more than routine maintenance is to be carried out, some form of suitable working area becomes essential.

It is appreciated that many an owner mechanic is forced by circumstances to remove an engine or similar item, without the benefit of a garage or workshop. Having done this, any repairs should always be done under the cover of a roof.

Wherever possible, any dismantling should be done on a clean flat workbench or table at a suitable working height.

Any workbench needs a vice: one with a jaw opening of 4 in (100 mm) is suitable for most jobs. As mentioned previously, some clean dry storage space is also required for tools, as well as the lubricants, cleaning fluids, touch-up paints and so on which become necessary.

Another item which may be required, and which has a much more general usage, is an electric drill with a chuck capacity of at least $\frac{5}{16}$ in (8 mm). This, together with a good range of twist drills, is virtually essential for fitting accessories such as wing mirrors and reversing lights.

Last, but not least, always keep a supply of old newspapers and clean, lint-free rags available, and try to keep any working area as clean as possible.

Spanner jaw gap comparison table

Jaw gap (in)	Spanner size
0·250	$\frac{1}{4}$ in AF
0·276	7 mm
0·313	$\frac{5}{16}$ in AF
0·315	8 mm
0·344	$\frac{11}{32}$ in AF; $\frac{1}{8}$ in Whitworth
0·354	9 mm
0·375	$\frac{3}{8}$ in AF
0·394	10 mm
0·433	11 mm
0·438	$\frac{7}{16}$ in AF
0·445	$\frac{3}{16}$ in Whitworth; $\frac{1}{4}$ in BSF
0·472	12 mm
0·500	$\frac{1}{2}$ in AF
0·512	13 mm
0·525	$\frac{1}{4}$ in Whitworth; $\frac{5}{16}$ in BSF
0·551	14 mm
0·563	$\frac{9}{16}$ in AF
0·591	15 mm
0·600	$\frac{5}{16}$ in Whitworth; $\frac{3}{8}$ in BSF
0·625	$\frac{5}{8}$ in AF
0·630	16 mm
0·669	17 mm
0·686	$\frac{11}{16}$ in AF
0·709	18 mm
0·710	$\frac{3}{8}$ in Whitworth; $\frac{7}{16}$ in BSF
0·748	19 mm
0·750	$\frac{3}{4}$ in AF
0·813	$\frac{13}{16}$ in AF
0·820	$\frac{7}{16}$ in Whitworth; $\frac{1}{2}$ in BSF
0·866	22 mm
0·875	$\frac{7}{8}$ in AF
0·920	$\frac{1}{2}$ in Whitworth; $\frac{9}{16}$ in BSF
0·938	$\frac{15}{16}$ in AF
0·945	24 mm
1·000	1 in AF
1·010	$\frac{9}{16}$ in Whitworth; $\frac{5}{8}$ in BSF
1·024	26 mm
1·063	$1\frac{1}{16}$ in AF; 27 mm
1·100	$\frac{5}{8}$ in Whitworth; $\frac{11}{16}$ in BSF
1·125	$1\frac{1}{8}$ in AF
1·181	30 mm
1·200	$\frac{11}{16}$ in Whitworth; $\frac{3}{4}$ in BSF
1·250	$1\frac{1}{4}$ in AF
1·260	32 mm
1·300	$\frac{3}{4}$ in Whitworth; $\frac{7}{8}$ in BSF
1·313	$1\frac{5}{16}$ in AF
1·390	$\frac{13}{16}$ in Whitworth; $\frac{15}{16}$ in BSF
1·417	36 mm
1·438	$1\frac{7}{16}$ in AF
1·480	$\frac{7}{8}$ in Whitworth; 1 in BSF
1·500	$1\frac{1}{2}$ in AF
1·575	40 mm; $\frac{15}{16}$ in Whitworth
1·614	41 mm
1·625	$1\frac{5}{8}$ in AF
1·670	1 in Whitworth; $1\frac{1}{8}$ in BSF
1·688	$1\frac{11}{16}$ in AF
1·811	46 mm
1·813	$1\frac{13}{16}$ in AF
1·860	$1\frac{1}{8}$ in Whitworth; $1\frac{1}{4}$ in BSF
1·875	$1\frac{7}{8}$ in AF
1·969	50 mm
2·000	2 in AF
2·050	$1\frac{1}{4}$ in Whitworth; $1\frac{3}{8}$ in BSF
2·165	55 mm
2·362	60 mm

A Haltrac hoist and gantry in use during a typical engine removal procedure

Jacking and towing

For normal wheel changing, the jack supplied with the car is adequate. There are two jacking points on each side of the car, one at each end of the sill panel. When using this method of jacking, always chock one of the wheels remaining on the ground and apply the car handbrake as an additional precaution.

When working beneath the car, never rely solely on the jack, regardless of the type of jack used, but always use axle-stands or blocks for additional support.

If the car is being towed ensure that if the front wheels are on the road the steering lock/ignition switch is in the 'I' position (Garage position on early cars). If the car is fitted with automatic transmission it should not be towed for long distances or at speeds above 30 mph (48 km ph) with the front wheels on the ground.

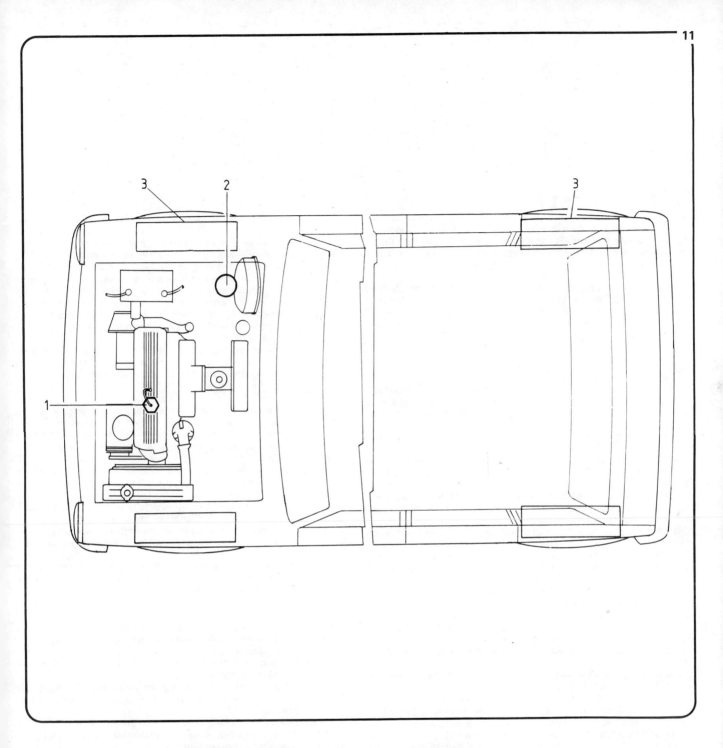

Recommended lubricants and fluids

Component or system	Lubricant type or specification	Castrol product
Engine/transmission (1)	Engine oil (SAE 20W/50)	**Castrol GTX**
Clutch and brake fluid (2)	Hydraulic fluid (SAE J1703)	**Castrol Girling Universal Brake and Clutch Fluid**
Front and rear wheel bearings (3)	Multi-purpose grease (NGL1 No 2)	**Castrol LM grease**
Steering rack	Hypoid gear oil (SAE 90EP)	**Castrol Hypoy**

Note: *The above are general recommendations only. Lubrication requirements vary from territory to territory. If in doubt, consult your nearest dealer or the operator's handbook supplied with the vehicle.*

Safety first!

Professional motor mechanics are trained in safe working procedures. However enthusiastic you may be about getting on with the job in hand, do take the time to ensure that your safety is not put at risk. A moment's lack of attention can result in an accident, as can failure to observe certain elementary precautions.

There will always be new ways of having accidents, and the following points do not pretend to be a comprehensive list of all dangers; they are intended rather to make you aware of the risks and to encourage a safety-conscious approach to all work you carry out on your vehicle.

Essential DOs and DON'Ts

DON'T rely on a single jack when working underneath the vehicle. Always use reliable additional means of support, such as axle stands, securely placed under a part of the vehicle that you know will not give way.

DON'T attempt to loosen or tighten high-torque nuts (e.g. wheel hub nuts) while the vehicle is on a jack; it may be pulled off.

DON'T start the engine without first ascertaining that the transmission is in neutral (or 'Park' where applicable) and the parking brake applied.

DON'T suddenly remove the filler cap from a hot cooling system — cover it with a cloth and release the pressure gradually first, or you may get scalded by escaping coolant.

DON'T attempt to drain oil until you are sure it has cooled sufficiently to avoid scalding you.

DON'T grasp any part of the engine, exhaust or catalytic converter without first ascertaining that it is sufficiently cool to avoid burning you.

DON'T syphon toxic liquids such as fuel, brake fluid or antifreeze by mouth, or allow them to remain on your skin.

DON'T inhale brake lining dust — it is injurious to health.

DON'T allow any spilt oil or grease to remain on the floor — wipe it up straight away, before someone slips on it.

DON'T use ill-fitting spanners or other tools which may slip and cause injury.

DON'T attempt to lift a heavy component which may be beyond your capability — get assistance.

DON'T rush to finish a job, or take unverified short cuts.

DON'T allow children or animals in or around an unattended vehicle.

DO wear eye protection when using power tools such as drill, sander, bench grinder etc, and when working under the vehicle.

DO use a barrier cream on your hands prior to undertaking dirty jobs — it will protect your skin from infection as well as making the dirt easier to remove afterwards; but make sure your hands aren't left slippery.

DO keep loose clothing (cuffs, tie etc) and long hair well out of the way of moving mechanical parts.

DO remove rings, wristwatch etc, before working on the vehicle — especially the electrical system.

DO ensure that any lifting tackle used has a safe working load rating adequate for the job.

DO keep your work area tidy — it is only too easy to fall over articles left lying around.

DO get someone to check periodically that all is well, when working alone on the vehicle.

DO carry out work in a logical sequence and check that everything is correctly assembled and tightened afterwards.

DO remember that your vehicle's safety affects that of yourself and others. If in doubt on any point, get specialist advice.

IF, in spite of following these precautions, you are unfortunate enough to injure yourself, seek medical attention as soon as possible.

Fire

Remember at all times that petrol (gasoline) is highly flammable. Never smoke, or have any kind of naked flame around, when working on the vehicle. But the risk does not end there — a spark caused by an electrical short-circuit, by two metal surfaces contacting each other, or even by static electricity built up in your body under certain conditions, can ignite petrol vapour, which in a confined space is highly explosive.

Always disconnect the battery earth (ground) terminal before working on any part of the fuel system, and never risk spilling fuel on to a hot engine or exhaust.

It is recommended that a fire extinguisher of a type suitable for fuel and electrical fires is kept handy in the garage or workplace at all times. Never try to extinguish a fuel or electrical fire with water.

Fumes

Certain fumes are highly toxic and can quickly cause unconsciousness and even death if inhaled to any extent. Petrol (gasoline) vapour comes into this category, as do the vapours from certain solvents such as trichloroethylene. Any draining or pouring of such volatile fluids should be done in a well ventilated area.

When using cleaning fluids and solvents, read the instructions carefully. Never use materials from unmarked containers — they may give off poisonous vapours.

Never run the engine of a motor vehicle in an enclosed space such as a garage. Exhaust fumes contain carbon monoxide which is extremely poisonous; if you need to run the engine, always do so in the open air or at least have the rear of the vehicle outside the workplace.

If you are fortunate enough to have the use of an inspection pit, never drain or pour petrol, and never run the engine, while the vehicle is standing over it; the fumes, being heavier than air, will concentrate in the pit with possibly lethal results.

The battery

Never cause a spark, or allow a naked light, near the vehicle's battery. It will normally be giving off a certain amount of hydrogen gas, which is highly explosive.

Always disconnect the battery earth (ground) terminal before working on the fuel or electrical systems.

If possible, loosen the filler plugs or cover when charging the battery from an external source. Do not charge at an excessive rate or the battery may burst.

Take care when topping up and when carrying the battery. The acid electrolyte, even when diluted, is very corrosive and should not be allowed to contact the eyes or skin.

If you ever need to prepare electrolyte yourself, always add the acid slowly to the water, and never the other way round. Protect against splashes by wearing rubber gloves and goggles.

Mains electricity

When using an electric power tool, inspection light etc which works from the mains, always ensure that the appliance is correctly connected to its plug and that, where necessary, it is properly earthed (grounded). Do not use such appliances in damp conditions and, again, beware of creating a spark or applying excessive heat in the vicinity of fuel or fuel vapour.

Ignition HT voltage

A severe electric shock can result from touching certain parts of the ignition system, such as the HT leads, when the engine is running or being cranked, particularly if components are damp or the insulation is defective. Where an electronic ignition system is fitted, the HT voltage is much higher and could prove fatal.

Routine maintenance

Routine maintenance is essential for safety and desirable for ensuring reliability and obtaining the best performance and economy from the vehicle. In many instances the largest element of maintenance is visual examination and a general sense of awareness of whether the vehicle is performing satisfactorily.

The maintenance summary is basically the same as that recommended by the vehicle manufacturer, but in certain instances has been altered when additional checks are thought to be advisable or when a timely renewal is likely to prevent a roadside breakdown.

reservoirs (photo). Top-up if necessary, using fluid of the correct specification. If the level has fallen drastically, or frequent topping up is required, investigate the loss of fluid urgently.
Examine the tyres for tread depth and look for damage such as cuts, bulges and exposed ply or cord structure.
Check the tightness of the wheel nuts.
Check the functioning of all lights, warning indicators, screen washer, windscreen wiper, direction indicators, and heated rear window (when fitted).

Weekly, and before a long journey

With the car standing on level ground, check the oil level. Top-up if necessary. Do not overfill, but always maintain the level at, or near the full mark.
Check the level of the battery electrolyte and top-up if necessary with distilled water (photo).
Top-up the windscreen washer reservoir with clean water. If necessary a proprietary brand of cleaning fluid may be added to prevent smearing, but the addition to the washer reservoir of household detergents is not recommended (photo).
When the tyres are cold (ie before a run) check their pressures, not forgetting the spare. The correct pressures are given in Chapter 11.
When the engine is cool, check the level of coolant. Top-up if necessary and if the system is filled with antifreeze, use the same strength antifreeze mixture for topping up.
Check the level of the fluid in the clutch and brake master cylinder

---

Every 3000 miles (5000 km) or three months

Check the condition of the fan belt and renew if frayed, or at the limit of its adjustment. The procedure for adjusting and renewing the belt is given in Chapter 2. In the interests of reliability the fan belt should be renewed after two years, regardless of its condition.
Check for any leakage of oil, fuel and hydraulic fluid. Remove the brake drums and also check around the calipers for any signs of brake fluid leakage. If any is present, refer to Chapter 9 for information about renewing the rubber seals.
Inspect all rigid and flexible pipes in the hydraulic and fuel systems for corrosion, chafing and general deterioration. Renew parts as necessary.
Check the condition of the radiator and heater hoses for signs of looseness of the hose clips and damage or deterioration of the hoses. Fit a new hose if any is suspect.
Check the condition of the gaiters on the steering rack, the drive shaft couplings and the suspension balljoints for deterioration.

Topping up the battery

Windscreen washer reservoir

Brake and clutch master cylinder reservoirs

Also check the joints for wear, making reference to Chapters 7 and 11 if necessary.

Check the exhaust system for security of fixing and any signs of joint leakage or blow holes in the silencer and pipes.

Check the brake discs for scoring and the pads for wear. Renew pads which have worn down to $\frac{1}{16}$ in (1.6 mm) or which are likely to have worn to this thickness before the next 3000 mile check.

Arrange for a headlamp alignment check to be carried out. Although the beams can be readily adjusted (see Chapter 10) the only accurate method is to use the proper optical alignment equipment.

Check the condition of the wiper blades and renew them if they do not give a satisfactory wiping action over the whole range of travel.

Check that there is no undue free travel on the brake pedal and handbrake lever. If any is found, check the adjustment of the rear brake shoes.

Check the condition of the seat belts and the security of the attachment points. If any fraying of the webbing is found, the belts should be renewed. If any corrosion around the attachment points is evident, seek the advice of a Leyland dealer without delay.

Check the condition of the interior and exterior rear view mirrors for adjustment, security of attachment and damage to the glass.

Road test the car to check for general preformance, satisfactory operation of the brakes and for general rattles and knocks.

Every 6000 miles (10 000 km) or 6 months

Drain the engine oil. Remove the oil filter and fit a new cartridge (photo), or element. Fill the engine with the recommended grade of oil.

Wipe the top of the carburettor dashpot(s) and unscrew the damper (photo). Check the level of the oil using the damper as a dipstick. The level should be $\frac{1}{2}$ in (12 mm) above the top of the hollow piston rod. Top-up if necessary with engine oil. Neglect of keeping the dashpot topped up will result in poor starting and lack of acceleration.

Remove the spark plugs and examine them to give information on engine condition and performance (see Chapter 4). Preferably have the plugs cleaned by a garage having a special cleaning machine, otherwise clean them with a wire brush. Check the gap and adjust if necessary before screwing them in again. Do not exceed the specified tightening torque.

Check the distributor points gap and the conditions of the points. Lubricate the distributor cam, spindle and weights.

Check the ignition timing and the operation of the automatic advance mechanism. This cannot be done satisfactorily without a stroboscopic timing light.

On models which have an adjustable clutch, check the clutch return stop clearance.

On models with automatic transmission check the operation of the parking pawl. With the car on level ground, move the selector to the "P" position and release the handbrake. Rock the car backwards and forwards to check that the transmission is locked. If the pawl does not hold, refer to Chapter 6.

On models with Hydrolastic suspension, check the suspension system for fluid leaks and check the suspension height (Chapter 11).

Examine the front tyres for signs of excessive, or uneven wear. If tyre wear is unsatisfactory, the front wheel alignment should be checked and this is a job which is best left to a garage.

Lubricate the handbrake mechanical linkages, the dynamo bearing (if the vehicle has a dynamo and not an alternator) and all locks and hinges except the steering lock.

Clean the battery connections and smear them with petroleum jelly.

Every 12 000 miles (20 000 km) or 12 months

Remove the air cleaner element and discard it. Fit a new element and check that the intake position is set for summer, or winter, as appropriate. A dirty air filter causes loss of performance and an increase in fuel consumption. It is a false economy not to renew it regularly.

Renew the element in the engine breather filter which is located on the flywheel housing. Remove the cover retaining screw (if fitted). Lift off the cover and filter and unscrew the adaptor, discarding all three items. Screw in a new adaptor and fit a new filter and cover.

Fit a new set of spark plugs, but ensure that the gap is set correctly before fitting them.

Fit a new contact breaker assembly. For the small additional cost involved it is also worth fitting a new condenser.

Every 24 000 miles (40 000 km) or 2 years

Discard the fan belt and fit a new one.

Drain out the antifreeze and discard it. Flush the cooling system thoroughly, fit new radiator and heater hoses and re-fill with fresh antifreeze mixture.

Every 36 000 miles (60 000 km) or 3 years

Renew all the rubber seals and flexible pipes in the brake and clutch hydraulic systems and fill the systems with fresh fluid

Fit a new brake servo filter (see Chapter 9)

Cartridge oil filter

Carburettor dashpot damper

Chapter 1 Engine

For modifications, and information applicable to later models, see Supplement at end of manual

Contents

Specifications

Engine – general

Designation	
1500	14H
1750	17H
Bore	3.0 in (76.2 mm)
Stroke	
1500	3.2 in (81.28 mm)
1750	3.77 in (95.75 mm)
Capacity	
1500	1485 cc (90.61 cu in)
1750	1748 cc (106.69 cu in)
Compression ratio	
1500 lc	8.0:1
1500 hc	9.0:1
1750	8.75:1
1750 twin carburettors	9.5:1
Firing order	1 3 4 2 (No 1 at timing chain end)
Idling speed	
1500 up to 1971	700 rpm
1500 1971 on	750 rpm
1750 single carburettor	650 rpm
1750 twin carburettors	750 rpm

Camshaft

Inlet valve:
- Opens .... 9° 4' BTDC*
- Closes .... 50° 56' ABDC*

Exhaust valve:
- Opens .... 48° 56' ABDC*
- Closes .... 11° 4' ATDC*

End thrust .... Taken on front and locating plate
Endfloat .... 0.002 to 0.007 in (0.05 to 0.17 mm)
- Bearings 3

Journal diameter:
- Front .... 1.9355 to 1.9356 inch (49.185 to 49.197 mm)
- Centre .... 1.9668 to 1.9678 inch (49.975 to 49.987 mm)
- Rear .... 1.998 to 1.999 inch (50.762 to 50.775 mm)

At 0.021 in (0.53 mm) valve clearances. 0.018 in (0.46 mm) on 1750 Twin carburettor models ;

Crankshaft

Main journal diameter .... 2.2515 to 2.2520 in (57.19 to 57.20 mm)
Crankpin journal diameter .... 1.8759 to 1.8764 in (47.62 to 47.64 mm)
Crankshaft endfloat .... 0.004 to 0.007 in (0.10 to 0.18 mm)
Diametrical clearance:
- No 4 main bearing .... 0.002 to 0.004 in (0.05 to 0.10 mm)
- All main bearings except No 4 .... 0.001 to 0.0035 in (0.03 to 0.08 mm)

Connecting rods

Length between centres .... 5.828 to 5.832 in (148.02 to 148.12 mm)
Endfloat on crankpin (nominal) .... 0.006 to 0.01 in (0.15 to 0.25 mm)
Small-end diameter .... 0.811 to 0.8115 in (20.59 to 20.61 mm)
Big-end bearing material .... Steel backed, reticular tin

Gudgeon pin

Type .... Press fit in small-end
Outside diameter .... 0.8123 to 0.8125 in (20.6 to 20.65 mm)

Pistons

Type .... Aluminium (slotted) solid skirt
Oversize .... 0.020 in (0.51 mm)
Clearance in cylinder:
- Top (below oil control groove) .... 0.0018 to 0.0024 in (0.045 to 0.061 mm)
- Bottom .... 0.001 to 0.0016 in (0.025 to 0.039 mm)
Width of ring grooves:
- Top .... 0.064 to 0.065 in (1.64 to 1.66 mm)
- Second .... 0.064 to 0.065 in (1.64 to 1.66 mm)
- Third (1500 models) .... 0.064 to 0.065 in (1.64 to 1.66 mm)
- Oil control .... 0.1565 to 0.1575 in (4.962 to 4.987 mm)

Piston rings

Compression rings
- Top .... Plain chrome
- Second .... Tapered
- Third (1500 only) .... Tapered
- Width .... 0.0615 to 0.0625 in (1.56 to 1.59 mm)
- Fitted gap .... 0.012 to 0.022 in (0.305 to 0.56 mm)
- Ring to groove clearance .... 0.0015 to 0.0035 in (0.03 to 0.08 mm)
Oil control ring
- Type .... Two chrome faced rings with expander
- Width .... 0.100 to 0.105 in (2.54 to 2.66 mm)
- Fitted gap .... 0.015 to 0.045 in (0.38 to 1.14 mm)

Valves

Seat angle .... 45½°
Head diameter:
- Inlet .... 1.5 in (38.1 mm)
- Exhaust .... 1.216 to 1.220 in (30.88 to 31.04 mm)
Stem diameter*
- Inlet .... 0.3110 to 0.3115 in (7.89 to 7.91 mm)
- Exhaust .... 0.3100 to 0.3105 in (7.87 to 7.89 mm)
Stem to guide clearance:*
- Inlet .... 0.002 in (0.051 mm)
- Exhaust .... 0.003 in (0.076 mm)
Stem diameter**
- Inlet .... 0.3115 to 0.3120 in (7.91 to 7.93 mm)
- Exhaust .... 0.3115 to 0.3120 in (7.91 to 7.93 mm)

Stem to guide clearance**

Inlet	0.0015 in (0.038 mm)
Exhaust	0.0015 in (0.038 mm)

Valve lift:

All models except 1750 twin carburerrors	0.36 in (9.14 mm)
1750 twin carburettors	0.393 in (9.98 mm)

Early engines up to engine number 14H/283EH/39163, 14H/288EH/1102
**All other engines*

Valve springs

Free length	1.797 in (45.70 mm)
Fitted length	1.38 in (35.05 mm)
Load at top of lift	96 lb (43.5 kg)
Number of working coils	$5\frac{1}{2}$

Valve clearances

Standard setting (cold) for all models:

Inlet	0.016 to 0.018 in (0.41 to 0.46 mm)
Exhaust	0.020 to 0.022 in (0.51 to 0.56 mm)

Minimum setting before adjustment necessary:

All models	0.012 in (0.31 mm)

Oil pump

Type	Concentric (serviced as a unit)
Outer ring endfloat	0.004 to 0.005 in (0.10 to 0.12 mm)
Inner rotor endfloat	0.0045 to 0.0055 in (0.11 to 0.14 mm)
Outer ring to body clearance	0.011 in (0.28 mm)
Rotor lobe clearance	0.0035 in (0.089 mm)

Oil pressure

Idling	15 lbf/in^2 (1.05 kgf/cm^2)
Running	60 lbf/in^2 (4.2 kgf/cm^2)

Torque wrench settings

	lbf ft	kgf m
Renewable element oil filter bolt	20	2.8
Cylinder head bolts (thread oiled):		
Washer face diameter 0.73 in (18.5 mm)	60	8.3
Washer face diameter 0.81 in (20.6 mm)	65	9.0
Lifting bracket set screws	10 to 30	1.4 to 4.1
Cam carrier to cylinder head	22	3.0
Camshaft sprocket	35	4.8
Camshaft cover	6	0.8
Thermostat housing to cylinder head	8 to 10	1.1 to 1.4
Water outlet elbow	8 to 10	1.1 to 1.4
Manifold to cylinder head	18 to 20	2.5 to 2.8
Adaptor plugs	30	4.1
Carburettor studs	6 to 8	0.8 to 1.1
Water pump set screws	18 to 20	2.5 to 2.8
Plug – water pump body	35	4.8
Pulley	18	2.5
Front cover – studs	6	0.8
Front cover – nuts	17 to 19	2.4 to 2.6
Petrol pump –studs	6	0.8
Petrol pump – nuts	15 to 18	2.1 to 2.5
Flywheel housing – studs	6	0.8
Flywheel housing – nuts	17 to 19	2.4 to 2.6
Flywheel housing – set screws	17 to 19	2.4 to 2.6
Crankshaft pulley bolt	60 to 70	8.3 to 9.7
Timing cover	18 to 20	2.5 to 2.8
Timing chain guide strips	18 to 20	2.5 to 2.8
Pivot pin	18 to 20	2.5 to 2.8
Big-end nuts	30	4.1
Main bearing bolts	70	9.7
Flywheel bolts:		
Plain headed bolts	60	8.3
Washer headed bolts	100	13.8
Oil pump	18 to 20	2.5 to 2.8

1 General description

The Maxi is fitted with a four cylinder overhead camshaft engine, with either a single or twin SU HS6 carburettor(s). It is transversely mounted in the car and supported by rubber mountings.

Two valves per cylinder are mounted at an angle in the cast iron cylinder head. They are operated by tappets in direct contact with the camshaft lobes.

The cylinder head has all eight inlet and exhaust ports on one side of the cylinder head.

The cast iron cylinder block and upper half of the crankcase are cast together, whilst the bottom half of the crankcase is incorporated within the combined transmission casing and oil sump.

The flat top pistons are made from anodised aluminium with slotted solid skirts. Three compression rings are fitted to 1500 cc engines, only two compression rings are fitted to 1750 cc engines. One oil control ring located above the gudgeon pin is fitted to all pistons. The gudgeon pin is a tight press fit into the connecting rod small-end and fully floating in the piston bosses.

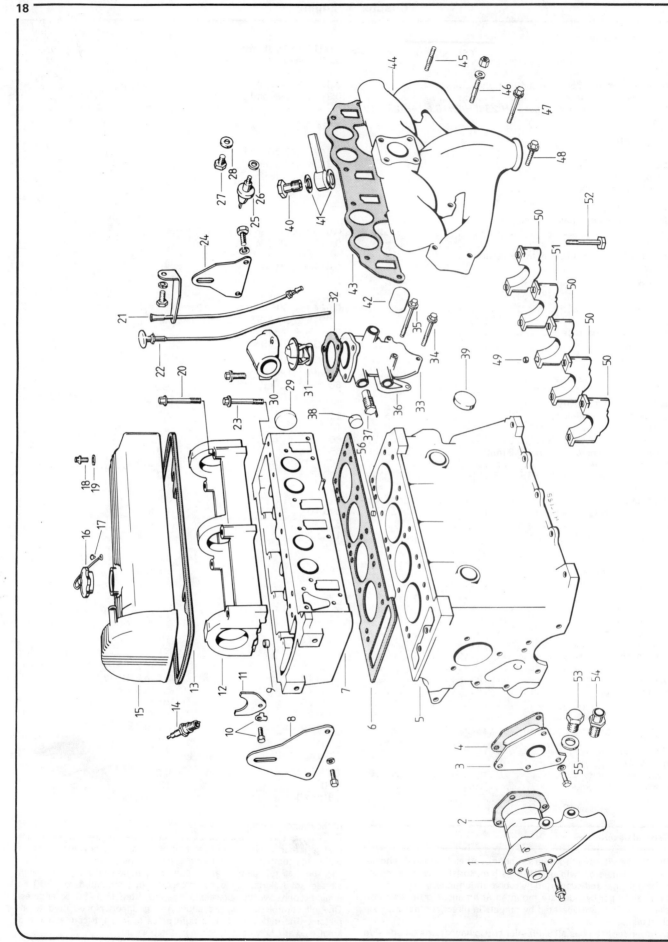

Fig. 1.1 Engine external components (Sec 1)

1 Water pump
2 Water pump gasket
3 Engine front cover
4 Front cover gasket
5 Cylinder block
6 Cylinder head gasket
7 Cylinder head
8 Engine front lifting bracket
9 Ring dowel
10 Bolt and lockwasher
11 Locating plate
12 Camshaft and tappets carrier
13 Gasket
14 Spark plug
15 Cylinder head cover
16 Oil filler cap
17 Rivet
18 Set screw
19 O-ring
20 Bolt for camshaft and tappet carrier
21 Oil dipstick tube
22 Oil dipstick
23 Cylinder head bolt
24 Engine rear lifting bracket
25 Oil pressure switch
26 Washer for oil pressure switch
27 Cylinder block drain plug
28 Drain plug washer
29 Cylinder head core plug
30 Water outlet elbow
31 Thermostat
32 Water outlet elbow gasket
33 Thermostat housing
34 Short bolt for thermostat housing
35 Long bolt for thermostat housing
36 Thermostat housing gasket
37 Thermal transmitter
38 Main oil gallery plug
39 Cylinder block core plug
40 Screw for servo banjo union
41 Washers for banjo union
42 Heater connection blanking plug
43 Gasket for inlet and exhaust manifold
44 Inlet and exhaust manifold
45 Short stud
46 Long stud
47 Long bolt
48 Short bolt
49 Main bearing cap dowel
50 Main bearing cap
51 No 4 (thrust) main bearing cap
52 Bolt for main bearing cap
53 Plug
54 Heater connection adaptor
55 Sealing washer
56 Cylinder head dowel

The crankshaft is machined from cast iron and runs in five main bearings. Fitted to the front of the crankshaft is a combined torsional vibration damper and crankshaft pulley. Situated behind this is the front oil seal followed by the camshaft chain driving sprocket and a skew gear, in mesh with a shaft, which drives the oil pump and distributor.

Located at the lower end of the shaft is a cam which operates the fuel pump via a short pushrod.

At the rear end of the crankshaft is bolted the flywheel and clutch which transmits engine torque via a single helical gear to the manual transmission mounted beneath the engine. The crankshaft main bearings run in reticular tin steel backed shell bearings.

Connecting the pistons to the crankshaft are four short connecting rods. The big-ends may be split horizontally like the crankshaft main bearings. The big-end bearings are of reticular tin steel back shell design.

Mounted onto the top face of the cylinder head is the aluminium casting in which the camshaft is fitted. The camshaft rotates in three bearings which are machined directly in the casting. Placed below each camshaft cam lobe is a large bore machined in the aluminium casting, and in each bore is a bucket type tappet. The hollow part of the tappet sits on the top of the valve stem and spring. There should be a clearance between the top of the tappet and cam lobe which may be adjusted by placing shims between the underside of the top of the tappet and the valve stem.

The camshaft is driven by a sprocket which is twice the size of the one fitted to the crankshaft.

Because of the length of drive chain, one automatic adjusting chain tensioner is used and two chain guides.

The centrifugal water pump and radiator cooling fan are driven, together with the generator, from the crankshaft pulley wheel by a rubber/fabric belt. The cooling fan is mounted on the front end of the water pump spindle.

Engine lubrication is accommodated by an oil pump which draws oil from the bottom of the transmission casing and passes it through a full flow renewable element oil filter and then to the oil gallery and distribution drillings within the engine. Oil pressure is controlled by a non-adjustable oil relief valve which is located in the transmission casing just below the filter head.

From the 'Specifications' given at the beginning of this Chapter it will be seen that two engine sizes are available, the increase in capacity being obtained by increasing the stroke.

2 Major operations with engine in place

1 No major operations can be carried out on the Maxi engine with it in place because it is impossible to drop the sump.
2 The following operations are possible however:

(a) Removal and refitting of the cylinder head assembly
(b) Removal and refitting of camshaft and carrier
(c) Removal and refitting of clutch and flywheel
(d) Removal and refitting of engine mountings

3 Major operations with engine removed

1 The following major operations can be carried out with the engine out of the body:

(a) Removal and refitting of the main bearings
(b) Removal and refitting of the crankshaft
(c) Removal and refitting of the oil pump
(d) Removal and refitting of the big-end bearings
(e) Removal and refitting of the pistons and connecting rods
(f) Removal and refitting of the camshaft drive sprocket and chain

4 Engine and transmission – removal (cable gear change)

The sequence of operations listed in this section is not critical as the position of the person undertaking the work, or the tool in his hand, will determine to a certain extent the order in which the work is

H13483

Fig. 1.2 Engine internal components (Sec 1)

1 Crankshaft
2 Keys for timing gear and sprocket
3 Dowel for flywheel
4 Main bearing shells
5 Retainer for water pump bearing
6 Crankshaft thrustwashers
7 Connecting rod
8 Big-end bearing cap
9 Big-end bearing shell
10 Big-end bolt
11 Nut for bolt
12 Gudgeon pin
13 Piston
14 Oil control ring
15 Tapered compression rings
16 Top compression ring
17 Distributor, oil pump and fuel pump drivegear
18 Distributor and fuel pump driveshaft
19 Oil pump drive coupling
20 Thrustwasher for shaft
21 Oil pump drive coupling
22 Oil pump rotor
23 Oil pump outer ring
24 Oil pump body
25 Oil strainer body
26 Gasket
27 Oil strainer
28 Oil strainer cover
29 Bolt for oil pump
30 Spring washer
31 Bolt for oil pump
32 Spring washer
33 Crankshaft sprocket
34 Oil thrower
35 Crankshaft front oil seal
36 Crankshaft pulley and vibration damper
37 Pulley bolt
38 Lockwasher for bolt
39 Chain for camshaft
40 Chain guide – tensioner side
41 Dowel bolt for guide
42 Washer for bolt
43 Chain guide – tight side
44 Adjuster for chain guide
45 Locknut for adjuster
46 Washer for nut
47 Chain tensioner assembly
48 Chain tensioner adaptor
49 Washer for adaptor
50 Bolt for adaptor
51 Washer for bolt
52 Setscrew for chain guides
53 Spring washer
54 Plain washer
55 Camshaft
56 Camshaft sprocket
57 Dowel for sprocket
58 Bolt for sprocket
59 Inlet valve
60 Exhaust valve
61 Valve cotters
62 Oil seal (inlet valve only)
63 Valve springs
64 Valve spring cup
65 Tappets
66 Shim for tappets
67 Water pump body
68 Water pump gasket
69 Bearing and shaft assembly
70 Seal for water pump
71 Vane for water pump
72 Bolt for water pump
73 Pulley for water pump and fan
74 Hub for fan and pulley
75 Fanbelt
76 Fan
77 Bolt for fan
78 Spring washer for bolt

tackled. Obviously the power unit cannot be removed until everything is disconnected from it and the following sequence will ensure nothing is forgotten.

1 Refer to Chapter 2 and drain the cooling system.
2 Preferably whilst the engine is warm, place a container having a capacity of at least 10 pints (6 litres) under the transmission unit drain plug and unscrew the drain plug. This is located on the radiator side of the transmission unit casing.
3 Using a soft pencil, mark the outline position of both the hinges at the bonnet to act as a datum for refitting.
4 With the help of a second person to take the weight of the bonnet, undo and remove the two lower stay retaining screws.
5 Undo and remove the hinge to bonnet securing bolts with plain and spring washers. There are two bolts to each hinge.
6 Lift away the bonnet and put in a safe place so that it will not be scratched.
7 Disconnect the positive and then the negative terminals from the battery.
8 Undo and remove the nuts and plain washers holding the battery clamp bar to the support rods and lift away the clamp bar and two rods.
9 Lift away the battery from its tray. The tray may next be lifted out.
10 Undo and remove the two nuts and shakeproof washers securing the air cleaner(s) to the carburettor air intake flange(s) (photo). Lift away the air cleaner(s).
11 Pull the HT lead from the centre of the ignition coil (photo).
12 Mark the high tension cables relative to the spark plugs for correct refitting, and disconnect the four leads.
13 Release the two distributor cap retaining clips and lift away the distributor cap and HT leads.
14 Undo and remove the two exhaust manifold to downpipe clamp securing nuts, bolts and washers. Lift away the clamp.
15 Make a note of the manner in which the throttle return spring(s) is fitted and unhook the spring(s) (photo). Put the spring in a safe place.
16 Release the throttle cable connector from the cable by slackening the centre screw and drawing the connector from the end of the cable (photo).
17 Pull the throttle outer cable from its support bracket (photo).
18 Slacken the choke cable connector centre screw and pull the inner cable from the connector. Lift away the connector (photo).
19 Draw the water temperature gauge thermal transmitter cable from the transmitter (photo).
20 Pull the distributor automatic advance/retard pipe connector from its union on the induction manifold side of the carburettor body (photo).
21 Pull the advance/retard pipe from the end of the distributor vacuum unit (photo). Lift away the complete pipe.
22 Slacken the clip securing the heater hose to the union on the water pump and carefully draw off the hose (photo).
23 Slacken the clip securing the second heater hose to thermostat (photo). Carefully draw off the hose.
24 Undo and remove the union bolt and copper washers securing the brake servo unit hose to the induction manifold (photo).
25 Apply the handbrake, chock the rear wheels, remove the front wheel trims, slacken the front wheel nuts, jack up the front of the car until the wheels are just off the ground and place on firmly based axle stands. Remove the front wheels.
26 Working under the right-hand wheel arch, soak with penetrating oil the four nuts securing the battery tray support to the inner wing panel. Undo and remove the four nuts and spring washers and lift away the support.
27 Note which way round the clutch release arm return spring is fitted and detach the spring (photo).
28 Undo and remove the two bolts with spring washers securing the clutch slave cylinder to the clutch/flywheel housing.
29 Carefully draw the clutch slave cylinder rearwards out of engagement of the pushrod and tie back out of the way. On no account depress the clutch pedal after this has been done.
30 Undo and remove the bolt and spring washer securing the battery earth strap to the clutch housing cover (photo).
31 Using a pair of pliers, release the clip securing the pipe to the expansion tank at the take off pipe on the radiator filter neck.
32 Undo and remove the two expansion tank clamp securing self tapping screws.
33 Lift away the expansion tank and connecting hose.
34 Pull the cable Lucar connector from the oil warning light switch

4.10 Removing the air cleaner

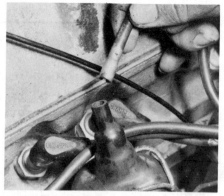

4.11 Removing the HT lead from the ignition coil

4.15 Throttle return spring

4.16 Disconnecting the throttle cable

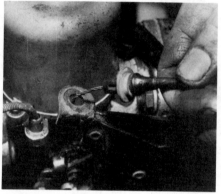

4.17 Throttle cable attachment to support bracket

4.18 Disconnecting the choke cable

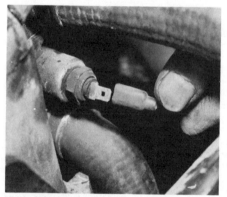

4.19 Disconnecting the temperature transmitter

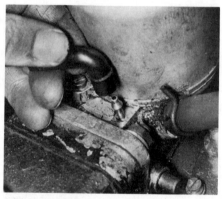

4.20 Distributor vacuum connection

4.21 Distributor vacuum connection

4.22 Heater hose connection (return)

4.23 Heater hose connection (flow)

4.24 Disconnecting the vacuum servo

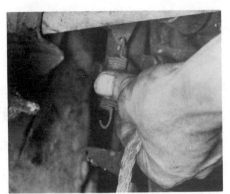
4.27 Clutch lever return spring

4.30 Earth strap connection

4.34 Oil pressure warning connection

4.36 Ignition coil connections

4.40 Dipstick bracket bolt

4.41 Fuel pump feed pipe

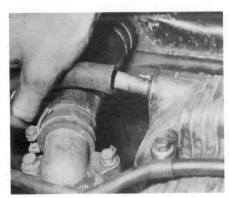
4.42 Camshaft cover breather

4.45 Engine steady-to-body fixing

4.46 Engine steady-to-engine fixing

located just beneath the ignition coil (photo).

35 Make a note of the cable connections to the rear of the dynamo and pull off the two Lucar connectors, or pull the plug off the alternator.

36 Ease back the cap on the ignition coil and note the low tension electrical cable connections. Carefully pull off the Lucar connectors (photo).

37 Pull off the Lucar connector from the side of the distributor body.

38 Undo and remove the nut securing the heavy duty cable to the terminal at the rear of the starter motor. Lift off the cable from the terminal.

39 If a pre-engaged starter motor is fitted, note the electrical cable connections and release the cables from the solenoid.

40 Undo and remove the one bolt securing the dip stick bracket to the ignition coil mounting bracket (photo).

41 With a pair of pliers, compress the ears of the fuel pump feed pipe flexible hose clip and carefully draw off the hose (photo).

42 Carefully pull off the breather pipe from the radiator end of the camshaft cover (photo).

43 Undo the camshaft cover securing bolts in a progressive manner and withdraw the bolts.

44 Carefully lift the camshaft cover and gasket from the top of the cylinder head.

45 Undo and remove the nut and bolt securing the engine steady bracket to the body (photo).

46 Undo and remove the nut and bolt securing the engine steady bracket to the mounting bracket on the side of the cylinder head (photo).

47 Fit lifting chains or strong rope to the two engine lifting brackets and, with an overhead hoist or crane, take the weight of the complete unit from the mountings.

48 Working under the car undo, but do not remove, the centre nut plain washer from the right-hand mounting.

49 Undo and remove the bolts with spring washers securing the

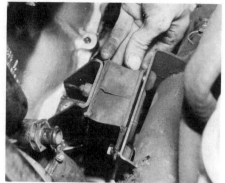
4.50 Left-hand engine to subframe mounting

4.53 Removing a gear cable gland nut

4.58 Disconnecting a gear cable

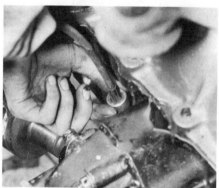
4.61 Disconnecting the speedometer cable

4.62 Disengaging the RH driveshaft

4.63 Disengaging the LH driveshaft

4.64 Lifting the transmission clear

4.65 Driveshafts tied to support them

right-hand mounting to the transmission unit.

50 Undo and remove the bolts with spring washers securing the left-hand mounting to the subframe (photo).

51 Move the gear change lever to the neutral position and mark the cables so that they may be refitted correctly.

52 Working under the car, unscrew the cable locking nut from each cable (if fitted).

53 Unscrew the outer cable gland nut from each cable (photo).

54 Pull the fifth/reverse cable outwards from the transmission unit.

55 Unscrew the inner cable gland nut and detach the cable.

56 Repeat the instructions given in paragraphs 54 and 55 for the first/second speed cable.

57 Push the first/second speed selector rod back into the neutral position using a suitable diameter metal rod.

58 Repeat the instructions given in paragraphs 54 and 55 for the third/fourth speed cable (photo).

59 Check that no electric cables or controls have been left connected, with the exception of the speedometer cable, and then raise the engine

about three inches. It will be necessary to lower the rear of the unit, so as to disengage the rear mounting.

60 Push the engine forwards as far as possible and then raise it sufficiently for the rear mounting to be completely disengaged.

61 Release the speedometer drive from the rear of the transmission unit.

62 Move the engine as far as possible to the left-hand side of the car and disengage the right-hand drive shaft (photo). Refer to Chapter 7 if necessary.

63 Move the engine to the right and disengage the left-hand drive shaft (photo).

64 Continue to raise the engine and transmission until the underside is just clear of the front panel (photo).

65 Tie the drive shafts to support their weight (photo) and push the car rearwards, or pull the crane forwards from the car until the complete power unit is clear of the car.

66 Carefully lower the power unit to the ground.

67 Thoroughly wash the exterior with paraffin or a water soluble

cleaner. Wash off with a strong water jet and dry thoroughly. The engine unit is now ready to have the radiator removed and then separated from the transmission as described in Section 8.

5 Engine and transmission – removal (rod gear change)

1 Follow the sequence given in Section 4 paragraphs 1 to 50 inclusive.

2 Undo and remove the large bolt and nut securing the steady rod to the differential housing. Separate the rod yoke from the casting and recover the two washers.

3 Undo and remove the two nuts and spring washers securing the exhaust bracket to the differential housing.

4 Slacken the exhaust bracket U-bolt nuts and slide the bracket down the exhaust pipe.

5 Undo and remove the two nuts, bolts and spring washers that secure the front left-hand mounting to the subframe bracket.

6 Undo and remove the two bolts that secure the rear left-hand mounting to the displacer housing.

7 Using a piece of metal bar, carefully release the two driveshafts from their locator rings. For this it may be necessary to jack up the lower suspension arms.

8 Slacken the two nuts and bolts that secure the rear engine mounting to the subframe bracket.

9 Undo and remove the two nuts retaining the rear engine mounting to the bracket on the clutch cover.

10 Using a parallel pin punch, carefully drift out the pin that retains the extension rod to the selector shaft.

11 Undo and remove the two nuts and spring washers that secure the damper mounting bracket to the transmission.

12 The removal procedure is now identical to that for cable operated gear change models. Refer to Section 4 and follow the sequence described in paragraphs 59 to 67 inclusive.

6 Engine and transmission – removal (automatic transmission)

The sequence of operations listed in this Section is not critical, as the position of the person undertaking the work, or the tool in his hand, will determine to a certain extent the order in which the work is tackled. Obviously, the power unit cannot be removed until everything is disconnected from it; the following sequence will ensure nothing is forgotten.

1 Remove the plastic ignition shield.

2 Refer to Chapter 2, and drain the cooling system.

3 Preferably whilst the engine is warm, place a container having a capacity of at least 10 pints (6 litres) under the transmission unit drain plug and unscrew the drain plug.

4 Using a soft pencil mark the outline position of both the hinges at the bonnet to act as a datum for refitting.

5 With the help of a second person to take the weight of the bonnet, undo and remove the two lower stay retaining screws.

6 Undo and remove the hinge to bonnet securing bolts with spring and plain washers. There are two bolts to each hinge.

7 Lift away the bonnet and put in a safe place so that it will not be scratched.

8 Disconnect the positive and then the negative terminals from the battery.

9 Undo and remove the nuts and plain washers holding the battery clamp bar to the support rods.

10 Lift away the clamp bar and two rods.

11 Lift away the battery from its tray. The tray may next be lifted away.

12 Undo and remove the two nuts and shake proof washers securing the air cleaner(s) to the carburettor air intake flange(s). Lift away the air cleaner(s).

13 Disconnect the fuel pipe, vacuum pipe and engine breather pipe from the carburettor(s).

14 Disconnect the 'kick-down' rod from the carburettor(s) linkage.

15 Remove the carburettor(s) from the manifold and tie it well clear of the engine.

16 Disconnect the exhaust downpipe from the exhaust manifold.

17 Disconnect the servo unit vacuum pipe from the inlet manifold.

18 Disconnect the engine steady from the subframe.

19 Detach the earth cable from the torque converter cover.

20 Disconnect the spill pipe from the radiator filler neck.

21 Remove the expansion tank.

22 Disconnect the heater hose from the thermostat housing.

23 Disconnect the heater hose from the water pump.

24 Disconnect the fuel feed pipe from the fuel pump.

25 The following cables should be disconnected: Thermal transmitter, oil pressure switch, inhibitor switch, distributor, ignition coil, dynamo/alternator, starter.

26 Remove the rubber strap that supports the thermal transmitter wire to the radiator top hose.

27 Chock the rear wheels, apply the handbrake, jack up the front of the car and support it under the lower suspension arms with axle stands.

28 Detach the engine damper from the bracket on the engine.

29 Undo and remove the bolts that secure the damper mounting bracket to the subframe and remove the bracket. Note that the right-hand top bolt secures the petrol pipe support clip and spacer.

30 Slacken the exhaust bracket U-bolt securing nuts.

31 Undo and remove the two nuts that secure the exhaust pipe bracket to the differential housing.

32 Now slide the exhaust pipe bracket down the exhaust pipe.

33 Move the gear selector lever to the 'D' position.

34 Remove the control cable retainer and then slacken the two outer control cable nuts.

35 Carefully pull the outer cables out of the transmission casing.

36 Disconnect the inner control cable from the end of the detent rod, and the second inner control cable from the park lock control rod.

37 Withdraw the control cables from the transmission casing.

38 Refer to Chapter 7, and release the driveshafts from their locator rings in the differential unit. It is important that when releasing the left-hand drive shaft the large rectangular block welded to the tool must face the left-hand roadwheel to avoid damage to the differential case.

39 The car may now be lowered to the ground again.

40 Using a rope or chain support the weight of the complete power unit.

41 Undo and remove the bolts that secure the engine left-hand rear mounting to the subframe.

42 Undo and remove the bolts that secure the engine left-hand front mounting to the subframe bracket.

43 Undo and remove the bolts that secure the engine right-hand mounting to the subframe bracket.

44 Undo and remove the bolts that secure the engine right-hand mounting to the plate attached to the torque converter cover. Remove the engine mounting.

45 Detach the rubber strap that supports the speedometer cable to the heater hose.

46 The power unit should now be lifted slightly until the converter cover plate is clear of the petrol pipe. Take care not to damage the servo vacuum pipe against the master cylinder as the power unit is lifted.

47 Disconnect the speedometer cable from the transmission unit.

48 Move the engine as far as possible to the right-hand side of the car and disengage the left-hand driveshaft.

49 Move the engine as far as possible to the left-hand side of the car and disengage the right-hand driveshaft.

50 Temporarily secure the driveshafts with string or wire to prevent damage or interference during final removal of the power unit.

51 The power unit may now be lifted up and away from the front of the car.

7 Engine and transmission with subframe – removal (cable gear change)

1 For this method of engine and transmission removal it is necessary to depressurise the hydrolastic suspension system. Refer to Chapter 11 for information on this subject.

2 Refer to Section 4 and follow the sequence given in paragraphs 1 to 47 inclusive.

3 Undo the two nuts and bolts securing the heat control valve to the subframe. Lift away the heat control valve.

4 Disconnect the speedometer cable from the rear of the transmission unit casing.

5 Undo and remove the bolt, nut and spring washer that secure the brake servo unit to the subframe.

6   Release the gear change lever knob locknut. Unscrew and remove the knob and the locknut.

7   Disconnect the cables to the reverse light switch located on the transmission unit casing.

8   Undo and remove the nut and bolt securing the exhaust pipe clip to the exhaust down pipe.

9   Undo and remove the four bolts securing the exhaust pipe to the silencer mountings.

10   Slacken the two nuts on the exhaust pipe to rear silencer joint clip and carefully remove the exhaust pipe.

11   Undo and remove the nuts and spring washers from the exhaust pipe and silencer heat shield.

12   Carefully lower the gear change control from the underside of the body.

13   With a scriber, or small file, mark the steering column flange and pinion so that the two parts may be correctly fitted on reassembly.

14   Disconnect the steering column from the coupling by undoing and removing the two nuts, bolts and spring washers.

15   Wipe the top of the brake master cylinder and unscrew the cap. Place a piece of thick polythene sheet over the top and refit the cap. This is to prevent hydraulic fluid syphoning out in subsequent operations.

16   Wipe the brake pipe connections at the joint between the front hub flexible hoses and main metal pipe lines and detach the brake pipes at these connections. Further information will be found in Chapter 9.

17   Open the boot lid and remove the boot compartment floor covering. Undo and remove the two self tapping screws securing each of the two suspension access plates to the floor. Remove the access plates.

18   The suspension may now be depressurised. For this it is usually necessary to use special equipment, but it may be done by unscrewing the valve cap, using a large jam jar to catch the fluid, and very carefully depressing the centre of the valve. Do not depress it fully as the Hydrolastic suspension is pressurised to approximately 245 lbf/in^2 (17.2 kgf/cm^2). Use a small screwdriver.

19   Using the same technique for the disconnection of brake flexible hoses, disconnect the suspension pipes at their front connectors.

20   Next release the flexible suspension pipes from the body clips.

21   Undo and remove the four bolts that secure the lower suspension arm bearings to the body.

22   Undo and remove the two bolts that secure the subframe to the toe board.

23   Undo and remove the three bolts, nuts and spring washers that secure each side of the subframe to the wing valance.

24   Very carefully lower the complete subframe assembly.

25   Place a rope sling, suitably padded, around the front of the body and raise the body to a sufficient height to clear the top of the engine. Either move the body rearwards and swing the front away from the complete power unit and subframe assembly, or draw the assembly forwards from under the car.

8   Engine and transmission with subframe – removal (rod gear change)

1   The sequence for removal is basically identical to that for removal of the cable operated gear change models as described in Section 7. The main difference is confined to the removal of the gear change remote control system. Full information will be found in Chapter 6. The following additional points should be carried out:

2   Remove the complete exhaust system from the underside of the car.

3   Slacken the screws that secure the front door kicking plates and completely remove the front carpeting.

4   When the subframe has been removed, recover the rubber mountings and sleeves from the subframe mounting points.

9   Engine – dismantling (general)

1   It is best to mount the engine on a dismantling stand, but if this is not available, stand the engine on a strong bench at a comfortable working height. Failing this, it can be stripped down on the floor.

2   During the dismantling process, the greatest care should be taken to keep the exposed parts free from dirt. As an aid to achieving this thoroughly clean down the outside of the engine, first removing all traces of oil and congealed dirt.

3   A water soluble cleaner will make the job much easier, for, after the cleaner has been applied and allowed to stand for a time, a vigorous jet of water will wash off the solvent and the grease with it. If the dirt is thick and deeply embedded, work the cleaner into it with a strong stiff brush.

4   Finally wipe down the exterior of the engine with a rag and only then, when it is quite clean, should the dismantling process begin. As the engine is stripped, clean each part in a bath of paraffin or petrol.

5   Never immerse parts with oilways in paraffin, eg crankshaft. To clean these parts, wipe down carefully with a petrol dampened rag. Oilways can be cleaned out with nylon pipe cleaners. If an air line is available, all parts can be blown dry and the oilways blown through as an added precaution.

6   Re-use of old gaskets is false economy. To avoid the possibility of trouble after the engine has been reassembled *always* use new gaskets throughout.

7   Do not throw the old gaskets away, for sometimes it happens that an immediate replacement cannot be found and the old gasket is then very useful as a template. Hang up the gaskets as they are removed.

8   To strip the engine, it is best to work from the top down. The crankcase provides a firm base on which the engine can be supported in an upright position. When the stage is reached where the crankshaft must be removed, the engine can be turned on its side and all other work carried out with it in this position.

9   Wherever possible, refit nuts, bolts and washers finger tight from wherever they were removed. This helps to avoid loss and muddle. If they cannot be refitted, then lay them out in such a fashion that it is clear from whence they came.

10   Engine – removing ancillary components

1   Before basic engine dismantling begins, it is necessary to strip it of ancillary components. These are as follows:-

(a) **Fuel system components**
     Carburettor(s) and manifold assembly
     Fuel pump
     Fuel lines

(b) **Ignition system components**
     Spark plugs
     Distributor
     Coil and mounting bracket

(c) **Electrical system components**
     Generator
     Starter motor

(d) **Cooling system components**
     Radiator and mountings
     Fan and hub
     Water pump
     Thermostat housing and thermostat
     Water temperature sender unit

(e) **Engine**
     Crankcase ventilation tube
     Oil pressure sender unit
     Oil level dipstick and guide tube
     Oil filler cap and camshaft cover
     Engine mountings

(f) **Clutch**
     Clutch pressure plate assembly
     Clutch friction plate assembly

2   All nuts and bolts associated with the foregoing.

3   Some of these items have to be removed for individual servicing or renewal periodically and details can be found under the appropriate Chapter.

11   Cylinder head removal – engine in car

1   Undo and remove the two nuts and spring washers securing the air cleaner(s) to the air intake flange of the carburettor(s). Lift away the air cleaner(s).

2   Detach the distributor automatic advance/retard pipe from the distributor vacuum unit and the induction side of the carburettor body. Lift away the pipe.

3 Detach the engine breather hose from the camshaft cover.
4 With a pair of pliers, compress the ears of the clip holding the fuel supply hose to the float chamber union. Pull off the fuel supply hose.
5 Make a note of the manner in which the throttle return spring(s) are fitted and unhook the spring(s). Put the spring(s) in a safe place.
6 Release the throttle cable connector from the cable by slackening the centre screw and drawing the connector from the end of the cable.
7 Pull the throttle outer cable from its support bracket.
8 Slacken the choke cable connector centre screw and pull the inner cable from the connector. Lift away the connector.
9 Undo the brake servo unit pipe union bolt from the induction manifold. Lift away the union bolt and remove the two copper washers.
10 Undo and remove the two nuts, bolts and washers from the clamp securing the exhaust down pipe to the exhaust manifold. Lift away the two halves of the clamp.
11 Refer to Chapter 2 and drain the cooling system.
12 Slacken the clips securing the radiator, water pump and heater hoses to the thermostat housing. Ease the hoses from the thermostat housing.
13 Disconnect the Lucar terminal from the temperature gauge thermal transmitter.
14 Mark the high tension cables relative to the spark plugs for correct refitting and disconnect the four leads.
15 Undo and remove the bolts and spring washers securing the engine steady arm bracket and right-hand lifting bracket to the cylinder head.
16 Undo and remove the bolts and spring washers securing the radiator bracket and left-hand lifting bracket to the cylinder head.
17 The six shaped bolts which hold the camshaft cover to the top of the cylinder head should now be unscrewed in a progressive diagonal manner. Lift away the cover and the gasket.
18 The crankshaft should now be turned until the timing marks 1/4 TDC on the flywheel of manual transmission models, or the 0° mark of those with automatic transmission are in line with their respective pointers and the piston of No 1 cylinder is at TDC on its firing stroke.
19 Carefully adjust the camshaft sprocket until the camshaft timing marks are in alignment. These are to be found on the back of the sprockets which have three holes in their web or on the front of sprockets with six hole webs and should be aligned with the mark on the top of the adjacent bearing boss.
20 Undo and remove the chain tensioner adaptor bolt and then, using an $\frac{1}{8}$ in Allen key placed through the bolt aperture, turn the tensioner plunger in a clockwise direction to retract the tensioner slipper from the chain.
21 Undo and remove the bolt and spring washer securing the camshaft sprocket to the camshaft and detach the sprocket from the camshaft.
22 Slacken the cylinder head securing bolts in a diagonal and progressive manner until all are free from tension. Remove the ten bolts noting that because of the shape of the bolt head no washers are used.
23 The cylinder head may now be removed by lifting upwards. If the head is jammed, try to rock it to break the seal. Under no circumstances try to prise it apart from the cylinder block with a screwdriver or cold chisel, as damage may be done to the faces of the cylinder head and block. If the head will not readily free, turn the engine over by the flywheel using the starter motor, as the compression in the cylinders will often break the cylinder head joint. If this fails to work, strike the head sharply with a plastic headed or wooden hammer, or with a metal hammer with an interposed piece of wood to cushion the blow. Under no circumstances hit the head directly with a metal hammer as this may cause the iron casting to fracture. Several sharp taps with the hammer, at the same time pulling upwards, should free the head. Lift the head off and place on one side.

12 Cylinder head removal – engine on bench

The procedure for removing the cylinder head with the engine on the bench is similar to that for removal when the engine is in the car, with the exception of disconnecting the controls and services. Refer to Section 11 and follow the sequence given in paragraphs 12, and 15 to 22 inclusive.
Instead of turning the crankshaft using the starter motor as mentioned in Section 11, use a large socket spanner on the pulley retaining bolt to turn the crankshaft.

13 Camshaft and tappets – removal

1 On automatic transmission models remove the plug from the timing aperture on the underside of the converter housing and ensure that the zero mark on the converter is aligned with the pointer and that No 1 cylinder piston is about to start its firing stroke. Turn the engine in the normal direction of rotation to align the marks.
2 On vehicles with manual transmission, remove the two bolts and spring washers securing the flywheel housing timing cover and remove the cover. Align the 1/4 TDC mark on the flywheel with the pointer when the piston of No 1 cylinder is starting its firing stroke. On later models there are timing marks on the crankshaft pulley and timing case, in which case the removal of the flywheel cover plate is not necessary.
3 Undo and remove the six bolts which hold the camshaft cover onto the cylinder head. The bolts should be loosened progressively in a diagonal sequence. Lift off the cover and gasket (Fig. 1.3).
4 Carefully align the mark on the camshaft sprocket with the mark on the top of the adjacent bearing cap. On sprockets with three holes in the web, the timing mark is on the rear face and on sprockets with six holes in the web, the mark is on the front face. If necessary, turn the crankshaft in the normal direction of rotation until the marks do align correctly.
5 Remove the positive and negative terminals from the battery.
6 Undo and remove the nuts and plain washers holding the battery clamp bar to the support rods and lift away the clamp bar and two rods.
7 Lift away the battery from its tray. The tray may be lifted out next.
8 Undo and remove the bolts and spring washers securing the radiator stay and left-hand lifting bracket to the end of the cylinder head.
9 Undo and remove the bolts and spring washers securing the engine steady and right-hand lifting bracket to the end of the cylinder head.
10 Undo and remove the chain tensioner adaptor bolt and then, using an $\frac{1}{8}$ in Allen key placed through the bolt aperture, turn the tensioner plunger in a clockwise direction to retract the tensioner slipper from the chain.
11 Undo and remove the bolt and spring washer securing the camshaft sprocket to the camshaft and detach the sprocket from the camshaft.
12 Slacken the camshaft housing bolts in a diagonal and progressive manner until the valve spring pressure is released.
13 Lift up the camshaft housing by a sufficient amount for the tappets to fall clear of the camshaft. Give the housing a little shake if necessary.
14 Recover the tappets and place in order so that they can be refitted in their original positions.
15 The camshaft can be removed from the housing by the end opposite to the sprocket.

14 Valve – removal

1 The valves can be removed from the cylinder head by the following method. Compress each spring in turn with a valve spring compressor until the two halves of the collets can be removed (photo).
2 Release the compressor and remove the valve spring cup and spring (photo).
3 Lift away the oil seal fitted to inlet valves only (photo).
4 If, when the valve spring compressor is screwed down, the valve spring cup refuses to free and expose the split collet, do not continue to screw it down as there is a likelihood of damaging it.
5 Gently tap the top of the tool directly over the cup with a hammer. This will free the cup. To avoid the compressor jumping off the valve retaining cup when it is tapped, hold the compressor firmly in position with one hand.
6 It is essential that the valves are kept in their correct sequence unless they are so badly worn that they are to be renewed. If they are going to be used again, place them in a sheet of card having eight numbered holes corresponding with the relative positions of the valves when fitted. Also keep the valve springs, cups etc., in the correct order.
7 Should a case of noisy valve gear be under investigation on early

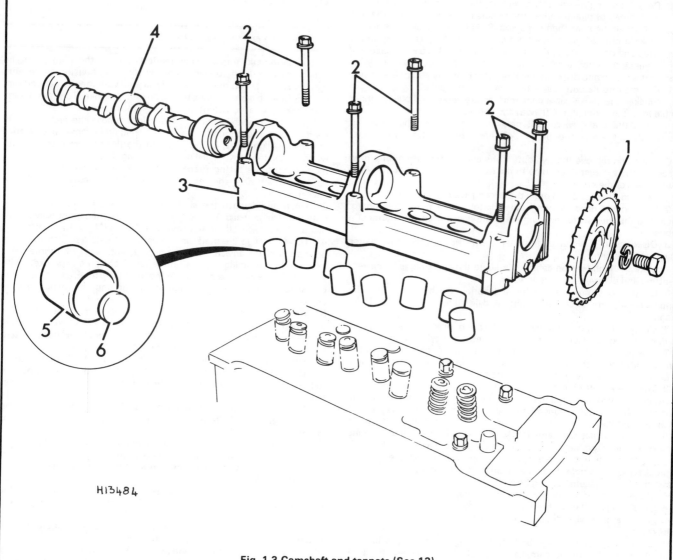

H13484

Fig. 1.3 Camshaft and tappets (Sec 13)

1 Camshaft sprocket	3 Camshaft housing	5 Tappet
2 Camshaft housing bolts	4 Camshaft	6 Tappet adjustment shim

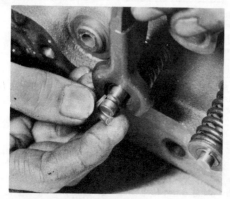

14.1 Removing a split collet

14.2 Removing a cup and spring

14.3 Removing an inlet valve oil seal

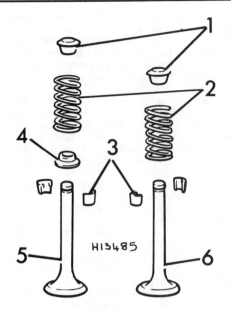

Fig. 1.4 Inlet and exhaust valve assemblies (Sec 14)

1	Valve spring cups	4	Oil seal (inlet valve only)
2	Valve springs	5	Inlet valve
3	Collets	6	Exhaust valve

engines up to engine number 14H/283EH/13472 the cause could be due to the valve stem either scuffing or picking up in the guide. If this is evident new valves must be fitted. On engines produced after this number, the finish of the guides and method of assembly into the cylinder head were changed to eliminate this problem.

15 Timing chain and sprockets – removal

1 Before starting, it should be noted that a special tool is required to split the chain. If this tool (Part No 18G 1151) cannot be borrowed, some other type of rivet extractor will be required.

2 Provided that the radiator and lower support bracket are removed to give access (see Chapter 2), this work may be done with the engine in the car. The fan belt and fan blades must also be removed.

3 Turn the crankshaft until the 1/4 TDC mark on the flywheel of manual transmission models, or the 0° mark on the torque converter of automatic transmission models is in alignment with its associated pointer and No 1 cylinder is at the start of its firing stroke.

4 With the transmission locked and using a starting nut spanner, or an impact wrench, undo and remove the crankshaft pulley bolt and lock washer.

5 Either lever the pulley off carefully, or preferably draw it off with a universal puller.

6 Remove the camshaft cover (Section 11). Check that the camshaft sprocket mark and the mark on the adjoining bearing cap are in alignment and if necessary turn the crankshaft in the normal direction of rotation to achieve this.

7 Undo and remove the chain tensioner adaptor bolt and with a $\frac{1}{8}$ in Allen key inserted through the bolt aperture, turn the tensioner plunger clockwise to retract the tensioner slipper from the chain.

8 Prevent the camshaft sprocket from rotating. Undo and remove the bolt and spring washer securing the camshaft sprocket and detach the sprocket from the camshaft.

9 Using a screwdriver, carefully prise the front oil seal from its location in the cylinder block.

10 Lift the oil thrower off the crankshaft and ease the crankshaft sprocket off (Fig. 1.6).

11 If the chain is to be removed, it must first be split. To do this, push out its rivets with either the special tool referred to in paragraph 1, or with a rivet extractor.

12 If a new chain is to be fitted, secure the new chain to the old one and feed in the new chain by pulling out the old one. Detach the old chain and join the new one as described in Section 50.

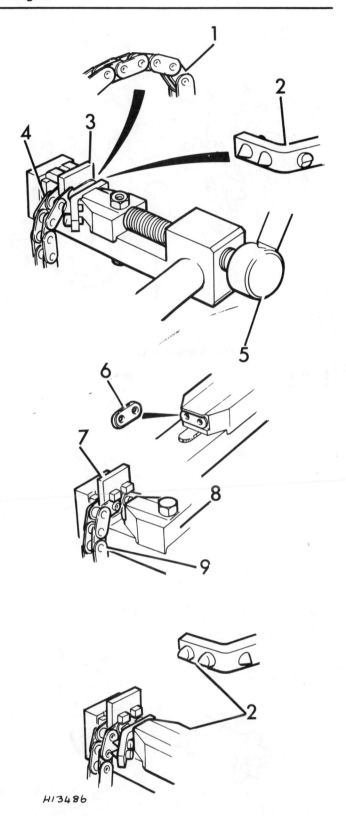

Fig. 1.5 Timing chain link remover/replacer (Sec 15)

1	Timing chain	6	Side plate fitted to moving jaw
2	Pointed extractor pins		
3	Loose bridge piece	7	Loose bridge piece reversed
4	Side plate removal	8	Moving jaw
5	Service tool 18G 1151	9	Press tightened onto pins

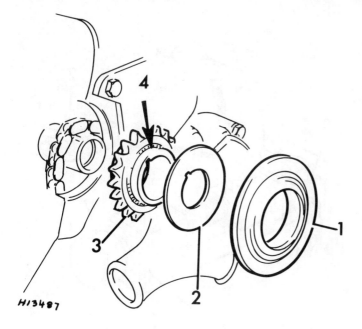

H13487

Fig. 1.6 Crankshaft sprocket removal (Sec 15)

1   Oil seal   4   Tapered face of sprocket to
2   Oil thrower   face forwards
3   Crankshaft sprocket

16 Chain tensioner – removal

1   This operation may be carried out with the engine still in the car.
2   Refer to Chapter 2 and remove the radiator and cowling.
3   Slacken the dynamo mountings and push the dynamo towards the cylinder block. Lift off the fan belt.
4   Undo the bolts that secure the fan blade hub to the water pump spindle and lift away the bolts, metal bushes and the fan blades.
5   Undo and remove the bolts and spring washers that secure the radiator lower support bracket. Lift away the support bracket.
6   Using a suitable sized socket, and to lock the flywheel a screwdriver inserted through the timing cover, undo and remove the crankshaft pulley securing bolt and lockwasher.
7   With either a universal puller or tyre levers, draw the crankshaft pulley from the end of the crankshaft.
8   Refer to Section 15 and follow the sequence described in paragraphs 6 to 9 inclusive.
9   Using a small open ended spanner, unscrew and remove the dynamo adjusting link pivot and spring washer.
10 Undo and remove the three bolts and spring washers securing the engine cover to the cylinder block just below the water pump. Lift away the cover and joint washer.
11 Unscrew and remove the chain tensioner adaptor and withdraw the tensioner through the front cover aperture.

17 Chain guides – removal

1   Refer to Chapter 2 and remove the radiator and cowling.
2   Remove the fan belt, fan blades, radiator lower support bracket and crankshaft pulley.
3   Unscrew and remove the two bolts and spring washers securing

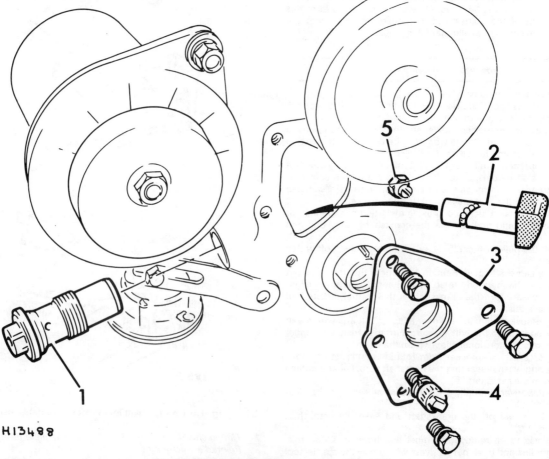

H13488

Fig. 1.7 Timing chain tensioner removal (Sec 16)

1   Tensioner adaptor   3   Engine front cover   5   Adjuster for RH chain guide
2   Tensioner   4   Generator link pivot bolt

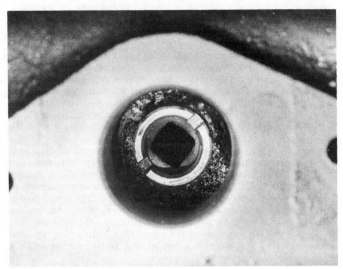

18.4 Distributor driveshaft

the timing cover to the flywheel housing.

4 Pull the breather hose from the radiator end of the crankshaft cover.

5 Unscrew the six camshaft cover securing bolts in a diagonal and progressive manner. Lift away the camshaft cover and its gasket.

6 Turn the crankshaft until the timing marks 1/4 TDC on the flywheel are in alignment with number 1 cylinder on the commencement of the firing stroke.

7 Carefully check that the camshaft sprocket and adjoining bearing boss marks align correctly and, if necessary, turn the crankshaft in the normal direction of rotation until the marks do align.

8 Undo and remove the chain tensioner adaptor bolt and then, using a $\frac{1}{8}$ in Allen key placed through the bolt aperture, turn the tensioner plunger in a clockwise direction to retract the tensioner slipper from the chain.

9 Undo and remove the bolt and spring washer securing the camshaft sprocket to the camshaft and detach the sprocket from the camshaft.

10 Undo and remove the dowel bolt and spring washer from the lower end of the fixed guide.

11 Undo and remove the two guide upper retaining bolts and spring washers.

12 The fixed guide (tensioner side) may now be lifted away from the engine.

13 Carefully detach the lower end of the adjustable guide from the eccentric adjuster, turn the guide through 90° and lift it from the engine.

18 Distributor and fuel pump driveshaft – removal

1 For this operation it is necessary to remove the power unit from the car.

2 Refer to Chapter 6 and separate the engine from the transmission unit.

3 Remove the camshaft and camshaft sprocket.

4 Make sure No 1 piston is at TDC on compression. Note the position of the distributor drive and the slot at the 2 o'clock position with the large lobe uppermost (photo).

5 The distributor drivegear may now be withdrawn from the crankshaft. Note that the drivegear shaft will turn through approximately 90° as the gear is withdrawn. Lift out the driveshaft and thrust washer.

19 Pistons, connecting rods and big-end bearings – removal

Unlike the conventional engine it is not possible to remove the pistons or connecting rods whilst the engine is still in the car as it is necessary first to remove the flywheel housing and primary drive gear cover and then separate the transmission unit as described in Chapter 6. The

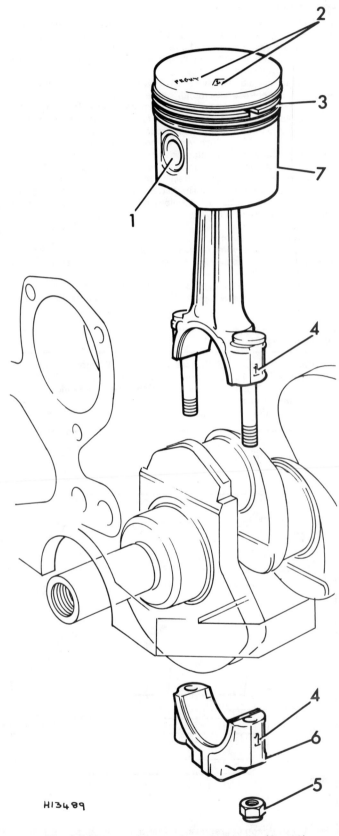

H13489

Fig. 1.8 Piston and connecting rod assembly (Sec 19)

1	Gudgeon pin	*identification number*
2	Piston identification marks	5 Big-end nut (early type)
3	Piston rings	6 Big-end cap
4	Connecting rod and cap/bore	7 Piston

cylinder head must also be removed.

1   Remove the big-end nuts and if they are hexagon shaped, discard them and obtain a set of the new 12-point nuts. If the nuts removed are of the new type they may be re-used, but lay the nuts out as they are removed so that each nut will be screwed back on to the stud from which it was removed.

2   Remove the big-end caps, taking care to keep them in the right order and the correct way round. Also ensure that the shell bearings are kept with their correct connecting rods and caps unless they are to be renewed. Normally, the numbers 1 to 4 are stamped on adjacent sides of the big-end caps and connecting rods, indicating which cap fits on which rod and which way round the cap fits (Fig. 1.8). If no numbers or lines can be found, then with a scriber or file scratch mating marks across the joint from the rod to the cap. One line for connecting rod No 1, two for connecting rod No 2 and so on. This will ensure that there is no confusion later. It is most important that the caps go back in the correct positions on the connecting rods from which they were removed.

3   If the big-end caps are difficult to remove, they may be gently tapped with a soft hammer.

4   To remove the shell bearings, press the bearing opposite the groove in both the connecting rod and its cap, and the bearings will slide out easily.

5   Withdraw the pistons and connecting rods through the top of the cylinder block and ensure they are kept in the correct order for fitting in the same bore.

20 Gudgeon pin – removal

1   A press fit gudgeon pin is used and a special BL tool No 18G1150 with adaptor 18G1150D is required to remove and refit it. The tool is shown in Fig. 1.9 and must be used in the manner described in the following paragraphs.

2   Securely hold the hexagonal body in a firm vice and screw back

the large nut until it is flush with the end of the main centre screw. Well lubricate the screw and large nut as they have to withstand high loading. Now push the centre screw in until the nut touches the thrust race.

3   Fit the adaptor number 18G1150D onto the main centre screw with the piston ring cut away positioned uppermost. Then slide the parallel sleeve with the groove end first onto the centre screw.

4   Fit the piston with the 'Front' or '$\triangle$' mark towards the adaptor, on the centre screw. This is important because the gudgeon pin bore is offset and irreparable damage will result if fitted the wrong way round. Next fit the remover/refitment bush on the centre screw with the flange end towards the gudgeon pin.

5   Screw the stop nut onto the main centre screw and adjust it until approximately 0.040 in (1.0 mm) endplay ('A' in Fig. 1.9) exists, and lock the stop nut securely with the lock screws. Now check that the remover/refitment bush and parallel sleeve are positioned correctly in the bore on both sides on the piston. Also check that the curved face of the adaptor is clean and slide the piston onto the tool so it fits into the curved face of the adaptor with the piston rings over the cut away.

6   Screw the large nut up to the thrust race and, holding the lock screw, turn the large nut with a ring spanner or long socket until the gudgeon pin is withdrawn from the piston.

21 Piston rings – removal

1   To remove the piston rings, slide them carefully over the top of the piston, taking care not to scratch the aluminium alloy; never slide them off the bottom of the piston skirt. It is very easy to break the cast iron piston rings if they are pulled off roughly, so this operation should be done with extreme care. It is helpful to make use of an old 0.020 in (0.5 mm) feeler gauge.

2   Lift one end of the piston ring to be removed out of its groove and insert under it the end of the feeler gauge.

3   Turn the feeler gauge slowly round the piston and, as the ring

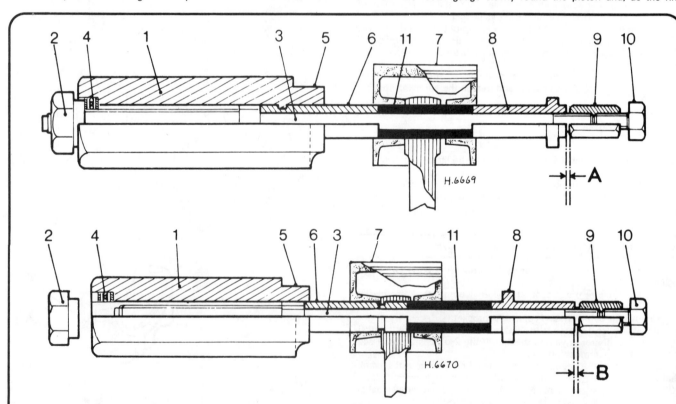

Fig. 1.9 Gudgeon pin removal and refitting (Sec 20 and 46) using service tool '18G 1150' to remove (upper illustration) and refit (lower illustration) gudgeon pin (Secs 20 and 46)

1 Hexagon body	4 Thrust race	7 Piston	10 Lockscrew
2 Large nut	5 Adaptor	8 Service tool bush	11 Gudgeon pin
3 Centre screw	6 Parallel sleeve	9 Stop nut	Dimension A and B = 0.040 in (1.0 mm)

comes out of its groove, apply slightly upward pressure so that it rests on the land above. It can then be eased off the piston with the feeler gauge stopping it from slipping into an empty groove if it is any but the top piston ring that is being removed.

22 Flywheel and flywheel housing – removal

Full details of this operation are given in Chapter 6.

23 Crankshaft and main bearings – removal

With the engine removed from the car and separated from the

transmission, remove the camshaft drive chain and sprocket. Also remove the crankshaft sprocket, flywheel and flywheel housing, big-end bearings and pistons. It will also be necessary to remove the distributor drivegear, the crankshaft primary gear and thrust washer.

1 Undo by one turn at a time the bolts which hold the five bearing caps.
2 Unscrew the bolts and remove them. Check that each bearing cap is marked as shown in Fig. 1.10. If no marks are evident these should be made with a file or scriber.
3 Remove the main bearing caps and the bottom half of each bearing shell, taking care to keep the bearing shells in the right caps.
4 When removing the number 4 main bearing cap, note the semicircular halves of the thrust washers, one half lying on either side of the main bearing. Lay them with the number 4 main bearing along the

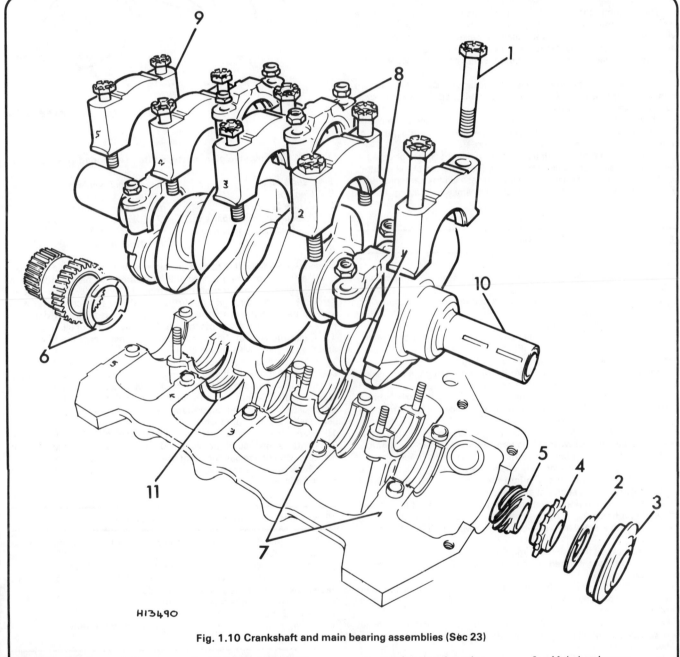

Fig. 1.10 Crankshaft and main bearing assemblies (Sec 23)

1 Main bearing cap bolt
2 Oil thrower
3 Front oil seal
4 Crankshaft sprocket
5 Distributor drivegear
6 Primary gear and thrustwasher
7 Main bearing cap and crankcase web mating marks
8 Big-end bearing caps
9 Main bearing cap
10 Crankshaft
11 Crankshaft thrustwashers

correct side.

5   Slightly rotate the crankshaft to free the upper halves of the bearing shells and thrust washers which can be extracted and placed over the correct bearing cap.

6   Remove the crankshaft by lifting it away from the crankcase. Recover the two remaining thrust washers.

24 Lubricating system – description

1   A forced feed system of lubrication is used so that oil circulates round the engine from the transmission unit below the cylinder block. The level of oil is indicated on the dipstick which is fitted to the front of the cylinder block.

2   The level of oil ideally should not be above or below the MAX mark. Oil is replenished via the filler cap on the top of the camshaft cover.

3   The oil pump, located in the transmission unit, draws oil from the supply in the transmission casing and passes it to a full flow oil filter which on early modles is of the renewable element type and on later models is a throw-away cartridge. To control the oil pressure, an oil pressure relief valve is located in the transmission unit under the filter head.

4   Oil passes from the filter to the main gallery, which runs the length of the cylinder block, and from there it is distributed by means of drillings to the various bearings.

5   Oil passes from the main gallery to the big-ends and main crankshaft bearings. A small hole in each connecting rod lets a jet of oil lubricate the cylinder wall on each revolution.

6   Oil passes up through a drilling in the cylinder head to lubricate the overhead camshaft and valve assemblies. From the top of the cylinder head, oil is able to pass back into the crankcase via the camshaft drive chain chest and from there into the transmission casing for recirculation.

25 Oil filter – removal and refitting

Renewable element type

1   The full flow oil filter is located at the front of the transmission casing in the vicinity of the fuel pump.

2   It is removed by first unscrewing the centre bolt and withdrawing the complete filter assembly.

3   Remove the filter head from the transmission casing.

4   Remove and discard the element and then remove the circlip. Withdraw the centre bolt and lift out the pressure plate, rubber washer, steel washer and spring from the casing.

5   Remove the old sealing ring from the filter head and the old gasket located between the filter head and transmission casing.

6   Thoroughly wash all components in petrol and wipe dry with a clean, lint-free rag. Make sure that the mating faces of the filter head and transmission casing are really clean.

7   Fit the centre bolt to the filter bowl and slide on the spring, steel washer and new rubber washer followed by the pressure plate (photo).

8   Secure the pressure plate in position with the circlip (photo).

9   Using a screwdriver, carefully ease a new sealing ring into the filter head by first fitting the ring into the groove at four equidistant points. Press it home a segment at a time (photo).

10   Do not insert the ring at just one point and work round the groove by pressing it home as, using this method, it is easy to stretch the ring and be left with a small loop of rubber which will not fit into the locating groove.

11   Insert a new oil filter element into the filter bowl (photo).

12   If a central seal is fitted to the filter head, discard it. **Do not** fit another one (photo).

13   Fit the filter head over the centre bolt, making sure that the filter bowl locates correctly on the rubber sealing ring in the filter head (photo).

14   Smear a little grease onto the transmission casing filter head mating face and fit the new gasket noting that the oil filter face is marked (photo).

15   Refit the complete filter assembly and secure with the centre bolt (photo).

Cartridge type

16   The disposable cartridge type filter is removed by unscrewing the

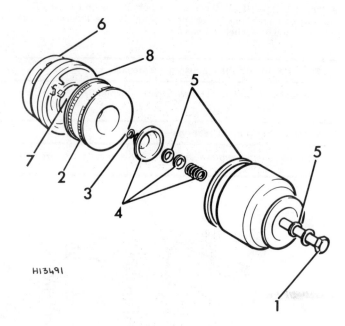

H13491

Fig. 1.11 Renewable element type filter – exploded view (Sec 25)

1	Centre bolt	5	Rubber washers and sealing
2	Element		ring
3	Centre bolt circlip	6	Gasket for filter head
4	Pressure plate, rubber and	7	Centre bolt sealing ring
	steel washers and spring		– discard if fitted
		8	Filter head

complete assembly. It is seldom possible to do this by hand and is normally achieved by using a special filter spanner, a chain wrench, or a strap wrench. If neither of these tools is available, drive a long screwdriver right through the cartridge and use the screwdriver as a tommy bar. Whatever method of removal is used, have a drip tray beneath the filter ready to catch up to 1 pint (0.6 litre) of oil.

17   Clean the face of the cylinder block against which the filter seals and then smear it with engine oil.

18   If the sealing ring is not already fitted to the new filter, smear the seal with oil and press it into the groove on the filter by first locating it at four equally spaced points on its circumference and then bedding it fully all round. Do not insert the seal at one point only and then bed it progressively round the circumference because this may result in the seal having a small hump which may leak.

19   Screw the cartridge onto the cylinder block by hand until the seal just contacts the face of the block and then tighten it by hand a further half turn. Do not use any tool to fit the filter and do not over tighten it.

20   Check and if necessary top-up the oil level. Start the engine and check for leaks.

26 Ventilation air filter – removal and refitting

1   To provide air for ventilating the engine, a filter is located on the flywheel housing.

2   At the specified intervals, renew the filter compounds. On early models, unscrew the cover retaining screw (later models do not have this screw). Lift off the cover and the element (photo).

3   Unscrew the valve from the crankcase.

4   Discard the old cover, filter and valve.

5   Fit the new components in the reverse order to removal.

27 Oil pressure relief valve

1   The oil pressure relief valve is non-adjustable so, if its operation is suspect, a new assembly must be obtained and fitted. It is located under the oil filter head.

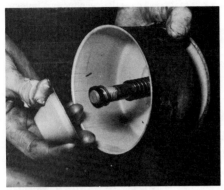

25.7 Relative positions of filter spring and washers

25.8 Fitting the pressure plate retaining circlip

25.9 Fitting the sealing ring

25.11 Inserting the filter

25.12 If a central seal is fitted, discard it

25.13 Fitting the filter head

25.14 Correct fitting of gasket

25.15 Refitting the filter assembly

26.2 Ventilation air filter assembly (early type)

2 Refer to Section 25 and remove the oil filter and head assembly.
3 Draw the oil pressure relief valve from its bore in the transmission case. Note the location of the release hole which must point downwards (photo).
4 There is a line scribed on the face of the pressure relief valve to act as a guide for refitting. This is shown in Fig. 1.12.
5 Refitting is the reverse procedure to removal.

28 Oil pump – removal and dismantling

Manual transmission

To gain access to the oil pump remove the complete power unit and then separate the transmission unit from the engine. Full information on this operation will be found in Chapter 6.

1 Bend back the tab washer locking the baffle plate securing bolt in the centre web of the transmission unit. Undo and remove the bolt, tab washer and baffle.
2 Unscrew the oil pump outlet connection which will be found under the oil filter head adjacent to the pressure relief valve. Although a special tool is recommended it is possible to remove it with a mole wrench provided it is clamped securely to the large boss of the outlet connection.
3 Undo and remove the two bolts with spring and plain washers that secure the oil pump to the side of the transmission unit.
4 The oil pump may now be lifted out of the transmission unit.
5 Should it be necessary to remove the oil pump pick up, it is necessary to remove the fifth speed gear.
6 To dismantle the oil pump, first undo and remove the three bolts and spring washers which secure the suction filter housing to the body.
7 Lift away the intake filter assembly.
8 The motor and shaft assembly and outer ring may now be withdrawn from the body.

27.3 Oil release hole in relief valve

H13492

Fig. 1.12 Oil pressure relief valve (Sec 27)

1   Relief valve
2   Mark to show position of release hole

9   Undo and remove the bolts and spring washers holding the two parts of the intake filter assembly together. Separate the two parts and lift away the strainer and joint washer.

Automatic transmission

10   Removal of the oil pump from cars fitted with automatic transmission is not covered in this manual due to the need for major dismantling of the transmission assembly.

29 Chain tensioner – dismantling

With the tensioner removed from the engine as described in

Section 16, fit a $\frac{1}{8}$ in Allen key to its socket in the cylinder and, holding the slipper and plunger firmly, turn the key clockwise to free the cylinder and spring from the plunger.

30 Engine – examination and renovation (general)

1   With the engine stripped down and all parts thoroughly clean it is time to examine everything for wear or damage. The items in Sections 31 to 41 following should be checked and where necessary renewed or renovated.
2   In any border line cases it is always best to decide in favour of a new part. Even if a part may still be serviceable its life will have been reduced by wear and the degree of trouble needed to renew it in the future must be taken into consideration.
3   This is a relative situation; it depends on whether a quick job is being done, or the car as a whole is being regarded as having many thousands of miles of useful and economical life remaining.

31 Crankshaft – examination and renovation

1   Look at the main bearing journals and the crankpins. If there are any scratches or score marks then the shaft will need regrinding. Such conditions will nearly always be accompanied by similar deterioration on the matching bearing shells.
2   Each bearing journal should also be round and can be checked with a micrometer or caliper gauge around the periphery at several points. If there is more than 0.001 in (0.025 mm) of ovality regrinding is necessary.
3   A BL garage or motor engineering specialist will be able to decide to what extent regrinding is necessary and supply the special undersize bearings to match.
4   Before taking the crankshaft for regrinding, check the cylinder bores and pistons, as it may be advantageous to have the whole unit done together.

32 Crankshaft, main bearings and big-end bearings – examination and renovation

1   With careful servicing and regular oil and filter changes, bearings will last for a very long time but they can still fail for unforeseen reasons. With big-end bearings, the indication of failure is a regular rhythmic loud knocking from the crankcase. The frequency depends on engine speed and is particularly noticeable when the engine is under load. This symptom is accompanied by a fall in oil pressure, although this is not noticeable unless an accurate oil pressure gauge is fitted. Main bearing failure is usually indicated by serious vibration, particularly at higher engine revolutions, accompanied by a more significant drop in oil pressure and a 'rumbling' noise.
2   Bearing shells in good condition have bearing surfaces with a smooth, even matt silver/grey colour all over. Worn bearings will show patches of a different colour when the bearing metal has worn and exposed the underlay. Damaged bearings will be pitted or scored. Always fit new shells. Their cost is relatively low. If the crankshaft is in good condition it is merely a question of obtaining another set of standard size shells. A reground crankshaft will need new bearing shells as a matter of course.

33 Cylinder bores – examination and renovation

1   A new cylinder bore is perfectly round and the walls parallel throughout its length. The action of the piston tends to wear the walls at right angles to the gudgeon pin due to side thrust. This wear takes place principally on that section of the cylinder swept by the piston rings.
2   It is possible to get an indication of bore wear by removing the cylinder head with the engine still in the car. With the piston down in the bore, first signs of wear can be seen and felt just below the top of the bore where the top piston ring reaches, and there will be a noticeable lip. If there is no lip evident, it is reasonable to expect that bore wear is not severe and any lack of compression or excessive oil consumption is due to either worn or broken piston rings, pistons, valves or guides.

3   If it is possible to obtain an internal micrometer, measure the bore in the thrust plane below the lip and again at the bottom of the cylinder bore in the same plane. If the difference is more than 0.003 in (0.076 mm) then a rebore is necessary. Similarly a difference of 0.003 in (0.076 mm) or more across the bore diameter is a sign of ovality calling for a rebore.

4   Any bore which is significantly scratched or scored will need reboring. This symptom usually indicates that the piston or rings are also damaged in that cylinder. In the event of any one cylinder being in need of reboring, it will still be necessary for all four to be bored and fitted with new oversize pistons and rings. Your BL garage or local motor engineering specialist will be able to rebore and obtain the necessary matched pistons. If the crankshaft is undergoing regrinding, it is a good idea to let the same firm renovate and reassemble the crankshaft and pistons to the cylinder block. A reputable firm normally gives a guarantee for such work. In cases where engines have been rebored already to their maximum, new cylinder liners are available which may be fitted. In such cases the same reboring processes have to be followed and the services of a specialist engineering firm are required.

34 Pistons and piston rings – examination and renovation

1   Worn pistons and rings can usually be diagnosed when the symptoms of excessive oil consumption and low compression occur and are sometimes, though not always, associated with worn cylinder bores. Compression testers that fit into the spark plug holes are available and these can indicate where low compression is occurring. Wear usually accelerates the more it is left, so when the symptoms occur early action can possibly save the expense of a rebore.

2   Another sympton of piston wear is piston slap – a knocking noise from the crankcase not to be confused with big-end bearing failure. It can be heard clearly at low engine speed when there is no load (idling for example) and is much less audible when the engine speed increases. Piston wear usually occurs in the skirt or lower end of the piston and is indicated by vertical streaks in the worn area which is always on the thrust side. It can be seen where the skirt thickness is different.

3   Piston ring wear can be checked by first removing the rings from the pistons as described in Section 21. Then place the rings in the cylinder bores from the top, pushing them down about 1.5 in (38 mm) with the head of a piston from which the rings have been removed) so that they rest squarely in the cylinder bore. Then measure the gap at

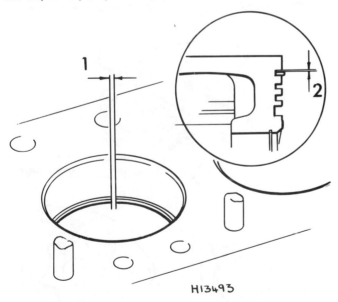

Fig. 1.13 Piston ring wear measurement (Sec 34)

1   Ring gap measurement   2   Ring groove measurement

the ends of the ring with a feeler gauge. If it exceeds 0.022 in (0.56 mm) for the compression rings or 0.045 in (1.2 mm) for the lower oil control ring, then they need renewal.

4   The grooves in which the rings locate in the piston can also become enlarged in use. The clearance between ring and piston, in the groove, should not exceed 0.0035 in (0.089 mm) for each ring.

5   However, it is rare that a piston is only worn in the ring grooves, and the need to renew them for this fault alone is hardly ever encountered. Whenever pistons are renewed, the weight of the four piston/connecting rod assemblies should be kept within the limit variations of 0.3 oz (8 grms) to maintain correct engine balance.

35 Connecting rods and gudgeon pins – examination and renovation

1   Gudgeon pins are a tight fit in the little-end of the connecting rods. Neither of these would normally need renewal unless the pistons are being changed, in which case the new pistons would automatically be supplied with new gudgeon pins.

2   Connecting rods are not subject to wear but, in extreme circumstances such as engine seizure, they could be distorted. Such conditions may be visually apparent, but where doubt exists they should be checked. The bearing caps should also be examined for indications of filing down which may have been attempted in the mistaken idea that bearing slackness could be remedied in this way. If there are such signs then the connecting rods should be renewed.

36 Camshaft and camshaft bearings – examination and renovation

1   The camshaft itself should show no sign of wear, but if very slight score marks on the cams are noticed, they can be removed by very gently rubbing down with very fine emery cloth or an oil stone. The greatest care should be taken to keep the cam profiles smooth.

2   Carefully examine the camshaft bearing surfaces for wear and, if evident, the camshaft must be renewed.

3   Check the camshaft fit in the cast aluminium housing and, if side movement is evident, a new housing must be obtained. The camshaft runs directly in the aluminium housing and does not have white metal bushes.

37 Tappets – examination and renovation

1   The little shims found inside the tappet bucket must be kept with the relative tappet and not interchanged.

2   The faces of the tappets which bear on the camshaft lobes should show no signs of pitting, scoring, fracturing or other forms of wear. They should not be a loose fit in the aluminium housing. Wear is normally encountered at very high mileages or in cases of neglected engine lubrication. Renew the tappets or housing as necessary.

38 Valves and valve seats – examination and renovation

1   With the valves removed from the cylinder head, examine the heads for signs of cracking, burning away and pitting of the edges where they seat in the ports. The seats of the valves in the cylinder head should also be examined for the same signs. Usually it is the valve that deteriorates first, but if a bad valve is not rectified the seat will suffer and this is more difficult to repair.

2   Provided there are no obvious signs of serious pitting, the valve should be ground into its seat. This may be done by placing a smear of carborundum paste on the edge of the valve head and using a suction type valve holder, grinding the valve in situ. Use a semi-rotary action; rotating the handle of the valve holder between the hands and lifting it occasionally to re-distribute the traces of paste. Start with a coarse paste and finish with a fine paste.

3   As soon as a matt grey unbroken line appears on both the valve and seat, the valve is 'ground in'. All traces of carbon should also be cleaned from the head and neck of the valve stem. A wire brush mounted in a power drill is a quick and effective way of doing this.

4   If the valve requires renewal, it should be ground into the seat in the same way as the old valve.

5   Another form of valve wear can occur on the stem where it runs in
the guide in the cylinder head. This can be detected by trying to rock
the valve from side to side. If there is any movement at all, it is an
indication that the valve stem or guide is worn. Check the stem first
with a micrometer at points along and around its length, and if they are
not within the specified size new valves will probably solve the
problem. If the guides are worn however, they will need reboring for
oversize valves or for fitting guide inserts. The valve seats will also
need recutting to ensure they are concentric with the stems. This work
should be given to your local BL garage or engineering works.
6   When the valve seats are badly burnt or pitted, requiring renovation, inserts may be fitted – or renewed if previously fitted – and once
again this is a specialist task to be carried out by a suitable engineering
firm.
7   When all valve grinding is completed, it is essential that every
trace of grinding paste is removed from the valves and ports in the
cylinder head. This should be done by thorough washing in petrol or
paraffin and blowing out with a jet of air. If particles of carborundum
paste should work their way into the engine this would cause havoc
with bearings or cylinder walls.

39 Timing sprockets and chain – examination and renovation

1   Carefully examine the teeth on both the crankshaft and camshaft
sprockets for wear. Each tooth forms an inverted V with the gear
wheel periphery and if worn, the side of each tooth under tension will
be slightly concave in shape when compared with the other side of the
tooth. If any sign of wear is present, the sprockets must be renewed.
2   Examine the links of the chain for side slackness and renew the
chain if any slackness is noticeable when compared with a new chain.
It is a sensible precaution to renew the chain at about 30 000 miles
(50 000 km) and at a lesser mileage if the engine is stripped down for
major overhaul. The actual rollers on a very badly worn chain may be
slightly grooved.

40 Flywheel starter ring – examination and renovation

1   If the teeth on the flywheel starter ring gear are badly worn, or if
some are missing, then it will be necessary to remove the ring. This is
achieved by splitting the oil ring with a cold chisel. The greatest care
must be taken not to damage the flywheel during this process.
2   To fit a new ring gear, heat it gently and evenly with an oxy-
acetylene flame until a temperature of approximately 350°C (660°F)
is reached. This is indicated by a light metallic surface colour. With the
ring gear at this temperature, fit it to the flywheel with the front of the
teeth furthermost from the clutch mounting face. The ring gear should
be either pressed or lightly tapped onto its register and left to cool
naturally when the contraction of the metal on cooling will ensure that
it is a secure and permanent fit. Great care must be taken not to over-
heat the ring gear as if this happens the temper of the ring will be lost.
3   Alternatively the local BL garage or engineering works may have a
suitable oven in which the ring gear can be heated. The normal
domestic oven will only give a maximum temperature of about 250°C
(480°F), except for the latest self cleaning type which will give a
higher temperature. With the former it may just be possible to fit the
ring gear with it at this temperature, but it is unlikely. No great force
should have to be used.

41 Oil pump – examination and renovation

1   Thoroughly clean all the component parts in petrol and then check
the rotor endfloat and lobe clearance.
2   Position the rotor and outer ring in the pump body and place the
straight edge of a steel rule across the joint face of the pump. Measure
the gap between the bottom of the straight edge and the top of the
rotor and outer ring as shown in Fig. 1.15(A). If the measurement
exceeds 0.005 in (0.13 mm) (outer ring) and 0.0055 in (0.14 mm)
(inner rotor) a new pump must be obtained as no individual parts are
obtainable.
3   Measure the gaps between the peaks of the lobes and peaks of the
outer ring with feeler gauges. If the measurement exceeds 0·0035 in
(0·09 mm) a new pump must be obtained, (Fig. 1.15 (B)).

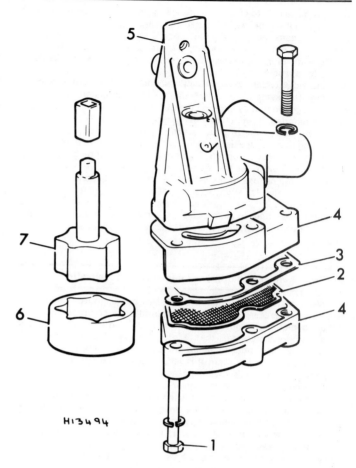

H13494

Fig. 1.14 Oil pump components (Sec 41)

1   Filter housing bolts
2   Filter
3   Gasket
4   Filter housing – upper and

     lower halves
5   Oil pump body
6   Outer ring
7   Rotor and shaft assembly

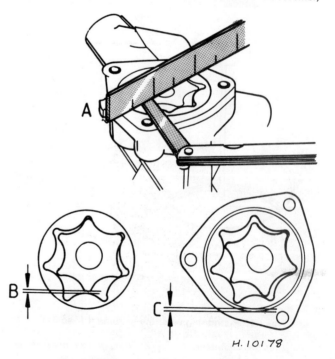

H. 10178

Fig. 1.15 Checking oil pump wear (Sec 41)

4   Measure the clearance betweeen the outer ring and the pump body and if it exceeds 0·011 in (0·28 mm) a new pump must be obtained (Fig. 1.15 (C)).

5   If all parts are satisfactory, assembly is the reverse sequence to dismantling as described in Section 28. Always make sure the strainer is clean and use a new joint washer between the two halves of the strainer body.

6   Tighten the pump securing bolts to the specified torque.

42 Cylinder head – decarbonising

1   This operation can be carried out with the engine either in or out of the car. With the cylinder head off, carefully remove, with a wire brush and blunt scraper, all traces of carbon deposits from the combustion spaces and the ports. The valve stems and valve guides should also be free from any carbon deposits. Wash the combustion spaces and ports down with petrol and scrape the cylinder head surface free of any foreign matter with the side of a steel rule or a similar article. Take care not to scratch the surfaces.

2   Clean the pistons and top of the cylinder bores. If the pistons are still in the cylinder bores, it is essential that great care is taken to ensure that no carbon gets into the bores as this could scratch the cylinder walls or cause damage to the piston and rings. To ensure that this does not happen first turn the crankshaft so that two of the pistons are at the top of the bores. Place clean lint-free rags into the two bores, or seal them off with paper and masking tape. The water and oil ways should also be covered with a small piece of masking tape to prevent particles of carbon entering the cooling system and damaging the water pump, or entering the lubrication system and causing damage to a bearing surface.

3   There are two schools of thought as to how much carbon ought to be removed from the piston crown. One is that a ring of carbon should be left around the edge of the piston and on the cylinder bore wall as an aid to keeping oil consumption low. The other is to remove all traces of carbon during decarbonisation, and leave everything clean.

4   If all traces of carbon are to be removed, press a little grease into the gap between the cylinder walls and the two pistons which are to be worked on. With a blunt scraper carefully scrape away the carbon from the piston crown, taking care not to scratch the aluminium. Also scrape away the carbon from the surrounding lip of the cylinder wall. When all carbon has been removed, scrape away the grease which will now be contaminated with carbon particles, taking care not to press any into the bores. To assist prevention of carbon build up, the piston crown can be polished with metal polish. Remove the rags or masking tape from the other two cylinders and turn the crankshaft so that the two pistons which were at the bottom are now at the top. Place rag into the other two bores, or seal them with paper and masking tape. Do not forget the waterways and oilways as well. Proceed as previously described.

5   If a ring of carbon is going to be left round the piston, this can be helped by inserting an old piston ring into the top of the bore to rest on the piston and ensure that carbon is not accidently removed. Check that there are no particles of carbon in the cylinder bores.

43 Engine – reassembly (general)

1   To ensure maximum life with minimum trouble from a rebuilt engine, not only must every part be correctly assembled, but everything must be spotlessly clean. All the oil-ways must be clear, locking washers and spring washers must always be fitted where indicated, and all bearings and other working surfaces must be thoroughly lubricated during assembly. Before assembly begins, renew any bolts or studs the threads of which are in any way damaged, and whenever possible use new spring washers.

2   Apart from your normal tools, a supply of lint-free rag, an oil can filled with engine oil, a supply of new spring washers, a set of new gaskets and a torque wrench should be collected together.

44 Crankshaft – refitting

Ensure that the crankcase is thoroughly clean and that all the oilways are clear. A thin drill is useful for clearing them out. If possible, blow them out with compressed air. Treat the crankshaft in the same fashion and then inject engine oil into the crankshaft oilways.

1   Replace the main bearing shells by fitting the five upper halves of the main bearing shells to their location in the crankcase, after wiping the location clean. If the old bearings are being used ensure that they are fitted in their original location.

2   Note that on the back of each bearing is a tab which engages in locating grooves in either the crank or the main bearing cap housing (photo).

3   New bearings are coated with protective grease; carefully clean away all traces of this with paraffin and then fit the bearings, noting that the bearing having a coloured edge is fitted to No 4 position.

4   With the five upper bearing shells securely in place, wipe the lower bearing cap housings and fit the five lower shell bearings to their caps ensuring that the right shell goes into the right cap, if the old bearings are being refitted (photo).

5   Wipe the recesses either side of the number 4 main bearing which locate the upper halves of the thrust washers.

6   Smear a little grease onto the recesses for the upper thrust washers within the crankcase. Fit the thrust washers with their grooves facing outwards (photo).

7   Fit the innermost Woodruff key to the nose of the crankshaft (photo).

8   Generously lubricate the crankshaft journals and the upper and lower main bearing shells and carefully lower the crankshaft into position. Make sure that it is the right way round (photo).

9   Fit the main bearing caps into position ensuring that they locate properly on the dowels and that the mating numbers correspond (photo).

10 Apply a little grease to the location for the thrust washers on number 4 main bearing cap. Fit the thrust washers with the grooves facing outwards. Refit the cap to the main bearing web (photo).

11 Refit the long bolts that secure the main bearing caps and screw them up finger tight.

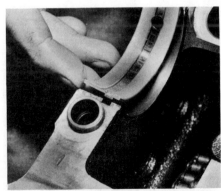
44.2 Fitting a crankcase bearing shell

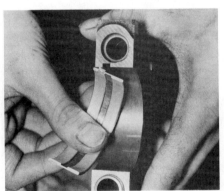
44.4 Fitting a bearing cap shell

44.6 Fitting a thrustwasher

44.7 Crankshaft Woodruff key

44.8 Fitting the crankshaft

44.9 Bearing cap identification mark and locating dowel

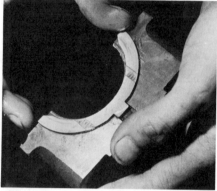
44.10 Bearing cap thrustwasher

44.14 Measuring crankshaft endplay

45.1 Fitting the distributor driveshaft thrustwasher

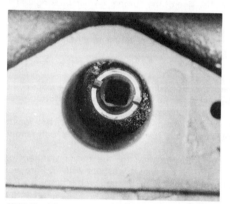
45.3 Position of slot in shaft before crankshaft gear is fitted

45.4 Fitting the gear to the crankshaft

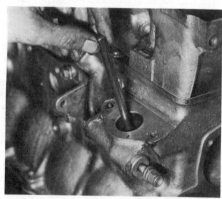
45.6 Inserting the oil pump driveshaft

48.3 Piston with gaps in rings staggered

48.4 Inserting a piston with ring compressor in place

49.5 Fitting a big-end bearing cap

12 Test the crankshaft for freedom of rotation. Should it be very stiff to turn, or posses high spots, a most careful inspection must be made, preferably by a skilled mechanic with a micrometer to trace the cause of the trouble. It is very seldom that any trouble of this nature will be experienced when fitting the crankshaft.
13 Tighten the main bearing bolts to the specified torque and recheck the crankshaft for freedom of rotation.
14 The endfloat of the crankshaft may next be checked. Using a screwdriver as a lever at one of the crankshaft webs and main bearing caps, move the crankshaft longitudinally as far as possible in one direction. Measure the gap between the side of number 4 journal and the thrust washer. Maximum endfloat should be between 0·004 and 0·007 in (0·10 and 0·18 mm) and is adjustable by means of selective thrust washers (photo).

45 Distributor and fuel pump driveshaft – refitting

1 Fit the thrust washer to the driveshaft (photo).
2 Turn the crankshaft until the No 1 and 4 big-end journals are parallel with the cylinder bores. This would be an equivalent TDC position for two of the four pistons.
3 Fit the driveshaft with the drive slot at the 10 o'clock position with the large lobe uppermost (photo).
4 Fit the distributor drivegear. It will be noticed that as the teeth mesh, the shaft will turn anti-clockwise through approximately 90° to bring the drive slot to the 2 o'clock position with the large lobe uppermost. (photo).
5 Refer to photo 18.4 which shows the correct position of the drive slot after the crankshaft gear has been fitted.
6 Insert the oil pump driveshaft into the distributor and fuel pump driveshaft (photo).
7 As a further check, temporarily refit the distributor and make sure that the rotor arm is set to fire on number 1 cylinder.

46 Piston and connecting rod – reassembly

If the same pistons are being used, then they must be mated to the same connecting rod with the same gudgeon pin. If new pistons are being fitted it does not matter with which connecting rod they are used, but the gudgeon pin must be kept matched to its piston.

Upon reference to Section 20 it will be seen that a special tool was required to remove the gudgeon pin from the piston and connecting rod assembly. This tool is now required to refit the gudgeon pin.

1 Unscrew the large nut and withdraw the centre screw from the body a few inches. Well lubricate the screw thread and correctly locate the piston support adaptor.
2 Carefully slide the parallel sleeve with the groove end last onto the centre screw, up as far as the shoulder. Lubricate the gudgeon pin and its bores in the connecting rod and piston with graphite oil.
3 Fit the connecting rod and piston, side marked 'front' or '△' to the tool, with the connecting rod entered on the sleeve up to the groove. Fit the gudgeon pin into the piston bore up to the connecting rod. Next fit the remover/refitment bush flange end towards the gudgeon pin.
4 Screw the stop nut onto the centre screw and adjust the nut to give a 0·040 in (1·0 mm) end play 'B' as shown in Fig. 1.9. Lock the nut securely with the lock screw. Ensure that the curved face of the adaptor is clean, and slide the piston on the tool so that it fits into the curved face of the adaptor with the piston rings over the adaptor cutaway.
5 Screw the large nut up to the thrust race. Adjust the torque wrench to a setting of 12 lbf ft (1·7 kgf m) which will represent the minimum load for an acceptable fit. Use the torque wrench previously set on the large nut, and a ring spanner on the lock screw. Pull the gudgeon pin into the the piston until the flange of the remover/refitment bush is 0·390 in (10 mm) for a gudgeon pin length of 2·75 in (69·85 mm) or 0·330 in (8·38 mm) for a gudgeon pin length of 2·62 in (66·59 mm) from the piston skirt.
6 Should the torque not exceed 12 lbf ft (1·7 kgf m) throughout the pull, the fit of the gudgeon pin in the connecting rod is not within limits and the parts must be renewed.
7 Ensure that the piston pivots freely on the gudgeon pin and it is free to slide sideways. Should stiffness exist, wash the assembly in paraffin, lubricate the gudgeon pin and recheck. Again if stiffness

exists, dismantle the assembly and recheck for signs of ingrained dirt and damage.

47 Piston rings – refitting

1 Check that the piston ring grooves and oilways are thoroughly clean and unblocked. Piston rings must always be fitted over the head of the piston and never from the bottom.
2 The easiest method to use when fitting rings is to wrap a long 0·020 in (0·5 mm) feeler gauge round the top of the piston and fit the rings one at a time, starting from the bottom oil control ring.
3 Fit the bottom rail of the oil control ring to the piston and position it below the bottom groove. Refit the oil control expander into the bottom groove and move the bottom oil control ring rail up into the bottom groove. Fit the top oil control rail into the bottom groove.
4 Ensure that the ends of the expander are butting, but not overlapping. Set the gaps of the rails and the expander at 90° to each other.
5 Refit the third and second tapered compression rings with the side marked top uppermost. Note: on 1750 engines the tapered compression ring is fitted into the second groove only.
6 Fit the chromium plated compression ring to the top groove.

48 Pistons – refitting

1 With a wad of clean lint-free rag wipe the cylinder bores clean.
2 The pistons, complete with connecting rods, are fitted to their bores from above.
3 Set the piston ring gaps so that the gaps are equidistant around the circumference of the piston (photo).
4 Well lubricate the top of the piston and fit a ring compressor or a jubilee clip of suitable diameter and shim steel (photo).
5 As each piston is inserted into its bore ensure that it is the correct piston/connecting rod assembly for that particular bore; that the connecting rod is the right way round; and that the front of the piston is towards the front of the bore ie, towards the chain chest of the engine. Lubricate the piston and bore generously.
6 The piston will slide into the bore only as far as the ring compressor. Gently tap the piston into the bore with a wooden or plastic hammer.

49 Connecting rod to crankshaft – refitting

1 Wipe clean the connecting rod half of the big-end bearing cap and the underside of the shell bearing, and fit the shell bearing in position with its locating tongue engaged with the corresponding groove in the connecting rod.
2 If the old bearings are nearly new and are being refitted then ensure they are fitted in their correct locations in the correct rods.
3 Generously lubricate the crankpin journals, and turn the crankshaft so that the crankpin is in the most advantageous position for the connecting rod to be drawn onto it.
4 Wipe clean the connecting rod bearing cap and back of the shell bearing and fit the shell bearing in position ensuring that the locating tongue at the back of the bearing engages with the locating groove in the connecting rod cap.
5 Generously lubricate the shell bearing and offer up the connecting rod cap to the connecting rod (photo).
6 Fit new multi-sided nuts to the connecting rod bolts and tighten to the specified torque (photo).
7 Repeat the above described procedures for the three remaining piston/connecting rod assemblies.

50 Timing chain, crankshaft sprocket and tensioner – refitting

1 If the chain was removed for renewal, fit the new chain into the cylinder block.
2 Rivet the chain, using a link connector riveter, or the specified tool (18G 1151).
3 Fit the second Woodruff key to the crankshaft nose and locate the crankshaft sprocket on the crankshaft with the tapered face outwards. Drift into its final position with a piece of tube.
4 Engage the chain into mesh with the crankshaft sprocket.

49.6 Fitted bearing cap showing multi-sided nuts and identification marks

50.7 Inserting the fixed guide

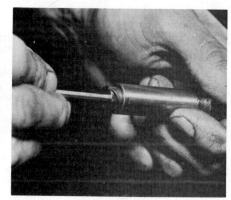
50.11 Compressing the plunger spring

50.12 Fitting the tensioner and adaptor

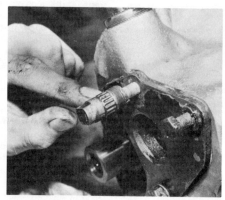
50.15 Fitting the cover plate

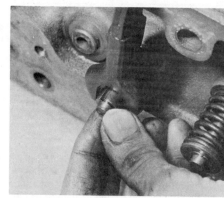
51.3 Inserting the split cotters

52.4 Fitting the cylinder head

53.1 Tappet and shim

53.4 Fitting the tappet housing

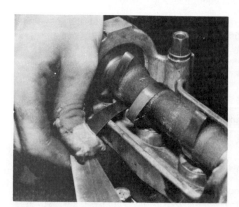
54.7 Measuring cam to tappet clearance

54.8 Turning the camshaft using a Mole wrench

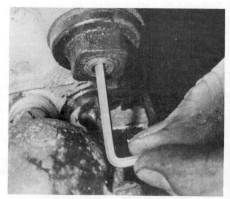
54.16 Retracting the chain tensioner

5   Fit the adjustable guide into the chain chest making sure that the lower end engages in the adjuster.

6   If the adjuster has been removed, check that it is correctly positioned so that the guide is not moved out of vertical alignment.

7   Fit the fixed guide and lightly tighten the two securing bolts, spring and plain washers (photo).

8   Tighten the adjuster screw until the guide is positioned vertically in the chain chamber and secure in position with the locknut.

9   Fully tighten the two bolts securing the chain guides.

10 Assemble the chain tensioner by inserting one end of the spring into the cylinder.

11 Compress the spring until the cylinder enters the plunger bore and ensure the peg in the plunger engages the helical slot. Insert and turn a $\frac{1}{8}$ in Allen key clockwise until the end of the cylinder is below the peg and the spring is held compressed (photo).

12 Insert the tensioner into the aperture at the front of the chain chamber and engage it into the adaptor. Screw in the adaptor (photo).

13 Clean the mating faces of the engine front cover and crankcase and fit a new gasket to the front cover.

14 Fit the cover in position and locate the long bolt so that it engages with the fixed chain guide.

15 Secure the front cover with the conventional bolt and dynamo adjustment link pivot, both using spring washers (photo). Tighten the bolts to the specified torque.

51 Valves and valve springs – reassembly

1   Rest the cylinder head on its side and insert each valve and valve spring in turn, wiping down and lubricating each valve stem as it is inserted into the same valve guide from which it was removed.

2   An oil seal is fitted between the cylinder head and valve spring on inlet valves only.

3   Fit the spring cups to the top of the valve springs and, with the base of the valve compressor on the valve head, compress the valve spring until the cotters can be slipped into place in the cotter grooves (photo).

4   Gently release the valve spring compressor.

5   Repeat this procedure until all eight valves and valve springs are fitted.

52 Cylinder head – refitting

After checking that both the cylinder block and cylinder head mating faces are perfectly clean, generously lubricate each cylinder.

1   Always use a new cylinder head gasket as the old gasket will be compressed and not capable of giving a good seal.

2   Never smear grease on either side of the gasket for when the engine heats up, the grease will melt and may allow compression leaks to develop.

3   Carefully lower the new cylinder head gasket into position. It is not possible to fit it the wrong way round.

4   With the gasket in position carefully lower the cylinder head onto the cylinder block (photo).

5   With the cylinder head in position fit the cylinder head bolts, having first oiled the threads, then screw in the bolts finger tight.

6   When all are in position, tighten in a diagonal and progressive manner to the specified torque.

53 Camshaft and tappets – refitting

Unless new parts have been fitted to the cylinder head, camshaft, or camshaft housing, the chances are that the valve clearances will not have to be reset as the original shims will be refitted to the tappet buckets which will also be refitted in their original positions. If new parts have been fitted, the camshaft and tappets must still be refitted and then the instructions followed as described in Section 54.

1   Smear the shims with petroleum jelly and then fit them into the tappets (photo).

2   Lubricate the camshaft bearings and carefully slide the camshaft into the housing.

3   Invert the camshaft housing and place the tappets in their respective bores in the order in which they were removed.

4   Place the fingers over the tappets as shown in this photograph and carefully refit the housing, taking care to seat the tappets onto the valve stems (photo).

5   Temporarily refit the camshaft sprocket to the camshaft, and turn the camshaft until the sprocket and housing marks align.

6   Fit the six housing securing bolts and tighten in a progressive and diagonal manner to the specified torque.

7   Refer to Section 54 and check the tappet clearance. If adjustment is necessary, remove the camshaft housing and lift out the relevant tappets. Recover the shim inside the tappet and by calculation select the correct shim. Reassemble the tappet and camshaft housing again.

54 Tappet adjustment

It is not usual for the tappets to need re-adjustment throughout the life of the engine because of the lack of moving parts normally found with overhead valve installations. The reason for this is that the camshaft bears directly on the top of the tappet which in turn is in direct contact with the valve stem. Should new parts have been fitted then it will be necessary to check the clearances and adjust as necessary.

1   Obtain a micrometer or very accurate vernier.

2   Open the bonnet and pull the breather hose from the cylinder head cover.

3   Pull the fuel feed pipe from the carburettor float chamber union and draw it through the thermostat housing clip.

4   Plug the end of the fuel pipe with a piece of tapered wood such as a pencil to stop fuel spurting out when the camshaft is rotated.

5   Pull off the ignition vacuum pipe from the manifold side of the carburettor body.

6   Undo and remove the six cylinder head cover securing bolts. Lift away the cover and the gasket.

7   Using a feeler gauge, check the clearance between the cam lobe and the tappet of each valve in the order given in the table (photo). Make a note of the results obtained.

8   The camshaft must only be turned **against** the normal direction of rotation. For this a Mole wrench will make the job easier (photo).

Check No 1 tappet with No 8 valve fully open
Check No 3 tappet with No 6 valve fully open
Check No 5 tappet with No 4 valve fully open
Check No 2 tappet with No 7 valve fully open
Check No 8 tappet with No 1 valve fully open
Check No 6 tappet with No 3 valve fully open
Check No 4 tappet with No 5 valve fully open
Check No 7 tappet with No 2 valve fully open

9   Once the readings have been tabulated for all valves it should be noted that, unless new parts have been fitted or the valve seats reground, adjustment of the valve tappet clearance to the standard setting is only necessary if the clearance of either inlet or exhaust is less than 0.012 in (0.3 mm).

10 On vehicles with automatic transmission, remove the plug from the timing aperture on the underside of the converter housing and ensure that the zero mark on the converter is aligned with the pointer and that No 1 cylinder is about to start its firing stroke. Turn the engine in its normal direction of rotation to achieve alignment.

11 On manual transmission models, remove the two bolts and spring washers securing the flywheel housing timing cover and remove the cover. Align the 1/4 TDC mark on the flywheel with the pointer when No 1 cylinder is about to start its firing stroke. On later models there are timing marks on the crankshaft pulley and the timing chain case and on these models it is not necessary to remove the flywheel housing timing cover.

12 Check that the camshaft sprocket and the housing marks align correctly.

13 Undo and remove the positive and then the negative terminal from the battery. Unscrew the battery clamp bar securing nuts and lift away the clamp bar and battery.

14 Undo and remove the four bolts and spring washers securing the combined top radiator stay and front lifting bracket. Lift away the bracket.

15 Undo and remove the two bolts and spring washers securing the engine steady and lifting bracket from the flywheel end of the cylinder head.

16 Remove the chain tensioner adaptor screw. Insert a $\frac{1}{8}$ in Allen key

into the screw aperture and turn it in a clockwise direction so as to retract the tensioner slipper (photo).

17 Undo and remove the bolt and spring washer securing the camshaft sprocket to the camshaft and withdraw the sprocket.

18 Undo and remove the six bolts which secure the camshaft housing to the cylinder head in a diagonal and progressive manner.

19 Carefully lift the camshaft housing sufficiently to allow the tappets to fall clear of the camshaft housing and remain in position on the valve stems. Draw the camshaft out of the housing from the flywheel end.

20 Remove the maladjusted tappet and recover the adjustment shim from within the tappet.

21 Note the thickness of the shim originally fitted (photo) and by using the following calculation determine the new thickness of shim required to give the correct valve clearance.

Clearance as determined in paragraph 7 = A inch
Thickness of shim removed = B inch
Correct clearance = C inch
New shim thickness required = A + B − C inch

22 Shims are available in the following thicknesses:

0.097 in (2.47 mm) 0.113 in (2.87 mm)
0.099 in (2.52 mm) 0.115 in (2.93 mm)
0.101 in (2.56 mm) 0.117 in (2.98 mm)
0.103 in (2.62 mm) 0.119 in (3.03 mm)
0.105 in (2.67 mm) 0.121 in (3.08 mm)
0.107 in (2.72 mm) 0.123 in (3.13 mm)
0.109 in (2.77 mm) 0.125 in (3.18 mm)
0.111 in (2.83 mm) 0.127 in (3.23 mm)

Thicker shims are available for 1750 twin carburettor models in eight sizes from 0.135 in (3.43 mm) to 0.149 in (3.78 mm) in increments of 0.002 in (0·05 mm).

23 Always check the shim thickness with a micrometer.

24 If a range of shims is not available and the clearance is less than 0.012 in (0·3 mm) it is possible to grind off a little metal from a shim using an oil stone, lubricated with paraffin. Keep a check on the thickness of metal being removed, using the micrometer.

25 Smear the shims in petroleum jelly and fit them into the tappets.

26 Refit the tappets into their respective guides and insert the camshaft into the camshaft housing from the flywheel end.

27 The sequence for reassembly is now the reverse sequence to removal. Further information may be found in Section 53.

28 Check that the crankshaft is positioned with No 1 piston at TDC on compression, and that the camshaft sprocket and carrier timing marks are in alignment.

29 With the camshaft sprocket engaged with the timing chain, refit it to the camshaft and tighten the retaining bolt to the specified torque.

30 Loosen the locknut of the adjustable chain guide, and turn the adjuster with a screwdriver until the timing chain is tight but not taut, then tighten the locknut.

31 Using a $\frac{1}{8}$ in Allen key, release the chain tensioner by turning it anti-clockwise. Remove the key and tighten the bolt into the adaptor.

32 The radiator stay, lifting bracket securing bolts and spring washers should be tightened to the specified torque.

33 The engine steady and flywheel end lifting bracket securing bolts and spring washers should be tightened to the specified torque.

55 Engine – refitting to transmission

Full information will be found in Chapter 6

56 Crankshaft pulley and vibration damper – refitting

1 Fit the pulley hub Woodruff key to the milled slot in the crankshaft (photo). This, and the operation in the next paragraph, can be done with the engine away from the transmission unit if considered more convenient.

2 Slide the oil slinger over the end of the crankshaft nose and push up against the crankshaft sprocket (photo).

3 With the engine bolted to the transmission unit, cut the protruding ends of the oil seals with a sharp knife. Take care they do not fall into the transmission casing (photo).

4 Lubricate the front seal and carefully push it into position. Note on

some seals the word TOP is marked on the front face (photo).

5 Ease the crankshaft pulley and vibration damper over the nose of the crankshaft and engage the keyway with the Woodruff key previously positioned on the crankshaft.

6 Refit the pulley securing bolt and a new tab washer (photo).

7 Tighten the pulley securing bolt to the specified torque.

8 To enable this operation to be carried out satisfactorily it will be necessary to lock the crankshaft using a screwdriver as shown (photo).

57 Engine – final reassembly

1 Fit a new combined inlet and exhaust manifold gasket taking care it is fitted the correct way round (photo).

2 Carefully refit the combined inlet and exhaust manifold and carburettor installation to the side of the cylinder head and secure in position with the nuts, spring washers and bolts. Tighten all fixings in a progressive and diagonal manner (photo).

3 Refit the oil pressure warning light switch to the right-hand side of the cylinder block (photo).

4 Ease the starter motor drive into position. Make sure the main terminal is away from the cylinder block for inertia type starter motors (photo).

5 Secure the starter motor with the two bolts and spring washers.

6 Refit the radiator top mounting to the top of the cylinder head and secure with the two bolts and spring washers (photo).

7 Refit the engine steady and lifting bracket to the flywheel end of the cylinder head. Secure with the two bolts and spring washers (photo).

8 Refit the radiator lower mounting and secure with the two bolts and spring washers (photo).

9 Slowly turn the crankshaft in the normal direction of rotation until the $\frac{1}{4}$ TDC mark on the flywheel is aligned with the pointer. No 1 cylinder should be at the top of the compression stroke and just about to commence the power stroke.

10 Fit the distributor with the clamp plate and engage the driving dog into the distributor driveshaft. The rotor arm should now point to the segment in the distributor cap which leads to No 1 spark plug (the one nearest the fan).

11 Refit the two distributor clamp bolts and washers and lightly tighten. The ignition should be accurately set when the engine is back in the car as described in Chapter 4.

12 Slide the dynamo or alternator adjustment link over its mounting on the cylinder block.

13 Thread the long dynamo or alternator mounting bolt through the cast web on the cylinder block and the front end bracket, and lightly secure with the spring washer and nyloc nut (photo).

14 Refit the rear mounting bolt, spring washer and nyloc nut.

15 Assemble the water pump pulley and fan and offer up to the water pump drive flange. Secure with the three bolts and spring washers (photo).

16 Refit the fan belt and adjust the position of the dynamo until there is 0·5 in (13 mm) of lateral movement at the mid point position of the belt run between the dynamo pulley and the water pump.

17 Clean the mating faces of the thermostat housing and cylinder head and fit a new gasket to the thermostat housing (photo).

18 Fit the housing to the cylinder head and tighten the three securing bolts.

19 Fit the thermostat into the housing (photo).

20 Make sure the mating faces of the top hose elbow and thermostat housing are clean and fit a new gasket.

21 Fit the three elbow securing bolts noting that one also retains the fuel pipe clip (photo). Tighten the three bolts to the specified torque.

22 Refit the dip stick guide tube union to the side of the transmission casing (photo).

23 Ease the fuel feed pipe onto the float chamber union.

24 Refit the ignition coil mounting bracket and any radio suppressor capacitors to the side of the cylinder block and secure with the two bolts, plain and spring washers (photo).

25 Fit the hose onto the water pump and position the clip so that it may be easily undone when the engine is back in the car.

26 Refit the mounting to the power unit at the rear of the cylinder block near to the left-hand end by the fan (photo). Secure with the nut, spring and plain washer.

27 Fit new spark plugs to the cylinder head. Do not forget to check

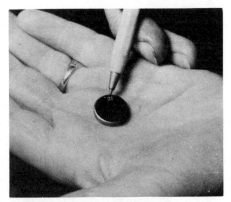
54.21 Thickness marking on shim

56.1 Crankshaft pulley key

56.2 Fitting the oil thrower

56.3 Trimming the crankcase oil seal

56.4 Fitting the front oil seal

56.6 Fitting the pulley, bolt and tab washer

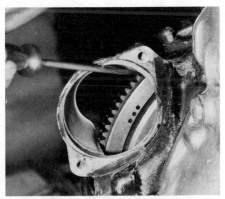
56.8 Preventing rotation of the flywheel

57.1 Fitting the manifold gasket

57.2 Fitting the manifold

57.3 Fitting the oil pressure switch

57.4 Fitting the starter motor

57.6 Fitting the radiator top mounting bracket

57.7 Fitting the engine steady bracket

57.8 Fitting the radiator lower mounting bracket

57.13 Fitting the dynamo

57.15 Fitting the water pump pulley and fan

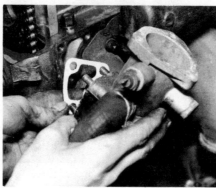

57.17 Thermostat housing and gasket

57.19 Fitting the thermostat

57.21 Fitting the thermostat cover

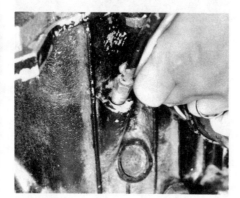

57.22 Fitting the dipstick guide

57.24 Fitting the ignition coil

the electrode gaps first.

28 Refit the radiator to the upper and lower mounting brackets and secure with the four bolts and plain washers (photo).

29 Tighten the top and bottom radiator hose clips.

30 Insert the fuel pump pushrod, and then the fuel pump. Secure with the two bolts and spring washers (photos).

31 The cylinder head cover should not be fitted until the complete power unit is in place, as it is easily damaged.

---

58 Engine and transmission – refitting

Although the engine can be refitted by one man and a suitable winch, it is easier if two are present, one to control the winch and the other to guide the engine into position so it does not foul anything. Generally speaking refitting is a reversal of the procedures used when removing the unit, but the following points are of special note:

1 Ensure all the loose leads, cables etc, are tucked out of the way. If

not, it is easy to trap one and so cause much additional work after the unit is fitted.

2 Carefully lower the engine whilst an assistant recouples the driveshafts to the final drive unit. When finally in position, refit the following:

    (a) Mounting nuts, bolts and washers
    (b) Speedometer drive cable
    (c) Clutch slave cylinder; check adjustment (early models)
    (d) Gear change linkage/cables
    (e) Wires to oil pressure switch, temperature gauge thermal transmitter, ignition coil, distributor and dynamo (or alternator)
    (f) Carburettor controls
    (g) Air cleaner and cylinder head cover
    (h) Exhaust system/down pipe to manifold
    (i) Earth and starter motor cables
    (j) Heater and servo hoses
    (k) Vacuum advance and retard pipe

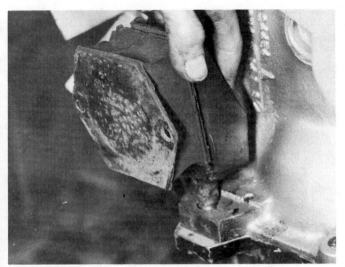

57.26 Fitting the LH engine mounting

57.28 Fitting the radiator

57.30A Inserting the fuel pump pushrod

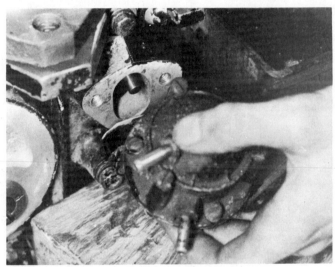

57.30B Fitting the fuel pump

(l) Distributor cap and HT leads
(m) Fuel pump
(n) Battery
(o) If applicable, bleed brake hydraulic system and pressurise the suspension

3   Check that the drain taps are closed and refill the cooling system with water. Full information will be found in Chapter 2.
4   Refill the power unit with engine oil.
5   On models fitted with automatic transmission, adjust the selector control cables as described in Chapter 6.

59 Engine – initial start-up after overhaul or major repair

1   Make sure that the battery is fully charged and that the oil, water and fuel are replenished.
2   If the fuel system has been dismantled it will require several revolutions of the engine on the starter motor to get the petrol up to the carburettor. An initial prime by pouring petrol down the carburettor feed pipe will help the engine to fire quickly thus relieving the load on the battery.
3   As soon as the engine fires and runs, keep it going at a fast tickover only (not faster) and bring it up to normal working temperature.
4   As the engine warms up there will be odd smells and some smoke from parts getting hot and burning off oil deposits. The signs to look for are leaks of oil or water which will be obvious, if serious. Check also the clamp connections of the exhaust pipes to the manifolds as these do not always find their exact gas tight position until the warmth and vibration have acted on them and it is almost certain that they will need tightening further. This should be done, of course, with the engine stopped.
5   When normal running temperature has been reached adjust the idling speed as described in Chapter 3.
6   Stop the engine and wait a few minutes to see if any lubricant or coolant is dripping out when the engine is stationary.
7   Road test the car to check that the timing is correct and giving the necessary smoothness and power. Do not race the engine – when new bearings and/or pistons and rings have been fitted it should be treated as a new engine and run in at reduced revolutions for the first 500 miles (800 km).

60 Fault diagnosis – engine

Symptom	Reason(s)
Engine fails to turn over when starter switch is operated	Discharged, or defective battery Dirty, or loose battery leads Defective solenoid, or starter switch Loose, or broken starter motor leads Defective starter motor
Engine spins, but does not start	Ignition components damp, or wet Disconnected low tension lead Dirty contact breaker points Faulty condenser Faulty coil No petrol, or petrol not reaching carburettor Faulty fuel pump Too much choke, leading to wet spark plugs
Engine stops and will not re-start	Ignition failure Fuel pump failure No petrol in tank Water in fuel system Carburettor dashpot piston stuck
Engine lacks power	Burnt exhaust valve Incorrect timing Blown cylinder head gasket Leaking carburettor gasket Incorrect mixture Blocked air intake, or dirty air filter Ignition automatic advance faulty
Excessive oil consumption	Defective valve stem oil seals Worn pistons and bores Blocked engine breather Oil leaks
Engine noisy	Incorrect tappet clearance Worn timing chain Worn distributor drive Worn bearings

Chapter 2   Cooling system

For modifications, and information applicable to later models, see Supplement at end of manual

Contents

Specifications

System type
.... Pressurised thermo-syphon, pump assisted and fan cooled. No loss type with separate expansion tank

Thermostat
Type .... Wax
Opening temperature
    Standard .... 82°C (180°F)
    Hot climate .... 74°C (165°F)
    Cold climate .... 88°C (190°F)

Expansion tank pressure cap setting .... 15 lbf/in² (1 kgf/cm²)

Coolant capacity
With heater .... 9 Imp pints (5.1 litres)
Without heater .... 7¼ Imp pints (4.1 litres)

Antifreeze
Type .... Ethylene glycol
Specification .... BS 3151 or BS 3152

Torque wrench settings

	lbf ft	kgf m
Thermostat housing to cylinder head bolts	8 to 10	1.1 to 1.4
Thermostat cover bolts	8 to 10	1.1 to 1.4
Water pump mounting bolts	18 to 20	2.5 to 2.8
Water pump body plug	35	4.8
Pulley to fan bolts	20	2.8
Generator mounting and adjuster bolts	18 to 20	2.5 to 2.8

1   General description

The engine is liquid cooled, using a pressurised, fan-assisted thermo-syphon system which is thermostatically controlled. The system is of the no loss type and is pressurised so that the coolant does not boil until it reaches a temperature of about 110° C (230° F).

When the engine is heated to the normal operating temperature, the coolant expands and some of its is displaced into the expansion tank. This displaced coolant collects in the tank and is returned to the radiator when the system cools.

The cooling system consists of an engine driven pump which circulates the coolant through the passages round the cylinders and combustion chambers to the thermostat. When the engine has achieved normal operating temperature and the thermostat is open, the coolant passes to the top of the radiator and in passing down the radiator is cooled by the flow of air resulting from the rotation of the fan behind the radiator. Coolant from the bottom of the radiator is fed to the inlet of the pump and is then recirculated.

2   Cooling system – draining

1   If the engine is hot, the pressure in the cooling system must be relieved before attempting to drain the system. Place a cloth over the pressure cap of the expansion tank and turn the cap anti-clockwise until it reaches its stop.

2   Wait until the pressure has escaped, then press the cap downwards and turn it further in an anti-clockwise direction. Release the downward pressure on the cap very slowly and after making sure that all the pressure in the system has been relieved, remove the cap.

3   If the coolant in the system is to be re-used, place a clean container beneath the radiator and also beneath the cylinder block drain plug by the starter motor.

4   With the car standing on level ground, remove the filler cap from the top of the radiator. On early models there is a drain plug on the bottom of the radiator and this should be unscrewed and removed.

5   If there is no radiator drain plug, slacken the hose clip and disconnect the bottom hose from the radiator.

6	Unscrew and remove the cylinder block drain plug.

## 3	Cooling system – flushing

1	In time, the cooling system will lose its efficiency as the radiator becomes choked with rust, scale deposits from the water and sediment.
2	To clean the radiator, disconnect the bottom hose and leave a hose running in the radiator filler cap neck until the water emerging from the bottom of the radiator is quite clean. In very bad cases, the radiator should be reverse flushed by fitting an adaptor to connect the hose to the bottom of the radiator and allowing the water to flow out of the filler cap neck. While doing this, it is advisable to cover the engine with a plastic sheet to prevent any water going on to parts of the ignition system.
3	To remove sediment from the cylinder block, remove the thermostat cover and lift out the thermostat.
4	Remove the cylinder block drain plug and run water from a hose into the thermostat housing and out of the cylinder block drain hole until the water emerging is quite clear.
5	Cleaning out a badly corroded cooling system can be aided by the use of a proprietary cleaning agent obtainable from garages and accessory shops. When using these, take care to read and follow the instructions on the package.

## 4	Cooling system – filling

1	Refit the cylinder block and radiator drain plug (or bottom hose if this was disconnected).
2	Fill the system slowly to ensure that no air locks develop. If a heater is fitted, check that the heater control valve is open, (knob pushed in), otherwise an air lock may form in the heater. The best type of water to use in the cooling system is rain water, use this whenever possible.
3	Completely fill the radiator, refit the cap, remove the expansion chamber cap and check that it is half full of coolant.

4	Replace the expansion chamber cap and turn it firmly in a clockwise direction to lock it in position.
5	Run the engine at a fast idle speed for approximately half a minute and remove the radiator filler cap slowly. Top-up if necessary to the top of the filler neck and refit the cap.
6	Run the engine until it reaches normal operating temperature. Stop the engine and allow the system to cool, then top-up the expansion tank to half-full.

## 5	Antifreeze

1	There is no provision for draining the heater, or the expansion tank, so it is essential to use antifreeze in the cooling system in freezing conditions.
2	Antifreeze should be of the ethylene glycol type, conforming to BS 3151, or BS 3152 and the degree of protection given by various concentrations is given in the Table.

Antifreeze solution	Commences to freeze	Frozen solid	Amount of antifreeze
25%	-13°C (9°F)	-26°C (-15°F)	2.25 pts (1.3 litres)
33⅓%	-19°C (-2°F)	-36°C (-33°F)	3 pts (1.7 litres)
50%	-36°C (-33°F)	-48°C (-53°F)	4.5 pts (2.6 litres)

3	Antifreeze can remain in the cooling system for up to two years, provided that its specific gravity is checked periodically and additional antifreeze added as necessary. After two years, drain and flush the system and use fresh antifreeze.
4	Whenever topping up the cooling system use an antifreeze solution of the same concentration as that used for filling the system, never use water only. Take care not to spill antifreeze on the paintwork and if any is spilled, wipe it off immediately.
5	After filling the system with antifreeze, add 0.25 pints (0.15 litres) of neat antifreeze to the expansion tank.

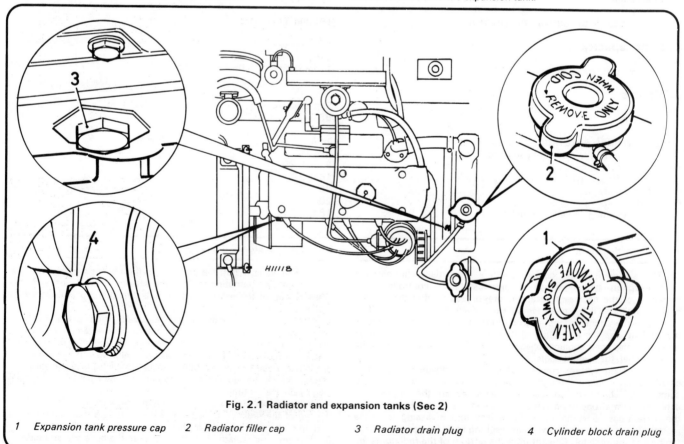

Fig. 2.1 Radiator and expansion tanks (Sec 2)

1	Expansion tank pressure cap		2	Radiator filler cap		3	Radiator drain plug		4	Cylinder block drain plug

6 Radiator – removal, inspection and cleaning

1   Drain the cooling system as described in Section 2 of this Chapter.
2   Slacken the top radiator hose clip at the radiator end of the hose and carefully draw off the hose.
3   Unwind the clip securing the overflow hose to the filler neck and carefully draw off the overflow hose.
4   Undo and remove the two radiator top fixing bracket bolts and washers.
5   Slacken the radiator bottom hose clip at the radiator end and carefully draw off the bottom hose.
6   Undo and remove the two radiator lower fixing bracket bolts, plain washers and rubber bushes.
7   Remove the six screws securing the cowl to the radiator. Remove the cowl. Lift out the radiator taking care not to damage the radiator core.
8   With the radiator out of the car, flush it out thoroughly and brush the dirt and debris from the outside. If the radiator requires repairing, it is preferable to have this done by a specialist repairer, or fit an exchange unit. For minor leaks, the addition of a proprietary radiator sealant to the cooling system is often all that is necessary.
9   Inspect the radiator hoses for damage and deterioration. Renew any hoses which are suspect. When filling the system with fresh antifreeze every two years, it may be worth fitting all new hoses and clips to decrease the risk of a breakdown. Do not overtighten the hose clips. After the clips are tight enough to prevent leaks, further tightening only damaged the hoses.
10 On models with a radiator drain plug, apply sealant to the threads of the plug before screwing it in and check that the fibre washer on the plug is in good condition.

7 Radiator – refitting

1   Refitting the radiator is the reverse of removal.
2   If new hoses are being fitted, it may be difficult to get them on to the parts to which they connect and the task is made easier if the bores of the hose ends are smeared with soap, or rubber grease.
3   Position the hose clips so that the clamp screws are in their most accessible position and the clips are only about 0.4 in (10 mm) from the end of the hose.
4   Ensure that the hoses are not kinked, or strained and that they are not over the flared ends of the radiator inlet and outlet pipes.

8 Thermostat – removal, testing and refitting

1   Drain enough coolant from the system to reduce the level to below the thermostat (about 4 pints)(2.3 litres).
2   Unscrew the three bolts securing the top cover to the thermostat housing.
3   Lift away the thermostat top cover and its gasket from the thermostat housing (photo).
4   Lift the thermostat from the housing (photo).

8.3 Removing the thermostat cover

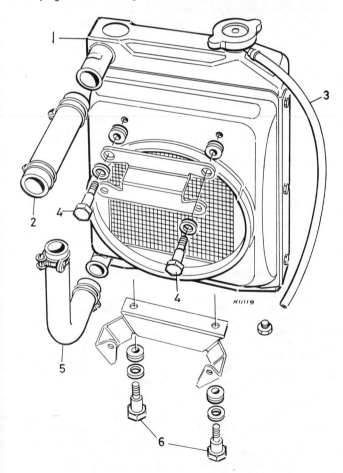

Fig. 2.2 Radiator and mountings (Sec 6)

1 Radiator and cowl	4 Top mounting bolts
2 Top hose	5 Bottom hose
3 Overflow hose	6 Bottom mounting bolts

8.4 Removing the thermostat

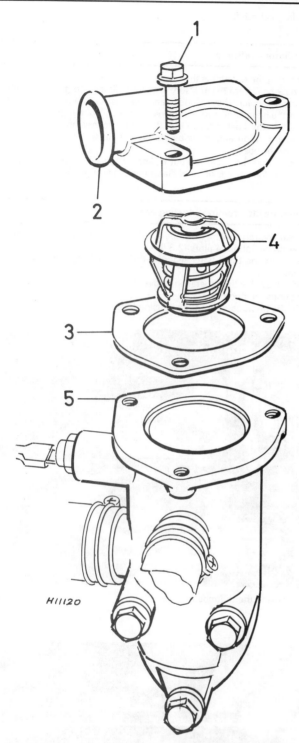

Fig. 2.3 Thermostat assembly (Sec 8)

1	Cover bolt	4	Thermostat
2	Cover	5	Thermostat housing
3	Gasket		

5   To test the thermostat for correct functioning, examine the thermostat when it is cold to check that it is closed. Place the thermostat in a pan of cold water with a thermometer and heat the water.

6   Note the temperature at which the thermostat starts to open. This should be the same as the temperature stamped on the bottom of the thermostat.

7   Continue heating the water and check that the thermostat opens fully.

8   If the thermostat is open when cold, or fails to operate correctly when heated, it must be rejected and a new one fitted. Do not attempt to re-calibrate, or repair a defective one.

9   Refitting the thermostat is the reverse of the removal sequence. Ensure that the thermostat assembly is clean and that the mating faces of the thermostat housing and cover are clean. Use a new gasket and tighten the housing cover bolts to the specified torque.

9   Thermostat housing – removal and refitting

1   Partially drain the cooling system (usually 4 pints (2.3 litres) is enough) as described in Section 2.

2   Detach the Lucar connector from the temperature transmitter.

3   Slacken the hose clips securing the heater hose, radiator top hose and water pump hose to the thermostat housing and carefully ease the three hoses from the housing.

4   Undo and remove the three bolts securing the thermostat housing to the cylinder head.

5   Carefully lift the thermostat housing away from the cylinder head (photo). Recover the gasket adhering to either the housing, or cylinder head.

6   Refitting the housing is the reverse sequence to removal. Make sure the mating faces of the housing and cylinder head are free of old gasket and jointing compound and always fit a new gasket.

7   Refill the cooling system as described in Section 4.

10   Water pump – removal and refitting

1   Drain the cooling system (Section 2).

2   Remove the radiator and its cowling (Section 5).

3   Slacken the mounting bolts and the adjusting link bolt of the dynamo, or alternator and remove the fan belt.

4   Unscrew and remove the three bolts securing the fan and pulley to the water pump hub. Lift away the fan and pulley (photo).

5   Slacken the hose clips and carefully detach the hoses from the water pump.

6   Undo the three bolts securing the water pump to the cylinder block front face. Lift away the water pump and its gasket.

7   Refitting is the reverse of removal. Use a new gasket and ensure that the mating faces of the pump and cylinder block are clean.

8   Tighten the bolts of the water pump and the fan to the specified torque.

9   Tension the fan belt (see Section 11) and refill the cooling system.

11   Fan belt – removal, refitting and tensioning

1   Slacken the mounting bolts and adjusting link bolt of the dynamo, or alternator, swivel it downwards to make the belt slack and pull the bolt off the pulley.

2   Release the belt from the crankshaft pulley and manoeuvre the belt over the fan blades and out through the recess in the radiator cowling (photo).

3   When fitting the belt, first pinch the sides of the belt together to make a tight loop to feed through the recess in the engine cowling and over one fan blade, then turn the fan and manoeuvre the belt over each of the other blades in turn. Guide the belt into the groove of the fan pulley, the crankshaft pulley and then the generator pulley.

4   If fitting a new belt, swivel the generator away from the engine until the belt is moderately tight and run the engine for five minutes at 1000 rpm. Stop the engine and apply finger pressure to the centre of the longest span of the belt. A correctly tensioned belt should deflect 0.5 in (13 mm).

5   An alternative means of checking, is to fit a torque spanner to the nut of the generator pulley retaining nut and apply a torque of 11 to 11.5 lbf ft (1.5 to 1.6 kgf m) in a clockwise direction. If the belt is tensioned correctly, the pulley will just slip at this torque.

6   Do not over tighten the belt because this will reduce belt life and will also cause damage to the generator bearings.

12   Water pump – dismantling, overhaul and reassembly

1   Before attempting to overhaul a water pump, make sure that a new seal and a new bearing and spindle assembly can be obtained. If

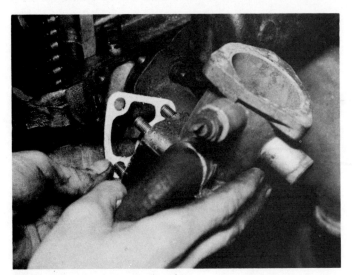

9.5 Removing the thermostat housing

10.4 Removing the fan and pulley

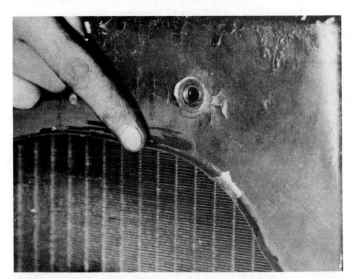

11.2 Recess for fanbelt fitting

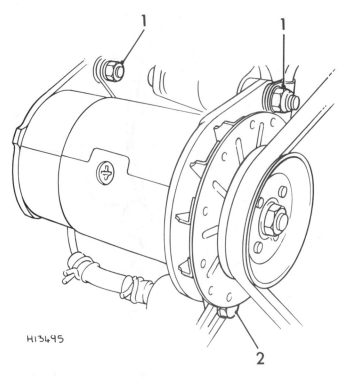

H13495

Fig. 2.4 Fanbelt adjustment (models with dynamo) (Sec 11)

1   Mounting bolts   *2   Adjusting link bolt*

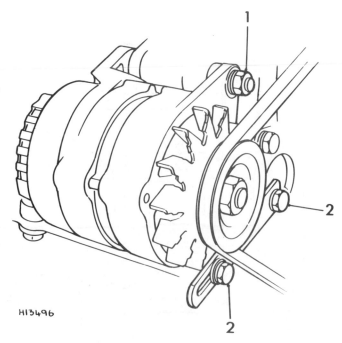

H13496

Fig. 2.5 Fanbelt adjustment (models with alternator) (Sec 11)

1   Mounting bolt   *2   Adjusting link bolts*

these are not obtainable a defective pump must be replaced by a new one or an exchanged unit.

2   Early 1500 models have a water pump with a plain spindle and a bearing assembly which is located by a wire clip (Fig. 2.6). Later 1500 and 1750 models have pumps with different spindle assembly and there is no locating clip for the bearing.

3   Using a universal puller, draw the pulley hub off the shaft.

4   If a bearing locating wire is fitted, lever it out with a screwdriver, or

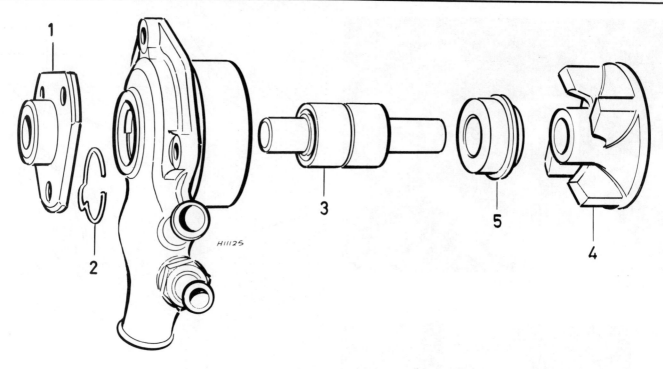

Fig. 2.6 Water pump components (early 1500 models) (Sec 12)

1 Pulley hub	3 Spindle bearing assembly	4 Impeller
2 Bearing locating wire		5 Seal

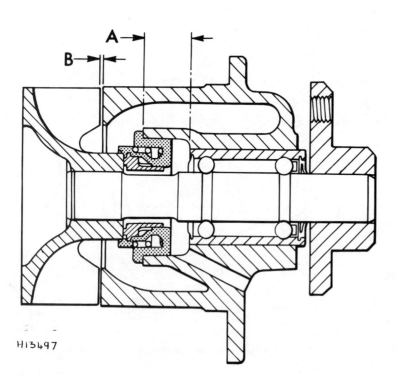

Fig. 2.7 Water pump sectional view (later 1500 and 1750 models) (Sec 12)

A   Bearing setting dimension
B   Impeller clearance dimension

pull it out with pliers.

5   Using a soft faced hammer, drive the bearing and spindle assembly rearwards out of the pump. If the bearing is too tight a fit to be driven out it will be necessary to have the assembly pressed out.

6   Draw the spindle off the shaft, or have the shaft pressed out and then remove the seal.

7   Check the fit of the pulley hub on the new spindle. If the fit is too loose, a new hub will be necessary. Press the spindle into the hub until the end of the spindle is flush with the front face of the hub.

8   Press the bearing and spindle assembly in to the case and on early 1500 models fit the bearing locating wire.

9   On models without a bearing locating wire adjust the position of the spindle bearing assembly so that the distance from the rear face of the bearing outer track to the seal housing shoulder (dimension A in Fig. 2.7) is 0.596 to 0.606 in (15.14 to 15.40 mm).

10 Fit a new seal and then press the impeller on to the spindle so that the clearance between the impeller and the body (dimension B in Fig. 2.7) is 0.010 to 0.020 in (0.25 to 0.51 mm).

13 Fault diagnosis – cooling system

Symptom	Reason(s)
Engine overheating	Insufficient coolant in system
	Fan belt slipping
	Radiator core blocked, or restricted
	Water hose kinked, restricting flow
	Thermostat defective
	Ignition timing incorrect (retarded)
	Carburettor setting incorrect (mixture too lean)
	Oil level in sump too low
	Blown cylinder head gasket causing loss of coolant
	Defective, or incorrect pressure cap
	Outside temperature excessively high
Engine too cool	Thermostat jammed open
	No thermostat
	Outside temperature excessively low
Loss of coolant	Loose clips or hose
	Water hoses perished and leaking
	Radiator core leaking
	Defective pressure cap
	Blown cylinder head gasket
	Leaking core plug
	Cracked cylinder block, or cylinder head

Chapter 3 Fuel and exhaust systems

For modifications, and information applicable to later models, see Supplement at end of manual

Contents

Specifications

Air cleaner

Type . . . . Renewable paper element

Carburettor

Type . . . . SU HS6 horizontal
Piston spring . . . . Red
Jet size . . . . 0.100 in (2.54 mm)

	1500 (1969 and 1970)	1500 (1971 onwards)	
		HC	**LC**
Carburettor specification number	AUD 258	AUD 468 or AUD 555	AUD 498 or AUD 556
Needle	KP	BAS	BAS

	1750 single carburettor		1750 twin carburettors
Carburettor specification number	AUD 462 AUD 558	AUD 528 AUD 557 AUD 529 or AUD 619	AUD 539
Needle	BAR	BBH	BBR

Idling speed

	Normal idle	Fast idle
1500 up to 1970	700 rpm	1100 to 1200 rpm
1500 1971 on	750 rpm	1300 rpm
1750 single carburettor models	650 rpm	1300 rpm
1750 twin carburettor models	750 rpm	1200 rpm

Fuel pump

Make . . . . SU mechanical

Type	**AUF 700**	**AUF 800**
Suction (minimum)	6 in (150 mm) Hg	9 in (230 mm) Hg
Delivery pressure (minimum)	3 lbf/in² (0.2 kgf/cm²)	4 lbf/in² (0.28 kgf/cm²)

Fuel tank capacity

1969 and 1970 models . . . . 9 Imp gall, 10.5 US gall, 41 litres
1971 onwards . . . . 10.5 Imp gall, 12.6 US gall, 48 litres

Torque wrench settings

	lbf ft	kgf cm
Manifold to cylinder head	16	2.2
Adaptor plugs	30	4.1
Carburettor studs	6 to 8	0.8 to 1.1
Petrol pump nuts	14 to 16	2.0 to 2.2
Petrol pump studs	6	0.8

1   General description

The fuel system comprises a fuel tank at the rear of the car, a mechanical fuel pump located on the bulkhead side of the crankcase next to the oil filter, and a single or twin horizontally mounted SU carburettor(s). A renewable paper element air cleaner is fitted which must be renewed at the recommended mileages.

2   Fuel pump – general description

The mechanically operated fuel pump is located on the front left-hand side of the transmission case and is operated by a separate lobe on the driveshaft via a short pushrod. As the pushrod moves horizontally to and fro, it actuates a rocker lever, one end of which is connected to the diaphragm operating rod. When the pushrod is moved outwards by the cam lobe, the diaphragm moves downwards, causing fuel to be drawn in through the filter, past the inlet valve flap and into the diaphragm chamber. As the cam lobe moves round, the diaphragm moves upwards under the action of a spring and fuel flows via the large outlet valve to the carburettor float chamber.

When the float chamber has the requisite amount of fuel in it, the needle valve in the top of the chamber shuts off the fuel supply, causing pressure in the fuel delivery line to hold the diaphragm down against the action of the diaphragm spring until the needle valve opens to admit more fuel.

3   Fuel pump – removal and refitting

1   Apply the handbrake, and raise the front of the car for access to the fuel pump, which is below the generator.
2   Remove the fuel inlet and outlet connections from the fuel pump.
3   Unscrew the two pump mounting flange nuts and remove them with the two spring washers.
4   Carefully slide the pump off the two studs, followed by the insulating block assembly and gaskets. Withdraw the pushrod from its location in the side of the transmission case.
5   Refitting of the pump is a reversal of the above procedure. Use new gaskets, but on no account alter the original total thickness of the insulating block and gaskets. Do not forget to insert the pushrod into the transmission case.

4   Fuel pump – dismantling, inspection and reassembly

1   Thoroughly clean the outside of the pump in paraffin and dry. To ensure correct reassembly, mark the upper and lower body flanges.
2   Remove the cover retaining screws, lift away the cover, followed by the sealing ring and fuel filter.
3   Remove the six screws holding the upper body to the lower body, making special note of the position of the three shorter screws. Separate the upper and lower parts.
4   As the combined inlet and outlet valve is a press fit into the body, very carefully remove the valve, taking care not to damage the very fine edge of the inlet valve.
5   With the diaphragm and rocker held down against the action of the diaphragm spring, tap out the rocker lever pivot pin, using a parallel punch. Lift out the rocker lever and spring.
6   Lift out the diaphragm and spring, having first well lubricated the lower seal to avoid damage as the spindle stirrup is drawn through it.
7   It is recommended that unless the seal is damaged, it be left in position, as a special extractor is required for removal.
8   Carefully wash the filter gauze in petrol and clean all traces of sediment from the upper body. Inspect the diaphragm for signs of distortion, cracking or perishing and fit a new one if suspect.
9   Inspect the fine edge and lips of the combined inlet and outlet valve and also check that it is a firm fit in the upper body. Finally, inspect the outlet cover for signs of corrosion, pitting or distortion and fit a new component if necessary.
10   To reassemble, first check that there are no sharp edges on the diaphragm spindle and stirrup and well lubricate the oil seal. Insert the stirrup and spindle into the spring, then through the oil seal and position the stirrup ready for rocker lever engagement.
11   Fit the combined inlet/outlet valve ensuring that the groove

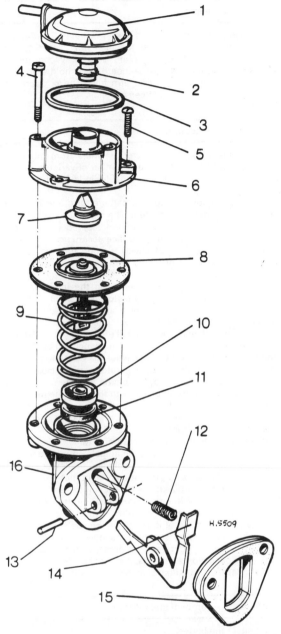

H.5509

Fig. 3.1 Exploded view of mechanical fuel pump (Sec 4)

1	Outlet cover	9 Diaphragm spring
2	Insert – outlet cover	10 Retaining cup
3	Sealing washer	11 Crankcase seal
4	Long screws	12 Rocker lever tension spring
5	Short screws	13 Rocker lever pivot pin
6	Upper body	14 Rocker lever
7	Inlet and outlet valve	15 Insulator and gasket
8	Diaphragm assembly	16 Lower body

registers in the housing correctly. Check that the fine edge of the inlet valve contacts its seating correctly and evenly.
12   Match up the screw holes in the lower body and holes in the diaphragm and depress the rocker lever until the diaphragm lies flat. Fit the upper body and hold in place by the three short screws, but do not tighten fully. Refit the filter, a new sealing washer and the outlet cover suitably positioned to connect to the outlet hose to the carburettor. Refit the three long screws and then tighten all screws firmly in a diagonal pattern.
13   Insert the rocker lever and spring into the crankcase and hold in position using the rocker lever pivot pin.

5 Fuel pump – testing

If the pump is suspect, or has been overhauled, it may be quickly dry tested holding a finger over the inlet nozzle and operating the rocker lever through three complete strokes. When the finger is released a sucking noise should be heard. Next hold a finger over the outlet nozzle and press the rocker arm fully. The pressure generated should hold for a minimum of fifteen seconds.

6 Carburettor – description

1 The variable choke SU carburettor differs from most other carburettors in that instead of having a number of various sized fixed jets for different conditions, only one variable jet is fitted to deal with all possible conditions.
2 Air passing rapidly through the carburettor draws petrol from the jet so forming the petrol/air mixture. The amount of petrol drawn from the jet depends on the position of the tapered carburettor needle, which moves up and down the jet orifice according to the engine load and throttle opening, thus effectively altering the size of jet, so that exactly the right amount of fuel is metered for the prevailing engine speed and load.
3 The position of the tapered needle in the jet is determined by engine vacuum acting on a sliding piston. The shank of the needle is held at its top end in the piston, which slides up and down the dashpot in resonse to the degree of manifold vacuum.
4 With the throttle fully open, the full effect of inlet manifold vacuum is felt by the piston, which has a vacuum connection to the choke tube on the outside of the throttle. This causes the piston to rise fully, bringing the needle with it. With the accelerator partially closed, only slight inlet manifold vacuum is felt by the piston and the piston only rises a little, blocking most of the jet orifice with the metering needle.
5 To prevent the piston fluttering and giving a richer mixture when the accelerator is suddenly depressed, an oil damper and light spring are fitted inside the dashpot.
6 The only portion of the piston assembly to come into contact with the piston chamber, or dashpot, is the actual central piston rod. All the other parts of the piston assembly, including the lower choke portion, have sufficient clearance to prevent any direct metal to metal contact and is essential if the carburettor is to function correctly.
7 The correct level of the petrol in the carburettor is determined by the level of the float chamber. When the level is correct, the float rises and a lever resting on top of it, closes the needle valve in the cover of the float chamber. This closes off the supply of fuel from the pump. When the level in the float chamber drops, as fuel is used in the carburettor, the float drops. As it does, the float needle is unseated, allowing more fuel to enter the float chamber and restore the correct level.

7 Carburettor – removal and refitting

1 Disconnect the battery.
2 Remove the air cleaner assembly.

Single carburettor
3 Unscrew the clamp screw of the throttle inner cable and pull the outer cable clear of the carburettor. Be careful that the clamp screw or nipple does not become detached from the throttle lever
4 Disconnect the choke cable in a similar manner to the throttle cable, again taking care not to lose the clamp screw, or nipple.
5 Disconnect the distributor vacuum pipe from the carburettor.
6 Unclamp and detach the fuel pipe to the float chamber.
7 Undo and remove the four nuts and washers securing the carburettor to the inlet manifold studs and carefully draw off the carburettor, insulator, gaskets and abutment bracket.
8 Refitting is the reverse of removal, but use new gaskets and ensure that the joint faces of the carburettor flange and inlet manifold are clean.
9 Adjust the throttle cable (Section 18)
10 Adjust the choke cable (Section 19)

Twin carburettors
11 Disconnect the throttle return springs from their anchor brackets.
12 Disconnect the throttle cable from the carburettor and remove the

cable trunnion and the return springs.
13 Disconnect the choke cable, taking care not to lose the clamp screw or nipple.
14 Disconnect the engine breather pipes from the Y-junction.
15 Unclamp and disconnect the fuel delivery pipe to the carburettor and the fuel bridge pipe.
16 Disconnect the vacuum advance pipe.
17 Undo and remove the four nuts from the flange of each carburettor.
18 Lift off the throttle cable abutment bracket and the return spring anchor brackets.
19 Lift off the the two carburettors as an assembly with their linkages attached.
20 Refitting is the reverse of removal, but use new gaskets and ensure that the joint faces of the carburettor flange and the inlet manifold are clean.
21 Adjust the throttle cable (Section 18)
22 Adjust the choke cable (Section 19)
23 If necessary, tune the carburettors (Section 17)

8 Carburettor – dismantling and reassembling

1 Unscrew the piston damper and lift it away from the chamber and piston assembly. Using a screwdriver, or small file, scratch identification marks on the suction chamber and carburettor body so that they may be fitted together in their original position. Remove the three suction chamber retaining screws and lift the suction chamber from the carburettor body, leaving the piston in the main body.

Fig. 3.2 Carburettor (early models) – exploded view (Sec 8)

1	Body	43	Tab washer for nut (1500 only)
2	Piston lifting pin		
3	Spring for pin	44	Jet assembly
4	Sealing washer	45	Nut
5	Plain washer	46	Washer
6	Circlip	47	Gland
7	Piston chamber	48	Ferrule
8	Screw for chamber	49	Jet bearing
9	Piston	50	Washer
10	Spring	51	Jet locking nut
11	Needle*	52	Spring
12	Needle locking screw*	53	Jet adjusting nut
13	Piston damper	54	Pick-up lever and link
14	Sealing washer	55	Screw for link
15	Throttle adjusting screw	56	Bracket for link
16	Spring for screw	57	Cam lever
17	Spacer	58	Washer
18	Gasket	59	Spring for cam lever
19	Progressive throttle linkage	60	Spring for pick-up lever
20	Gasket	61	Pivot bolt
21	Throttle return spring	62	Pivot tube – inner
22	Float chamber	63	Pivot tube – outer
23	Adaptor	64	Distance washer
24	Bolt for float chamber	65	Throttle lever rod
25	Spring washer	66	Bush
26	Plain washer	67	Washer (early 1500 only)
27	Float (1500 only)	68	Lockwasher
28	Hinge pin for float	69	Piston guide
29	Lid for float chamber	70	Screw for guide
30	Gasket	71	Tension spring
31	Needle and seat	72	Anchor tag
32	Screw for lid	73	Spring**
33	Spring washer	74	Needle**
34	Baffle plate	75	Support guide for needle**
35	Throttle spindle	76	Support guide locking screw**
36	Throttle disc		
37	Screw for disc	77	Plastic float**
38	Washer for spindle		
39	Throttle return lever		*Used on fixed needle carburettors
40	Cam stop screw		
41	Spring for screw		**Used on spring-loaded needle carburettors
42	Nut for spindle		

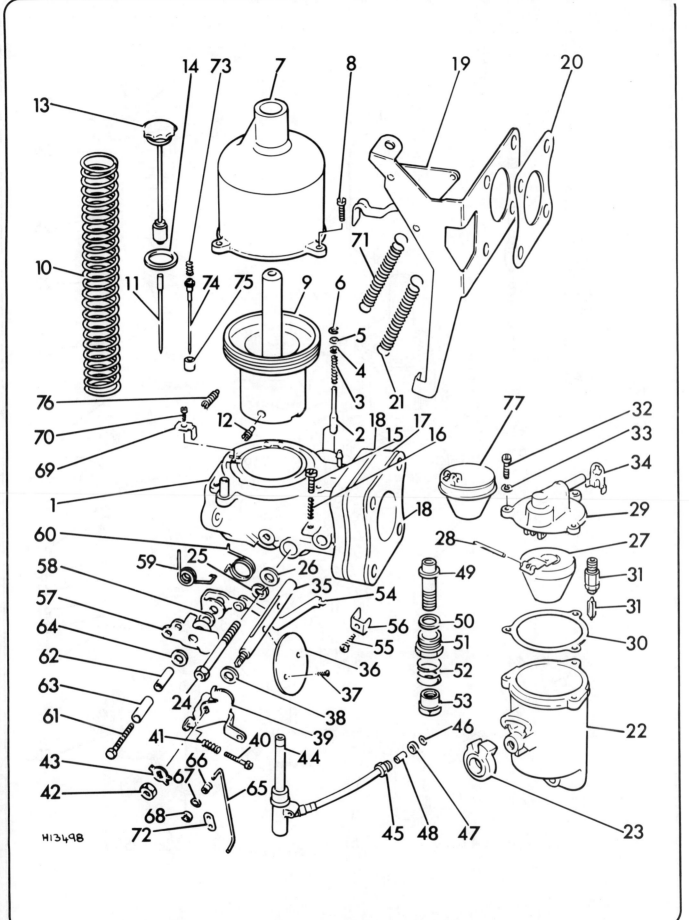

H13498

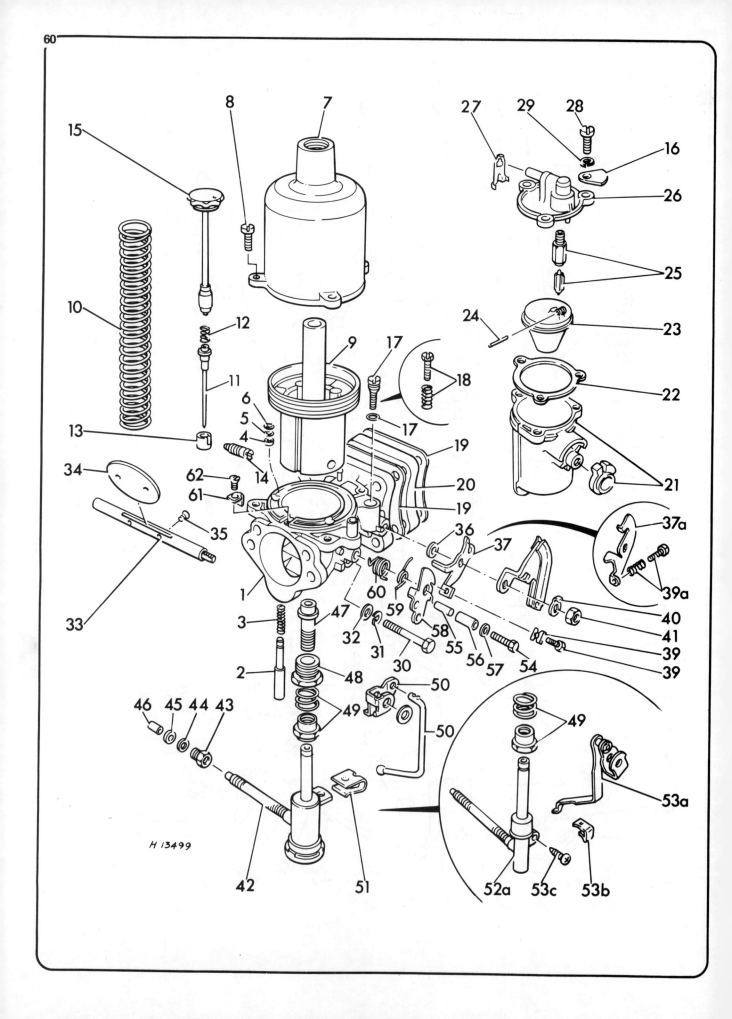

H 13499

Fig. 3.3 Carburettor (later models) – exploded view (Sec 8)

1 Body
2 Piston lifting pin
3 Spring for pin
4 Sealing washer
5 Plain washer
6 Circlip
7 Piston chamber
8 Screw
9 Piston
10 Spring
11 Needle
12 Spring
13 Support guide
14 Locking screw
15 Piston damper
16 Identification tag
17 Throttle adjusting screw and
    O-ring*
18 Throttle adjusting screw and
    spring
19 Joint washers
20 Insulator block
21 Float chamber and spacer
22 Joint washer
23 Float
24 Hinge pin
25 Needle and seat
26 Lid
27 Baffle plate
28 Screw
29 Spring washer
30 Bolt
31 Spring washer
32 Plain washer
33 Throttle spindle
34 Throttle disc
35 Screw
36 Washer
37 Throttle return lever*
37a Throttle return lever
38 Progressive throttle (snail
    cam)
39 Fast idle screw*
39a Fast idle screw and spring
40 Lockwasher
41 Nut
42 Jet assembly – capstat
43 Sleeve nut
44 Washer
45 Gland
46 Ferrule
47 Jet bearing
48 Jet locating nut
49 Jet adjustment nut and
    spring
50 Rod link and pick-up lever
51 Spring clip
52a Jet assembly
53a Pick-up lever
53b Link   non-capstat
53c Screw
54 Pivot bolt
55 Pivot bolt tube – inner
56 Pivot bolt tube – outer
57 Distance washer
58 Cam lever
59 Spring
60 Spring
61 Guide
62 Screw

*Used with sealed adjustment
carburettors*

2   Lift the piston spring from the piston, noting which way round it is fitted and remove the piston. Invert it and allow the oil in the damper bore to drain out. Place the piston in a safe place, so that the needle will not be touched, or the piston roll onto the floor. It is recommended that the piston be placed on the neck of a narrow jam jar with the needle inside, so acting as a stand.
3   Mark the position of the float chamber lid relative to the body and unscrew the three screws holding the float chamber lid to the float chamber body. Remove the lid and withdraw the pin, releasing the float and float lever. Using a spanner, or socket, remove the needle valve assembly.
4   Disconnect the jet link from the base of the jet and unscrew the nut holding the flexible nylon tube into the base of the float chamber. Carefully withdraw the jet and nylon connection tube.
5   Unscrew the jet adjustment nut and lift it away with its locking spring. Also unscrew the jet locknut and lift it away together with the brass washer and jet bearing.
6   Remove the bolt securing the float chamber to the carburettor body and separate the two parts.
7   To remove the throttle and actuating spindle, release the two screws holding the throttle in position in the slot in the spindle. Make a note of the tapered eges of the throttle and slide it out of the spindle from the carburettor body.
8   Reassembly is a straight reversal of the dismantling sequence.

9 Carburettor – examination and repair

1   The SU carburettor, generally speaking, is most reliable, but even so it may develop one of several faults which may not be apparent unless a careful inspection is carried out. The common faults the carburettor is prone to are:

    (a) Piston sticking
    (b) Float needle sticking
    (c) Float chamber flooding
    (d) Water and dirt in the carburettor

2   In addition, the following parts are susceptible to wear after high mileages and as they vitally affect the economy of the engine, they should be checked and renewed where necessary, every 24 000 miles (39 000 km).
3   **The carburettor needle.** If this has been incorrectly fitted at some time, so that it is not centrally located in the jet orifice, the needle will have a tiny ridge worn on it. If a ridge can be seen, the needle must be renewed. SU carburettor needles are made to very fine tolerances and should a ridge be apparent, no attempt should be made to rub the needle down with fine emery paper. If it is wished to clean the needle, it can be polished lightly with metal polish.
4   **The carburettor jet.** If the needle is worn it is likely that the rim of the jet will be damaged where the needle has been striking it. It should be renewed, as otherwise fuel consumption will suffer. The jet can also be badly worn, or ridged on the outside, from where it has been sliding up and down between the jet bearing every time the choke has been pulled out. Removal and renewal is the only satisfactory solution.
5   Check the edges of the throttle and the choke tube for wear. Renew if worn.
6   The washers fitted to the base of the jet and under the float chamber lid may leak after a time and can cause a great deal of fuel wastage. It is wisest to renew them automatically when the carburettor is stripped down.
7   After high mileages, the float chamber needle and seat are bound to be ridged. They are not expensive items to replace and must be renewed as a set. They should never be renewed separately.

10 Carburettor – piston sticking

1   The hardened piston rod which slides in the centre guide tube in the middle of the dashpot is the only part of the piston assembly which should make contact with the dashpot. The piston rim and the choke periphery are machined to very fine tolerances so that they will not touch the dashpot, or the choke tube walls.
2   After high mileages wear in the centre guide tube may allow the piston to touch the dashpot wall. This condition is known as sticking.
3   If piston sticking is suspected and it is wished to test for this condition, rotate the piston about the centre guide tube and at the same

time slide it up and down inside the dashpot. If any portion of the piston makes contact with the dashpot wall, that portion of the wall must be polished with metal polish until clearance exists. In extreme cases, fine emery cloth can be used.

4   The greatest care should be taken to remove only the minimum amount of metal to provide the clearance, as too large a gap will cause air leakage and will upset the functioning of the carburettor. Clean down the walls of the dashpot and the piston rim and ensure that there is no oil on them. A trace of oil may be applied to the piston rod.

5   If the piston is sticking, under no circumstances try to clear it by trying to alter the tension of the light return spring.

11 Carburettor – float needle sticking

1   If the float needle sticks, the carburettor will soon run dry and the engine will stop, despite there being fuel in the tank.

2   The easiest way to check a suspected sticking float needle is to remove the inlet pipe at the carburettor and with the ignition turned OFF turn the engine over on the starter motor by pressing the solenoid rubber button.

3   If fuel spurts from the end of the pipe the fault is almost certain to be a sticking float needle. When doing this, take care to ensure that the fuel cannot be ignited.

4   Remove the float chamber, dismantle the valve and clean the housing and float chamber out thoroughly. If the float needle is ridged, fit a new needle.

12 Carburettor – float chamber flooding

If fuel emerges from the small breather hole in the cover of the float chamber, this is known as flooding. It is caused by the float chamber needle not seating properly in its housing; normally this is because a piece of dirt or foreign matter is jammed between the needle and the needle housing. Alternatively the float may have developed a leak or be maladjusted so that it is holding open the float chamber needle valve even though the chamber is full of petrol. Remove the float chamber cover, clean the needle assembly, check the setting of the float as detailed later in this Chapter and shake the float to verify if any fuel has leaked into it.

13 Carburettor – clearance of water, or dirt

1   Because of the size of the jet orifice, water or dirt in the carburettor is normally easily cleared. If dirt in the carburettor is suspected, start the engine (the jet is never completely blocked) and with the throttle fully open, blank off the air intake. This will cause a partial vacuum in the choke tube and help suck out any foreign matter from the jet tube. Release the throttle as soon as the engine speed alters considerably. Repeat this procedure several times.

2   If this failed to do the trick then there is no alternative but to remove and blow out the jet.

14 Carburettor – jet centering of fixed needle jet

1   This operation is always necessary if the carburettor has been dismantled, but to check if it is necessary on a carburettor in service, first screw up the jet adjusting nut as far as it will go without forcing it, lift the piston and then let it fall under its own weight. It should fall onto the bridge making a soft metallic click. Repeat the above procedure, but this time with the adjusting nut screwed right down. If the soft metallic click is not audible in either of the two tests, proceed as follows:

2   Disconnect the jet link, (Fig. 3.4) from the bottom of the jet and the nylon flexible tube from the underside of the float chamber. Gently slide the jet and the nylon tube from the underside of the carburettor body. Next unscrew the jet adjusting nut and lift away the nut and the locking spring. Refit the adjusting nut without the locking spring and screw it up as far as possible without forcing. Replace the jet and tube, but there is no need to reconnect the tube at this stage.

3   Slacken the jet locking nut so that it may be rotated with the fingers only. Unscrew the piston damper and lift away the damper. Gently press the piston down onto the bridge and tighten the locknut.

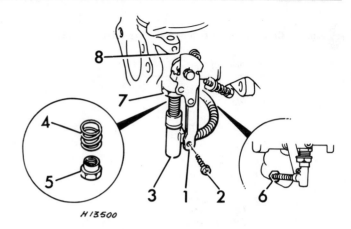

H 13500

Fig. 3.4 Jet centering of fixed needle jet (Sec 14)

1	Jet link	5	Adjusting nut
2	Jet link securing screw	6	Fuel feed pipe to jet
3	Jet	7	Jet locknut
4	Spring	8	Lifting pin

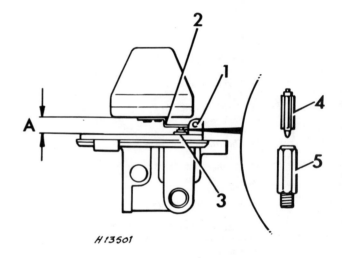

H 13501

Fig. 3.5 Float level adjustment (Sec 15)

1	Float lever pivot pin	4	Needle
2	Float lever	5	Valve body
3	Needle valve	A	Setting dimension

Lift the piston, using the lifting pin and check that it is able to fall freely under its own weight. Now lower the adjusting nut and check once again. If this time there is a difference in the two metallic clicks, repeat the centering procedure until the sound is the same for both tests.

4   Gently remove the jet and unscrew the adjusting nut. Refit the locking spring and jet adjusting nut. Top-up the damper with oil, if necessary, and refit the damper. Connect the nylon flexible tube to the underside of the float chamber and finally reconnect the jet link.

15 Carburettor – float level adjustment (float with metal lever)

1   It is essential that the fuel level in the float chamber is always correct as otherwise excessive fuel consumption may occur. On reassembly of the float chamber, check the fuel level before refitting the float chamber cover in the following manner.

2   Invert the float chamber cover so that the needle valve is closed. It should be possible to place a round bar of 0·12 to 0·18 in (3·0 to 4·6 mm) diameter (A: Fig. 3.5) parallel to the float chamber cover without

fouling the float. If the float stands proud of the bar, it is necessary to bend the float level slightly until the clearance is correct. **Note**: *A No 31 drill is 0·12 in (3·0 mm) and No 15 drill is 0·18 in (4·6 mm)*

16 Carburettor – needle renewal

1   Should it be found necessary to fit a new needle, first remove the piston and suction chamber assembly, marking the chamber for correct reassembly in its original position.
2   Slacken the needle, or support guide locking screw and withdraw the needle, or support guide/needle assembly from the piston.
3   Upon refitting a new needle it is important that the shoulder on the shank, or the lower edge of the guide is flush with the underside of the piston. Use a straight edge such as a metal rule for the adjustment. On the spring loaded type of needle, ensure that the guide on the needle is positioned so that the locking screw will tighten on to the flat machined on to the guide
4   Refit the piston and suction chamber and check the piston for freedom of movement.

17 Carburettor – tuning and adjustment

1   Before any adjustments are made to the carburettor, it is essential that the ignition timing, tappet clearances, contact breaker and spark plug gaps are checked and set within the specified limits.
2   In territories which have exhaust emission control regulations, carburettor adjustments should not be carried out unless using a tachometer, an exhaust gas analyser (CO meter) and for twin carburettors, a balancing meter.
3   Ensure that the engine is at the normal operating temperature.

Single carburettor
4   Release the speedometer cable clip from the air cleaner intake tube. Unscrew the centre bolt and remove the air cleaner assembly.
5   Check the oil level of the carburettor piston damper and top it up if necessary.
6   Check that the throttle operates smoothly over its entire range
7   Check that the choke is fully open when the control knob is pushed in fully and that the control has a free movement of 0·063 in (1·5 mm) before the cable starts to pull the carburettor choke lever.
8   Check that there is a small clearance between the fast idle screw and its cam.
9   Use a finger to raise and lower the piston over its full range of travel. If the movement is not free and smooth, overhaul the carburettor before proceeding further.
10   If a tachometer is available, connect it in accordance with its maker's instructions
11   Select P on models with automatic transmission and neutral on models with manual transmission. Start the engine and run it at fast idle speed until it attains the normal running temperature. Leave the engine running at this speed for a further five minutes, then increase the speed to 2500 rpm for 30 seconds, after which the speed should be allowed to fall to the normal idling speed and tuning can be started. If tuning cannot be completed within three minutes, again increase the engine speed to 2500 rpm for 30 seconds and repeat this bout of increased speed every three minutes until timing has been completed.
12   Check that the normal idling speed is as given in the Specification and if necessary adjust it by turning the idling screw.
13   Turn the jet adjusting nut on the carburettor one flat at a time first in one direction and then in the other, until the fastest speed is obtained. Turning the nut upwards weakens the mixture and turning it downwards makes the mixture richer.
14   From the nut position for maximum speed, turn the nut upwards, weakening the mixture, until the speed of the engine just starts to decrease and then screw the nut down very slowly by the minimum amount necessary to regain maximum speed.
15   Check that the normal idling speed is as given in the Specification and adjust it if necessary with the throttle adjusting screw.
16   For cars fitted with emission control equipment, the percentage CO in the exhaust should now be checked with a CO meter. If the reading is outside the limits permitted (2 to 4%), turn the jet adjusting nut by the minimum amount necessary to bring the CO percentage within the limits.
17   Unscrew the fast idle screw until it is well clear of the cam and

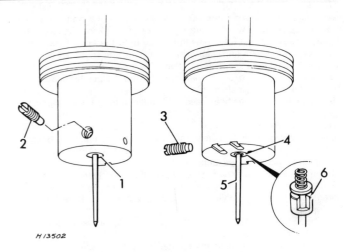

H/3502

Fig. 3.6 Carburettor needle fixing (Sec 16)

1	Needle shoulder flush with bottom of piston
2	Needle securing screw
	Fixed needle
3	Support guide locking screw
4	Support guide flush with bottom of piston
5	Needle
6	Assembly of spring, support guide and needle
	Spring – loaded needle

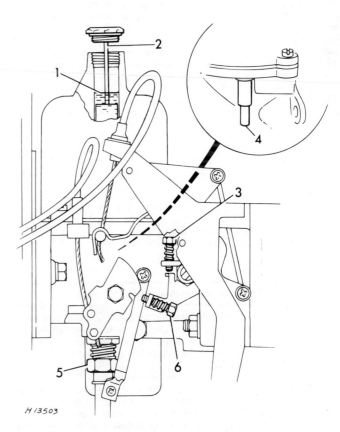

H/3503

Fig. 3.7 Carburettor adjustments (Sec 17)

1	Oil level in dashpot	4	Piston lifting pin
2	Damper	5	Jet adjusting nut
3	Idle speed adjustment screw	6	Fast idle screw

then pull out the choke control knob until the linkage is on the point of moving the jet downwards. With the choke control knob locked in this position, turn the fast idle adjusting screw until the end of the screw just touches the cam and then continue to turn the screw slowly until the specified fast idling speed is obtained.

18 Return the choke control knob to its fully IN position. Stop the engine and refit the air cleaner.

19 If a tachometer has been used, disconnect it from the engine.

Twin carburettors

20 It is very difficult to balance twin carburettors unless a balance meter is used. If you are unable to borrow one, it is worth buying one as they are reasonably inexpensive.

21 Unscrew the two wing nuts and take off the air cleaner assembly.

22 Proceed with the sequence for tuning a single carburettor in paragraphs 5 to 12, applying the operations to each carburettor when appropriate.

23 Check that the air intake of the two carburettors is the same, by testing them with a balance meter.

24 If they are not balanced, release the clamp on the throttle connecting linkage and turn the throttle adjusting screw of one carburettor until the correct balance is obtained. When the balance is correct, adjust the idling speed by turning the throttle adjusting screw of each carburettor the same amount and the same direction. When the idling is correct, recheck the balance and then tighten the clamp on the throttle connecting linkage. If a smooth idle at the correct speed and balance cannot be obtained, the idle speed mixture needs to be adjusted and this is done as follows.

25 Stop the engine and remove the suction chamber and piston of both carburettors. Be careful to ensure that the parts are marked so that they will be refitted to the carburettor from which they were removed and that the suction chambers are fitted the same way round as they were before removal.

26 Turn the adjusting nut of each carburettor until the top of the jet is flush with the bridge. If the jet cannot be raised this high, turn the nut to raise the jet as far as it will go. It is important that the top of the jet is not raised above bridge height and that if one jet cannot be screwed as high as the bridge, the jet of the other carburettor is set to exactly the same height. From this position screw each jet downwards exactly two complete turns and then refit the pistons and suction chambers. Top-up the level of oil in the piston dampers.

27 Turn the jet adjusting nut of each carburettor by the same amount, one flat at a time to adjust each of them in the same way as for a single carburettor described in paragraphs 13 and 14.

28 Recheck the idle speed and the carburettor balance and make further adjustments if necessary.

29 For cars fitted with emission control equipment, proceed as in paragraph 16, but ensure that each jet is turned by exactly the same amount.

30 Slacken one of the levers on the throttle interconnecting linkage. Ensure that the link pin on each end of the linkage is just in contact with the lower edge of its throttle lever and then tighten the lever. This ensures that both throttles open simultaneously.

31 Carry out the operations of paragraphs 17 to 19.

---

18 Throttle cable – removal, refitting and adjustment

1 Disconnect the inner cable from the carburettor throttle spindle.

2 Release the outer cable from the carburettor abutment bracket.

3 Release the inner cable from the accelerator pedal arm by drawing the nipple from its location 'in the top of the pedal arm and lifting the cable from the slot in the arm.

4 Detach the throttle cable from the servo pipe clip.

5 Withdraw the inner and outer cable as an assembly out of the servo mounting plate, pulling them out from the front of the car.

6 Refitting the cable is the reverse of the removal sequence. It will however be necessary to adjust the cable as described in the following paragraphs.

7 Slacken the throttle cable trunnion bolt.

8 Carefully pull down on the inner cable until all free movement of the accelerator pedal has been removed.

9 While holding the cable taut, on the linkage type throttle, raise the cam operating lever until it just makes contact with the cam.

10 On the linkage type throttle, move the trunnion up the cable until it

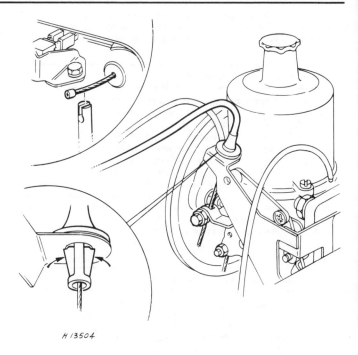

H 13504

Fig. 3.8 Throttle cable attachments (Sec 18)

contacts the operating lever. Tighten the trunnion bolt on both types of throttle.

11 Depress the accelerator pedal and check that approximately 0·063 in (1·5 mm) free movement takes place on the throttle cable before the cam operating lever begins to move.

---

19 Choke control – removal, refitting and adjustment

Cable gear change models

1 Disconnect the battery.

2 Disconnect the choke control from the carburettor.

3 Undo and remove the securing screws from below the instrument panel.

4 Disconnect the speedometer cable from the rear of the speedometer head.

5 Detach the wiring plug from the rear of the instrument panel and draw the instrument panel away from the facia.

6 Undo the nut and shakeproof washer securing the outer cable to the facia panel.

7 The inner and outer cable assembly may now be withdrawn from the body grommet.

8 Refitting the cable is the reverse of the removal sequence. It is important that the inner cable trunnion is connected to the lower of the two holes on the carburettor choke lever. The cable must be adjusted as described later in this Section.

Rod gear change models

9 Disconnect the battery.

10 Disconnect the choke cable from trhe carburettor.

11 Undo and remove the screws securing the glovebox lid support to the facia.

12 Undo and remove the screws and washers securing the glovebox lid striker.

13 Undo and remove the side and lower glovebox retaining screws and washers, and withdraw the glovebox.

14 Remove the grub screws securing the control knobs to the heater controls and withdraw the knobs.

15 Carefully prise away the heater control masking plate using a knife or thin, wide-bladed screwdriver.

16 Undo and remove the two screws securing the heater controls to the facia panel.

17 Remove the nut and shakeproof washer securing the outer cable to the facia panel.

18 The inner and outer cable may now be withdrawn from the body grommet. Note that this cable uses the same grommet as the bonnet release cable.

19 Refitting is the reverse of removal. Note that the inner cable trunnion is connected into the lower of the two holes on the carburettor choke lever. It will be necessary to adjust the cable as described later in this Section.

Adjustment

20 Slacken the cable trunnion bolt.

21 Make sure that the choke control knob is pushed in fully.

22 Adjust the fast idle adjusting screw so that a small clearance exists between the end of the screw and the cam.

23 Adjust the position of the trunnion so as to give a free movement of the cable of 0·063 in (1·5 mm) before the cam lever begins to move (Fig. 3.9).

24 Pull out the choke control knob approximately 0·5 in (13 mm) until the linkage is just about to move the jet.

25 Start the engine and allow to warm up to the normal operating temperature.

26 Turn the fast idle screw to give an engine speed of between 1100 and 1200 rpm.

27 Return the choke control knob to its fully closed position and check that there is a small gap between the end of the fast idle adjusting screw and the cam.

20 Accelerator pedal – removal and refitting

1 Detach the throttle cable from the pedal arm by drawing the nipple from its location in the top of the pedal arm and lifting the cable from the slot in the arm.

2 Extract the split pin and lift away the washer from the pedal pivot.

3 Very carefully lever the pivot from the mounting bracket sufficiently for the pedal to be withdrawn.

4 Check the accelerator pedal arm and pivot for wear, and if evident, a new pedal assembly should be fitted.

5 Refitting is the reverse sequence to removal. Lubricate the pedal pivot with a little grease.

21 Fuel tank – removal and refitting

1 Petrol tanks are a potential source of serious explosions and great care should be exercised both during removal and when they are off the vehicle. It is safest to do the work in the open, or in a well ventilated place and not over a pit.

2 As far as is possible, use up the fuel in the tank by using the vehicle.

3 Disconnect the battery.

4 Remove the access panel from the floor of the boot and disconnect the fuel gauge unit cable (Fig. 3.11).

5 Squeeze the ends of the fuel pipe clip with a pair of pliers and detach the pipe from the tank outlet.

6 Remove the filler cap from the tank neck.

7 On models up to 1970, detach the breather pipe from its clip on the rear flange of the tank and push the breather pipe back through the body grommet.

8 On models from 1971 onwards, remove the nut securing the exhaust pipe clip to the rear mountings and detach the clip from the mountings.

9 Support the tank and undo and remove the securing bolts and washers.

10 Lower the tank and disengage the filler neck from the body grommet.

11 Empty the remaining fuel out of the tank and store the tank well away from sources of heat or sparks.

12 Refitting is the reverse of removal, but the following points should be noted.

13 First pass the neck of the tank through the body grommet and ensure that the body grommet is properly seated before raising the fuel tank fully.

14 On models up to 1970, the breather pipe should be fed through the body grommet as the tank is raised.

15 On 1971 and later models, the left-hand rear bolts of the fuel tank also secure the exhaust pipe mounting bracket.

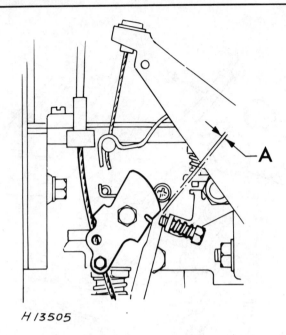

H 13505

Fig. 3.9 Choke control adjustment (Sec 19)

A   Free movement

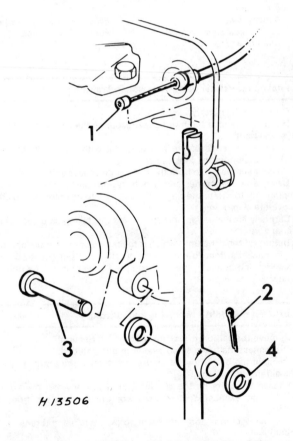

H 13506

Fig. 3.10 Accelerator pedal assembly (Sec 20)

1   Inner cable   3   Pedal pivot
2   Split pin   4   Spacer washer

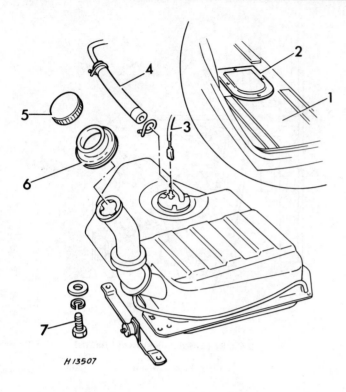

Fig. 3.11 Fuel tank assembly (Sec 21)

1   Boot floor
2   Access panel
3   Sender unit electric cable
4   Main fuel pipe
5   Filler cap
6   Filler neck body grommet
7   Fuel tank fixing bolt

22   Fuel gauge sender unit – removal and refitting

1   Disconnect the battery.
2   Undo and remove the four screws securing the access panel in the floor of the boot.
3   Squeeze the ends of the fuel pipe clip with a pair of pliers and detach the pipe from the tank outlet.
4   Disconnect the cable from the fuel gauge sender unit.
5   Using a light hammer and a drift, tap on one of the lugs of the clamping ring to rotate the ring anti-clockwise to its unlocked position. Remove the clamp ring.
6   Carefully lift the gauge unit out of the tank, taking care not to bend the float wire.
7   Before refitting the unit, which is the reverse of the removal procedure, inspect the float to make sure that it is not punctured. Discard the sealing ring between the tank and the flange plate of the unit and fit a new sealing ring.

23   Exhaust manifold – removing and refitting

1   Remove the carburettor(s), as described in Section 7.
2   Disconnect the brake servo pipe from the manifold.
3   Remove the bolt from the bracket connecting the exhaust system to the differential housing.
4   Loosen the bolts on the clamp of the joint between the exhaust manifold and exhaust system and separate the system from the manifold.
5   Remove the bolts and nuts securing the manifold and remove the manifold.
6   When refitting the manifold, use new gaskets and ensure that the joint faces of the manifold and the cylinder head are clean and undamaged. Use sealing compound on the bolts.
7   On twin carburettor models, ensure that the twin exhaust stubs of the manifold enter the exhaust pipe to a depth of 2·1 in (52 mm).

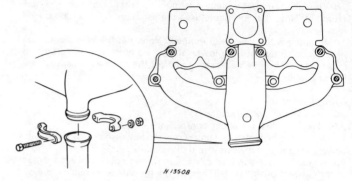

Fig. 3.12 Exhaust manifold and pipe joint (single carburettor) (Sec 23)

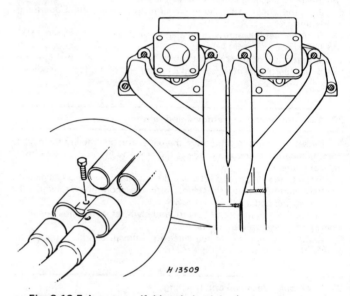

Fig. 3.13 Exhaust manifold and pipe joint (twin carburettors) (Sec 23)

24   Exhaust system – removal and refitting

Models up to 1970
1   Remove the clip securing the exhaust pipe to the manifold.
2   Remove the bolt from the strap securing the exhaust pipe to the differential housing.
3   Remove the bolt from each side of the mounting of the front silencer.
4   Remove the rear suspension tie plate.
5   Remove the nuts and washers attaching the exhaust pipe to the two rear rubber mountings.
6   Remove the nut and washer securing the tail pipe to its mounting rubber and remove the exhaust system complete.
7   To refit the system, start by attaching the exhaust pipe to the manifold with the clamp fitted loosely.
8   Fit the remaining attachments working towards the tail pipe, but do not tighten any of the fixings.
9   Remove the exhaust pipe to manifold clamp and coat the mating surfaces of the manifold and pipe with exhaust sealant. Align the pipe and manifold, fit the clamp and tighten the bolts.
10   Starting at the front and working towards the rear, tighten the remaining fixings, ensuring that neither the exhaust system, nor any mounting, is under strain.

1971 and later models
11   Disconnect the exhaust pipe(s) from the manifold.
12   Remove the nuts and U-bolt securing the exhaust pipe to the

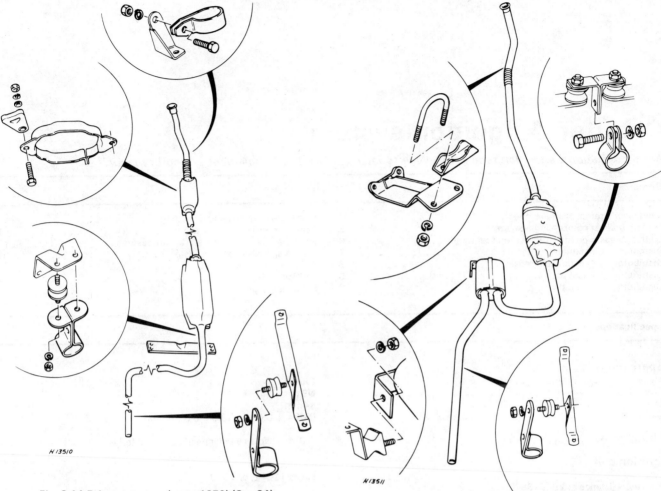

Fig. 3.14 Exhaust system (up to 1970) (Sec 24)

Fig. 3.15 Exhaust system (1971 onwards) (Sec 24)

differential housing, and the bolt from the intermediate mounting.

13 Remove the nut and washer from the mounting securing the small silencer.

14 Remove the nut and washer securing the tail pipe to its mounting rubber and remove the exhaust system complete.

15 On vehicles with a single carburettor, refit the exhaust system in a similar manner to that described in paragraphs 7 to 10.

16 For twin carburettor models, start by coating the exhaust stubs with exhaust sealant and then enter them in to the exhaust pipes to a depth of 2·1 in (52 mm). Slide the clamp into place, but do not tighten the bolt at this stage.

17 Complete the installation by attaching all the fixings loosely and then starting at the front, tighten all the fixings, ensuring that neither the exhaust system, nor any mounting, is under strain.

25 Fault diagnosis – fuel system

Symptom	Reason(s)
Smell of petrol with engine stopped	Leaking fuel tank Leaking fuel pipe, or joints
Smell of petrol with engine running	Leaking fuel pipe Carburettor needle valve set wrongly, or punctured float
Excessive fuel consumption without obvious petrol leakage	Worn needle Sticking needle Dirty air filter element
Failure to start, or difficult starting	Choke not operating properly Fuel blockage Fuel pump defective Intake manifold gasket leaking Carburettor loose on manifold Carburettor piston stuck Leak in vacuum line to distributor

Chapter 4 Ignition system

For modifications, and information applicable to later models, see Supplement at end of manual

Contents

Specifications

Spark plugs

Make	Champion
Type	N9Y
Size	14mm
Gap	0.024 to 0.026 in (0.61 to 0.66 mm)

Firing order

1-3-4-2 (No 1 cylinder nearest to radiator)

Ignition coil

Type	Lucas 11C12, or 16C6
Primary resistance at 20°C (68°F):	
11C12	3.0 to 3.4 ohms
16C6	1.43 to 1.58 ohms

Distributor

Type	Lucas 25D4, Lucas 45D4, or Ducellier
Rotation	Anti-clockwise
Contact breaker gap	0.014 to 0.016 in (0.36 to 0.41 mm)
Dwell angle:	
25D4	60° ± 3°
45D4	51° ± 5°
Ducellier	57°
Condenser capacity	0.18 to 0.24 mF
Automatic advance	Vacuum and centrifugal

Centrifugal advance – deceleration (vacuum pipe disconnected)

HC engines	LC engines
20° to 24° at 6000 rpm	28° to 32° at 6000 rpm
14° to 18° at 4000 rpm	22° to 26° at 4000 rpm
8° to 12° at 2000 rpm	8° to 12° at 2000 rpm
6° to 10° at 1500 rpm	4° to 8° at 1500 rpm
0° to 1° at 900 rpm	0° to 3° at 900 rpm
Zero advance below 800 rpm	Zero advance below 500 rpm

Vacuum advance

	HC engines	LC engines
Starts	6 in (152 mm) Hg	4 in (101mm) Hg
Finishes	16° at 14 in (356 mm) Hg	16° at 12 in (305 mm) Hg

Stroboscopic ignition setting

1500 models 1969, 1970 and 1500 LC models 1971 onwards	12° BTDC at 1000 rpm (vacuum pipe disconnected)
1500 HC models 1971 onwards, and 1750 single carburettor models	13° BTDC at 1000 rpm (vacuum pipe disconnected)
1750 twin carburettor models	11° BTDC at 1000 rpm (vacuum pipe disconnected)

Torque wrench settings

	lbf ft	kgf m
Distributor to plate	10	1.4
Distributor clamp bolt	3.0	0.41
Spark plugs	18	2.5

1 General description

For an engine to run at maximum efficiency, the spark must ignite the fuel/air charge in the combustion chamber at exactly the right moment for the particular engine speed and load conditions.

The ignition system consists of the ignition coil, which is two windings which are coupled electromagnetically; and the distributor, which is a mechanically operated switch. The distributor contacts apply battery voltage to the low voltage winding of the coil and at the instant when the low voltage, or primary winding is switched off, a very high voltage is induced in the high tension assembly winding. This very high voltage is switched to the appropriate cylinder by the distributor rotor and jumps to earth across the electrodes of the spark plug.

A vacuum diaphragm, which is controlled by the suction of the inlet manifold, causes the instant of switching of the low voltage winding of the coil to be varied according to inlet manifold suction and therefore engine load, while a centrifugally operated cam produces a variation in switching which is dependent upon engine speed.

2 Contact breaker points – adjustment

1 Release the two clips securing the distributor cap, lift off the cap and remove the rotor arm.
2 Gently prise the contact breaker points open, to examine the condition of their faces. If they are rough, pitted or dirty, it will be necessary to remove them and although the contacts can be resurfaced with a file, it is better to fit a new contact assembly.
3 If the condition of the contacts is satisfactory, turn the crankshaft slowly until the heel of the contact breaker is on the highest part of one of the cam lobes. In this position, a 0.015 in (0.4 mm) feeler gauge should just fit between the points, but ensure that the feeler gauge is free from dirt and grease before inserting it.
4 If the gap is incorrect, adjustment should be made in the following way.

Lucas distributor

5 Slacken the screw which clamps the contact breaker. Insert a screwdriver into the notch in the contact breaker plate (Fig. 4.1) and twist the screwdriver to open and close the points.
6 While holding the feeler gauge between the points, twist the screwdriver until the feeler gauge will just slide between the points and then tighten the clamp screw. Recheck the gap and readjust if necessary.

Ducellier distributor

7 Slacken the screw securing the fixed contact. Hold the feeler gauge between the contacts and push the fixed contact towards, or away from the moving contact until the feeler gauge will just slide between them. Tighten the clamp screw, recheck the gap and readjust if necessary.

All distributors

8 Before refitting the distributor cap, fit the rotor arm, wipe the inside of the distributor cap and check that the carbon brush in the centre of the cap is free to move in its hole.

3 Contact breaker points – removal and refitting

1 If the contact breaker points are burned, pitted, or badly worn, they must be removed. Although it is possible to file the contacts, the result is seldom satisfactory and it is preferable to fit a new contact breaker assembly.
2 Each of the different types of distributor has a different contact breaker assembly and the individual procedures are as follows.

Lucas 25D4 distributor

3 Unscrew and remove the nut from the terminal post on the contact breaker assembly and remove the steel washer and fibre washer, or the insulating bush beneath it.
4 Lift the LT lead and the condenser lead off the terminal post.
5 Remove the screw, plain washer and spring washer which clamp the contact breaker assembly to the base plate and lift the contact

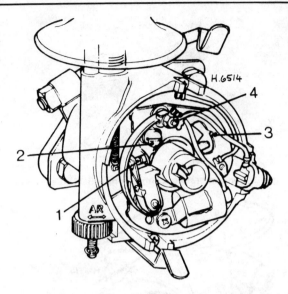

Fig. 4.1 Contact breaker adjustment (Lucas) (Sec 2)

1 Contact breaker points
2 Contact plate securing screw
3 Screwdriver slot
4 Moving contact spring and terminals securing nut

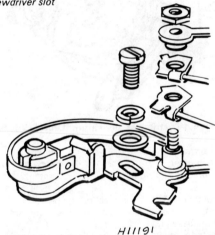

Fig. 4.2 Contact breaker connections (25D4) (Sec 3 and 4)

breaker assembly clear.
6 If fitting a new contact breaker assembly, first wipe the faces of the contacts with a piece of clean, dry rag, because the contacts may be coated with preservative.
7 Locate the pivot of the moving contact on the small post projecting from the base plate. Fit the spring washer, then the plain washer to the clamp screw. Insert the clamp screw and tighten it until it just grips the plate.
8 Connect the LT lead, condenser lead, and bush to the terminal post and clamp them. Note that the two leads must be in electrical contact with the spring of the moving contact, but not with any other metal part of the distributor.
9 Adjust the contact breaker gap, as described in the previous Section and lubricate the pivot (Section 5).

Lucas 45D4 distributor

10 The method is similar to that for the 25D4, except for the way in which the LT and condenser leads are connected.
11 The two leads are cold welded to a common plate which is clipped to the moving contact spring (Fig. 4.3).

Ducellier distributor

12 Disconnect the LT lead to the distributor.
13 Remove the spring clip and the insulating washer from the pivot of

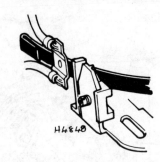

Fig. 4.3 Contact breaker connections (45D4) (Sec 3 and 4)

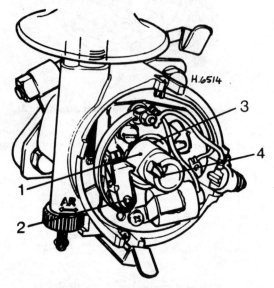

Fig. 4.4 Distributor lubrication (Lucas) (Sec 5)

1 Cam surface	weights
2 Contact pivot	4 Screw or pad in cam
3 Apertures to centrifugal	spindle

the moving contact and lift the contact off the pivot.
14 Remove the clamp screw from the fixed contact and lift the contact from the base plate.
15 Fit contacts by reversing the operations necessary for removal. If fitting new contacts, first wipe their faces with a piece of clean, dry rag because they may be coated with preservative.
16 Adjust the contact breaker gap, as described in the previous Section prior to having the dwell angle set by a Leyland agent with the necessary electronic equipment.

4   Condenser – removal and refitting

1   The purpose of the condenser is to ensure that when the contact breaker contacts interrupt the current in the primary circuit of the ignition coil, there is no arcing between the points. In addition to causing the points to burn away quickly, arcing reduces the efficiency of the coil and the spark produced at the spark plug is weaker.
2   The condenser is fitted in parallel with the contact breaker points. If a condenser becomes open circuited, or disconnected, the engine will become difficult to start and there will be excessive wear of the contact breaker points. If the condenser short circuits, the primary circuit of the ignition coil will not be interrupted when the contact breaker points open and no spark will be produced at the spark plug.
3   Testing a condenser requires a high voltage insulation tester so if one is thought to be suspect it is generally easier to substitute a different condenser, preferably a new one, in place of the suspect component.
4   To remove the condenser from a Lucas distributor remove the distributor cap and rotor arm. On 25D4 models, unscrew the nut securing the leads to the moving contact and lift off the orange wire.

On 45D4 models, which have the condenser wire cold-welded to the terminal plate (Fig. 4.3), cut the orange wire off. In both cases, remove the condenser clamping screw and lift the condenser out.
5   Refitting is the reverse of removal. On the 25D4 model, the tag on the end of the condenser lead must be placed with the primary lead beneath the insulating bush (Fig. 4.2). On 45D4 models the condenser wire should be soldered to the terminal plate. Ensure that the condenser and the contact breaker baseplate are free from dirt, oil and grease and clamp the condenser into place with its fixing screw.
6   To remove the condenser from a Ducellier distributor, disconnect the condenser lead from the contact breaker primary lead and remove the screw securing the condenser to the vacuum unit. Refitting is the reverse of removal, but it is necessary to ensure that the mating surfaces of the condenser fixing clip and the vacuum unit are free from dirt, oil and grease, so that there is a good electrical connection.

5   Distributor – lubrication

1   Regular lubrication of the distributor is essential because lack of lubricant can result in a loss in performance due to the centrifugal advance mechanism not working and excessive wear on the cam follower. Nevertheless, excessive lubrication must be avoided because excess oil may contaminate the contact faces of the points and cause misfiring, or ignition failure.
2   Each of the three types of distributor fitted has slightly different lubrication requirements, but the preliminary steps are the same in all cases.
3   Remove the ignition shield, release the retaining clips and remove the distributor cap. Pull the rotor arm off the cam spindle.

Lucas 25D4
4   Very lightly smear the surface of the cam and the pivot post of the moving contact with grease. Allow about four drops of oil to fall through the gap between the cam spindle and the contact plate to lubricate the centrifugal weights. Apply two or three drops of oil around the edge of the screw in the centre of the cam spindle, but do not remove the screw and do not allow the oil to run out of the slot in the cam.

Lucas 45D4
5   Lubrication is the same as the 25D4 distributor except that the oil for the cam spindle is applied to the felt pad which covers the screw in the centre of the cam spindle. Do not oil the felt pad which bears against the face of the cam.

Ducellier
6   Lightly smear the face of the cam with grease and apply grease to the pressure pad which is in contact with the cam. Add two or three drops of oil to the felt pad in the top of the cam spindle. Turn the crankshaft until the pivot post of the centrifugal weight is visible through the cut out in the base plate and lubricate the pivot post with a drop of oil. Repeat the operation for the opposite pivot post.
7   In all cases, wipe away any surplus lubricant and ensure that the contact breaker points are clean and dry.
8   Wipe the inside and outside of the distributor cap, particularly the inside between the electrodes. Refit the rotor arm, distributor cap and ignition shield.

6   Distributor – removal and refitting

1   Before removing the distributor, remove the flywheel housing cover plate on manual transmission models, or the converter housing plug on models with automatic transmission. Note the position on the distributor cap of the lead to No 1 cylinder, which is the cylinder nearest to the fan.
2   Release the two clips securing the distributor cap to the body and lift away the distributor cap.
3   Turn the crankshaft slowly in the normal direction of rotation until the 1/4 TDC mark on the flywheel, or the 0^0 mark on the torque converter is aligned with the pointer and the distributor rotor is pointing to the lead to No 1 cylinder. (Later models, see Fig. 4.13).
4   Disconnect the low tension cable from the side of the distributor.
5   Mark the plug leads to show the plug to which they were connected and then disconnect the leads from the plugs. Disconnect the

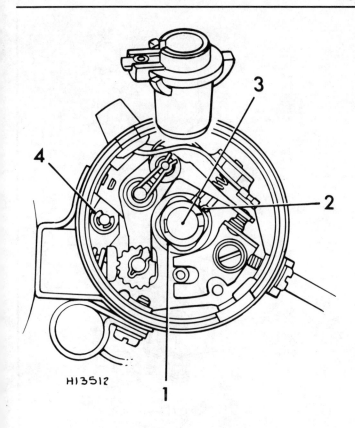

Fig. 4.5 Distributor lubrication (Ducellier) (Sec 5)

1	Cam face	3	Cam spindle pad
2	Pressure pad	4	Centrifugal weight pivot

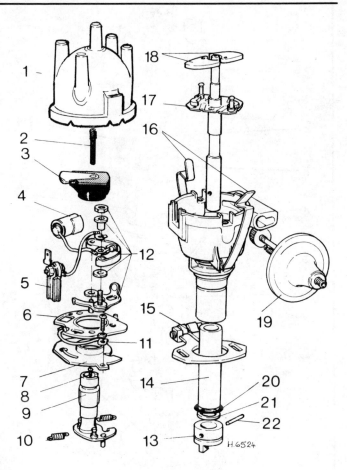

Fig. 4.6 Exploded view of the Lucas 25D4 distributor (Sec 7)

1	Distributor cap	12	Contact breaker points
2	Brush and spring	13	Driving dog
3	Rotor arm	14	Bush
4	Condenser	15	Clamp plate
5	Terminal and lead	16	Cap retaining clips
6	Moving baseplate	17	Shaft and action plate
7	Fixed baseplate	18	Bob weights
8	Cam screw	19	Vacuum unit
9	Cam	20	O-ring oil seal
10	Advance spring	21	Thrust washer
11	Earth lead	22	Taper pin

high tension lead from the ignition coil and remove the distributor cap with leads attached.

6   Disconnect the vacuum pipe from the distributor vacuum unit.

7   Remove the two bolts and washers from the distributor clamp plate and lift the distributor and clamp plate from the cylinder block. If the distributor is removed in this way, the ignition timing will not be altered. If the pinch bolt on the clamp plate is loosened and the distributor is removed leaving the clamp plate in place, it will be necessary to reset the ignition timing.

8   Before refitting the distributor, ensure that the flywheel or torque converter is still in the same position as when the distributor was removed and turn the rotor arm so that it is pointing to the lead to No 1 cylinder.

9   Fit the distributor by reversing the operations necessary for removal, taking care to reconnect the low tension and all the high tension leads correctly.

7   Distributor – dismantling

Lucas 25D4 distributor

1   Pull off the rotor arm.

2   Unscrew the nut from the moving contact anchor pillar and disconnect the low tension and condenser leads.

3   Lift off the moving contact if it is a separate component, otherwise unscrew the fixed contact securing screw. Remove the screw with its flat and spring washer and lift away the moving contact with the fixed contact.

4   Remove the screw securing the condenser and remove the condenser.

5   Unscrew the two screws securing the base plate and note that one of them also secures the earth lead. Unhook the vacuum unit link from the pillar on the base plate and lift out the base plate.

6   Make a mark on the drive dog on the bottom of the spindle to show the position of the dog relative to the rotor arm slot in the cam spindle. If this is not done, the distributor arm can be reassembled with the engine timing 180° out.

7   Mark the ends of the centrifugal advance springs and the pins to which they are connected, so that the springs will be refitted to their original position exactly and then unhook one end of each spring.

8   Hold the drive dog, or cam to prevent it from rotating and remove the screw from the centre of the cam.

9   Hold the cam to prevent it from falling off and turn the distributor upside down. Carefully lift the distributor body off the cam and the centrifugal weights will stay on their pivots on the cam. Note the position of each of the weights and then remove the weights.

10   Remove the small clip from the end of the vacuum unit adjuster. Remove the nut and spring and also the small spring clip against which the milled surface of the nut bears. Separate the vacuum unit from the distributor body.

11   Mark the position of the drive dog relative to its shaft. Check to see whether the dog is attached with a taper pin, or a spring pin. Drive the pin out with a pin punch and remove the dog, thrust washer and spindle.

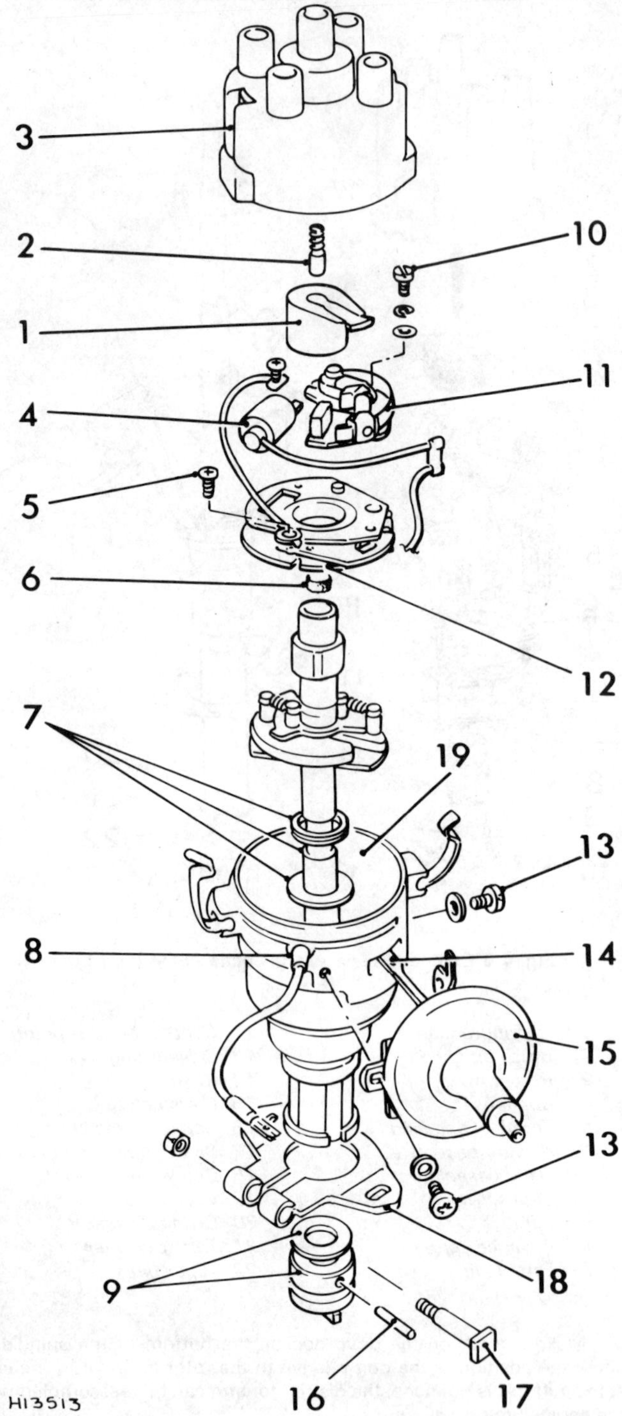

H13513

Fig. 4.7 Distributor 45D4 (exploded view) (Sec 7)

1	Rotor	10	Contact set securing screw
2	Carbon brush and spring	11	Contact set
3	Cap	12	Base plate
4	Condenser (capacitor)	13	Vacuum unit retaining screws and washers
5	Baseplate securing screw	14	Vacuum unit link
6	Felt pad	15	Vacuum unit
7	Shaft assembly with steel washer and spacer	16	Parallel pin
8	Low tension lead and grommet	17	Pinch bolt and nut
9	Drive dog and thrust washer	18	Lockplate
		19	Distributor body

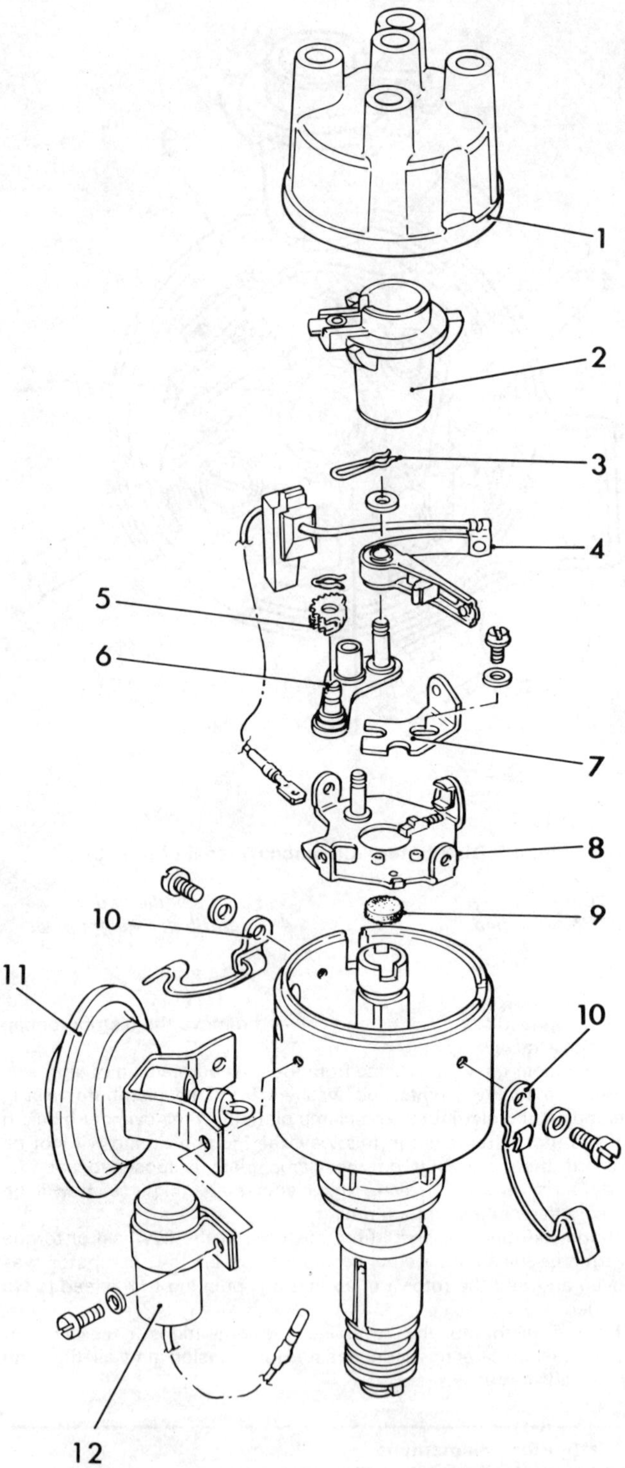

H13514

Fig. 4.8 Exploded view of Ducellier distributor (Sec 7)

1	Cap	7	Fixed contact
2	Rotor	8	Baseplate
3	Rocker arm clip	9	Felt pad
4	Moving contact assembly	10	Cap retaining clips
5	Serrated cam	11	Vacuum unit
6	Eccentric D-post	12	Condenser

Lucas 45D4 distributor

12 Remove the rotor arm and lift the felt pad out of the centre of the cam.

13 Remove the two screws securing the vacuum unit, tilt the vacuum unit to disengage the operating arm and remove the vacuum unit.

14 Push the low tension lead and its grommet into the inside of the distributor body.

15 Remove the screw securing the base plate. Lever the slotted segment of the base plate out of its groove and remove the base plate assembly.

16 Remove the drive dog as described in paragraph 11.

17 Remove the shaft, complete with automatic advance mechanism, steel washer and spacer.

18 Push the spring of the moving contact inwards and detach the low tension connector from the spring loop.

19 Remove the screw to release the condenser and the earth lead.

20 Remove the screw securing the contact set and remove the contact set.

Ducellier distributor

21 Remove the rotor arm and lift the felt pad out of the centre of the cam.

22 Remove the two screws retaining the vacuum unit and condenser and release the clip from the eccentric D-post retaining the serrated cam.

23 Mark the position of the serrated cam relative to the spring seat of the vacuum operated link. This is very important, because otherwise the vacuum advance setting will be different on reassembly.

24 Disengage the vacuum operated link and serrated cam from the eccentric D-post and carefully remove the vacuum unit.

25 Release the retaining clip, remove the securing screws and take off the contact breaker assembly.

26 Remove the base plate securing screw and lift out the base plate. Be careful to retain the nylon pressure pad and spring.

8 Distributor – inspection and repair

1 Examine all components for damage and excessive wear and obtain new parts when necessary.

2 Clean the distributor cap and inspect it for cracks and signs of tracking or burning of the insulation. Check that the central brush moves freely in its holder.

Lucas 25D4 distributor

3 If the clearance between the shaft and body is excessive, a new bush may be fitted if facilities are available for pressing out the old one and pressing in the new one. New bushes must be soaked in engine oil for 24 hours before fitting and must then be pressed into the body with the smaller diameter of the bush leading. The bottom of the bush should be flush with the end of the body shank and the upper end will protrude into the body slightly.

4 Using the hole in the body shank as a guide, drill a hole of the same diameter as the drain hole through the bush.

5 Do not ream the bush after it has been fitted, but lubricate the shaft and fit it to the body. Mount the assembly securely and rotate the shaft for 15 minutes by driving it with an electric drill, or a lathe. Remove the shaft again, wipe and lubricate it.

Lucas 45D4 distributor

6 Do not dismantle the advance mechanism beyond removing the control springs. The springs may be renewed, but if any of the moving parts of the cam assembly are worn, or damaged, the complete shaft assembly must be renewed.

7 Check the fit of the shaft in its bearing. If the side play is excessive the complete distributor must be renewed.

8 Check the base plate assembly. If the spring between the plates is damaged, or if the plates do not move freely, fit a new assembly.

Ducellier distributor

9 Inspection and repair of the Ducellier distributor is broadly similar to that for the Lucas 45D4 distributor, but note that the distributor drive dog is retained loosely on the driveshaft to allow for any misalignment.

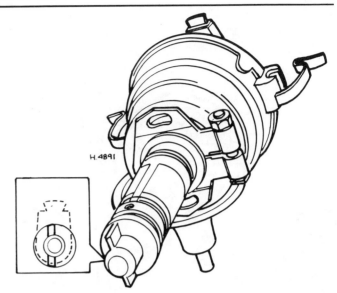

Fig. 4.9 Correct position of drive dog (45D4) (Sec 9)

9 Distributor – reassembly

1 Reassembly is a reversal of the operations necessary for dismantling, but there are a number of points which require particular attention.

2 Lubricate the centrifugal weights and other parts of the advance mechanism, the spindle and the cam as described in Section 5.

3 When fitting the condenser, ensure that the body makes good contact with the distributor body.

Lucas 25D4 distributor

4 Take great care to ensure that the mating marks on the shaft, dog and cam are aligned when reassembling so that the distributor is not assembled with the timing 180° out.

5 When fitting the vacuum unit, fit the small spring clip on to the distributor body before fitting the vacuum unit spring and nut.

6 After screwing on the nut, fit the small clip to the shaft end and squeeze it into its groove, then adjust the nut so that the vacuum unit is at the mid point of its micrometer scale.

Lucas 45D4 distributor

7 The thrust washer has raised pips on one side of it and these must be towards the drive dog.

8 Fit the drive dog so that the driving tongues are parallel with the rotor arm electrode and to the left of its centre line when the rotor arm points upwards (Fig. 4.9).

9 Position the base assembly so that the two downward pointing prongs will straddle the screw hole below the cap clip. Press the base plate into the body until it engages the undercut.

10 Take an accurate measurement across the distributor cap register on the body at right angles to the slot in the base plate (Fig. 4.10). Position the earth lead and fit and tighten the base plate securing screw. Remeasure across the cap register and if the measurement has not increased by at least 0.006 in (0.15 mm), fit a new base plate assembly.

11 Check that the base plate prongs still straddle the screw hole before refitting the vacuum unit.

Ducellier distributor

12 On reassembly, set the contact breaker points to 0.015 in (0.4 mm) as an initial setting. Final setting of the contact breaker dwell angle and vacuum advance adjustment must be carried out with electronic test equipment which Leyland agents should have.

10 Ignition – timing

1 If the clamp plate pinch bolt has been loosened on the distributor and the static timing lost, or if for any other reason it is wished to set

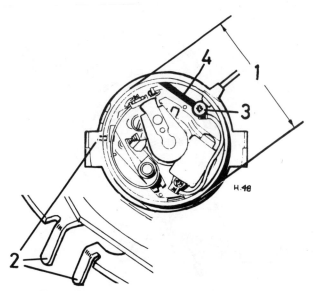

Fig. 4.10 Installing the baseplate (45D4) (Sec 9)

1   Dimension across distributor cap register
2   Downward pointing prongs on baseplate
3   Earth lead
4   Slot in baseplate

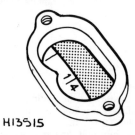

Fig. 4.11 Timing marks – manual transmission (Sec 10)

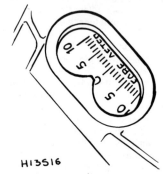

Fig. 4.12 Timing marks – automatic transmission (Sec 10)

the ignition timing, proceed as follows:

2   Refer to Section 2 and check the contact breaker points. Reset as necessary.

3   Assemble the clamp plate to the distributor body, but do not tighten the pinch bolt fully. Where the distributor has a knurled micrometer adjustment nut, set this to approximately the mid-position of its travel range.

4   Slowly turn the crankshaft in the normal direction of rotation until the 1/4 TDC mark on the flywheel of manual transmission models, or the 0° mark on the torque converter of models with automatic transmission is aligned with the housing pointer. No 1 cylinder should be at the top of the compression stroke and just about to commence the power stroke. On later models the timing marks consist of a groove in the crankshaft pulley and a scale on the timing case, therefore the removal of the flywheel cover plate is not necessary.

5   Fit the distributor and engage the driving dog into the distributor driveshaft. Provided the distributor driveshaft has not been disturbed or has been refitted correctly, the rotor arm should now point to the segment in the distributor cap which leads to No 1 spark plug (the one nearest the fan).

6   Refit the two distributor clamp bolts and washers but do not tighten fully yet.

7   Rotate the crankshaft anti-clockwise approximately 20° then turn it clockwise again until the timing pointer indicates 1° less than the specified stroboscopic timing setting. This allows for approximately 1° of centrifugal advance at 1000 rpm.

8   Rotate the distributor body anti-clockwise a little, then rotate it slowly clockwise until the points just commence to open. Now tighten the clamp bolts. Difficulty is sometimes experienced in determining exactly when the contact breaker points open. This can be ascertained most accurately by connecting a 12 volt bulb in parallel with the contact breaker points (one lead to earth and the other from the distributor low tension terminal). Switch on the ignition, and turn the advance and retard adjuster until the bulb lights up, indicating that the points have just opened.

9   Refit the distributor cap and reconnect the spark plug leads. Do not forget the HT lead to the centre of the ignition coil.

10   If it was not found possible to align the rotor arm correctly, one of two things is wrong: either the distributor driveshaft has been incorrectly refitted, in which case it must be removed and replaced as described in Chapter 1, or the distributor has been dismantled and the distributor cam spindle refitted 180° out. To rectify, it will be necessary to partially dismantle the distributor, lift the camshaft pins from the centrifugal weight holes and turn the camshaft through 180°. Refit the pins into the weights and reassemble.

11   It should be noted that the adjustment which has been made is nominal and the final adjustment should be made under running conditions.

12   First start the engine and allow to warm up to normal running temperature, and then accelerate in top gear from 30 to 50 mph, listening for heavy pinking of the engine. If this occurs, the ignition needs to be retarded slightly until just the faintest trace of pinking can be heard under these operating conditions. If the distributor has a micrometer adjuster, this can be used, but where there is no adjuster, the distributor will have to be rotated slightly anti-clockwise.

13   The specified ignition settings are correct for the grade of fuel recommended by the manufacturers and the use of a different grade of fuel necessitates the timing being advanced 1° for every unit increase in octane number, with a corresponding retarding of the ignition if a lower grade fuel is used. For example, an engine timed for 4 star fuel (97 octane rating) should have the ignition retarded 2° if run on 3 star (95 octane rating).

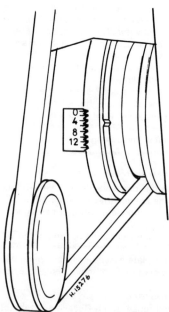

Fig. 4.13 Timing marks on crankshaft pulley and timing case – later models (Sec 10)

Measuring plug gap. A feeler gauge of the correct size (see ignition system specifications) should have a slight 'drag' when slid between the electrodes. Adjust gap if necessary

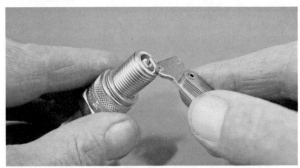

Adjusting plug gap. The plug gap is adjusted by bending the earth electrode inwards, or outwards, as necessary until the correct clearance is obtained. Note the use of the correct tool

Normal. Grey-brown deposits, lightly coated core nose. Gap increasing by around 0.001 in (0.025 mm) per 1000 miles (1600 km). Plugs ideally suited to engine, and engine in good condition

Carbon fouling. Dry, black, sooty deposits. Will cause weak spark and eventually misfire. Fault: over-rich fuel mixture. Check: carburettor mixture settings, float level and jet sizes; choke operation and cleanliness of air filter. Plugs can be re-used after cleaning

Oil fouling. Wet, oily deposits. Will cause weak spark and eventually misfire. Fault: worn bores/piston rings or valve guides; sometimes occurs (temporarily) during running-in period. Plugs can be re-used after thorough cleaning

Overheating. Electrodes have glazed appearance, core nose very white — few deposits. Fault: plug overheating. Check: plug value, ignition timing, fuel octane rating (too low) and fuel mixture (too weak). Discard plugs and cure fault immediately

Electrode damage. Electrodes burned away; core nose has burned, glazed appearance. Fault: pre-ignition. Check: as for 'Overheating' but may be more severe. Discard plugs and remedy fault before piston or valve damage occurs

Split core nose (may appear initially as a crack). Damage is self-evident, but cracks will only show after cleaning. Fault: pre-ignition or wrong gap-setting technique. Check: ignition timing, cooling system, fuel octane rating (too low) and fuel mixture (too weak). Discard plugs, rectify fault immediately

14 The foregoing will enable the ignition timing to be set sufficiently accurately for the engine to start and run, but will not necessarily give optimum performance. Accurate setting of the timing requires a stroboscopic timing light. These can be purchased from accessory shops and are not expensive. The procedure is described in Chapter 13.

11 Spark plugs and HT leads

1 An engine will not run correctly and efficiently unless the spark plugs are of the correct grade, are clean and properly adjusted.
2 At the recommended maintenance intervals, the plugs should be removed, cleaned and examined. If they are in poor condition, it is a false economy not to fit a new set.
3 If possible, get the plugs cleaned by a garage having a spark plug cleaning machine, otherwise clean them with a wire brush and adjust the gap to the specified dimension.
4 The appearance of the spark plugs gives a lot of information about the condition of the engine and the way in which it is operating.
5 Plug leads require no routine attention other than being kept clean and the plug leads, plug caps and the outside of the plug porcelain insulator should be wiped with a clean dry cloth at intervals of 6000 miles (10 000 km). During damp, misty weather, it is particularly important to have clean plug leads and insulators, because under these conditions dirt and moisture will result in the engine failing to start.

12 Fault diagnosis – ignition system

1 There are two distinct symptoms of ignition faults. Either the engine will not start, or fire; or it starts with difficulty and does not run normally.
2 If the starter motor spins the engine satisfactorily, there is adequate fuel and yet the engine will not start, the fault is more likely to be on the LT side and will most probably result from a bad, or broken electrical connection.
3 If the engine starts, but does not run satisfactorily, the fault is more likely to be on the HT side.

13 Fault diagnosis – engine fails to start

1 If the starter motor spins the engine satisfactorily, but the engine does not start, first remove the fuel pipe to the carburettor(s), spin the engine and check that fuel is being pumped to the carburettor(s). Be very careful to eliminate any chance of the fuel being ignited. Check that the carburettor piston damper is not stuck, by pressing the pin on the underside of the carburettor body (see Chapter 3).
2 Check that none of the LT wires to the coil, or to the contact breaker have broken away from their connecting tags, then connect a 12V lamp across the LT terminals of the ignition coil and see whether the lamp flashes on and off as the engine spins. If it does, there is no LT fault. If it does not, check the contact breaker, condenser and LT wiring.
3 If the engine does not spin normally, but the battery is known to be in good condition, check the battery terminals for cleanliness and tightness.
4 If the engine fails to start and it is proved that the LT circuit is satisfactory, remove one of the spark plugs and with its HT lead attached, lodge it so that the plug casing is in contact with the engine. Spin the engine to see if there is a spark at the plug. If there is no spark, check that the HT lead is pushed securely into the ignition coil and that the carbon brush in the distributor cover is making contact with the rotor arm. If both these checks are made without revealing a fault, the coil could be defective, but this is a rare occurrence.

14 Fault diagnosis – engine starts, but misfires

1 Bad starting and intermittent misfiring can be an LT fault such as an intermittent connection of either the distributor, ignition coil LT leads, or a loose condenser clamping screw.
2 If these are satisfactory, look for signs of tracking and burning inside the distributor cap, then check the plug leads, plug caps and plug insulators for signs of damage.
3 If the engine misfires regularly, it indicates that the fault is on one particular cylinder. While the engine is running, grip each plug cap in turn with a piece of clean, dry rag to avoid getting an electric shock and pull the cap off the plug. If there is no difference in engine running when a particular plug cap is removed, it indicates a defective plug, or lead. Stop the engine, remove the suspect plug and insert it in a different cylinder. Repeat the test, to see whether the plug performs satisfactorily in a new position and whether a different plug is satisfactory in the position from which the suspect one was removed.

Chapter 5 Clutch

Contents

Specifications

Manufacturer	Borg and Beck
Type	Diaphragm
Diameter	7.75 in (197 mm)
Clutch release bearing	Ball journal

Torque wrench settings	lbf ft	kgf m
Clutch cover to flywheel	15 to 18	2.1 to 2.5
Thrust plate to diaphragm	5	0.7
Diaphragm to pressure plate	12	1.6
Slave cylinder bolts	18 to 20	2.5 to 2.8
Flywheel bolts:		
Plain headed bolts	60	8.3
Washer headed bolts	100	13.8

1 General description

The main parts of the clutch assembly are the flywheel and pressure plate, the driven plate and the release bearing assembly.

The diaphragm and pressure plate assembly is bolted to the flywheel via three spring straps, and the driven plate, which is splined to the gearbox primary gear, is sandwiched between the flywheel and the pressure plate, causing the gear to rotate with the crankshaft.

When the clutch pedal is depressed, the clutch release bearing applies thrust to the diaphragm and this overcomes the spring force between the flywheel and the pressure plate. This causes them to separate and as the driven plate is no longer clamped between them, the driven plate ceases being driven, which disconnects the crankshaft from the transmission.

The clutch operating mechanism is hydraulic, with a combined reservoir and master cylinder connected to the clutch pedal and a slave cylinder connected by a pushrod to the clutch operating lever. On later models the clutch is self-adjusting and requires no routine maintenance except topping up the fluid in the reservoir. Early models have an adjustable stop on the clutch lever and the clearance between the stop and the lever must be maintained at the specified amount.

2 Clutch – adjustment

1   On early models, identified by having a clutch slave cylinder with horizontal mounting lugs, a clearance of 0.052 in (1.32 mm) must be maintained between the clutch release lever and its return stop.

2   Pull the release lever away from the slave cylinder until all free movement has been eliminated and then check the clearance between

Fig. 5.1 Clutch adjustment (Sec 2)

A   Clearance checking point   *B   Locknut*

the release lever and the end of the stop bolt, using feeler gauges (Fig. 5.1).

3   If adjustment is required, release the locknut and turn the stop lever clockwise to increase the clearance and anti-clockwise to decrease the clearance. When the adjustment is correct, hold the bolt stationary and tighten the locknut.

4   On later models, having angled mounting lugs on the slave cylinder, the release bearing is kept in contact with the diaphragm spring fingers by the design of the slave cylinder and no adjustment is required throughout the life of the clutch.

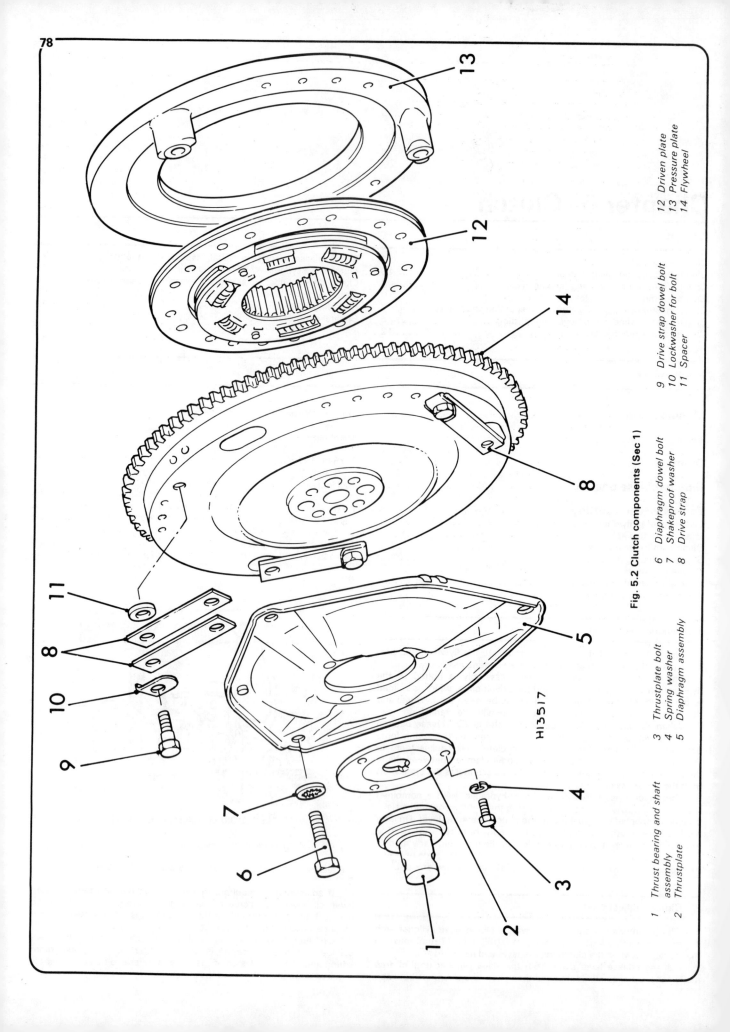

Fig. 5.2 Clutch components (Sec 1)

1 Thrust bearing and shaft
   assembly
2 Thrustplate
3 Thrustplate bolt
4 Spring washer
5 Diaphragm assembly
6 Diaphragm dowel bolt
7 Shakeproof washer
8 Drive strap
9 Drive strap dowel bolt
10 Lockwasher for bolt
11 Spacer
12 Driven plate
13 Pressure plate
14 Flywheel

H13517

3 Clutch system – bleeding

Whenever the clutch hydraulic system has been overhauled, a part renewed, or the level in the reservoir is too low, air will have entered the system necessitating its bleeding. During this operation the level of hydraulic fluid in the reservoir should not be allowed to fall below half full, otherwise air will be drawn in again.

1 Obtain a clean and dry jam jar, plastic tubing at least 12 in (30 cm) long and able to fit tightly over the bleed screw of the slave cylinder, a supply of clean hydraulic fluid and an assistant.
2 Check that the master cylinder reservoir is full and if not, fill it. Cover the bottom inch (25 mm) of the jar with hydraulic fluid.
3 Remove the rubber dust cap (if fitted) from the bleed screw on the slave cylinder and, with a suitable spanner, open the bleed screw one turn.
4 Place one end of the tube securely over the end of the bleed screw and insert the other end in the jar so that the tube end is below the level of the fluid.
5 The assistant should now pump the clutch pedal up and down quite quickly until the air bubbles cease to emerge from the end of the tubing. He should also check the reservoir frequently to ensure that the hydraulic fluid does not drop too far so letting air into the system.
6 When no more air bubbles appear, tighten the bleed screw at the end of a downstroke.
7 Refit the rubber dust cap over the bleed nipple. **Note:** *Never re-use the fluid bled from the hydraulic system*

4 Clutch slave cylinder – removal and refitting

1 It is not necessary to drain the clutch master cylinder when removing the slave cylinder. If fluid is to be left in the master cylinder, however it is necessary to seal the vent hole in the reservoir cap. Wipe the top of the reservoir and unscrew the cap. Place a piece of thick polythene over the top of the reservoir and refit the cap.
2 Wipe the hydraulic pipe union at its connection on the slave cylinder with a clean, lint-free rag. Unscrew the union nut with an open ended spanner and wrap the exposed end in a piece of clean, lint-free rag to prevent dirt ingress.
3 If the clutch lever has a return spring, note the way in which it is fitted and then disconnect it from the slave cylinder. Undo and remove the two bolts with spring washers that secure the slave cylinder to the clutch housing. Carefully withdraw the slave cylinder leaving the pushrod attached to the clutch operating lever.
4 Refitting is the reverse of removal and on completion the hydraulic system must be bled.

5 Clutch slave cylinder – dismantling, examination and reassembly

1 The slave cylinder may be of Girling, or Lockheed manufacture and their components are not interchangeable. When obtaining spares it is important to specify the cylinder manufacturer and if a new bleed screw, or flexible hose is being fitted it is necessary to ascertain the thread form of the mating components. The way in which UNF and metric threaded components can be identified is given in Chapter 13.
2 Clean the exterior of the cylinder using a clean, lint-free rag.
3 Peel the dust cover off the end of the cylinder. Remove the piston and stop cap (Girling) which is held in place by a crimp retainer, or remove the circlip from the end of the bore (Lockheed),
4 Remove the piston, piston seal and the spring. The Lockheed cylinder has a seal expander which must be removed in addition to the other components. On the Girling cylinder the seal must be removed from the piston by pulling it off with the fingers.
5 Wash all the metal parts in methylated spirit, or clean brake fluid. Examine the piston and cylinder bore for signs of scoring, or corrosion. If their condition is not satisfactory, a new assembly must be fitted.
6 If the piston and cylinder are sound, fit the spring and new seal, with the lip of the seal towards the closed end of the cylinder. Lubricate the cylinder and the seal with clean hydraulic fluid before inserting the seal and piston in to the bore. On the Girling cylinder the smaller diameter end of the spring fits on to the stem of the piston. When inserting the lip of the seal, east it in gently, taking care that the lip is not folded back.
7 Fit the bore circlip, or cylinder end cap and then a new dust cover.

6 Clutch master cylinder – removal and refitting

1 Drain the hydraulic fluid from the clutch hydraulic system by attaching a length of suitable size plastic tubing to the bleed screw on the slave cylinder. Place the other end in a clean jam jar. Open the bleed screw, with an open ended spanner, one complete turn and depress the clutch pedal. Tighten the bleed screw and allow the pedal to return. Repeat this procedure until the system has been drained.
2 Using a pair of pliers, extract the brake pedal to pushrod clevis pin split pin and lift away the plain washer. Withdraw the clevis pin from the pushrod yoke.
3 Slacken the clip and disconnect the right-hand demister tube from the heater unit.
4 Using an open ended spanner, undo the flexible hydraulic pipe connection at the slave cylinder.
5 Undo and remove the two nuts and spring washers securing the

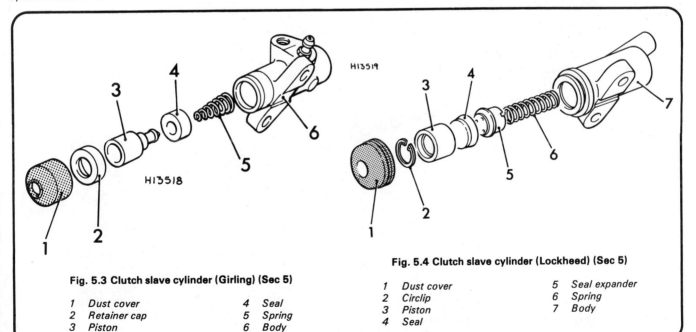

Fig. 5.3 Clutch slave cylinder (Girling) (Sec 5)

1 Dust cover	4 Seal
2 Retainer cap	5 Spring
3 Piston	6 Body

Fig. 5.4 Clutch slave cylinder (Lockheed) (Sec 5)

1 Dust cover	5 Seal expander
2 Circlip	6 Spring
3 Piston	7 Body
4 Seal	

master cylinder and carefully withdraw it together with the flexible hydraulic pipe.
6   Using an open ended spanner, undo the flexible hydraulic pipe connection at the master cylinder.
7   The master cylinder refitting procedure is the reverse of removal, but care must be taken when offering up to the bulkhead that the pushrod is in line with clutch pedal. Once connections have been made the hydraulic system must be bled as described in Section 3.

7   Clutch master cylinder – dismantling, inspection and reassembly

1   Peel off the dust cover. Remove the circlip from the mouth of the bore and extract the pushrod and retaining washer.
2   Extract the piston and valve assembly from the cylinder.
3   Separate the piston and valve assembly by prising up the tang of the piston return spring retainer so that it can be disengaged from the piston.
4   Compress the spring by pushing the thimble and then disengage the valve stem from the elongated hole in the thimble.
5   Withdraw the thimble, spring, valve spacer and curved washer from the valve stem and pull the seals from the piston and piston rod.
6   Clean all the metal parts in methylated spirit and examine them for signs of damage or scoring. If the piston, or cylinder bore are damaged, a new master cylinder assembly must be fitted.
7   Thoroughly wet all parts in clean brake fluid and reassemble in the following order using new seals and the other components supplied in a repair kit.
8   Fit the piston seal to the piston so that the lip will enter the cylinder bore first.
9   Fit the valve seal to the valve in the same manner as in (8) above.
10 Place the valve spring seal washer so that its convex face abuts against the valve stem flange and then fit the seat spacer and spring.
11 Fit the spring retainer to the spring, which must then be compressed so the valve stem can be re-inserted into the retainer.
12 Refit the front of the piston in the retainer and then press down the retaining leg so it locates under the shoulder at the front of the piston.
13 With the valve assembly well lubricated with clean hydraulic fluid, carefully insert it in the master cylinder bore taking care that the rubber seal is not damaged, or the lip reversed as it is pushed into the bore.

14 Fit the pushrod and washer in place and secure with the circlip. Smear the sealing areas of the dust cover with rubber grease and also pack the cover with rubber grease to act as a dust trap and fit to the master cylinder body.

8   Clutch – removal and refitting (engine in car)

The sequence for removing the clutch when the engine is in the car differs slightly when the later type rod gear change system is utilised instead of cables. These differences are fully described where applicable.

1   Open the bonnet and disconnect the two battery terminals. Release the battery clamp bar securing nuts and ease back the clamp. Lift away the battery tray from the engine compartment.
2   Undo and remove the nut securing the heavy duty cable to the rear of the starter motor and withdraw the cable from the terminal. On pre-engaged starter motors make a note of the electrical cable connections at the rear of the solenoid and disconnect the three cables.
3   Undo and remove the two bolts and spring washers securing the starter motor to the flywheel housing. Carefully draw the starter motor out of engagement of the flywheel and lift away from the engine.
4   Place a piece of soft wood on a jack located on the underside of the transmission case. Raise the jack until the weight of the complete power unit is just taken from the mountings.

Cable gear change models only
5   Undo and remove the nut and large diameter washer securing the engine rear mounting centre bolt to the mounting.
6   Undo and remove the three bolts with spring washers that secure the engine rear mounting bracket to the clutch housing cover. Lift away the engine rear mounting bracket.

Rod gear change models only
7   Slacken the bolts that secure the engine rear mounting to the subframe bracket.
8   Undo and remove the three bolts and spring washers that secure the engine rear mounting bracket to the subframe.
9   Undo and remove the two nuts and spring washers that secure the engine rear mounting to the bracket on the clutch housing cover. The engine rear mounting assembly may now be lifted away.

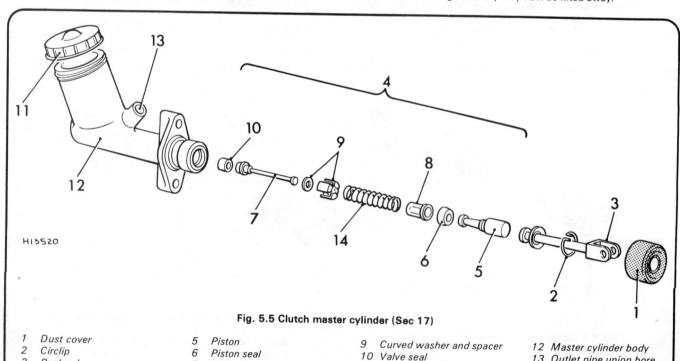

H15520

Fig. 5.5 Clutch master cylinder (Sec 17)

1 Dust cover	5 Piston	9 Curved washer and spacer	12 Master cylinder body
2 Circlip	6 Piston seal	10 Valve seal	13 Outlet pipe union bore
3 Pushrod	7 Valve stem	11 Master cylinder cap	14 Spring
4 Piston and valve assembly	8 Spring retainer		

Both models

10 If the clutch lever has a return spring, note the way in which it is fitted and then disconnect it from the slave cylinder and the release lever.

11 Undo and remove the ten bolts and spring washers that secure the clutch housing cover to the flywheel housing. Lift away the clutch housing cover having first carefully withdrawn the pushrod from the slave cylinder.

12 With a scriber or file, mark the position of the clutch thrust plate relative to the diaphragm so that it may be refitted in its original position. Undo and remove the three bolts and spring washers securing the clutch thrust plate to the diaphragm.

13 Undo and remove the four bolts that secure the flywheel to the end of the crankshaft. These can be tight so, to stop the crankshaft rotating, chock the front wheels and select top gear.

14 Move the gear change lever back to neutral and, turning the flywheel a quarter of a turn at a time, drive the flywheel from the dowels in the end of the crankshaft with a hard wood block and hammer, or a large diameter soft metal drift. Take care that the flywheel does not drop, by having an assistant ready to catch it.

15 Mark the relative positions of the diaphragm, flywheel and pressure plate so they may be refitted in their original positions upon reassembly. Then undo and remove the three shaped diaphragm retaining bolts and star washers.

16 Lift away the diaphragm and flywheel from the pressure plate.

17 Note which way round the driven plate is fitted and lift from the pressure plate.

18 The clutch and flywheel assembly is now ready for inspection as described in Section 10.

19 Whilst the clutch is away from the engine, check the crankshaft primary gear endfloat. Full information on this check will be found in Chapter 6.

20 To reassemble the clutch, first lay the pressure plate on a flat surface with the three securing lugs facing upwards.

21 Place the driven plate on the pressure plate with the larger damper spring boss uppermost. This is identified by the two words 'Flywheel Side' (photo).

22 Lower the flywheel over the pressure plate and driven plate, making sure that the previously made marks on the pressure plate are aligned. There is a letter 'A' stamped on the diaphragm, pressure plate and flywheel of some models which will also assist refitting correctly (photo).

23 Refit the diaphragm aligning the previously made marks. Refit the three shouldered bolts and star washers, but do not tighten fully (photo).

24 Note the location of the larger dowel in the end of the crankshaft and its mating hole in the flywheel. Line up the dowel with the hole and fit the flywheel and clutch assembly to the flywheel.

25 Oil the threads of the four bolts which secure the flywheel. Insert the bolts and tighten them progressively and in diagonal sequence to the specified torque.

26 Tighten the three diaphragm securing bolts to the specified torque.

27 Fit the clutch thrust bearing plate to the diaphragm aligning the previously made marks and secure with the three bolts and spring washers.

28 Fit the clutch housing cover and insert the ten securing bolts. Tighten the bolts in diagonal pairs to the specified torque setting.

29 Refit the clutch slave cylinder and pushrod if removed. If a return spring was removed, refit it as before.

Rod gear change models only

30 Fit the engine rear mounting to the bracket on the clutch housing cover and secure with the two nuts and spring washers.

31 Fit the engine rear mounting bracket to the subframe and secure in position with the three bolts and spring washers, tightened to the specified torque.

32 Tighten to the specified torque the bolts which secure the engine rear mounting to the subframe bracket.

Cable gear change models only

33 Carefully engage the engine rear mounting to its centre bolt.

34 Refit and tighten the three bolts with spring washers that secure the engine rear mounting to the clutch housing cover.

35 Finally refit the nut and large plain washer to the engine rear mounting centre bolt. Tighten the nut fully.

36 Remove the hydraulic jack supporting the weight of the complete power unit.

37 Refit the starter motor, battery tray and battery, remaking the necessary electrical connections.

38 On models which have an adjustable strap, set the stop to give the correct clearance between the stop and the operating lever.

9 Clutch – removal and refitting (engine out of the car)

The procedure is basically identical to that for working with the engine in the car, with the exceptions of the initial preparatory work and release of the engine rear mounting. Follow the instructions given in Section 8, paragraph 3, 10 to 29, 37 and 38.

10 Clutch – inspection and overhaul

1 Thoroughly clean all parts by wiping with a rag to remove any dust.

2 Examine the clutch disc friction linings for wear, loose or broken springs and rivets. The linings must be proud of the rivets and light in appearance with the material structure visible. If it is dark in appearance, further investigation is necessary, as it is a sign of oil contamination caused by oil leaking past the crankshaft rear seal.

3 Check the machined faces of the flywheel and pressure plate for signs of grooving. If evident, new parts should be fitted. Inspect the pressure plate for signs of hair line cracks, usually caused by overheating due to clutch slip.

4 Inspect the three driving straps and, if they show signs of distortion, overheating or looseness, fit a complete set.

5 Carefully fit the clutch disc to the crankshaft primary drive gear and check for wear of the splines. If evident a new disc should be tried to ensure the wear is on the disc splines and not on the primary drivegear. Should the latter splines also be worn, a new gear must be fitted and the endfloat adjusted by means of a selective fit thrust washer. Full information will be found in Chapter 6.

6 Carefully inspect the diaphragm for signs of overheating or cracking. If evident, a new diaphragm must be obtained.

8.18 Marking to show flywheel side of clutch plate

8.19 Alignment marks on diaphragm and pressure plate

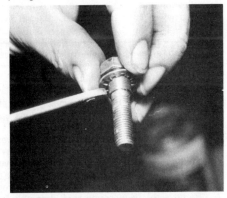

8.20 Shouldered bolts of diaphragm

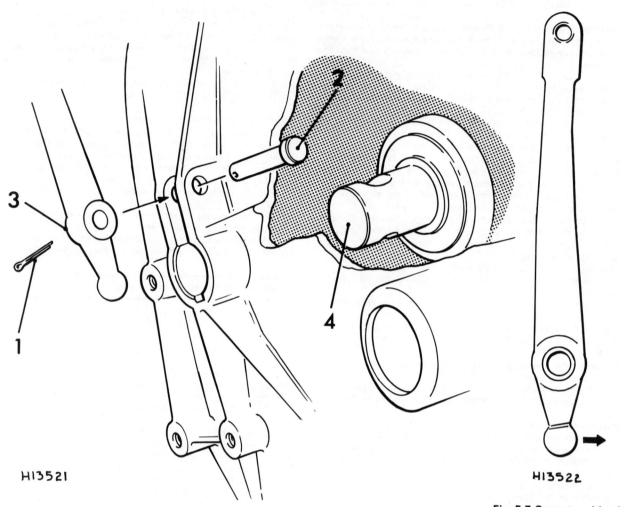

H13521

H13522

Fig. 5.6 Clutch release lever and bearing (Sec 11)

1   Split pin   3   Operating lever
2   Operating lever pivot pin   4   Shaft and bearing assembly

Fig. 5.7 Correct position for release lever with part shown arrowed towards clutch (Sec 11)

7   Check the clutch release bearing for wear or roughness when the inner track is held and the outer track rotated. If it is blue in colour, it is an indication that it has overheated due to incorrect clutch adjustment. Obtain a new bearing and fit as described in Section 11.

11 Clutch release bearing – removal, inspection and refitting

Press fit bearing

1   Refer to Section 8 or 9, depending on whether the engine is in or out of the car, and follow the instructions up to and including the removal of the clutch housing cover.
2   Using a pair of pliers remove the clutch lever pivot pin split pin and withdraw the lever pivot pin noting which way round the pin head is fitted. Also note which way round the clutch lever is fitted.
3   Pull the clutch lever out of engagement of the release bearing shaft and lift it away from the clutch housing cover.
4   Remove the bearing and shaft assembly from the clutch housing cover.
5   Check the clutch release bearing for wear or roughness when the

inner track is held and the outer track rotated. If it is blue in colour, it is an indication that it has overheated due to incorrect clutch adjustment.
6   To remove the release bearing, using a bench vice and suitable metal packing, press the old bearing from the shaft.
7   Refitting and reassembling the release bearing is the reverse sequence to removal. Take care that the clutch lever is fitted the correct way round. Finally, adjust the clutch clearance between the withdrawal lever and stop as described in Section 2.

Self-aligning bearing

8   Remove the clutch housing cover as in paragraph 1.
9   Prise the locking ring from the bearing shaft and remove the release bearing. Check the bearing as in paragraph 5
10 To fit a new bearing, wedge the release lever so that the shoulder on the shaft protrudes through the cover. Place the bearing on the plunger shaft and either by hand pressure, or using a tubular drift press a new self-locking ring over the plunger flange. Check that the bearing has been clamped by the ring and leave the wedge in position until the slave cylinder has been fitted.
11 If the clutch has an adjustable stop, make the necessary adjustments as described in Section 2.

12 Clutch pedal – removal and refitting

1 If it is wished to remove the complete pedal bracket assembly, including the brake pedal and the pivot shaft, refer to Chapter 9. To remove the clutch pedal alone, proceed as follows.
2 Access will be easier if one or both front seats are removed.
3 Remove the spring clip which secures the clevis pin to the clutch pedal. Withdraw the clevis pin, retrieving the washer from the spring clip side.
4 Remove the split pin from the left-hand end of the pivot shaft.
5 Unhook the clutch pedal from its return spring and slide it off the left-hand end of the pivot shaft. Note the arrangement of washer and bushes.
6 Refitting is a reversal of the removal procedure. Lubricate the bushes and the pivot shaft with a little multi-purpose grease.

13 Fault diagnosis – clutch

Symptom	Reason(s)
Squealing noise when clutch is depressed	Worn clutch release bearing
Clutch slips	Friction plate worn down to rivets Oil on clutch facing Incorrect adjustment (if clutch is adjustable) Clutch plate splines need lubrication
Gears difficult to engage, even though clutch pedal is depressed fully	Air in hydraulic system Defective seal in master or slave cylinder Clutch plate facing sticky due to partially burnt oil Clutch plate splines in need of lubrication Diaphragm spring needs renewing
Clutch judder	Engine or gearbox rubber mountings defective Oil on friction faces of driven plate

Chapter 6 Transmission

Contents

Specifications

Part A Manual transmission

Type . . . .   Manual, cable or rod remote control, 5 forward and 1 reverse gear with synchromesh on all forward speeds

Ratios	1500 models	1750 models
Fifth	0.80:1	0.87:1
Fourth	1.00:1	1.00:1
Third	1.37:1	1.37:1
Second	2.00:1	2.00:1
First	3.20:1	3.20:1
Reverse	3.47:1	3.47:1

Overall ratios		
Fifth	3.34:1	3.38:1
Fourth	4.2:1	3.89:1
Third	5.76:1	5.33:1
Second	8.42:1	7.79:1
First	13.54:1	12.45:1
Reverse	14.56:1	13.49:1

Primary drive ratio 1.066:1   1.066:1

Final drive ratio 3.938:1   3.647:1

Torque wrench settings	lbf ft	kgf m
Flywheel bolts:		
Plain headed bolts	60	8.3
Washer headed bolts	100	13.8
Drain plug	27	3.7
Flywheel housing		
Studs	6	0.8
Nuts	17 to 19	2.4 to 2.6
Set screws	17 to 19	2.4 to 2.6
Transmission case to block		
$\frac{5}{16}$ in bolts	20 to 25	2.8 to 3.4
$\frac{3}{8}$ in bolts	30	4.1
Detent plug		
Small	15 to 20	2.1 to 2.8
Large	35 to 40	4.8 to 5.5
Access plug – 3rd/4th fork (cable gear change)	55 to 60	7.6 to 8.3

	lbf ft	kgf m
First motion shaft nut	120	16.6
Layshaft nuts	120	16.6
Third motion shaft nut	150	20.7
Bellcrank levers pivot nut (rod gear change)	25	3.5

Part B Automatic transmission

Type	Torque converter and planetary gear train with 4 forward and 1 reverse gear

Ratios
Fourth	1.00:1
Third	1.45:1
Second	1.81:1
First	2.61:1
Reverse	2.61:1

Overall ratios
Fourth	3.80:1
Third	5.49:1
Second	6.87:1
First	9.93:1
Reverse	9.93:1

Primary drive ratio 1.066:1

Final drive ratio 3.800:1

Torque wrench settings
	lbf ft	kgf m
Converter to crankshaft bolts (threads oiled)	60	8.3
Input bearing housing bolts.............	18	2.5
Input sprocket retaining nut	110	15.2
Output shaft nut	125	17.3
Torque converter housing bolts.............	18	2.5

Part A MANUAL TRANSMISSION

1 General description

The transmission unit has five forward speeds and one reverse speed. Synchromesh is incorporated on all five forward speeds. Fourth gear is a direct drive ratio and fifth a 'gearing-up' ratio to provide high speed cruising at reduced engine revolutions.

Engine torque at the rear of the crankshaft is transmitted to the first motion shaft gear by primary gears located on the engine side of the flywheel housing. The first motion shaft is supported in two bearings and has inside the inner end a needle roller bearing, into which is located the left-hand end of the third motion shaft. The first motion shaft inner gear is in constant mesh with the largest gear of the layshaft cluster. This means that whenever the first motion shaft is rotating, the first four forward speed and the reverse speed laygears also rotate. The synchroniser for the fifth speed gear is splined to the right-hand end of the layshaft. This fifth speed gear is free to rotate on the layshaft and is mounted on needle roller bearings instead of bushes.

When the gear change lever is moved from fourth to fifth position, the outer sleeve of the synchroniser is moved to the left and dogs are meshed so as to provide transmission of power from the layshaft to the fifth speed gear and then on to the final drive pinion.

The first, second and third speed gears are free to rotate on the third motion shaft and yet are in constant mesh with their matching gears on the layshaft. This means that whenever the first motion shaft is rotated, these gears also rotate on the third motion shaft.

When one of these gears is selected, movement of the outer synchromesh sleeves and dogs to either the left or right will select the required gear, and lock it to the third motion shaft.

Reverse gear may be engaged between the straight toothed gear on the sleeve of the synchroniser and the small straight toothed gear in the centre of the layshaft, via the reverse idler gear.

The synchroniser sleeves are splined to hubs, which are also splined to the shafts, so that when the dogs on the sleeve are engaged with any required gear, that selected gear is then coupled to the shaft.

Cone clutches in the form of baulk rings enable the speeds of the dogs on the gears and sleeves to synchronise to ensure easy and quiet gear changing.

The remote control system is connected to the gear selectors by either cables (early models) or rods (later models).

As usual in BL transverse power units, the transmission unit, final drive and engine share a common lubrication system.

Whenever the transmission unit or engine is being worked upon it will be necessary to use information contained in both this Chapter and Chapter 1. For any major work to be carried out on the transmission unit or flywheel housing the unit must be removed from the car and then separated into the two major assemblies.

2 Crankshaft primary gear endfloat – adjustment

It is possible to adjust the crankshaft primary gear endfloat with the power unit either in or out of the car. Both methods are given.

Engine in car
1   Refer to Chapter 5 and remove the clutch and flywheel assembly.
2   Using a vernier depth gauge, or sets of feeler gauges, measure the depth of the crankshaft recess in the flywheel (Fig. 6.2).
3   Fit the existing thrust washer and gear to the end of the crankshaft if they have been removed previously.
4   With the fingers, push the gear firmly towards the engine as far as possible and again using either a vernier depth gauge or sets of feeler gauges, measure the length of crankshaft boss protruding from the gear.
5   Select a new thrust washer so that the measurement obtained in paragraph 4 gives a reading of 0.004 to 0.006 in (0.10 to 0.15 mm) more than that obtained in paragraph 2.

HI3523

Fig. 6.1 Manual transmission (sectional view) (Sec 1)

1 Nut for first motion shaft gear
2 Nut lockwasher
3 First motion shaft gear
4 Ball-bearing
5 Roller-bearing
6 Needle-roller bearing
7 First motion shaft
8 Circlip
9 Selective spacer
10 Baulk ring
11 3rd and 4th speed synchronizer
12 Baulk ring
13 Spacer for bearing
14 Needle-roller bearing
15 3rd speed gear
16 2nd speed gear
17 Needle-roller bearing
18 Spacer for bearing
19 Baulk ring
20 1st and 2nd speed synchronizer
21 Baulk ring
22 Bearing spacer
23 Needle-roller bearing
24 1st speed gear
25 Hub for gear
26 Casing centre web
27 Circlip
28 2nd speed gear
29 Roller-bearing
30 Circlip
31 Final drive pinion
32 Nut lockwasher
33 Pinion nut
34 Third motion shaft
35 Speedometer pinion
36 Circlip
37 Gearbox front cover
38 Nut for layshaft – rear
39 Circlip
40 Ball-bearing
41 Spacer
42 Laygear
43 Layshaft
44 Circlip
45 Reverse selector lever
46 O-ring
47 Circlip
48 Reverse selector pivot pin
49 Roller-bearing
50 Hub for gear
51 5th speed gear
52 Needle-roller bearing
53 Baulk ring
54 Bearing spacer
55 5th gear synchronizer
56 Retainer for synchronizer
57 Nut lockwasher
58 Nut for layshaft – front

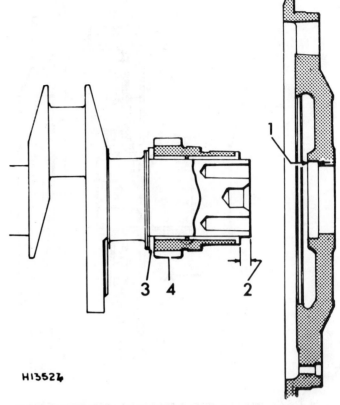

H13524

Fig. 6.2 Crankshaft primary gear endfloat measurements (engine in car) (Sec 2)

1 Depth of crankshaft recess in flywheel
2 Crankshaft boss protrusion
3 Selective thrustwasher
4 Crankshaft primary gear

6 Thrust washers are available in the following thicknesses:

0.153 to 0.155 in (3.89 to 3.94 mm)
0.156 to 0.158 in (3.96 to 4.01 mm)
0.159 to 0.161 in (4.04 to 4.09 mm)
0.162 to 0.164 in (4.11 to 4.17 mm)
0.165 to 0.167 in (4.19 to 4.24 mm)
0.168 to 0.170 in (4.27 to 4.32 mm)

7 Reassembly is the reverse sequence to dismantling.

Engine out of car

8 Remove the clutch and flywheel assembly (Chapter 5).
9 Bend back the locking tabs on the four shaped tab washers and then undo and remove the housing retaining bolts and nuts from inside and outside the clutch housing.
10 Wrap some sticky tape around the splines of the primary gear to prevent damage to the oil seal and carefully draw the flywheel housing from the rear of the engine and transmission unit.
11 Fit the existing thrust washer and gear to the end of the crankshaft if they have been previously removed.
12 Refit the flywheel to the end of the crankshaft and secure with the four bolts which should be tightened to the specified torque.
13 Using feeler gauges determine the clearance 'A' between the boss face of the crankshaft and the rear face of the primary gear (Fig. 6.3).
14 Select a thrust washer to give the correct clearance of 0·004 to 0·006 in (0·10 to 0·15 mm).
15 Thrust washers are available in the sizes given earlier in this Section.
16 Reassembly is the reverse sequence to dismantling.

---

3 Crankshaft primary gear oil seal – removal and refitting

It is possible to remove and refit the oil seal with the power unit in the car although it is far easier to do if the power unit is out of the car.

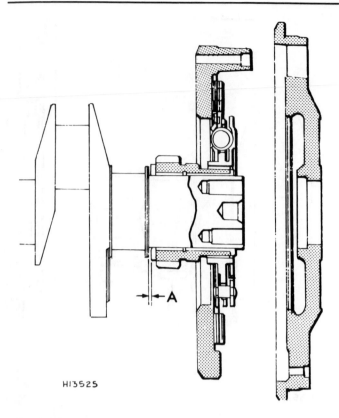

H13525

Fig. 6.3 Crankshaft primary gear endfloat measurement (engine out of car) (Sec 2)

A – clearance between crankshaft boss face and rear face of primary gear

Both methods are given.

Engine in car

1　Refer to Chapter 5 and remove the clutch and flywheel assembly.
2　Using a small three legged universal puller with thin feet, locate the feet behind the splines of the primary drivegear and very carefully draw the primary drivegear and oil seal from the end of the crankshaft.
3　Well lubricate the new seal.
4　Wrap some adhesive tape around the splines of the primary gear to prevent damage to the oil seal and enter the oil seal onto the primary gear, lip facing innermost.
5　Using a small soft metal drift very carefully tap the new seal into position, together with the drivegear.
6　Refer to Section 2 and check the primary gear end float. Adjust as necessary.
7　Reassembly is now the reverse sequence to dismantling.

Engine out of car

8　With the power unit out of the car, refer to Section 2 paragraphs 1 to 4 inclusive and remove the clutch and flywheel assembly and the flywheel housing.
9　Using a screwdriver carefully remove the old seal noting which way round it is fitted.
10　Well lubricate the new seal and fit to the flywheel housing using a suitable diameter tube.
11　Refer to Section 2 and check the primary gear endfloat. Adjust as necessary.
12　Reassembly is the reverse of dismantling.

4　Transmission – separation from engine

Before commencing work, clean the exterior of the engine and transmission unit thoroughly using paraffin, or a water soluble cleaner. After the cleaner has been applied and allowed to stand for a time, a vigorous jet of water will wash off the solvent together with all grease and dirt. If the dirt is thick and deeply embedded, work the cleaner into it with a wire brush. Finally wipe down the exterior of the unit with a dry lint-free rag. The transmission unit may be separated from the engine.

1　Unscrew the union securing the dipstick guide tube to the side of the transmission casing. Lift away the guide tube and dipstick.
2　Undo and remove the two bolts securing the distributor body clamp to the cylinder block and carefully lift away the distributor. Withdraw the oil pump driveshaft.
3　Undo and remove the two bolts and spring washers securing the starter motor to the flywheel housing. Lift away the starter motor.
4　Undo the centre bolt securing the oil filter to the side of the transmission casing and lift away the oil filter. Be prepared to catch oil which will seep from the filter when it is withdrawn.
5　Undo and remove the two nuts and spring washers that secure the fuel pump to the side of the transmission casing. Withdraw the pump and insulator block from the two mounting studs and then recover the operating pushrod.
6　The eight bolts and spring washers securing the clutch housing cover to the flywheel housing may next be removed. Lift away the clutch housing cover.
7　Unscrew the three bolts securing the thrust plate and lift away the thrust plate.
8　Remove the two bolts and spring washers securing the flywheel housing cover to the housing and lift away the cover.
9　Using a screwdriver, lock the flywheel, then undo and remove the four bolts securing the flywheel to the end of the crankshaft.
10　Working through the starter motor aperture drive the flywheel from the dowels in the inside of the end of the crankshaft using a soft metal drift or hard wood block.
11　Bend back the flywheel housing securing bolt lock tabs and undo and remove the nuts and bolts from inside and outside the housing.
12　Wrap some sticky tape around the splines on the primary drive gear to prevent damage to the oil seal and carefully remove the flywheel housing (photo).
13　Undo and remove the bolts and spring washers that secure the transmission casing to the mounting flange of the crankcase.
14　Drive out the locating dowels accurately mating the transmission casing to the crankcase.
15　Carefully lift the engine from the transmission casing (photo).

5　Transmission (cable gear change) – dismantling

1　If the splash shield has not already been removed, bend back the locking tab washer and undo the securing bolt. Lift away the splash shield, bolt and tab washer.
2　Undo and remove the two nuts and spring washers securing the front mounting to the front cover securing studs. Lift away the front mounting.
3　Undo and remove the further one nut and spring washer and then the five bolts and spring washers securing the front cover to the transmission case. Lift away the front cover and its gasket (Fig. 6.4).
4　Remove the old gasket from the front cover and traces of any jointing compound.
5　Unscrew and remove the two long bolts and plain and spring washers that secure the oil pump to the transmission casing.
6　Using a piece of metal shaped as shown in Section 8, photo 8:102 and gripped with a Mole wrench, undo and remove the pump outlet.
7　Unscrew the magnetic drain plug from the bottom of the front face of the transmission casing.
8　Using a large socket unscrew the speedometer drive gear housing and lift away from the transmission unit.
9　Undo the two nuts and spring washers that secure the bracket to the differential casing. Lift away the bracket.
10　Refer to Chapter 8 and remove the differential unit from the transmission casing. Using feeler gauges inserted between the third speed gear and the shoulder on the shaft, measure the gear endfloat and record it for adjustment, if necessary, on reassembly. The correct endfloat is 0·005 to 0·008 in (0·13 to 0·20 mm).
11　Using a pair of circlip pliers, remove the circlip that retains the speedometer pinion on the end of the third motion shaft.
12　Ease the speedometer drive pinion from the end of the third

4.12 Removing the flywheel housing

4.15 Separating the engine and transmission

motion shaft using a screwdriver. Take care not to damage the gear teeth.

13 Extract the Woodruff key from the keyway in the end of the third motion shaft.

14 Using a pair of circlip pliers, remove the outer bearing retaining circlip located on the end of the first motion shaft.

15 Ease the spigot bearing from the end of the first motion shaft using a screwdriver. Take care not to damage the bearing.

16 Again using a pair of circlip pliers, remove the circlip in front of the gear on the first motion shaft, this being exposed once the spigot bearing has been removed.

17 Withdraw the idler gear and shaft from the transmission case. It may be necessary to ease it out of its fitted position with a screwdriver (Fig. 6.6).

18 Recover the inner thrust washer from the back of the idler gear.

19 Using a pair of circlip pliers, remove the idler gear bearing inner and outer retaining circlips.

20 To remove the idler gear bearing, carefully drift out using a soft metal drift and driving it out from within the transmission unit. This will, of course, only be necessary if the bearing is to be renewed.

21 Using a chisel, bend back the lockwasher ears locking the nut on the end of the first motion shaft.

22 It will now be necessary to lock two gears together by moving two synchromesh collars into mesh.

23 Using a socket or large ring spanner unscrew the nut on the end of the first motion shaft. *Note this nut has a left-hand thread.*

24 Remove the lockwasher exposed once the nut has been removed.

25 Using two screwdrivers, or small tyre levers, carefully draw the first motion shaft gear from the first motion shaft. Using feeler gauges inserted between the first and second speed gears and the shaft shoulders, measure the gear endfloat for adjustment, if necessary, on reassembly. The correct endfloat is 0·005 to 0·008 in (0·13 to 0·20 mm). If the endfloat is incorrect with either first or second gear, or the third gear (see Paragraph 10), renewal of the gear assemblies or of the third motion shaft will be necessary.

26 Bend back the lockwasher securing the nut on the rear end of the layshaft and, with a socket, unscrew the nut. *Note this nut has a left-hand thread.*

27 Using a socket and extension bar, undo the nut on the front end of the layshaft after bending back the lockwasher.

28 Bend back the lockwasher securing the nut on the end of the third motion shaft and, using a large socket, undo and remove the nut followed by the lockwasher.

29 Unscrew and remove the plug retaining the first and second speed detent plunger and spring in the transmission case. Recover the spring and plunger. Note this plug has three washers under its head (Fig. 6.8).

30 Release the locknut and unscrew the taper bolt securing the third and fourth speed selector fork to the selector rod (Fig. 6.9). (Remove the access plug if still in position).

31 Disengage the two synchromesh collars previously locked and carefully withdraw the third and fourth speed selector rod. It will be of assistance to screw a bolt into the exposed end and pull out using a Mole wrench.

32 Undo and remove the reverse and fifth speed detent plunger and spring retaining cap nut and lift away the spring and detent plunger. Note this cap nut has a fibre washer under its head.

33 Remove the nut and lockwasher from the front of the layshaft.

34 The retainer may now be lifted out of the centre of the fifth and reverse speed synchromesh unit.

35 Using a screwdriver, carefully ease the final drive pinion from the end of the third motion shaft.

36 Release the locknut and unscrew the taper bolt securing the fifth and reverse speed selector fork to the selector rod.

37 Screw a bolt into the threaded end of the fifth and reverse speed selector rod and draw the selector rod from the transmission casing. Gripping the bolt with a Mole wrench will make this job easier.

38 Lift away the fifth and reverse speed selector fork from the synchromesh unit collar.

39 Lift the fifth speed synchromesh hub and collar assembly from the end of the layshaft. Recover the fifth speed baulk ring from the cone on the front of the fifth speed gear.

40 Lift the fifth speed from the bearing on the layshaft.

41 Using a small diameter parallel pin punch, carefully drift out the spring pin securing the reverse idler shaft collar to the idler shaft.

42 Using a soft metal drift as well as a screwdriver, carefully remove the idler shaft.

43 Recover the collar and reverse idler.

44 Using a screwdriver, carefully lift the bearing spacer from the layshaft.

45 Slide the fifth speed gear bearing and hub from the layshaft.

46 Using a suitable diameter drift and soft faced hammer, tap the layshaft out of the transmission casing.

47 By carefully using a narrow soft metal drift, tap the layshaft front bearing from its housing in the centre web of the transmission casing.

48 Using a soft metal drift, release the bearing assembly retaining ring from its location on the front of the first motion shaft bearing assembly.

49 Working from the inside of the transmission casing, carefully drive out the first motion shaft complete with the ball and roller bearing assemblies.

50 Remove the ball and roller bearings from the first motion shaft using a universal three legged puller and suitable thrust pad. This operation will only be necessary if the bearings are to be renewed (see Section 7).

51 Lift away the baulk ring from the synchroniser collar exposed when the first motion shaft has been removed.

52 Using a pair of circlip pliers, remove the third and fourth speed synchroniser spacer retaining circlip from the end of the third motion shaft.

53 Slide the spacer from the third motion shaft.

54 Carefully remove the third and fourth speed synchronizer assembly

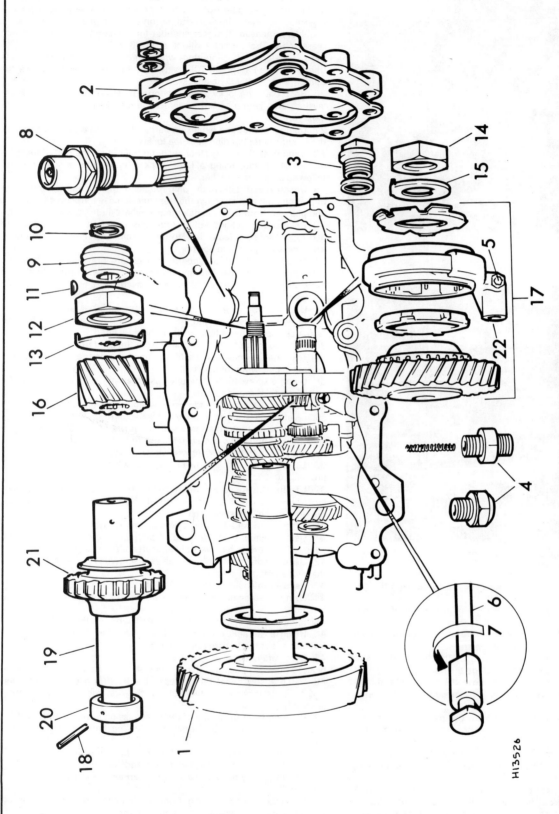

Fig. 6.4 Front cover, reverse idler and fifth speed assemblies (Sec 5)

H13526

1	Idler gear		
2	Front cover		
3	Fifth/reverse selector rod plug		
4	Fifth/reverse selector detent plug		
5	Fifth speed selector fork screw	9	Speedometer drivegear
6	Selector rod	10	Circlip
7	Removal of selector rod by rotating through 180°	11	Woodruff key
8	Speedometer pinion	12	Final drive pinion nut
		13	Lockwasher
	assembly	14	Layshaft front nut
		15	Lockwasher
		16	Final drive pinion
		17	Fifth speed synchronizer assembly
		18	Spring pin
		19	Reverse idler shaft
		20	Collar
		21	Reverse idler gear
		22	Fifth speed selector fork

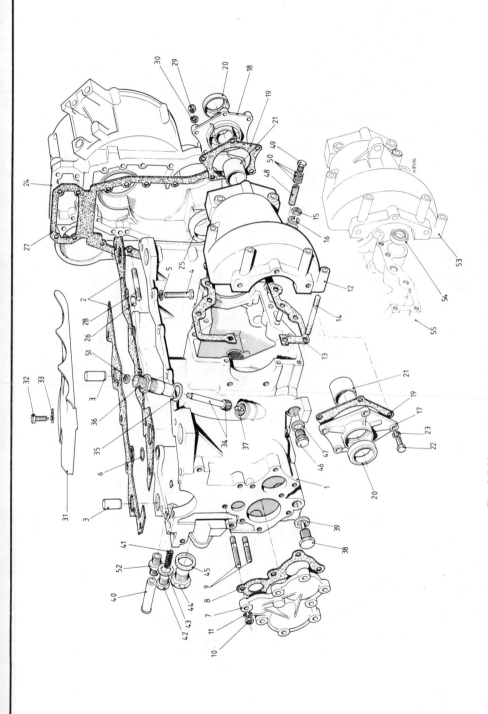

Fig. 6.5 Manual transmission external components (Sec 5)

1 Gearbox casing – cable gearchange
2 Gasket for casing
3 Dowel for cylinder block
4 Gearbox to cylinder block bolt
5 Spring washer
6 Oil sealing ring
7 Gearbox front cover
8 Gasket for cover
9 Stud for cover
10 Nut for stud
11 Spring washer for nut
12 Differential housing

13 Gasket for housing
14 Stud for housing
15 Nut for stud
16 Spring washer
17 Differential side cover – LH
18 Differential side cover – RH
19 Gasket for side cover
20 Oil seal for side cover
21 Bush for side cover
22 Bolt for side cover
23 Spring washer for bolt
24 Flywheel housing

25 Ring dowel for housing
26 Dowel for housing
27 Gasket for housing
28 Stud for housing
29 Nut for stud
30 Spring washer for stud
31 Gearbox baffle
32 Bolt for reverse shaft and baffle
33 Lockwasher for bolt
34 Speedometer pinion
35 Thrustwasher for pinion
36 Adaptor for pinion
37 Thrust pad for

38 Magnetic drain plug
39 Washer for drain plug
40 Oil pressure relief valve
41 Reverse and 5th detent spring
42 Reverse and 5th detent plug
43 Washer
44 3rd and 4th fork access plug
45 Washer for plug
46 1st and 2nd selector plug

47 Washer for plug
48 1st and 2nd detent spring
49 1st and 2nd detent plug
50 Washers for plug
51 Seal for driveshaft
52 Detent plug – rod gearchange
53 Differential housing – rod gearchange
54 Oil seal for selector shaft – rod gearchange
55 Gearbox casing – rod gearchange

driveshaft

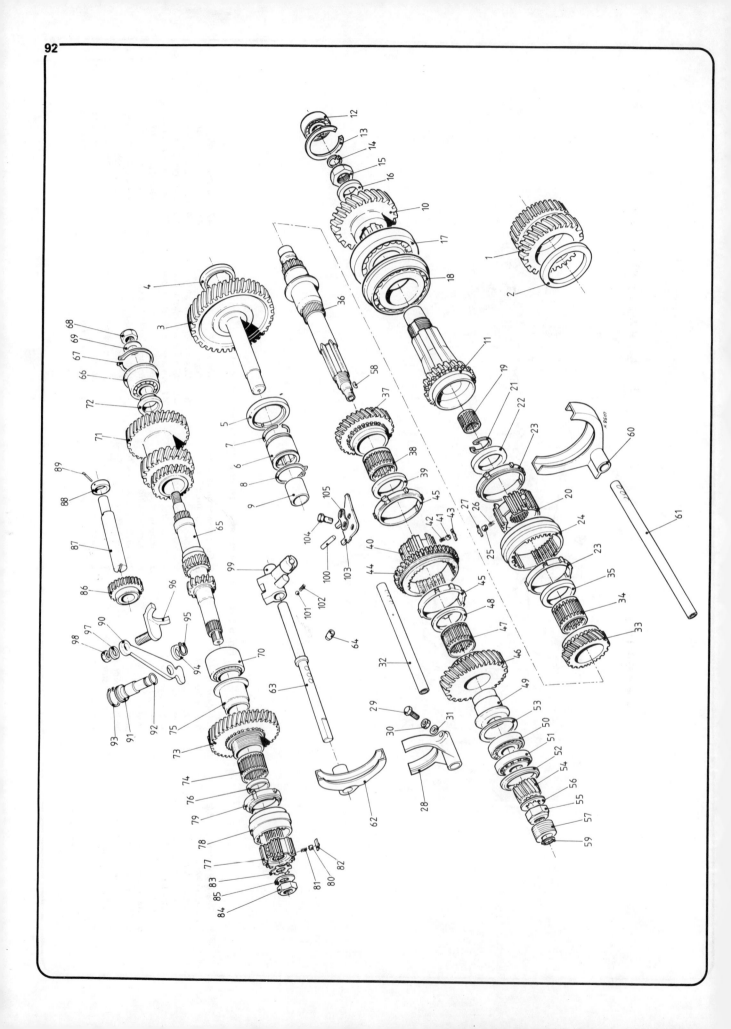

Fig. 6.6 Manual transmission internal components (cable gearchange) (Sec 5)

1 Primary gear – crankshaft
2 Thrustwasher for gear
3 Idler gear
4 Thrustwasher for idler gear
5 Thrustwasher for idler gear
6 Bearing for idler gear
7 Circlip for bearing
8 Circlip for bearing
9 Bearing for idler gear
10 First motion shaft gear (input)
11 First motion shaft
12 Bearing for shaft – spigot
13 Circlip for bearing outer track
14 Circlip for bearing inner track
15 Nut for first motion shaft
16 Lockwasher for nut
17 Ball bearing for shaft
18 Roller bearing for shaft
19 Needle roller bearing for shaft
20 Synchronizer
21 Circlip for synchronizer
22 Spacer for synchronizer
23 Baulk ring
24 Synchronizer collar
25 Plunger for synchronizer
26 Spring for plunger
27 Key
28 1st and 2nd speed selector fork
29 Bolt
30 Locknut
31 Washer for locknut
32 1st and 2nd speed selector rod
33 3rd speed gear
34 Bearing for gear
35 Spacer for bearing
36 Third motion shaft
37 2nd speed gear
38 Bearing for gear
39 Spacer for bearing
40 Synchronizer hub
41 Plunger for synchronizer
42 Spring for plunger
43 Key
44 Synchronizer collar/reverse (selective)
45 Baulk ring
46 First speed gear
47 Bearing for gear
48 Spacer for bearing
49 Hub for gear
50 Ball bearing for 3rd motion shaft
51 Roller bearing for 3rd motion shaft
52 Circlip for roller bearing
53 Circlip for ball bearing
54 Final drive pinion
55 Nut for pinion
56 Lockwasher for nut
57 Speedometer pinion
58 Key for pinion
59 Circlip for pinion
60 3rd and 4th speed selector fork
61 3rd and 4th speed selector fork
62 5th and reverse speed selector fork
63 5th and reverse speed selector fork
64 Detent plunger for selector rod
65 Layshaft
66 Bearing for layshaft
67 Circlip for bearing
68 Nut for layshaft
69 Lockwasher for nut
70 Bearing for layshaft
71 Laygear
72 Spacer for laygear
73 5th speed gear
74 Bearing for gear
75 Hub for gear
76 Spacer for bearing
77 Synchronizer hub
78 Synchronizer collar
79 Baulk ring
80 Plunger for synchronizer
81 Spring for plunger
82 Key
83 Retainer for synchronizer
84 Nut for layshaft
85 Lockwasher for nut
86 Reverse idler gear
87 Shaft for gear
88 Collar for shaft
89 Roll pin for collar
90 Reverse selector lever
91 Pivot pin for lever
92 O-ring for pin
93 Circlip for pin
94 Washer for pin
95 Circlip for pin
96 Reverse selector fork
97 Washer
98 Nut
99 Reverse selector interlock
100 Plunger for interlock
101 Ball for interlock
102 Spring for ball
103 Reverse interlock plate
104 Bolt for plate
105 Lockwasher

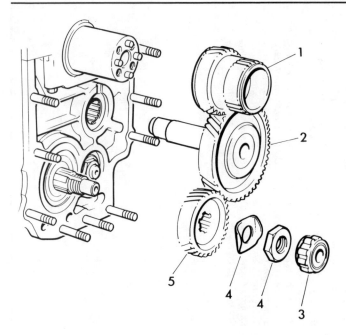

Fig. 6.7 Arrangement of primary gears (Sec 5)

1   Crankshaft primary gear   bearing
2   Idler gear   4   Nut and lockwasher
3   First motion shaft spigot   5   First motion shaft gear

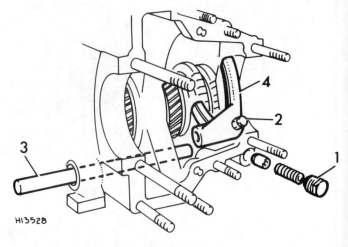

Fig. 6.8 First/second speed selector fork and plunger assembly
(Sec 5)

1   First/second speed detent plug
2   First/second speed selector fork retaining screw
3   First/second speed selector rod
4   First/second speed selector fork

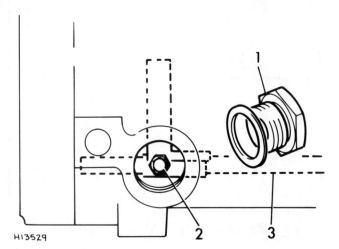

Fig. 6.9 Third/fourth speed selector fork and access plug (Sec 5)

1   Third/fourth speed selector fork access plug
2   Third/fourth speed selector fork retaining screw
3   Third/fourth speed selector rod

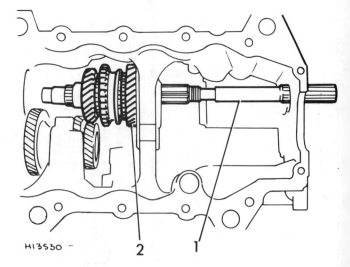

Fig. 6.10 Mainshaft removal (Sec 5)

1   Metal drift
2   First/second speed synchronizer and gears

transmission casing.
60 Lift out the remaining first and second speed gear cluster from the
transmission casing. Note the way the gears are fitted together so that
on reassembly they are fitted the correct way round.
61 Lift the second speed gear assembly from the synchronizer hub
and first speed gear assembly.
62 Remove the bearing, spacer and baulk ring from the second speed
gear.
63 Lift the synchronizer hub assembly from the first speed gear and
recover the baulk ring.
64 Lift out the bearing spacer from the hub of the first speed gear.
65 Separate the hub, bearing and baulk ring from the first speed gear.
66 Using a pair of circlip pliers, remove the circlip that retains the
twin track ball race in the outer end of the transmission case.
67 Using a thin soft metal drift, tap out the twin track ball race sufficiently to position two screwdrivers behind the outer track flange
whereupon the bearing can be levered out of its housing.
68 Using a screwdriver, carefully ease out the circlip that is located in
front of the roller race situated in the centre web of the transmission
casing.

from the third motion shaft. It will be necessary to release the collar
from the selector fork.
55 Remove the baulk ring located on the cone at the front of the third
speed gear.
56 Using a screwdriver, ease out and remove the bearing spacer from
within the hub of the third speed gear.
57 Slide the third speed gear and bearing from the third motion shaft.
58 Using a suitable diameter drift, carefully drift the third motion shaft
from the transmission casing.
59 Lift out the third and fourth and speed selector fork from the

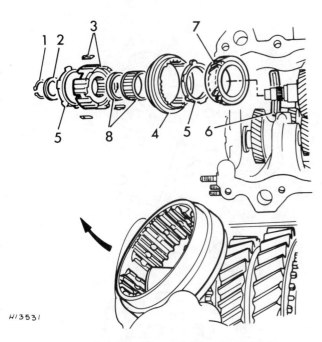

Fig. 6.11 Third/fourth speed assembly (Sec 5)

1 Circlip
2 Spacer
3 Synchronizer hub and keys
4 Synchronizer collar

5 Baulk ring
6 Third/fourth selector fork
7 Third speed gear
8 Spacer and bearing

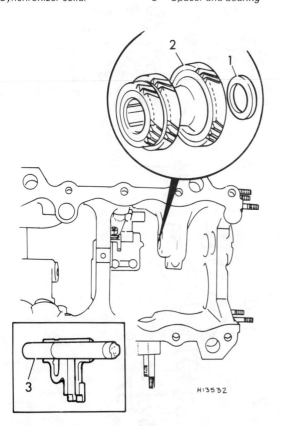

Fig. 6.12 Laygear and fifth/reverse selector rod assemblies (Sec 5)

1 Spacer
2 Laygear

3 Rod to retain ball and spring

69 With a narrow soft metal drift, carefully tap out the roller and ball bearing races from the centre web of the transmission casing. Note which way round the races are fitted.
70 Lift out the laygear from the transmission casing.
71 Recover the spacer from the end of the laygear.
72 Bend back the tabs locking the two reverse interlock securing bolts and then undo and remove the two bolts.
73 Carefully lift away the interlock selector and plate, taking care to recover the ball bearing, spring and plunger.
74 Lift out the oil pump pick-up pipe from the bottom of the transmission casing.

6 Transmission (rod gear change) – dismantling

1 With the transmission removed from the engine, remove the final drive as described in Chapter 8
2 Remove the oil pressure relief valve from the transmission case as described in Chapter 1, Section 25.
3 Bend back the lockplate from the baffle plate lock bolt. Remove the lock bolt and baffle. The oil pump outlet connection which is adjacent to the oil pressure relief valve hole must now be unscrewed. If a suitable tool is not available, use a pair of grips clamped securely to the outer edge of the large boss of the outlet connection. Now unscrew the two long mounting bolts and withdraw the oil pump.
4 Unbolt the left-hand engine mounting and safety bracket from the transmission case bracket.
5 Unbolt the transmission case bracket and remove it.
6 Unbolt and remove the front cover from the transmission case.
7 Withdraw the now exposed idler gear together with inner and outer thrust washers.
8 Carefully insert a drift through the idler gear needle roller bearing and drive out the inner bearing bush. Only carry out this operation if the bush is worn.
9 Extract the circlip which retains the idler gear needle roller bearing.
10 Withdraw the idler gear bearing from the transmission case. It will come out complete with its outer circlip.
11 Unscrew the end plugs from the 5th/reverse selector rod.
12 Unscrew and remove the 5th/reverse detent plug and extract the spring and plunger.
13 Slacken the locknut and unscrew the 5th shift fork locking screw.
14 Turn the 5th selector rod through 180° (half a turn) so that the flat on the end of the rod will clear the reverse selector arm when it is withdrawn.
15 Withdraw the selector rod to disengage it from the 5th shift fork but not so far that it disengages from the reverse selector interlock.
16 Turn the 5th speed shift fork through 180° (half a turn) and remove it.
17 Unscrew and remove the speedometer drive pinion.
18 Extract the circlip which retains the speedometer drivegear to the third motion shaft. Remove the drivegear and key.
19 Extract the circlip which retains the spigot bearing to the first motion shaft and then remove the bearing from the shaft.
20 Release the lockwasher tabs on the first motion shaft nut, the layshaft front and rear nuts and the final drive gear nut.
21 Lock two gears together by moving 1st and 5th synchro sleeves into mesh using a screwdriver.
22 With the gear train locked up, unscrew the final drivegear nut (left-hand thread).
23 Unscrew the layshaft front nut (right-hand thread).
24 Slacken, but do not remove, the layshaft rear nut (left-hand thread) and the first motion shaft nut (left-hand thread).
25 Disengage the locked up gears.
26 Remove the retainer from 5th gear synchronizer, then withdraw the synchro assembly, 5th gear, bearing and hub.
27 Extract the roll pin from the collar of the reverse idler shaft then remove the reverse idler shaft, collar and gear.
28 Unscrew and remove the previously slackened layshaft rear nut.
29 Using a suitable drift, drive the layshaft complete with front bearing out of the transmission case.
30 Unscrew the previously slackened first motion shaft nut and remove it.
31 Remove the first motion shaft input gear and extract the retaining ring.
32 Push 5th/reverse selector rod in towards the front of the transmission case until it clears the laygear.

H13533

Fig. 6.13 Manual transmission internal components (rod gearchange) (Sec 6)

1 Primary gear
2 Thrustwasher
3 Idler gear
4 Thrustwasher for idler gear
5 Thrustwasher for idler gear
6 Bearing for idler gear
7 Circlip for bearing
8 Circlip for bearing
9 Bearing for idler gear
10 First motion shaft gear (input)
11 First motion shaft
12 Bearing for shaft
13 Circlip for bearing outer track
14 Circlip for bearing inner track
15 Nut for first motion shaft
16 Lockwasher for nut
17 Ball-bearing for shaft
18 Roller-bearing for shaft
19 Needle-roller bearing for shaft
20 Synchronizer hub
21 Circlip for synchronizer
22 Spacer for synchronizer (selective)
23 Baulk ring
24 Synchronizer collar
25 Plunger for synchronizer
26 Spring for plunger
27 Key
28 Baulk ring
29 Slotted spring pin
30 1st to 4th speed selector rod
31 1st and 2nd speed fork
32 3rd and 4th speed selector fork
33 3rd speed gear
34 Bearing for gear
35 Spacer for bearing
36 Third motion shaft
37 2nd speed gear
38 Bearing for gear
39 Spacer for bearing
40 Synchronizer hub
41 Plunger for synchronizer
42 Spring for plunger
43 Key
44 Synchronizer collar/reverse mainshaft gear
45 Baulk ring
46 First speed gear
47 Bearing for gear
48 Spacer for bearing
49 Hub for gear
50 Ball bearing for 3rd motion shaft
51 Roller bearing for 3rd motion shaft
52 Circlip for roller bearing
53 Circlip for ball bearing
54 Final drive pinion
55 Nut for pinion
56 Lockwasher for nut
57 Speedometer pinion
58 Key for pinion
59 Circlip for pinion
60 5th and reverse speed selector fork
61 Washer for locknut
62 Locknut for bolt
63 Bolt for fork
64 5th and reverse speed selector rod
65 Layshaft
66 Bearing for layshaft
67 Circlip for bearing
68 Nut for layshaft
69 Lockwasher for nut
70 Bearing for layshaft
71 Laygear
72 Spacer for laygear
73 5th speed gear
74 Bearing for gear
75 Hub for gear
76 Spacer for bearing
77 Synchronizer hub
78 Synchronizer collar
79 Baulk ring
80 Plunger for synchronizer
81 Spring for plunger
82 Key
83 Retainer for synchronizer
84 Nut for layshaft
85 Lockwasher for nut
86 Reverse idler gear
87 Shaft for gear
88 Collar for shaft
89 Roll pin for collar
90 Reverse selector lever
91 Pivot pin for lever
92 O-ring for pin
93 Circlip for pin
94 Washer for pin
95 Circlip for pin
96 Reverse selector fork
97 Washer
98 Nut
99 Reverse selector interlock
100 Plunger for interlock
101 Ball for interlock
102 Spring for ball
103 Reverse interlock plate
104 Reverse operating lever
105 Circlip for reverse operating lever
106 Bolt for plate
107 Lockwasher for bolt
108 Selector shaft
109 Interlock spool
110 Torsion spring
111 Circlip for interlock spool
112 Retaining collar for interlock spool
113 Pin
114 Pivot post
115 O-ring seal
116 Bush for bellcrank levers
117 Washer
118 Nut
119 Spacer for bellcrank levers
120 Lower bellcrank lever
121 Centre bellcrank lever
122 Upper bellcrank lever

6.47A Self tapping screw inserted into roll pin

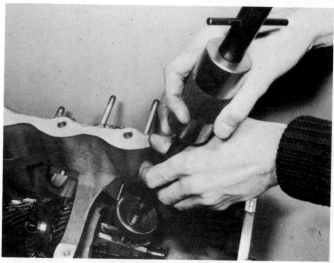

6.47B Withdrawing the roll pin

33 Insert a feeler gauge between 3rd speed gear and the shoulder on the shaft and check the endfloat of the gear. Compare with the end-float given in the Specifications and record for adjustment on reassembly.

34 Move the laygear out of mesh with 4th speed gear and clear of the synchro teeth.

35 Remove the 1st motion shaft complete with bearings and bearing outer track.

36 Using a feeler gauge, inserted between the 2nd speed gear and the shoulder on the shaft check the endfloat of the 1st and 2nd speed gears. If when compared with the tolerances in Specifications the end-float is incorrect, then the 3rd motion shaft, 1st speed gear assembly, 2nd speed gear assembly or synchro assembly will have to be renewed as necessary.

37 Extract the circlip which retains 3rd/4th speed synchro. Remove the synchro spacer.

38 Remove 3rd/4th synchro hub, catching the synchro keys as they fall.

39 Turn the selector shaft in an anti-clockwise direction and move the 3rd/4th selector fork into 4th gear position.

40 Turn the 3rd/4th synchro collar until one of its cut-outs will allow the collar to pass between the end of the shaft and the transmission case.

41 Remove 3rd speed gear bearing and the bearing spacer.

42 Drive the third motion shaft rearwards out of the transmission case.

43 Remove 2nd speed gear, bearing and the bearing spacer from the transmission case.

44 Remove 1st/2nd speed synchro assembly.

45 Remove the bearing spacer, the bearing, 1st speed gear and hub.

46 Extract the stepped circlip which retains the third motion shaft roller bearing. Withdraw the bearing from the transmission case.

47 The roll pin which retains the 1st/2nd and 3rd/4th selector rod in the transmission case must now be withdrawn. There is a special tool for removing this, but this pin can be removed without the special tool if a slide hammer is available. Screw a self tapping screw into the top of the pin, but do not insert the screw into that part of the pin which is in the casting (photo). Grip the top of the screw with the jaws of a slide hammer and gently impact the screw out (photo). Because the pin is spring steel, it is not possible to drill it out.

48 Unscrew and remove the 1st/2nd, 3rd/4th selector rod end plugs.

49 Cover the transmission case with a cloth or piece of plastic sheet-ing to avoid losing the springs and balls. Then apply a drift to the slotted end of the 1st/2nd, 3rd/4th selector rod and drive it from the transmission case. As it is removed, the interlock springs and balls will fly out and the 1st/2nd and 3rd/4th shift forks can be removed.

50 Lift the laygear and spacer from the transmission case.

51 Extract the circlip which retains the layshaft rear bearing and then remove the bearing from the transmission case.

52 Again cover the transmission case with a cloth or piece of plastic

sheeting to avoid losing the interlock balls and springs during the next operation.

53 Drive out the 5th/reverse selector rod from the transmission case so that the slotted end emerges first.

54 Unlock and unscrew the bolts which hold the reverse interlock plate.

55 Remove the reverse interlock plate, the interlock, the detent plunger, spring and ball.

56 Remove the C-clip and washer which retains the reverse selector lever assembly to its pivot.

57 Remove the reverse selector lever from its pivot.

58 Remove the circlip which retains the selector pivot in the transmission case. Withdraw the pivot complete with O-ring seal.

59 Unscrew the pivot post nut and remove the plain washer.

60 Rotate the selector shaft in an anti-clockwise direction and remove the bellcrank lever assembly.

61 Remove the bush from the pivot post.

62 Remove the collar which retains the interlock spool.

63 Withdraw the interlock spool from inside the transmission case.

64 Drive the pivot post complete with O-ring seal out of the transmis-sion case.

65 Remove the oil pump pick-up.

66 Clean all components and examine for wear, as detailed in Section 7. Renew worn or damaged components. If either 1st or 2nd speed gear or their baulk rings are being renewed, renew the gear and its baulk ring as a pair.

67 Dismantle the interlock spool by removing the selector shaft and then extracting the circlip to release the spring from the interlock spool.

---

7 Transmission components – examination and renovation

1 Carefully clean and examine all the component parts, for general wear, distortion and damage.

2 Examine the gear wheels for excessive wear and chipping of the teeth and renew them as necessary. It is advisable to renew the mating gear as well.

3 Examine the condition of all ball and roller races used. If there is looseness between the inner and outer races, the bearings must be renewed.

4 Ensure that the ball and roller races are a good fit in their housings.

5 Inspect the baulk rings and test them with their mating tapers on the gears. If they slip before they contact the edge of the dog teeth on the gear, the hub and baulk ring must be renewed. Check all sync-hromesh unit plungers to ensure they are not pitted or worn.

6 Check the locking detent plungers are not pitted or worn and that the springs when compared with a new one (if available) have not weakened.

7   Even if there have been no signs of oil leaks, new seals and gaskets must be fitted.

8   Examine all bushes for wear and, if suspect, fit new ones.

9   Inspect the transmission case very carefully for signs of cracking or damage, especially on the underside, as well as at all mating surfaces, bearing housings and stud or bolt holes.

10 Once the synchromesh units have been dismantled for inspection they should be reassembled as follows:

(a) Fit the springs and plungers into the hub pockets

(b) Align the cutaways in the collar with those of the hub and then fit the hub to the collar

(c) Press the keys into their slots with the raised ridge towards the collar

(d) Note that the third/fourth and fifth speed synchronizer keys are shorter than those fitted to the first/second speed synchronizer and must not be interchanged. The third/fourth speed synchronizer keys are identical to those fitted to the fifth speed and may be interchanged

(e) When new, the baulk rings for all synchronizers on early gearboxes are identical

8   Transmission (cable gear change) – reassembly

1   Always use new washers, gaskets and joint washers throughout reassembly. Generously lubricate all the gears, brushes and bearings with oil as they are being assembled.

2   Check that all oil ways are clear. Also ensure that the interior of the casing is clean and that there are no burrs on studs or bolt holes in the bearing housings.

3   Place the oil pump pick-up in the bottom of the transmission casing (photo).

4   Position the reverse interlock plate in the bottom of the transmission casing followed by the two hole tab washer and the two securing bolts. Do not tighten the bolts fully yet (photo).

5   Fit the spring and ball bearing into the reverse selector interlock and retain with a piece of metal rod or radio interference suppressor. Fit the interlock plunger into the reverse interlock and locate in position on the interlock plate. Tighten the two interlock plate securing screws and bend up the two locking tabs (photo).

6   Fit the spacer into the end of the laygear (photo).

7   Carefully lower the laygear into approximate position in the transmission case (photo).

8   Using a pair of circlip pliers, fit the third motion shaft ball bearing race retaining clip into the centre web of the transmission case. Insert the ball race with the stepped track side against the circlip.

9   Fit the roller bearing next to the ball bearing race

10 Using a soft metal drift, carefully tap the roller race in so that it will be possible to fit the retaining circlip of the roller race into the groove in the web.

11 Fit the roller race retaining circlip, making sure that it seats correctly in its groove. Selective circlips are available to eliminate bearing endfloat and the circlip should be fitted so that the step on it faces away from the bearing (photo).

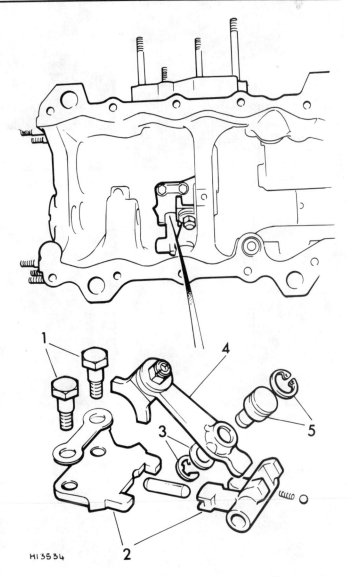

HI3534

Fig. 6.14 Selector forks (cable gearchange) (Sec 8)

1   Selector assembly securing bolts
2   Interlock plate and interlock assembly
3   Circlip and washer
4   Reverse selector lever and fork
5   Selector pivot and retaining circlip

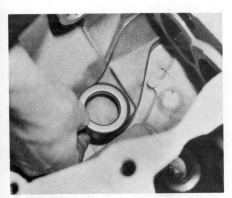

8.3 Fitting the oil pump pick-up pipe

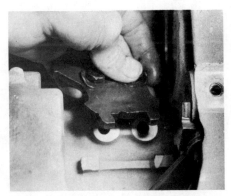

8.4 Positioning the reverse interlock plate

8.5 Reverse interlock bolt tabs

8.6 Fitting the laygear spacer

8.7 Inserting the laygear

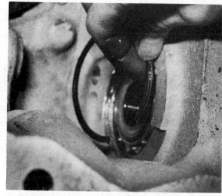
8.11 Third motion shaft bearing circlip

8.12 Installing the layshaft bearing

8.14 Fitting the layshaft bearing circlip

8.15 First speed gear, bearing and hub

8.16 First gear bearing spacer

8.17 Fitting first speed gear to its synchronizer

8.18 Second speed gear, bearing and spacer

8.19 Assembling first and second speed gears

8.20 Inserting first motion shaft temporarily

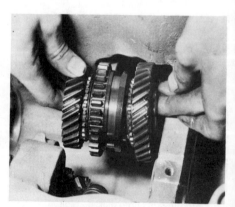
8.21 Installing first and second gear cluster

Circlip shoulder thickness

	Identification colour
0.0635 to 0.0645 in (1.62 to 1.65 mm)	*Orange*
0.065 to 0.066 in (1.66 to 1.69 mm)	*Blue*
0.0665 to 0.0675 in (1.70 to 1.72 mm)	*Self-finish*
0.068 to 0.069 in (1.74 to 1.76 mm)	*Green*

12 Fit the layshaft twin track ball race to the outer end of the transmission case (photo).
13 Using a piece of soft wood, carefully drift the twin track ball race into position so that it will be possible to fit the race retaining circlip into its groove in the transmission case.
14 Using a pair of circlip pliers, contract the circlip and fit it into its groove, making sure that it seats correctly (photo). Two thicknesses of circlip are available and if the thicker one will fit, it should be used.

Circlip thickness

	Identification colour
0.070 to 0.072 in (1.78 to 1.83 mm)	*Self-finish*
0.072 to 0.074 in (1.83 to 1.88 mm)	*Orange*

15 Assemble the first speed gear bearing, hub and baulk ring to first speed gear. If the cutaway parts of the hub are stepped, the steps should be towards the gear end of the collar (photo).
16 Fit the bearing spacer into the baulk ring end of the first speed gear (photo).
17 Fit the synchronizer hub assembly to the baulk ring on the first speed gear (photo).
18 Assemble the second speed gear bearing, spacer and baulk ring to the second speed gear (photo).
19 Fit the second speed gear assembly to the synchronizer hub and first speed gear assembly (photo).
20 Insert the third motion shaft through the previously assembled gear cluster and then fit on the third speed gear. This will give an idea of how the assembled gear cluster will look when assembled into the transmission case. Remove the third motion shaft again (photo).
21 Carefully lower the first and second speed gear cluster into the transmission case (photo).

22 Fit the securing bolt and locknut to the third and fourth speed selector fork (photo).
23 Place the third and fourth speed selector fork into the bottom of the transmission case.
24 Carefully insert the third motion shaft into the first and second speed gear assemblies (photo).
25 It will probably be necessary to use a piece of wood and hammer to finally position the third motion shaft.
26 This photograph shows what the assembled gears and third motion shaft should look like at this stage.
27 Lock the end of the third motion shaft with a screwdriver or piece of metal bar, in preparation for the next operation (photo).
28 Using a soft metal drift, carefully drive the inner roller race of the third motion shaft onto the third motion shaft (photo).
29 Fit the third speed gear and bearing onto the third motion shaft (photo).
30 Locate the bearing spacer in the hub of the third speed gear (photo).
31 Carefully manipulate the synchronizer collar onto the end of the third motion shaft (photo).
32 Slide the baulk ring through the synchronizer collar and then engage the collar with the third/fourth speed selector fork and push the collar up into mesh with the dog teeth on the third speed gear (photo). Note the boss on the baulk ring which locates in the grooves in the synchronizer collar.
33 Place the plungers and springs in the bores of the synchronizer hub (photo).
34 Slide the synchronizer hub half way onto the third motion shaft (photo) aligning the cutaways with the bosses on the baulk ring as shown in photograph 8.32. Make sure that the synchronizer assembly is fitted with the oilgrooves on the hub facing third speed gear.
35 It will be necessary to depress the spring loaded plungers for them to pass into synchronizer collar (photo).
36 Insert each of the three synchromesh unit keys into the synchronizer hub. The raised part must face outwards (photo).
37 Place the selective spacer for the synchronizer onto the third motion shaft (photo). The spacer is to stop any end-float of the synchromesh unit and is available in five different thicknesses:

8.22 Third/fourth selector fork bolt and locknut

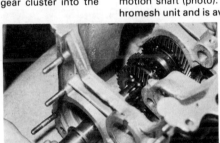
8.24 Installing third motion shaft

8.26 Third motion shaft installed

8.27 Restraining the third motion shaft

8.28 Driving home the third motion shaft inner race

8.29 Fitting third speed gear bearing ...

8.30 ... and spacer

8.31 Manipulating the synchronizer collar over the end of third motion shaft

8.32 Fitting the baulk ring and selector fork to the collar

8.33 Inserting the synchronizer springs and plungers

8.34 Installing the synchronizer hub

8.35 Depressing the plungers

8.36 Inserting a synchronizer key

8.37 Fitting the selective spacer

8.38 Fitting the spacer circlip

8.39 Inserting the detent plunger ...

8.40 ... and spring

8.41 Inserting third/fourth selector rod

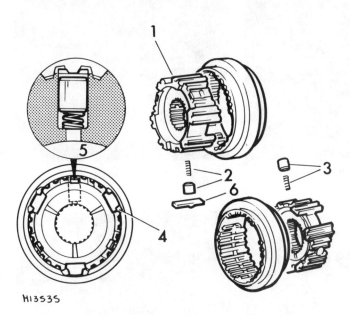

Fig. 6.15 Synchronizer assembly (Sec 8)

H1353S

1 Hub
2 Plunger and spring
3 Plunger and spring
4 Cutaway in collar aligned with cutaway in hub
5 Cross section with plunger and spring assembled
6 Key

Spacer thickness	Identification colour
0.093 to 0.094 in (2.36 to 2.38 mm)	Yellow
0.095 to 0.096 in (2.41 to 2.43mm)	Self finish
0.097 to 0.098 in (2.45 to 2.48mm)	Black
0.099 to 0.100 in (2.51 to 2.53mm)	Orange
0.101 to 0.102 in (2.56 to 2.58mm)	Blue
0.103 to 0.104 in (2.61 to 2.63mm)	Green

38 Fit the spacer retaining circlip making sure it is seating correctly (photo).

39 Insert the detent plunger, tapered end first, into its bore in the transmission case (photo).

40 Refit the detent plunger spring (photo).

41 Carefully insert the third and fourth selector rod into the transmission case, engaging the selector fork with the selector rod (photo).

42 Refit the plunger and spring retaining plug noting that two washers are fitted under the head. Tighten to the specified torque (photo).

43 Tighten the selector fork to rod securing tapered bolt making sure the taper enters the hole in the selector rod. Lock by tightening the locknut (photo).

44 Fit the baulk ring to the synchronizer collar (photo).

45 Using a suitable diameter tube, carefully drift the plain roller bearing onto the first motion shaft.

46 Insert the first motion shaft into the transmission casing, taking care to engage it with the end of the third motion shaft (photo).

47 Using a soft metal drift, carefully tap the bearing outer track into position (photo).

48 Fit the outer ball bearing race to the first motion shaft. (photo).

49 Carefully tap the ball bearing inner track into position using a soft metal drift (photo).

50 Fit the bearing assembly retaining ring, if necessary tapping it into its final position with a soft faced hammer (photo). If a new, or reconditioned, transmission assembly, transmission case or flywheel housing is to be fitted, the bearing assembly retaining ring must be checked as follows:

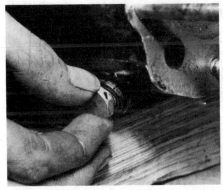

8.42 Screwing in the detent plug

8.43 Tightening the selector fork bolt

8.44 Fitting the baulk ring

8.46 Inserting the first motion shaft assembly

8.47 Driving in the bearing outer track

8.48 Installing the outer bearing ...

8.49 ... and tapping it into position

8.50 Fitting the bearing retaining ring

8.51 Inserting the layshaft

8.52 Tapping the layshaft bearing in

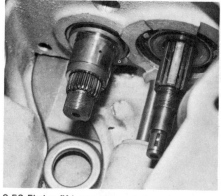
8.53 Fitting fifth speed gear hub, ...

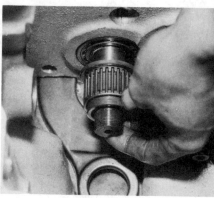
8.54 ... bearing

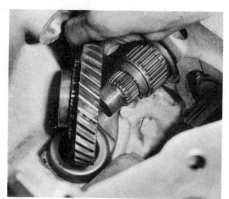
8.55 ... and gear

8.56 Fitting the layshaft bearing spacer

8.57 Fitting the baulk ring to fifth speed gear

8.58 Installing the reverse idler gear

8.59 Inserting the idler gear shaft ...

8.60 ... and collar

(a) Double check that the first motion shaft bearings are firmly pressed home in their housing

(b) Refer to Fig. 6.18 and measure the depth of the bearing housing from the face of the bearing to the outer face of the casing (A)

(c) Measure the depth of the ring recess in the first motion shaft gear pocket of the flywheel housing (B)

(d) Add 0.007 in (0.178 mm) to the sum of the measurements made in sub paragraphs (b) and (c). This is the compressed thickness of a new gasket

(e) Select a ring equal in thickness to the dimension calculated in (d)

(f) Rings are available in the following thicknesses:
0.337 to 0.339 in (8.56 to 8.61 mm)
0.339 to 0.341 in (8.61 to 8.66 mm)
0.341 to 0.343 in (8.66 to 8.71 mm)
0.343 to 0.345 in (8.71 to 8.76 mm)
0.345 to 0.347 in (8.76 to 8.81 mm)

51 Support the weight of the laygear and carefully insert the layshaft into the transmission casing (photo).

52 Using a suitable diameter tube, drift the front layshaft bearing into the transmission casing web (photo).

53 Fit the fifth speed gear hub onto the layshaft so that the large diameter is next to the bearing (photo).

54 Slide the fifth speed gear bearing onto the hub (photo).

55 Fit the fifth speed gear to the bearing (photo).

56 Push the bearing fully home and then fit the bearing spacer to the layshaft (photo).

57 Place the baulk ring onto the fifth speed gear hub (photo).

58 Place the reverse idler gear in the transmission case and hold it in its approximate fitted position with the selector fork guide facing the centre web (photo).

59 Fit the reverse selector to the idler fork guide and insert the reverse idler gear shaft so that the locking taper bolt hole will line up with the threaded hole in the centre web (photo). Fit the taper bolt and lockwasher.

60 Fit the reverse idler shaft collar to the shaft (photo), making sure

that the larger boss (between the pin hole and edge) is towards the gear.

61 With a small parallel pin punch, or screwdriver, position the idler shaft collar so that its locking pin hole aligns with the hole in the shaft.

62 Carefully insert the shaft collar locking pin and tap home fully with a suitable diameter drift (photo).

63 Fit the fifth speed baulk ring to the gear and then slide the synchromesh hub and collar assembly onto the end of the layshaft (photo). Check that the oil grooves on the hub face fifth gear.

64 Place the fifth and reverse gear selector fork onto the synchromesh unit collar (photo).

65 The fifth and reverse speed selector rod may now be fitted to the transmission case (photo).

66 Carefully insert the fifth and reverse speed selector rod, taking care to engage it with the reverse selector interlock and the fifth and reverse selector fork. The interlock ball and spring retainer previously placed in the reverse selector interlock must be recovered, as the selector rod is inserted into the reverse selector interlock.

67 Screw a suitable threaded bolt into the end of the fifth and reverse speed selector rod and tap the head of the bolt to assist in the final location (photo).

68 Line up the selector fork securing bolt hole with the hole in the fifth and reverse speed selector rod using a screwdriver, and then carefully fit the bolt and locknut. Tighten these fixings securely.

69 Slide the final drive pinion onto the end of the third motion shaft (photo). If necessary, pre-heat the pinion by immersing it in boiling water.

70 Fit a new lockwasher and refit the large securing nut (photo).

71 Place the fifth and reverse speed synchromesh unit retainer to the layshaft (photo).

72 Fit the retainer lockwasher and nut to the end of the layshaft (photo).

73 Insert the reverse and fifth speed detent plunger into the transmission case (photo).

74 Follow the detent plunger with the spring and secure in position with the cap nut and fibre washer (photo).

75 Fit the third and fourth speed selector rod to the transmission

8.62 Inserting the collar roll pin

8.63 Installing fifth gear synchronizer

8.64 Installing fifth/reverse selector fork ...

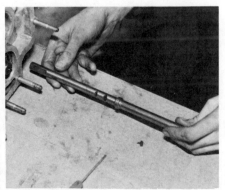
8.65 ... and rod

8.67 Tapping in the fifth/reverse selector rod

8.69 Installing the final drive pinion ...

8.70 ... lockwasher and nut

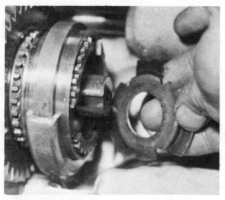

8.71 Installing the synchronizer retainer ...

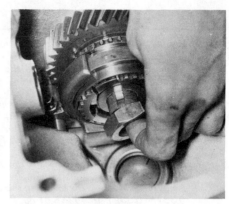

8.72 ... washer and locknut

8.73 Inserting fifth/reverse detent plunger ...

8.74 ... spring and cap nut

8.75 Inserting third/fourth speed selector rod

8.76 Securing the selector fork to the rod

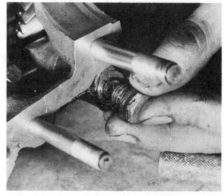

8.77 First/second gear detent plunger assembly

8.78A Tightening the layshaft nut ...

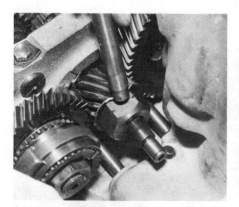

8.78B ... and locking the tab

8.80 The layshaft rear nut lockwasher

8.81 Installing the gear on the first motion shaft

case, taking care to line up the securing bolt holes in the selector fork and selector rod (photo).

76 Fit the taper bolt and locknut to the selector fork; carefully tighten the securing bolt and lock the locknut (photo).

77 Insert the first and second speed detent plunger and spring into the bore in the transmission case and secure in position with the plug and three washers (photo).

78 Remove the final drive pinion retaining nut, apply Loctite 270 to the shaft threads, refit the nut and tighten it to the specified torque. **Note** *that the nut has a left-hand thread (photos).*

79 Tighten the front nut on the end of the layshaft to the specified torque.

80 Fit the layshaft rear nut lockwasher and nut to the end of the layshaft and tighten to the specified torque. Bend over the lockwasher (photo). **Note** *this nut has a left-hand thread.*

81 Place the first motion shaft gear onto the first motion shaft (photo).

82 Using a suitable size socket, drift the first motion shaft gear into its final position on the first motion shaft.

83 Place the lockwasher onto the end of the first motion shaft with the ears facing outwards (photo).

84 Refit the nut and tighten it to the specified torque. It will be necessary to lock two gears together by moving two synchromesh collars into mesh with a screwdriver. **Note:** *This nut has a left-hand thread.*

85 Using a chisel bend over the lock washer ears.

86 Fit the idler gear bearing to the transmission casing (photo).

87 Tap the bearing into its final position with a piece of soft wood.

88 Fit the idler gear bearing inner and outer retaining circlip (photo). If the original idler gear bearing bush was removed because of wear, fit a new bush, making sure that it does not protrude. After installing the bush it must be reamed to $\frac{7}{8}$ in (22.23 mm), using clean paraffin as a lubricant. Do not allow any swarf to fall into the casing.

89 Slide the inner thrust washer onto the idler gear (photo).

90 Fit the idler gear and shaft into the transmission case, carefully meshing it with the first motion shaft gear (photo).

91 Refit the inner bearing circlip onto the end of the first motion shaft and then, using a piece of soft wood, drift on the spigot bearing (photo).

92 Fit the outer bearing circlip to the outermost end of the first motion shaft (photo).

93 Refer to Chapter 8 and fit the differential unit to the transmission casing.

94 Fit the Woodruff key to the end of the third motion shaft.

95 Slide the speedometer pinion onto the end of the third motion shaft.

96 Fit the speedometer pinion retaining circlip (photo).

97 Fit the bracket to the differential housing, if this has not already been done (photo).

98 Carefully insert the speedometer cable drive gear and housing into the transmission casing screw into the housing (photo).

99 Tighten the drivegear housing, using a socket.

100 Clean the magnetic drain plug and screw into the transmission casing.

101 Refit the oil pump and screw in the pump outlet connection (photo).

102 Using a piece of metal gripped with a Mole wrench, tighten the pump outlet connection (photo).

103 Secure the oil pump with the two long bolts with plain and spring washers.

104 Fit a new gasket to the front cover and slide into position over the two studs.

105 Refit the front mounting, and secure the front cover and mounting with the five bolts and spring washers and two nuts and spring washers.

106 The transmission unit is now ready to have the splash shield refitted and then for refitting to the engine as described in Section 10.

8.83 First motion shaft lockwasher

8.86 Installing the idler gear bearing

8.88 Fitting the bearing circlip

8.89 Installing the idler gear thrustwasher

8.90 Installing the idler gear and shaft

8.91 Installing the spigot bearing ...

8.92 ... and outer circlip

8.96 Speedometer pinion and circlip

8.97 Fitting the differential housing bracket

8.98 Inserting the speedometer drivegear

8.101 Inserting the oil pump outlet ...

8.102 ... and tightening it

9   Transmission (rod gear change) – reassembly

1   Use new washers, gaskets and seals throughout reassembly and lubricate all components generously with oil as they are assembled.
2   Check that oilways are clear and that the interior of the transmission case is clean. Renew any studs which are bent, or whose threads are damaged.
3   Fit a new O-ring seal to the selector bellcrank levers pivot post and then drive the pivot post in to the case.
4   Refit the interlock spool, retaining it with the collar (photo). A new spring, of the same pattern as the one removed should be fitted and the legs of the spring should be located on opposite sides of the stop pin (photo).
5   Refit the bush, bellcrank levers and flat washer onto the pivot post. Secure them with the self-locking nut after having checked that

(a) *There are spacers on either side of the centre bellcrank lever and that the lever has chamfers on its upper and lower faces*
(b) *The upper bellcrank lever is chamfered on its top face*
(c) *The lower bellcrank lever is chamfered on its bottom face*

Tighten the nut to the specified torque (photo).
6   Fit a new O-ring seal to the selector lever pivot, fit the pivot to the casing and retain it with the circlip. Make sure that oil is applied to the O-ring.
7   Fit the selector lever to the pivot, fit the plain washer and C-clip.
8   Fit the interlock spring and ball into the interlock arm and retain them in place with a suitably sized cylinder of wood, or metal (photos).
9   Assemble the plunger to the interlock and install the interlock and interlock plate in the transmission case (photos). Use new lockplates under the bolt heads and bend up the tabs of the lockplates when the bolts have been tightened.
10 Drive the 5th/reverse selector rod into the transmission case, entering the plain end of the rod first and positioning the rod so that the machined flat face at the other end is facing towards the bottom of the case. Drive the rod through the reverse interlock until the temporary retainer used for the ball is displaced and recover the

temporary retainer. Continue to drive in the rod until its leading end enters the central web of the transmission case, but do not drive it beyond the web at this stage (photo).
11 Fit the layshaft rear bearing into the transmission case and fit a bearing circlip which is thick enough to eliminate bearing endfloat. Circlips are available in the following thickness.

Circlip thickness	Colour code
0.070 to 0.072 in (1.78 to 1.83 mm)	Self-finish
0.072 to 0.074 in (1.83 to 1.88 mm)	Orange

12 Fit the third motion shaft bearing retaining circlip into the transmission case.
13 Refit the third motion shaft bearing into the transmission case, making sure that the stepped face of the bearing butts against the circlip.
14 Fit the outer track of the third motion shaft thrust bearing so that it locates against the first bearing.
15 Fit the thickest circlip, chosen from those available, to eliminate bearing endfloat and fit the circlip so that its stepped face is away from the bearing. Circlips are available in the following thicknesses.

Shoulder thickness	Colour code
0.0635 to 0.0645 in (1.62 to 1.65 mm)	Orange
0.065 to 0.066 in (1.66 to 1.69 mm)	Blue
0.0665 to 0.0675 in (1.70 to 1.72 mm)	Self-finish
0.068 to 0.069 in (1.74 to 1.76 mm)	Green

16 Refit the third motion shaft thrust bearing.
17 Lower the laygear into the bottom of the transmission case (photo).
18 Fit a new detent spring and ball into the 1st/2nd shift fork. Retain them in position with a piece of rod (photos).
19 Fit a new detent spring and ball into the 3rd/4th shift fork and retain it in a similar manner to that used previously.
20 Hold the 3rd/4th shift fork in position in the transmission case and insert the plain end of the 1st/2nd – 3rd/4th selector rod through the rear end of the case and tap the rod through the shift fork, ejecting the temporary detent ball retaining rod.
21 Hold the 1st/2nd shift fork in position in the transmission case and

9.4A Interlock spool retaining collar

9.4B Legs of spring on either side of stop pin

9.5 Installed position of bellcrank levers

9.8A Interlock arm, spring and ball

9.8B Spring and arm retained by wooden dowel

9.9A Interlock before installation

9.9B Interlock installed

9.10 Fifth/reverse selector rod in initial position

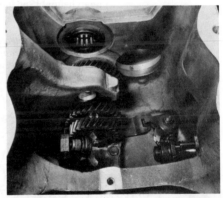
9.17 Laygear installed in the bottom of the transmission case

9.18A First/second shift fork, spring and ball

9.18B Ball retained temporarily

9.21 Shift forks before insertion of shift rod

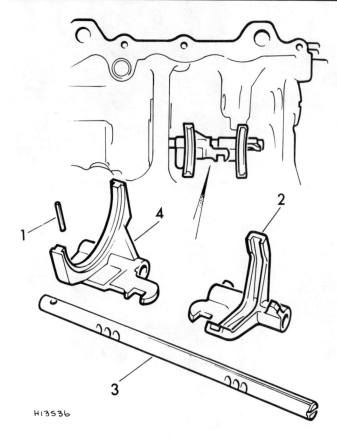

H13536

Fig. 6.16 First/second and third/fourth selector forks and rod (rod gearchange) (Sec 9)

1   Spring pin
2   Third/fourth speed selector fork
3   First/second selector rod
4   First/second speed selector fork

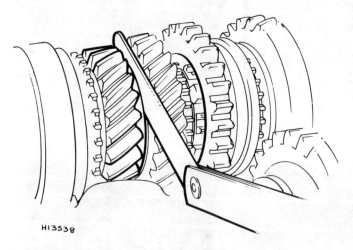

H13538

Fig. 6.17 Measuring 3rd speed endfloat (Sec 9)

pass the selector rod through it in a similar way to that just described in the preceding paragraph (through the shift fork and into the central web of the transmission casing) (photo).
22 Align the hole in the end of the selector rod with the hole in the transmission case and tap in a new roll pin.
23 Assemble the 1st/2nd speed synchro unit. This unit has baulk rings with larger bores than those fitted to the 3rd/4th or 5th units. Fit the springs and plungers to the synchro hub. Align the cutaways in the

sleeve with those in the hub and engage both components. If the cutaways in the synchro hub are stepped, make sure that the steps are towards the gear end of the sleeve. Press the keys into their slots so that their raised ridges are towards the collar. It should be noted that the 3rd/4th and 5th speed synchro keys are shorter than those used in the 1st/2nd unit. Do not interchange them.
24 Assemble the 5th speed synchro unit in a similar way to that described in the preceding paragraph.
25 Fit the baulk rings to the 1st/2nd and 5th speed synchro units. The 1st/2nd baulk ring has six oil grooves whilt the 5th speed baulk ring has only three grooves.
26 Assemble 1st gear, 1st/2nd synchro and 2nd gear.
27 Fit the spacer, bearing and hub to the 1st speed gear and the spacer and bearing to the 2nd speed gear.
28 Position 1st and 2nd speed gear assembly in the transmission case, so that the synchro sleeve engages with the 1st/2nd shift fork (photo) and then thread the third motion shaft through the gears on into the shaft bearings. With a hammer and a piece of hardwood, tap the shaft in fully, taking care not to displace the bearings (photo).
29 To the third motion shaft, fit the 3rd speed gear, the bearing, spacer and 3rd/4th speed synchro baulk ring (photos).
30 Slide the shift fork to the 4th gear position and then fit the 3rd/4th synchro sleeve (photo).
31 Insert the springs and plungers into the 3rd/4th synchro hub (photo). Fit the hub and refit the keys (photos) (refer to previous paragraph 23). Make sure that the oil grooves in the synchro hub face the 3rd speed gear.
32 Select a spacer from the available thicknesses to eliminate all end-float of the 3rd speed gear and 3rd/4th synchro unit. Spacers are available in the following thicknesses.

Thickness	Colour code
0.093 to 0.094 in (2.36 to 2.38 mm)	*Yellow*
0.095 to 0.096 in (2.41 to 2.43 mm)	*Self-finish*
0.097 to 0.098 in (2.45 to 2.48 mm)	*Black*
0.099 to 0.100 in (2.51 to 2.53 mm)	*Orange*
0.101 to 0.102 in (2.56 to 2.58 mm)	*Blue*
0.103 to 0.104 in (2.61 to 2.63 mm)	*Green*

Fit the spacer and circlip (photo).
33 If the first motion shaft bearings were removed from the shaft because of wear, fit new ones. Fit the new ones by installing the inner track of the roller bearing to the shaft. Press the bearings on to the shaft with the roller bearing nearest to the gear.
34 Fit the needle roller spigot bearing to the third motion shaft (photo).
35 Fit the first motion shaft and bearing assembly in the transmission case (photo), tapping the bearing inner and outer tracks in sequence, using a brass, or copper drift.
36 Fit the retaining ring. If a new, or reconditioned transmission is being fitted, or if the flywheel housing, or gearcase has been changed, the retaining ring must be checked in the following way. Check that the first motion shaft bearings are fully home in their seats. Measure the depth of the bearing track from the face of the bearing to the outer face of the transmission case (Dimension A) (Fig. 6.18). Measure the depth of the retaining ring recess in the flywheel housing (Dimension B). To the sum of dimensions A and B, add 0.007 in (0.18 mm) which is the thickness of an average flywheel housing gasket. Select a retaining ring equal to this total measurement from the sizes available, which are:

0.337 to 0.339 in (8.56 to 8.61 mm)
0.339 to 0.341 in (8.61 to 8.66 mm)
0.341 to 0.343 in (8.66 to 8.71 mm)
0.343 to 0.345 in (8.71 to 8.76 mm)
0.345 to 0.347 in (8.76 to 8.81 mm)

37 Fit first motion shaft input gear so that the boss on the gear is towards the bearing.
38 Fit a new lockwasher and screw the nut *(left-hand thread)* until it is finger tight.
39 If the layshaft bearing was removed because of wear, press a new one on to the shaft.
40 Fit the oil pump pick-up.
41 Fit the thrust washer to the end of the laygear.
42 Refit the layshaft from the front of the transmission case (photo). Fit a new lockwasher and screw on the nut *(left-hand thread)* finger tight.

9.28A First/second gear assembly with shift fork engaged

9.28B Third motion shaft installed

9.29A Third speed gear bearing and spacer

9.29B Third speed gear and baulk ring

9.30 Installing 3rd/4th synchro sleeve

9.31A Installing the synchro springs and plungers

9.31B Installing the hub

9.31C Inserting the keys

9.32 Third gear spacer circlip

9.34 Third motion shaft spigot bearing and first motion shaft assembly

9.35 Installing the first motion shaft assembly

9.42 Installing the layshaft

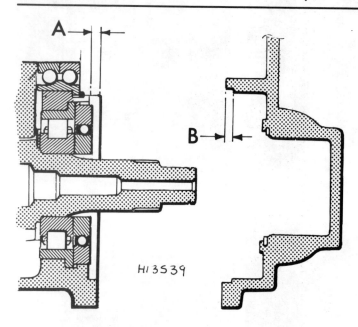

Fig. 6.18 First motion shaft bearing ring dowel (Sec 9)

A   Depth of bearing housing from face of bearing to outer face of
    casing
B   Depth of ring dowel recess in first motion shaft gear pocket of
    flywheel housing

43 Refit reverse idler shaft and gear, engaging the gear with the
reverse shift fork (photo)
44 Fit the collar to the reverse idler shaft so that the end which is
furthest from the roll pin hole is nearest to the gear (photo).
45 Align the holes in the collar and shaft and tap in a new pin.
46 Refit the 5th speed gear hub, 5th speed gear, gear bearing and 5th
speed synchro unit to the layshaft.
47 Fit 5th speed synchro retainer, the lockwasher and the layshaft
front nut (right-hand thread) and screw the nut on finger tight.
48 Fit the final drive gear to the third motion shaft. If the gear is a
tight fit, heat it in boiling water. Fit a new lockwasher, smear the
threads of the third motion shaft with a thread locking compound and
screw on the nut (left-hand thread) finger tight (photo).
49 Turn the selector shaft in an anti-clockwise direction and select
1st and 5th gears to lock the gear train.
50 Tighten the shaft nuts to the specified torque wrench settings in
the following sequence:

   (a) Layshaft front nut (right-hand thread)
   (b) Final drive gear nut (left-hand thread)
   (c) Layshaft rear nut (left-hand thread)
   (d) First motion shaft nut (left-hand thread)

51 Disengage the 1st and 5th gears and bend up the tabs on the nut
lockplates.

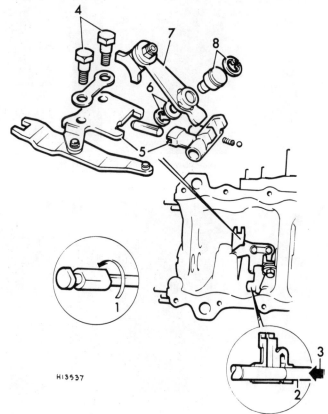

Fig. 6.19 Fifth/reverse selector forks and rod (rod gearchange)
(Sec 9)

   1   Rotate fifth/reverse selector rod 180°
   2   Metal rod to retain ball and spring in interlock assembly
   3   Push retainer into interlock
   4   Selector assembly securing bolts
   5   Interlock plate and interlock assembly
   6   C-clip and washer
   7   Selector lever and fork
   8   Selector pivot and retaining circlip

52 Locate the 5th speed shift fork over the 5th speed synchro sleeve
and rotate the fork through 180°.
53 Push the 5th speed selector rod into engagement with the 5th
speed shift fork.
54 Turn the selector rod through 180°, so that the machined flat is
uppermost (photo).
55 Tighten the fork back screw and locknut (photo).
56 Fit the speedometer drive key, drivegear and circlip to the end of
the third motion shaft (photos).
57 Fit the speedometer drive pinion into the transmission case,

9.43 Installing the reverse idler shaft and gear

9.44 Fitting the collar and roll pin

9.48 Fifth gear and final drive pinion installed

9.54 Fifth speed selector rod with machined flat uppermost

9.55 Selector fork lock screw

9.56A Speedometer drive key ...

9.56B ... gear and circlip

9.58A Fifth reverse detent ...

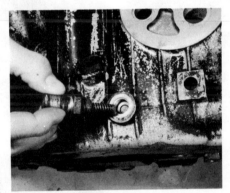

9.58B ... spring and plunger

9.67 Baffle plate and reverse idler shaft locking bolt

screwing it in until it is fully home.

58 Fit the 5th/reverse detent, spring and plunger in to the transmission case (photos).

59 Screw in the 5th/reverse selector rod end plugs.

60 Fit the first motion shaft spigot bearing and secure it with its circlip. If the bearing was renewed, extract the outer track of the old bearing from the flywheel housing and tap the track of the new bearing into position.

61 Fit the outer circlip to the new idler gear needle roller bearing and draw the bearing in to the casing, using a bolt, nut, washers and a distance piece. Fit the inner retaining circlip.

62 Fit a new idler gear bearing bush, making sure that it does not protrude on either side of the case. This operation will only be necessary if the old bush has been removed because of wear. The new bush must be reamed to $\frac{7}{8}$ in (22.22 mm) after installation and lubricated with paraffin while being reamed. Do not allow any swarf

from reaming to drop into the casing.

63 Fit the idler gear and the inner and outer thrust washers.

64 Rotate the reverse idler shaft as necessary to align its hole with the corresponding one in the web of the transmission case. Do not fit the locking bolt at this stage.

65 Refit the oil pump outlet connection and the oil pump. Tighten the oil pump bolts to the specified torque.

66 Refit the oil pressure relief valve (Chapter 1, Section 27).

67 Refit the baffle plate, making sure that the locking bolt passes through the hole in the reverse idler shaft (photo). Bend up the tabs of the bolt lock plate.

68 Refit the front cover of the transmission case, using a new gasket.

69 Refit the transmission case bracket, the left-hand engine mounting and safety bracket.

70 Refit the differential unit after reference to Chapter 8, Section 2.

71 Screw in and tighten the drain plug.

10 Transmission – refitting to engine

1   Refit a new oil sealing ring to the transmission casing (photo).

2   Locate new sealing strips into the slots on either side of the front oil seal location (photo).

3   Fit the splash shield if not yet fitted and secure in position with the bolt and tab washer (photo).

4   Bend up the tab washer, so locking the splash shield securing bolt.

5   Smear a little grease onto the mating faces of the transmission casing and carefully locate new joint washer halves to the mating face.

6   With the help of an assistant, carefully lift the engine and then place on the transmission casing. Loosely fit the engine to transmission bolts in the following places – above the oil filter, above the fuel pump boss and the centre bolts above the differential housing. These bolts cannot be inserted after the engine has been bolted to the transmission case.

7   Refit the crankshaft primary gear thrust washer to the end of the crankshaft (photo).

8   Refit the idler gear outer thrust washer and retain in position with a dab of grease (photo).

9   Smear a little grease onto the flywheel housing-to-engine and transmission case mating face and fit a new joint washer.

10   Lubricate the end of the crankshaft ready for the primary gear to be fitted.

10.1 Oil sealing ring

10.2 Front oil seal sealing strips

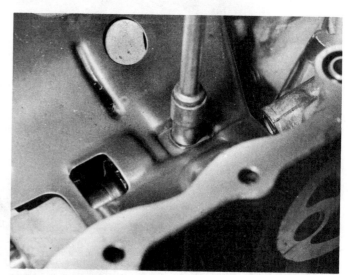

10.3 Fitting the splash shield

10.7 Fitting the primary gear thrustwasher

10.8 Idler gear outer thrustwasher

10.11 Installing the primary gear

10.20 Flywheel master dowel

11 Wrap some adhesive tape around the primary gear splines to prevent damage to the oil seal, and smear on a little grease. Slide on the primary gear (photo). Refer to Section 2 and check the endfloat.
12 If a new flywheel housing oil seal is to be fitted, this should be done as described in Section 3. If a new, or a reconditioned transmission assembly, transmission case, or flywheel housing has been, or is being fitted, the first motion shaft bearing ring dowel must be checked as described in Section 8, paragraph 50.
13 Carefully fit the flywheel housing to the engine and transmission casing.
14 Using a sharp knife, cut away the adhesive tape from the splines of the primary gear.
15 Refit the flywheel housing bolts, fit the nuts and tab washers, but do not tighten the nuts at this stage.
16 Fit the remaining transmission casing to crankcase securing bolts and spring washers, but do not tighten the bolts yet.
17 Carefully tap up the dowels to locate the transmission casing and crankcase mating flanges accurately.
18 Tighten the transmission to crankcase bolts to the torque wrench setting appropriate to the particular diameter of bolt.
19 Tighten the bolts and nuts securing the flywheel housing to the engine/transmission case to the specified torque and then bend over the lockwasher tabs.
20 Before fitting the clutch/flywheel assembly, note that there is a master dowel in the end of the crankshaft which is of larger diameter than the other three (photo).
21 Refit the clutch/flywheel assembly to the crankshaft and drive the flywheel fully home.
22 Locate the spacer plate on the inside of the clutch and fit the four securing bolts.
23 Tighten the flywheel retaining bolts to the specified torque.
24 Fit the clutch thrust plate, secure it with the three bolts and spring washers and tighten the bolts to the specified torque.
25 Fit the clutch housing cover and its eight bolts and spring washers. Tighten the bolts progressively to the specified torque.
26 Insert the fuel pump operating pushrod and fit the fuel pump and insulator. Fit the two nuts and spring washers and tighten the nuts to the specified torque.
27 Fit the oil filter and tighten it.
28 Refit the starter motor with its two bolts and spring washers. Tighten the bolts to the specified torque.
29 Insert the oil pump driveshaft and refit the distributor. Secure the distributor with two bolts and spring washers.
30 Refit the dipstick guide tube and secure it with the union nut.

11 Remote control (cable gear change) – removal and refitting

1 Place a container having a capacity of at least ten pints (5·6 litres) under the engine/transmission unit drain plug. Unscrew and remove

the drain plug and allow all the oil to drain out.
2 Unscrew the cable locking nut from each of the cables at the transmission unit end (Fig. 6.20).
3 Unscrew the outer cable gland nut from each of the cables.
4 Carefully pull out the fifth speed/reverse outer cable from the transmission.
5 Unscrew the inner cable gland nut and detach the cable from the transmission.
6 Repeat the operations in paragraphs 4 and 5 but for the first and second speed cable.
7 Screw a long bolt into the end of the first and second speed selector rod and push the rod into the neutral position.
8 Repeat the operations in paragraphs 4 and 5 but for the third and fourth speed cable.
9 Unscrew and remove the nut and spring washer that secures the heat shield front mounting.
10 Undo and remove the four nuts and spring washers that secure the silencer mounting brackets to the body.
11 Undo and remove the four bolts and spring washers that secure the change speed control to the heat shield.
12 Pull off the Lucar connectors from the two terminals on the reverse light switch.
13 Unscrew the knob from the gear change lever.
14 Move the carpeting from around the gear change lever area and then undo and remove the six screws and washers that secure the change speed lever control.
15 Lift away the cover and rubber gaiter from over the top of the gear change lever.
16 The complete change speed remote control assembly and cables may now be lifted away from the car.
17 Refitting the assembly is the reverse sequence to removal but it will be necessary to pull out the selector rods before the inner cables can be reconnected.
18 The cables must be adjusted as described in Section 16.
19 Finally refill the engine/transmission unit with oil.

12 Remote control (rod gear change) – removal and refitting

1 Unscrew the gear change lever knob.
2 Using a small diameter parallel pin punch remove the spring pin that retains the extension rod to the selector shaft.
3 Undo and remove the nyloc nut and long bolt that secures the steady rod to the transmission casing. Recover the two plain washers located either side of the transmission casing boss.
4 Pull off the Lucar connectors from the two terminals on the reverse light switch.
5 Undo and remove the nyloc nut and long bolt that secures the remote control to the mounting bracket.
6 Lift away the remote control from the car.

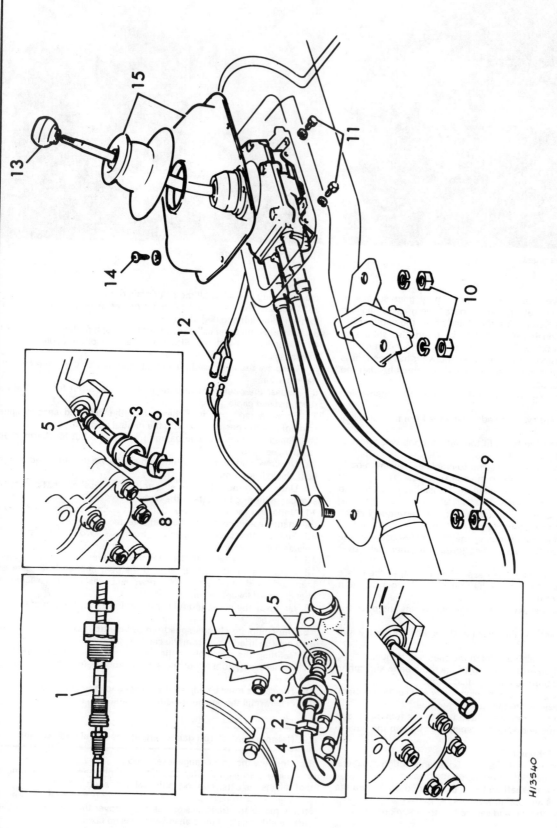

HI/3540

Fig. 6.20 Cable gearchange assembly (Sec 11)

1 Transmission unit end of cable
2 Cable locknut
3 Outer cable gland nut
4 Fifth/reverse cable
5 Inner cable gland nut
6 First/second cable
7 First/second selector rod in neutral position using long bolt
8 Third/fourth cable
9 Heat shield front securing nut and washer
10 Silencer box mounting nuts and washers
11 Remote control to heat shield securing bolts and washers
12 Reverse light switch cables
13 Gearchange lever knob
14 Remote control cover securing bolts and washers
15 Remote control cover and rubber gaiter

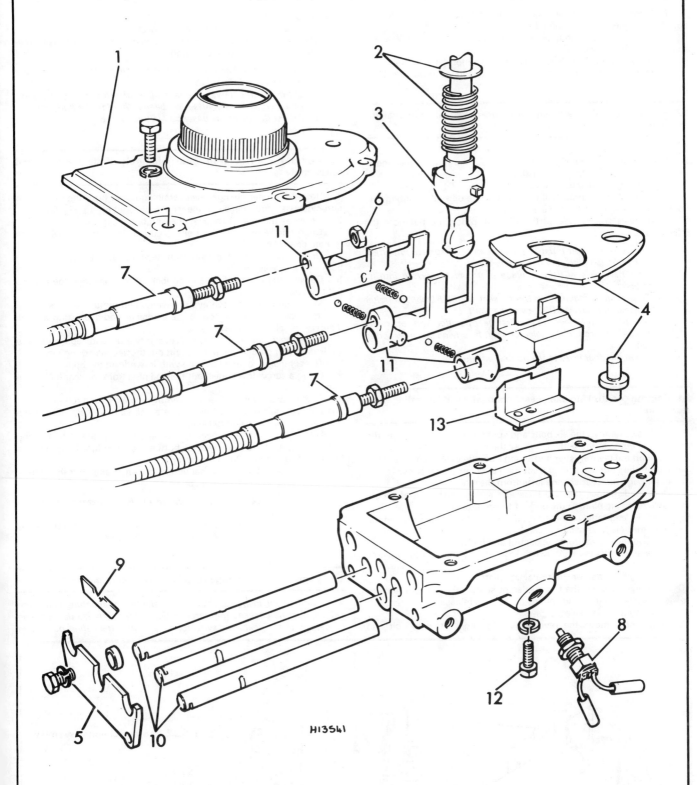

H13541

Fig. 6.21 Cable gearchange components (Sec 11)

1	Remote control cover	5	Cable retaining plate	9	Selector shaft retaining plate	12	Reverse selector stop
2	Spring and washer	6	Cable inner nuts	10	Selector shafts		retaining screw
3	Gearchange lever	7	Cables	11	Selector jaws	13	Reverse stop and dowel
4	Interlock and pivot	8	Reverse light switch				

7   Refitting is the reverse sequence to removal but the following additional points should be noted:
8   Always use a new spring pin when securing the selector extension rod to the selector shaft.
9   Adjust the reverse switch as described in Section 18.
10 The remote control must be adjusted as described in Section 16.

13 Remote control selector shaft (rod gear change) – removal and refitting

1   Select first gear.
2   Using a small pin punch, carefully drive out the spring pin connecting the selector rod to the selector shaft.
3   Move the gear lever to second gear position.
4   Use a hooked, pointed tool to hook out the oil seal, ensuring that no pieces of seal are left in the seal recess.
5   Refitting is the reverse of the removal procedure but note the following:

   (a) *The selector shaft must be cleaned and any surface imperfection removed with very fine emery cloth*
   (b) *Fit a new oil seal using a piece of tubing to press it into its recess*
   (c) *To provide protection for the oil seal, fit the BL special gaiter (part number DAM 3022) over the shaft*
   (d) *Return the gear lever to the first gear position and reconnect the selector rod to the selector shaft by driving in a new spring pin*
   (e) *Move the gear lever to the neutral position*

14 Remote control (cable gear change) – dismantling and reassembly

1   Undo and remove the six bolts and spring washers that secure the control unit cover to the body. Lift away the cover (Fig. 6.21).
2   Slide off the plain washer and spring from the gear change lever.
3   Lift off the interlock and its pivot from the control unit body.
4   Disengage the gear change lever from the interlock.
5   Undo and remove the two bolts and spring washers that secure the cable retaining plate to the body of the control unit.
6   Unscrew and remove the inner nuts and lockwashers securing the cables to the selector jaws.
7   Remove the cables from the control unit body.
8   Release the reverse light switch locknut and unscrew the reverse light switch.
9   Lift away the selector shaft retaining plate.
10 Carefully withdraw the three selector shafts taking precautions to collect the ball bearings and springs as they are released.
11 Lift away the three selector jaws.
12 Undo and remove the reverse selector stop retaining bolt and spring washer.
13 Lift away the reverse stop and its dowel.
14 Reassembly is the reverse sequence to dismantling but the following additional points should be noted;

   (a) *Apply a non-hardening sealer to the cable retaining plate before it is refitted to the body*
   (b) *Lubricate the jaws, shafts and lever with a graphite base grease once these parts have been refitted to the body*
   (c) *Adjust the cables as described in Section 16*

15 Remote control (rod gear change) – dismantling and reassembly

1   Rotate the gear change lever retaining dome from the body in an anti-clockwise direction so to release the bayonet fitting (Fig. 6.23).
2   Lift away the gear change lever assembly.
3   Undo and remove the six bolts securing the bottom cover to the remote control body.
4   Undo and remove the nyloc nut securing the steady rod to the body and lift away the steady rod.
5   Release the reverse light switch locknut and unscrew the reverse light switch.
6   Move the extension rod eye rearwards and remove the spring pin that retains the extension rod to the extension rod eye, using a small diameter parallel pin punch.
7   Now move the extension rod eye forwards and, again using a small diameter parallel pin punch, drift out the second spring pin.
8   The extension rod may now be withdrawn from the body.
9   Using a screwdriver, ease out the end plug from the rear end of the body.
10 Withdraw the support rod and remove the extension rod eye.
11 Using a pair of circlip pliers, or a small screwdriver, remove the circlip from the extension rod eye.
12 Lift away the ball-end bearing seat and then separate the bearing from the seat. If the later type of bottom cover is fitted, remove the baulk plate and spring from the cover.
13 Reassembly is the reverse sequence to dismantling, but the following two additional points should be noted:

   (a) *Always use new spring pins to retain the extension rod and support rod*
   (b) *The bottom cover should be fitted so that the reverse stop is towards the front of the remote control body*

16 Remote control change speed cables – adjustment

If difficulty is being experienced in selecting or changing gears, the cables must be checked for correct adjustment otherwise damage can be caused to the gears and synchronizers. Also, if the cables have been

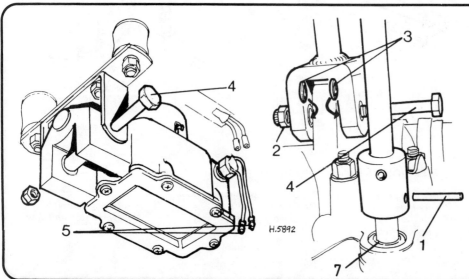

H.5892

Fig. 6.22 Rod gearchange assembly (Sec 13)

1   *Spring pin*
2   *Nyloc nut*
3   *Washers*
4   *Bolts*
5   *Reversing light switch connectors*
7   *Oil seal*

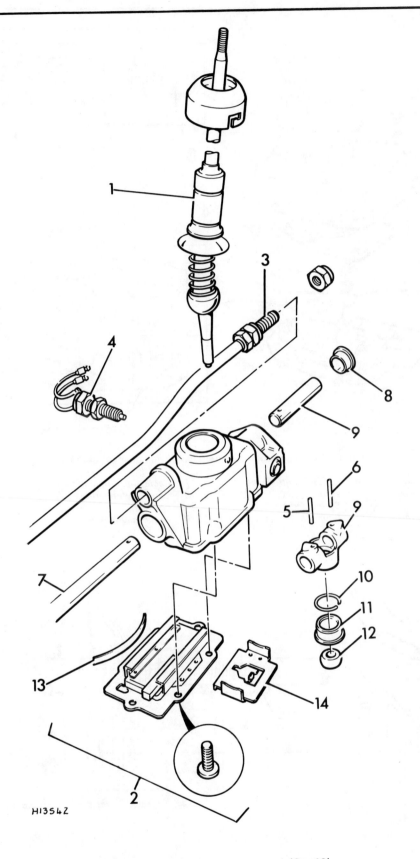

H1354Z

Fig. 6.23 Rod gearchange components (Sec 13)

1	Gearchange lever	5	Spring pin	9	Extension rod and eye	13	Baulk plate spring (later models)
2	Bottom cover	6	Spring pin	10	Circlip	
3	Steady rod	7	Extension rod	11	Ball end bearing seat	14	Baulk plate (later models)
4	Reverse light switch	8	End plug	12	Ball end bearing	

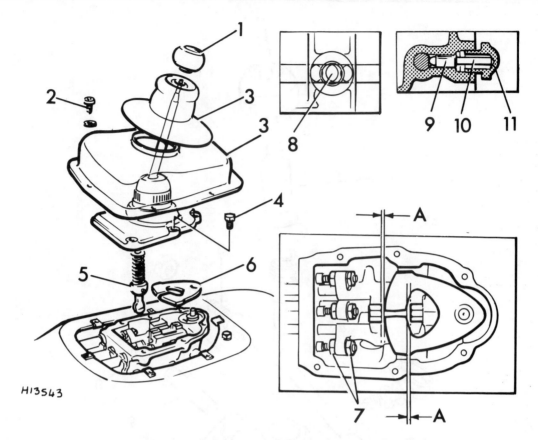

H13543

Fig. 6.24 Gear control adjustment (cable gearchange) (Sec 16)

1	Gearchange lever knob	4	Remote control cover	7	Cable adjustment nuts	10	Spacer rod
2	Cover securing screw and		securing bolt	8	Centre detent groove (neutral	11	Detent plug
	washer	5	Spring and washer		position)	A	Selector jaw alignment
3	Cover and rubber gaiter	6	Interlock	9	Detent plunger		

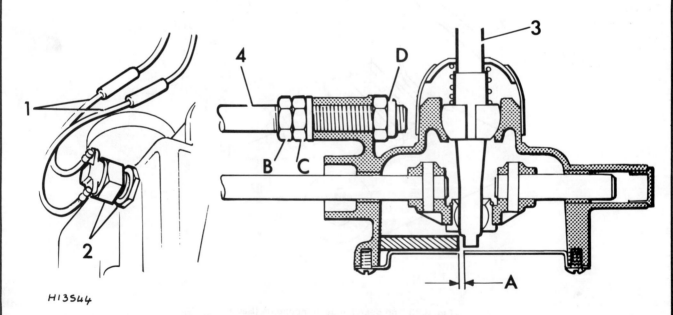

H13544

Fig. 6.25 Gear control adjustment (rod gearchange) (Sec 17)

1	Reverse light switch cables	3	Gearchange lever	A	0.03 inch	C	Rear locknut
2	Reverse light switch and	4	Steady rod	B	Front locknut	D	Adjustment locknut
	locknut						

detached from the transmission or remote control, they must be checked and reset as necessary.

1 Move the gear change lever to the neutral position (Fig. 6.24).
2 Unscrew the knob from the end of the gear change lever.
3 Move the carpeting away from the floor around the base of the gear change lever.
4 Undo and remove the six bolts and washers that secure the cover to the floor panel.
5 Ease the cover and rubber up the gear change lever and lift away.
6 Undo and remove the six bolts and spring washers that secure the control unit cover to the body. Lift away the cover.
7 Remove the plain washer and spring from the gear change lever.
8 Disengage the gear change lever from the interlock.
9 Using a spanner, slacken the cable adjustment nuts on each cable.
10 Remove the transmission unit detent plugs, springs and plungers for each of the selector rods.
11 Place each selector rod so that the neutral (centre) detent groove is exactly central in the end of the plunger bore. For this a torch and a mirror is useful.
12 Fit the plungers back in their respective bores.
13 Make up three metal rods 0·25 in (6·4 mm) diameter and 1·2 in (30 mm) long and fit one into each bore.
14 Remove the sealing washers from each detent plug. Note that three washers are used under the head of the first/second speed detent plug when it is finally refitted.
15 Screw in each plug in its respective bore finger tight so making sure that the selector rods are retained in their neutral positions.
16 Use the adjustment nuts attached to the cables in such a manner that the selector jaws align in the neutral position and also the interlock passes freely through the jaws with an equal clearance at each side.
17 Remove the detent plugs, recover the metal rods and refit the springs and plugs using the correct washers.
18 Reassemble the gear change lever and top cover to the body, refit the floor cover, carpeting, and finally the gear change lever knob.

17 Remote control (rod gear change) – adjustment

1 Disconnect the reversing light switch.
2 Slacken the locknut of the reversing light switch and partially unscrew the switch.
3 Move the gear change lever to its neutral position and unscrew the six screws from the bottom cover. Remove the cover.
4 Make a gauge bar 1·890 ± 0·005 in (47·90 ± 0·13 mm) long. This is to simulate the reverse stop, plus the gear lever clearance of 0·005 to 0·015 in (0·13 to 0·38 mm), dimension A in Fig. 6.25.
5 Position the gauge bar behind the front face of the housing and move the gear change lever in the neutral plane when it should just touch the end of the gauge bar.
6 If adjustment is necessary, slacken the steady rod nuts and adjust them until the gauge bar fit is correct.
7 Tighten the two innermost nuts on the steady rod until they lock against the faces of the housing. While holding the nut adjacent to the front face in a spanner to prevent it from rotating, tighten the lock nut against it.
8 Lubricate the following parts of the mechanism, using Shell Alvania R1 grease, or an equivalent.

   (a) The hemispherical fulcrum surface
   (b) The selector rod eye
   (c) The selector rod bearings
   (d) The upper surface of the bottom cover
   (e) The gear lever stub end stem, adjacent to the hole in the plastic cover
   (f) The helical spring

9 Remove the gauge bar and refit the bottom cover, making sure that the reverse stop is positioned towards the front of the remote control assembly.
10 Reconnect the reversing light switch and adjust it as described in Section 18.

18 Reversing light switch – adjustment

1 Move the gear change lever to the reverse gear position.
2 Slacken the reverse light switch locknut.
3 Switch on the ignition.
4 Slowly screw in the reverse light switch until the revese lights come on. Screw in the switch a further five hexagon flats.
5 Tighten the reverse light switch locknut, switch off the ignition and move the gear change lever to the neutral position.

19 Fault diagnosis – manual transmission

Symptom	Reasons(s)
Weak, or ineffective synchromesh	Baulk rings worn, or damaged Synchromesh dogs worn, or damaged
Jumps out of gear	Broken gearchange fork rod spring Broken or weak detent spring Selector fork rod worn Selector fork rod securing screw and locknut loose
Excessive noise	Lack of oil, or incorrect grade of oil Worn bearings Damaged, or excessively worn teeth on gears Worn laygear thrust washer, allowing excessive play

Part B AUTOMATIC TRANSMISSION

20 General description

The automatic transmission fitted to models covered by this manual incorporates a three element hydraulic torque converter, with a maximum torque conversion ratio of 2:1, coupled to a bevel gear train which provides four foward gears and reverse.

Power from the engine is transmitted from the crankshaft converter output gear to the transmission unit by a drive chain.

The final drive is transmitted from a drivegear to a conventional type differential unit which in turn transmits engine power through driveshafts employing constant velocity joints to the wheels.

The complete gear train assembly, including the reduction gear and differential unit runs below and parallel to the crankshaft and is housed in the transmission casing which also serves as the engine sump.

The sequence for checking the oil level, draining and refilling the engine/automatic transmission unit is basically identical to that for manual transmission models. The total oil capacity is larger, however. It is very important that no oil additives are used otherwise operation of the automatic transmission unit will be impaired.

The gear trains are controlled by a selector lever within a gated quadrant marked in seven positions. It is mounted centrally on the floor panel.

The reverse, neutral and drive positions are for normal automatic driving with the first, second, third and fourth positions used for manual operation or override as required by the driver.

This allows the system to be used as a fully automatic four speed transmission, from rest to maximum speed with the gears changing automatically according to throttle position and load. Should a lower ratio be required to obtain greater acceleration, an instant full throttle position (kick-down) on the accelerator immediately produces a ratio change.

Complete manual control of all four forward gears by the use of the selector lever provides rapid changes. However, it is very important that downward changes are effected at the correct road speeds otherwise serious damage may result to the automatic transmission unit. The second, third and top gears provide engine braking whether in automatic or manual control positions. In first gear a free wheel condition exists when decelerating.

Manual selection to third or second gear gives the engine braking and also allows the drive to stay in a particular lower gear to suit road conditions or when descending steep hills.

Due to the complexity of the automatic transmission unit, if performance is not up to standard, or overhaul is necessary, it is imperative that this be undertaken by the local BL garage who will have the equipment for accurate fault diagnosis and rectification. It is important that the fault is diagnosed before the unit is removed from the car.

The contents of the following Sections is therefore solely general and servicing information.

21 Automatic transmission – removal and refitting

1   The automatic transmission unit must be removed from the car with the engine and must then be separated from the engine.
2   Clean all dirt and oil from the outside of the engine and transmission and wipe dry.
3   Undo and remove the nine bolts and washers that secure the end cover to the converter housing. Note that the engine earth strap is retained by one of the bolts.
4   Undo and remove the four bolts and lock washers that secure the torque converter to the crankshaft.
5   A special tool (18G 1246) is necessary to remove the torque converter from the crankshaft. Unless the tool is used, there is a likelihood of the converter being damaged. For early models the tool number is 18G 1222.
6   Undo and remove the bolts and washers and lift away the torque converter housing, complete with the starter motor. Note the converter low pressure valve drain tube and the oil connection in the crankcase.
7   Withdraw the forward clutch oil feed pipe from the clutch input shaft and the transmission unit.
8   Unlock and remove the nut from the clutch input sprocket.
9   Withdraw the primary drive chain and sprockets from the engine and transmission unit.
10 Undo and remove the two bolts and washers securing the fuel pump to the side of the casing. Lift away the fuel pump, distance piece and joint washers.
11 Recover the fuel pump pushrod.
12 Remove the distributor (Chapter 4).
13 Withdraw the oil pump driveshaft from the distributor drive.
14 Remove the oil filter.
15 Remove the oil pressure relief valve from the transmission unit.
16 Unlock and then unscrew the starter inhibitor switch from the side of the transmission unit.
17 Undo and remove the two nuts and ten bolts that secure the engine and automatic transmission to each other.
18 Separate the engine and transmission.
19 Recover the O-ring from the oil feed joint between the crankcase and the transmission unit.
20 Refitting the transmission is the reverse of removal, but the following points should be noted.
21 Fit the torque converter housing with the bolts finger tight only at first. Temporarily fit the torque converter, then tighten the exposed housing bolts to the specified torque. Remove the converter and tighten the remaining bolts, then finally refit the converter.
22 The spigot of the crankshaft which enters the torque converter must be coated with Loctite grade HVX, or equivalent.
23 The oil pressure relief valve and oil filter must be fitted as described in Chapter 1.

22 Starter inhibitor switch – adjustment

1   Ensure that the selector cable is correctly adjusted (Section 24) and then move the selector lever to the N or P position.
2   Disconnect the two cable connections from the inhibitor switch and slacken the switch locknut.
3   Connect a test lamp and battery, or a continuity meter across the switch terminals.
4   Unscrew the switch from the transmission casing until the switch opens.
5   Screw the switch into the transmission casing until the switch contacts close. Screw the switch in a further one flat and tighten the locknut.
6   Check that the switch is ON only when the selector lever is in the P and N positions.
7   Disconnect the test equipment and reconnect the cables to the switch.
8   Select D, apply the hand and foot brakes firmly and hold the ignition key in the START position. Move the selector lever slowly through each gear position and note the lever position in relation to the selector gate when the engine can be started. This should only be possible when the lever is fully in the N and the P positions.
9   Stop the engine.
10 Select R and again hold the ignition key in the start position. Move the selector lever towards N and note the point at which the engine will start. This should not be possible until the lever is fully in the N position.
11 Repeat the operations of paragraph 10, except that this time move the lever towards P instead of N and check that starting is only possible when the lever is fully engaged in the P position. Any other condition is unacceptable and indicates that the inhibitor switch or selector cable adjustments are incorrect.

23 Reversing light switch – removal, refitting and adjustment

1   Disconnect the battery.
2   Note the terminals to which the two switch leads are connected and then disconnect them.
3   Slacken the locknut and unscrew the switch from the selector housing.
4   Refitting the switch is the reverse of removal, but the switch will need adjustment as follows.
5   Move the selector to the R position.
6   If not already disconnected, note the terminals to which the two switch leads are connected and then disconnect them.
7   Slacken the locknut, unless this has been done previously.
8   Connect a test light or meter across the switch terminals. Unscrew the switch from the selector lever mechanism until the switch contacts open.
9   Screw the switch into the selector housing until the switch just comes ON. Screw the switch in a further half turn and tighten the locknut.
10 Check that the light comes on only when the selector lever is in the R position.
11 Disconnect the test lamp, or meter and reconnect the wiring harness leads to the switch.

24 Selector cables – removal, refitting, checking and adjusting

1   For safety, disconnect the battery.
2   Move the gear selector lever to the D position.
3   Unscrew the knob from the control lever.
4   Carefully pull the nacelle from the selector mechanism.
5   Drain the engine/transmission oil.
6   Undo and remove the bolts and spring washers securing the access cover to transmission unit. Lift away the access cover and gasket.
7   Carefully pull the oil strainer off the end of the pick-up pipe.
8   Undo and remove the bolt and spring washer securing the park lock guide lug from the valve block.
9   Undo and remove the bolt and spring washer securing the control cable retainer to the rear of the automatic transmission unit.
10 Disconnect the control cable from the detent rod and the park lock

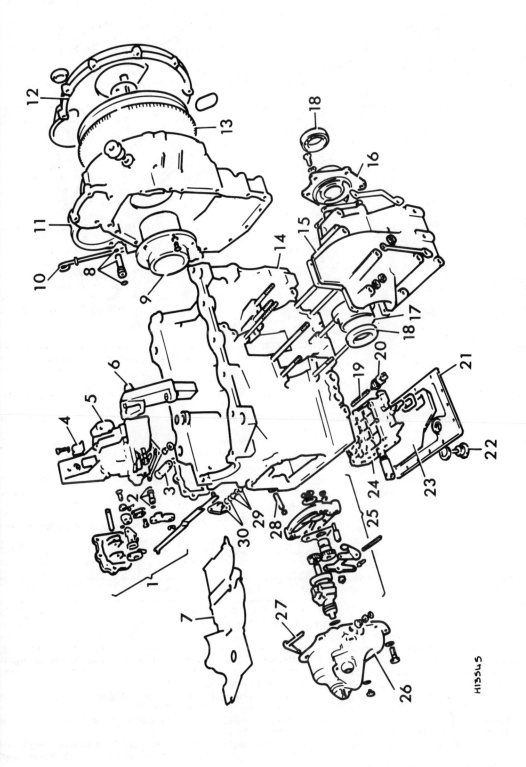

Fig. 6.26 Automatic transmission – internal components (Sec 21)

1 Park lock mechanism and mounting plate
2 Lubricant feed transfer tube and O-ring seals
3 Oil pressure relief valve
4 Retainer for forward clutch pipe
5 Oil pump
6 Oil pick-up
7 Baffle
8 Oil connection (valve) – engine to converter
9 Carrier for stator and low pressure valve
10 Oil dipstick
11 Converter housing
12 Converter cover
13 Converter
14 Transmission case
15 Differential housing
16 Differential end cover
17 Differential end sleeve
18 Oil seal
19 Inhibitor switch pushrod
20 Inhibitor switch
21 Access cover
22 Drain plug
23 Oil strainer
24 Valve block
25 Governor assembly
26 Governor housing
27 Lever and spindle
28 Reverse engagement valve
29 Reverse servo transfer tube retaining and O-ring
30 Reverse servo transfer tube retaining and O-ring

H13545

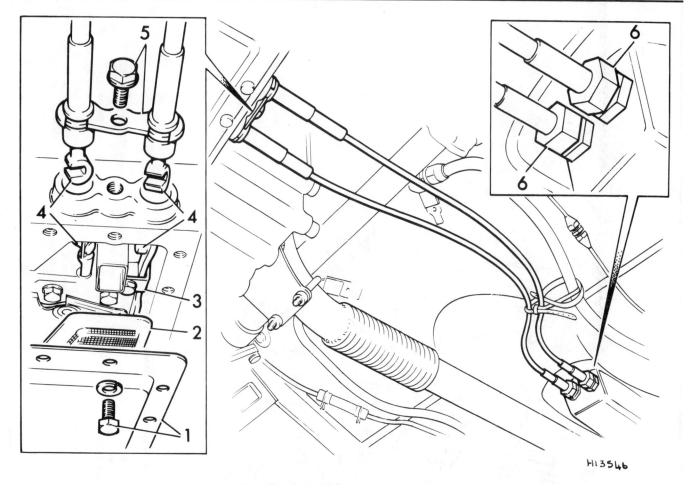

H13546

Fig. 6.27 Automatic transmission control cables (Sec 24)

1	Access cover and securing bolts	3	Park lock guide lug		and park lock		securing bolt
		4	Control cables, detent rod	5	Control cable retainer	6	Outer cable nuts
2	Oil strainer						

control rod.

11 The control cables may now be withdrawn from the transmission casing.

12 Unscrew the two outer cable securing nuts from the selector mechanism.

13 Unscrew the two inner cables from the selector assembly and remove the cable from the assembly.

14 To refit the cable first screw the two inner cables into their forks in the selector assembly. Make quite sure that each cable is fully screwed in. To allow for subsequent alignment at the transmission end, unscrew the cables one complete turn only.

15 Screw on the two outer cable nuts and tighten finger tight.

16 Refitting is now the reverse sequence to removal. It will be necessary to adjust the control cables as described later in this Section. Finally, check the adjustment of the reverse light and starter inhibitor switches as described in previous Sections.

17 To check the cable adjustment first move the selector lever to the P position and then release the brakes. Rock the car to-and-fro to ascertain if the parking pawl has engaged. If it has the park lock cable adjustment is correct.

18 Move the selector lever to the N position and start the engine.

19 Select the '1' position, release the brakes and drive the car forwards slowly. Once the car starts to move select N. The drive should now be disconnected.

20 Stop the car, select R and drive the car backwards. As the car begins to move backwards, select N. Disconnection of the drive should be felt as N is selected.

21 If the drive is felt to disconnect as N is selected from both directions, the gear selector cable adjustment is correct.

22 If any adjustment is necessary, stop the engine and move the selector lever to R.

23 Slacken the box nut on whichever cable requires adjustment. Hold the cable close to the box nut and pull the cable out from the selector mechanism.

24 When the cable cannot be pulled out any further, tighten the box nut.

25 Check the cable adjustment and also check that the engine can only be started when the selector lever is in the P or N position.

25 Kickdown linkage – adjustment

1 For this adjustment to be correctly achieved a special gauge tool kit is required. It has a BL part number '18G 1234'. If this tool is available follow the details given in this Section, otherwise leave to the local BL garage.

2 Check that the slots in the kickdown lever and its spindle are in line.

3 Remove the plug from the governor housing and screw in the spindle from the special tool until a stop is felt. The governor should now be fully collapsed.

4 Clean the setting holes in the bellcrank lever and transmission case.

5 Rotate the bellcrank lever anti-clockwise and insert the peg of the special tool through the lever and into the hole in the transmission case.

6 Using the special gauge check the length of the kickdown spring. If necessary, slacken the locknut and rotate the adjuster to set the spring length to match the gauge. Tighten the locknut again.

7 Check that the throttle is fully open. If not slacken the locknut on the carburettor rod and adjust the rod until the throttle is fully open and then retighten the locknut.

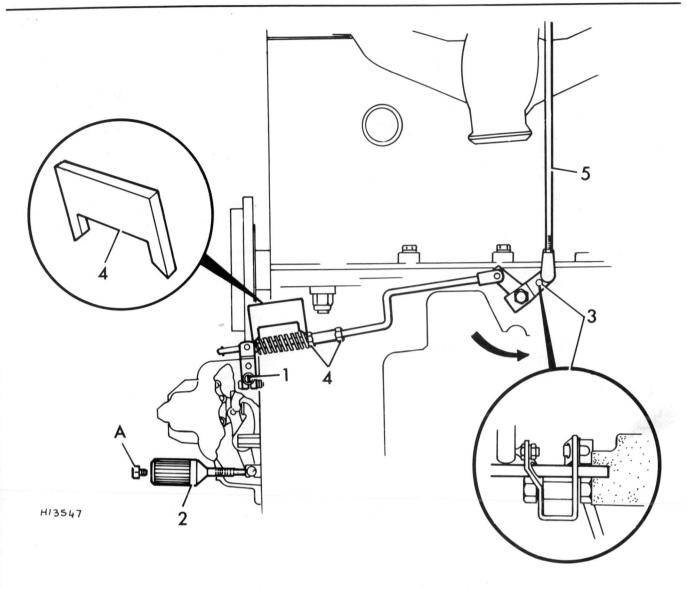

Fig. 6.28 Kickdown linkage adjustment (Sec 25)

1	Kickdown lever and spindle	lever and transmission	4 Gauge tool and spring	5 Carburettor rod
2	Tool spindle	case	adjuster	A Plug
3	Setting hole in bellcrank			

8 Remove the peg and spindle of the special tool. Refit the plug to the governor housing.

9 Make sure that the throttle is fully open when the throttle pedal is fully depressed. If necessary adjust the throttle cable.

10 The car should now be driven and the kickdown change speeds noted. These should occur at the following speeds when D is selected:

(a) 1 – 2 change at 26 to 33 mph (42 to 53 kph)
(b) 2 – 3 change at 37 to 43 mph (60 to 70 kph)
(c) 3 – 4 change at 57 to 65 mph (92 to 105 kph)

11 If the gearchanges occur at low speeds, slacken the locknut and rotate the adjuster to increase the kickdown spring load. Retighten the locknut.

12 If the gearchanges occur at high speeds, slacken the locknut and rotate the adjuster to decrease the kickdown spring load. Retighten the locknut.

26 Selector lever mechanism – removal and refitting

1 Disconnect the battery.

2 Remove the selector cables (Section 24).
3 Remove the reversing light switch (Section 23).
4 Slacken the locknut and unscrew and remove the control knob and its locknut from the selector lever (Fig. 6.29).
5 Carefully remove the nacelle from the hand selector mechanism.
6 Detach the nacelle light wiring from the wiring harness at the snap connectors inside the car (Fig. 6.30).
7 Undo and remove the six screws and nuts which secure the selector mechanism to the floor panel and lower the mechanism down beneath the car.
8 Unclip and remove the bulb holders and wiring from the selector mechanism.
9 Refitting the selector mechanism is the reverse of removal.

27 Selector mechanism – dismantling and reassembly

1 Remove the selector mechanism from the car (Section 26)
2 Undo the two cable connectors from the selector mechanism.
3 Undo and remove the set bolt which secures the selector mechanism to its housing and lift away the selector mechanism.
4 Carefully remove the E-clip and withdraw the forward pin.

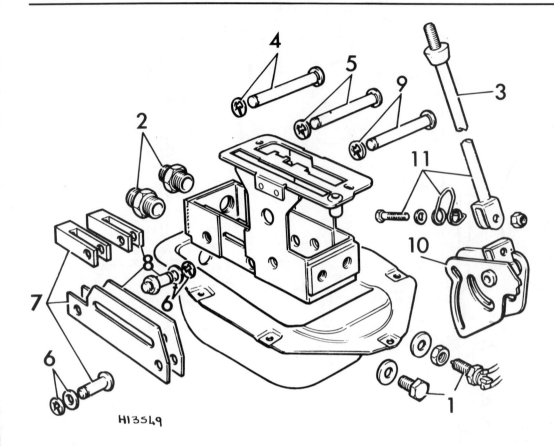

**Fig. 6.29 Selector
mechanism – exploded view
(Sec 26)**

1   *Reverse light switch and
    screw*
2   *Connectors*
3   *Knob locknut*
4   *E-clip and forward pin*
5   *E-clip and centre pin*
6   *E-clip and short pin*
7   *Left-hand fork assembly*
8   *Right-hand fork assembly*
9   *E-clip and actuator pivot
    pin*
10 *Actuator assembly*
11 *Selector lever and spring
    assembly*

H13549

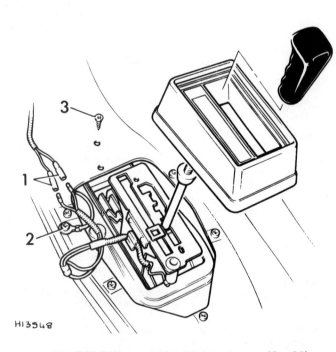

H13548

Fig. 6.30 Selector mechanism attachments (Sec 26)

1   *Electrical cable snap connectors*
2   *Earth cable securing screw*
3   *Mechanism securing screw*

5   Carefully remove the E-clip and withdraw the centre pin.
6   Carefully remove the E-clip and washer from the outside of each of
the two short pins.
7   Move the left-hand fork to the bottom of its actuating slot and
remove the pin, fork and plate.
8   Move the right-hand fork to the top of its actuating slot and
remove the pin, fork and plate.
9   Carefully remove the E-clip and withdraw the actuator pivot pin.
10 Remove the actuator assembly from the frame.
11 Undo and remove the bolt and separate the spring from the
actuator.
12 Reassembly of the selector lever assembly is the reverse of
removal. It is recommended that new E-clips are used for reassembly.
13 Lubricate all sliding and moving surfaces with Duckhams Laminol
O grease, or its equivalent.

28 Fault diagnosis – automatic transmission

A complete fault diagnosis requires the use of special test equipment, but before seeking expert advice the following items should be
checked.

(a) *engine oil level*
(b) *engine idle speed*
(c) *adjustment of selector lever cables, inhibitor switch and
    kickdown linkage*
(d) *throttle is fully open when accelerator pedal is fully depressed*

If these items are correct and the fault persists, it is likely that the
transmission will need to be removed from the vehicle, but this should
not be done before seeking specialist advice.

Chapter 7 Driveshafts and universal joints

Contents

Specifications

Inner joint
Type
    Early . . . .   Hooke's joint with needle rollers
    Later . . . .   Constant velocity with ball cage
Lubricant . . . .   Shell Tivella 'A' grease

Outer joint
Type . . . .   Constant velocity with ball cage
Lubricant . . . .   Duckhams Bentone Grease Q5795

Torque wrench settings

	lbf ft	kgf m
Hub nut	200	27.6
Balljoint nuts	25	3.4
Brake caliper to hub bolts	40 to 50	5.5 to 6.9

1 General description

Drive is transmitted from the differential unit to the front wheels by two driveshafts which have universal joints at each of their ends to permit vertical and radial movement of the front wheels.

The outer universal joints are of the constant velocity type with the driveshaft splined to the inner part of the coupling which is a cage containing six steel balls. The outer part of the coupling, which is integral with the wheel axle, has curved grooves machined parallel to the axis of the shaft, on its inside. The steel balls of the cage locate in the grooves in the outer part of the coupling. The joint is packed with a special grease and the assembly is enclosed in a rubber boot.

The inner universal joints on early models consist of a pair of needle roller bearings, located in bearing caps which fit into a tubular housing. Like the outer joints, the inner joints are packed with special grease and are enclosed in a rubber boot. The inner universal joints on later models are of the constant velocity type already described.

2 Hub and driveshaft – removal and refitting

1   Chock the rear wheels, apply the handbrake, remove the front wheel trims, and slacken the wheel nuts.
2   Jack up the front of the car and support on firmly based axle stands located under the main longitudinal members. Remove the wheels nuts and lift away the roadwheel.
3   Extract the split pin locking the hub nut. Undo and remove the hub nut (Fig. 7.1).
4   Using a jack, or other suitable means, support the weight of the lower suspension arm.
5   Undo and remove the two upper swivel balljoint securing bolts. Disengage the brake hydraulic pipe bracket (Fig. 7.2).
6   Undo and remove the two bolts and washers securing the brake caliper unit, lift it clear and, using some string or wire, support its weight away from the disc, so that the flexible hose is not strained.
7   Using a large universal puller and suitable thrust pad, pull the disc and driving flange assembly from the hub.

8   Undo and remove the nut securing the steering arm swivel balljoint and using a universal balljoint separator, detach the balljoint from the steering arm.
9   Undo and remove the lower suspension arm balljoint securing bolts.
10 Using the universal puller and suitable thrust pad, carefully pull the hub assembly from the driveshaft.
11 Refer to Fig. 7.4 and using a metal lever as shown, carefully detach the driveshaft from the differential and lift away the complete driveshaft assembly.
12 Refitting the hub and driveshaft is the reverse sequence to removal, but the content of the following paragraphs should be noted.
13 Make sure that the chamfers on the end of the shaft and the shaft splines are free from damage or burrs before entering the shaft into the differential unit.
14 Should any difficulty be found in engaging the shaft into the differential circlip, fit a 3.5 in (90 mm) diameter worm drive clip round the pot joint housing and applying an even and sustained pressure by hand onto the shaft, use a drift located on the worm drive clip to drive the shaft into its full engagement position.
15 Enter the end of the driveshaft into the hub bearing and then draw the shaft through as far as possible. If no means of pulling in the shaft can be found with parts already to hand, there is a special tool, Part No 18G 1104 A (Fig. 7.5). Refer also to Chapter 9 Section 12.

3 Ball type universal joint – dismantling, inspection and overhaul

There is little point in dismantling the outer constant velocity joints if they are known to be badly worn. In this case it is better to remove the old joint from the shaft and fit a new unit.

1   Remove the driveshaft from the car and separate it from the front hub as described in Section 2 of this Chapter. Wire the driveshaft and pot housing to stop the joint separating.
2   Thoroughly clean the exterior of the driveshaft and rubber gaiter.
3   Mount the driveshaft vertically in between soft faces in a vice with the joint facing outwards. Using a screwdriver, prise off the large

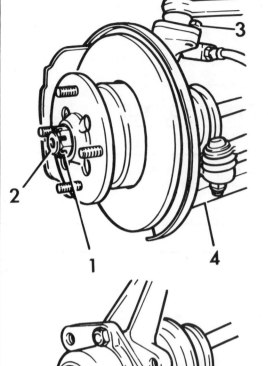
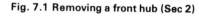
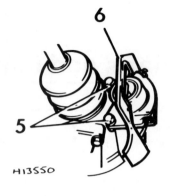

Fig. 7.1 Removing a front hub (Sec 2)

1   Split pin
2   Hub nut
3   Upper balljoint bolts
4   Lower suspension arm
5   Brake caliper bolts
6   Brake caliper

H13550

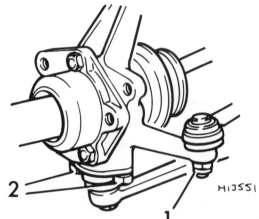

Fig. 7.2 Steering arm and lower suspension arm connections (Sec 2)

1   Balljoint nut   2   Lower balljoint nuts

H13551

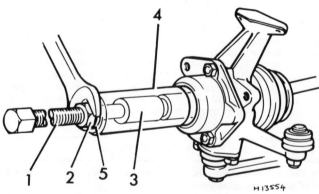

H13552

Fig. 7.3 Tool for levering the driveshaft from the differential (Sec 2)

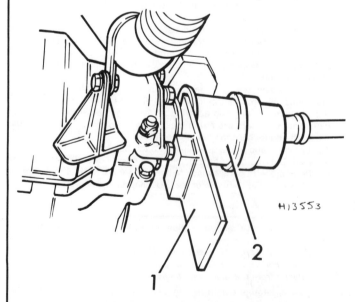

H13553

Fig. 7.4 Removing the driveshaft (Sec 2)

1   Special tool   2   Joint housing

H13554

Fig. 7.5 Drawing the driveshaft through the hub bearing (Sec 2)

1   Long bolt   4   Metal tube
2   Hexagon nut   5   Washer
3   Tubular nut

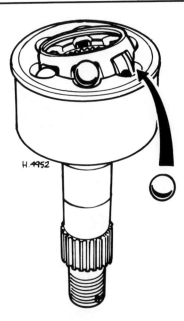

Fig. 7.6 Position of cage for removal of balls (Sec 3)

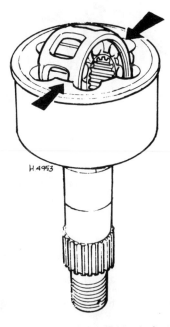

Fig. 7.7 Position of cage for removal of cage (Sec 3)

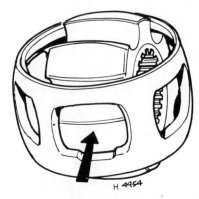

Fig. 7.8 Position of cage for removal of inner track (Sec 3)

diameter aluminium gaiter retaining ring towards the stub axle. Also prise off the small diameter aluminium ring and discard the rings. Turn back the gaiter and cut it off. A new gaiter and ring will be required for reassembly.

4   Before the joint can be dismantled it must be removed from the driveshaft. This is easily done by firmly tapping the outer edge of the constant velocity joint with a hide or plastic headed hammer. Alternatively, use a copper drift located on the inner member and give the drift a sharp blow. Whichever method is used, the inner spring ring will be contracted so releasing the joint from the shaft. Be sure to make mating marks on the shaft and on the joint before removing the joint and line the marks up when the joint is refitted to the shaft.

5   Ease off the round section spring ring and, when reassembling, use the new one supplied in the service kit.

6   Mark the position of the inner and outer races with a dab of paint, so that upon reassembly the mated parts can be correctly refitted.

7   Refer to Fig. 7.6 and tilt the inner race until one ball bearing is released. Repeat this operation easing out each ball bearing in turn, using a small screwdriver.

8   Manipulate the cage until the special elongated slot coincides with the lands of the bellhousing. Drop one of the lands into the slot and lift out the cage and race assembly (Fig. 7.7).

9   Turn the inner race at right angles to the cage and in line with the elongated slot. Drop one land into the slot and withdraw the inner race out from the chamfered end of the cage (Fig. 7.8).

10   Thoroughly clean all component parts of the joint by washing in paraffin.

11   Examine each ball bearing in turn for cracks, flat spots or signs of the surface pitting. Check the inner and outer tracks for widening which will cause the ball bearings to be a loose fit. This, together with excessive wear in the ball cage, will lead to the characteristic 'knocking' on full lock. The cage, which fits between the inner and outer races, must be examined for wear in the ball cage windows and for cracks which are likely to develop across the narrower portions between the outer rims and the holes for the ball bearings. If wear is excessive then all parts must be renewed as a matched set.

12   To reassemble, first ensure that all parts are perfectly clean and then lubricate with two packs of Duckhams Bentone Grease, No Q5795 which is supplied under part number AKD1457. Do not, under any circumstances, use any other grease. Provided that all parts have been cleaned and well lubricated, they should fit together easily without force.

13   Refit the inner race into the cage by manipulating one of the lands into the elongated slot in the cage. Insert the cage and inner race assembly into the balljoint by fitting one of the elongated slots over one of the lands in the outer race. Rotate the inner race to line up with the bellhousing in its original, previously marked position.

14   Taking care not to lose the position, tilt the cage until one ball bearing can be inserted into a slot. Repeat this procedure until all six ball bearings are in their correct positions. Ensure that the inner race moves freely in the bellhousing throughout its movement range, taking care that the ball bearings do not fall out.

15   Using the remainder of the special grease, pack the joint evenly. Smear the inside of a new rubber boot with the special grease and fit the rubber boot and a new circlip to the end of the shaft.

16   Hold the shaft in a vice and locate the inner race on the splines. By pressing the constant velocity joint against the circlip, position the ring centrally and contract it in the chamber in the inner race leading edge with two screwdrivers. Using a soft faced hammer, sharply tap the end of the stub shaft to compress the ring and then tap the complete assembly onto the driveshaft. Double check that the shaft is fully engaged and the circlip fully locked against the inner race.

17   Ease the rubber boot over the constant velocity joint and ensure the moulded edges of the boot are seating correctly in the retaining groove of the shaft and bellhousing. Secure in position with the large and small clips. Check that the tab of the large clip is pulled away from the direction of rotation as shown in Fig. 7.9. Do not use wire instead of the proper clips, because wire will damage the rubber boot and cause premature failure of the joint.

---

4   Roller type universal joint – dismantling, inspection and overhaul

1   Carefully remove the wire or clip that secures the pot joint rubber boot and roll back the rubber boot.

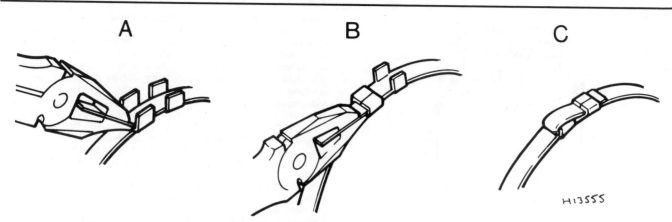

A   B   C

H13555

Fig. 7.9 Method of fitting rubber boot clips (Sec 3)

2   With a scriber, or file, mark the shaft and pot housing so that they may be refitted in their original positions and draw the shaft from the pot housing.
3   Lift away the bearing caps from the driveshaft cross piece and lift away the needle bearings.
4   If the rubber boot is to be renewed, it may be cut off the shaft, otherwise, leave it where it is.
5   Wash all parts in paraffin and wipe dry with a clean lint-free rag.
6   Examine the bearings and bearing surfaces of the pot joint for damage, grooving or excessive wear. If evident, new parts must be obtained.
7   Inspect the rubber boot for signs of cuts, splits or perishing. If evident, a new rubber boot must be obtained as if dirt finds its way into the joint, the joint will fail prematurely.
8   Reassembly is the reverse sequence to removal. All components must be smeared with Shell Tivella 'A' grease, Part Number AKF 1950, which contains the correct quantity of 120 cc for smearing the parts and packing one joint.
9   Position the rubber boot over the joint, with the ribs registering in the groove of the shaft and over the ridge of the joint housing.

5   Constant velocity joint gaiter – removal and refitting

1   At regular intervals the rubber boots which protect the outer universal joints should be inspected for damage. If they are torn, split, or damaged, they must be renewed as soon as possible, as the entry of road dust, grit, or water will lead to rapid deterioration of the ball bearings in the joint.
2   Should a new rubber boot be necessary, it requires the removal of the outer driveshaft and front hub assembly, as described in Section 2.
3   Mount the outer driveshaft centrally in a bench vice fitted with soft jaws.
4   Using a screwdriver, prise off the larger diameter aluminium gaiter retaining ring towards the stub axle.
5   Prise off the small diameter aluminium ring, again using a screwdriver. Turn back the gaiter and if a new gaiter is to be fitted, cut the old one off and discard it.
6   Before a new rubber gaiter may be fitted, the joint must be separated from the driveshaft. This is done by firmly tapping the outer edge of the constant velocity joint with a hide, or plastic headed hammer. Alternatively, use a copper drift located on the inner member and give the drift a sharp blow. Whichever method is used, the inner spring will be contracted, releasing the joint from the shaft.
7   Ease off the round section spring ring and when reassembling, use the new one supplied in the service kit.
8   Wipe the splines clean with a lint-free rag and smear with some Duckhams Bentone Grease, Number Q5795 which is supplied under part number AKD1457. Do not use any other grease.
9   Slide the new gaiter, small end first, onto the shaft, taking care not

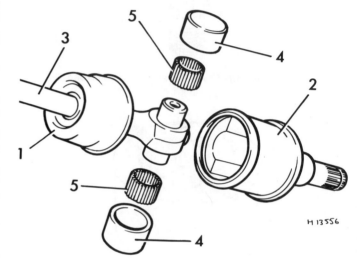

H13556

Fig. 7.10 Roller type universal joint components (Sec 4)

1	Rubber boot	4	Bearing cap
2	Joint housing	5	Needle rollers
3	Driveshaft		

to nick it on the circlips. Push it down the shaft, clear of the joint.
10 The constant velocity joint must contain 1 ounce of Duckhams Bentone Grease, so if it has not been dismantled and has not lost any through a damaged gaiter, add a little through the central splined hole. If the joint has lost grease the full quantity of two packs must be inserted.
11 Mount the joint assembly vertically in a bench vice fitted with soft jaws.
12 By pressing the constant velocity joint against the circlip, position the ring centrally and compress it into the chamfer in the inner race leading edge, with two screwdrivers. Using a soft faced hammer, sharply tap the end of the stub shaft to compress the ring and then tap the complete assembly on to the drive shaft. Double check that the shaft is fully engaged and the circlip fully locked against the inner race.
13 Ease the rubber boot over the constant velocity joint and ensure the moulded edges of the boot are seating correctly in the retaining groove of the shaft and bellhousing. Secure in position with the large and small clips. Check that the tab of the large clip is pulled away from the direction of rotation as shown in Fig. 7.9. Do not use wire instead of the proper clips, because wire will damage the rubber boot and cause premature failure of the joint.

Chapter 8 Final drive

Contents

Specifications

Type	Helical gears and differential

Ratio

1500	3.94:1
1750	
Manual transmission models	3.65:1
Automatic transmission models	3.80:1

Torque wrench settings

	lbf ft	kgf m
Differential cover		
$\frac{5}{16}$ in nuts	17 to 19	2.4 to 2.6
$\frac{3}{8}$ in nuts	24 to 26	3.0 to 3.6
Studs	6	0.8
Differential end cover set screws	18	2.5
Final drive pinion nut	150	20.7
Crownwheel bolts	40 to 50	5.5 to 7

1 General description

The differential unit is located on the bulkhead side of the combined engine and transmission unit. It is held in place by nuts and
studs. The crownwheel, or drivegear, together with the differential
gears, are mounted in the differential unit. The drive pinion is mounted
on the third motion shaft.

All repairs can be carried out to the component parts of the
differential unit only after the engine/transmission unit has been
removed from the car. If it is wished to attend to the pinion, it will be
necessary to separate the transmission casing from the engine.

The differential housing and gearbox casings are machined as a
matched pair when assembled so that they can only be removed as a
pair, not separately. Also the final drive gear and pinion are mated and
must be changed as a pair and not as individual gears.

2 Differential unit (manual transmission) – removal and refitting

1   Remove the engine and transmission assembly as described in
Chapter 1.
2   Remove the bolts and spring washers holding the differential side
covers in position on the transmission and differential housing. Mark
the side covers so that they may be refitted in their original positions
and then remove them (photo). Recover any shims fitted under the
left-hand side cover (Fig. 8.2).
3   Bend back the differential housing securing nut locking tabs and
remove the eight nuts and tab washers.
4   Using a soft faced hammer, carefully tap the differential housing
from the securing studs. Lift away the housing (photo).
5   Remove the collar retaining the interlock spool (rod gear change
only) and withdraw the complete differential assembly (photo).
6   If the side covers were showing signs of oil leaks, the oil seals
should be drifted out and new ones fitted with the lips facing inwards.
Lubricate the new seals before refitting.

2.2 Removing a side cover

7   Remove the selector shaft oil seal from the differential housing if it
shows signs of leaking, lubricate the new seal with oil and drift it in
(rod gear change only).
8   To refit, first fit the locating collar into the groove of the interlock
speed (rod gear change models only).
9   Place the differential assembly into the transmission casing with
the assembly positioned slightly towards the right-hand side.
10 Refit the differential housing, fit new tab washers and tighten the
nuts sufficiently tight to hold the bearings firmly, yet not so tight as to
prevent the differential from being moved laterally when the right-
hand cover is refitted.

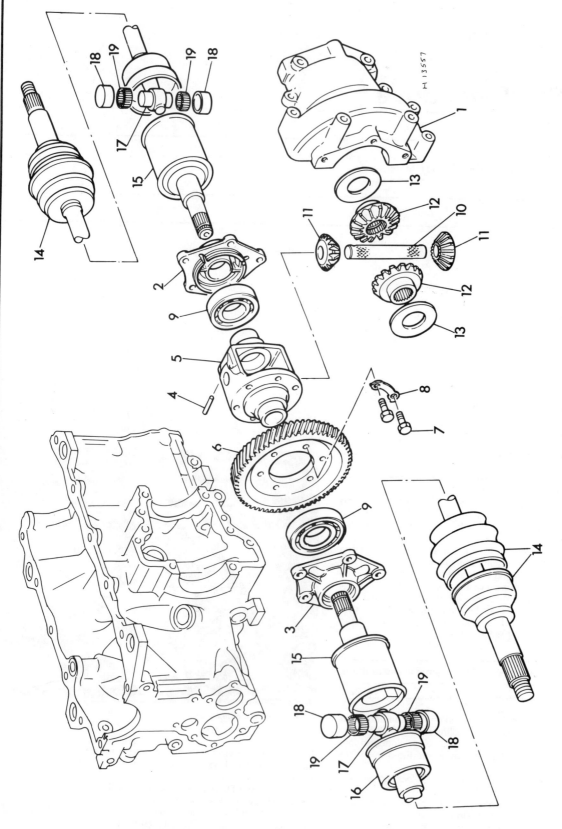

Fig. 8.1 Final drive assembly components (Sec 1)

1 Differential housing
2 Differential side cover — RH
3 Differential side cover — LH
4 Roll pin for differential pin
5 Differential cage

6 Crownwheel
7 Crownwheel securing bolt
8 Bolt lockwasher
9 Differential carrier bearing
10 Differential pin

11 Differential pinion
12 Differential gear
13 Thrustwasher
14 Constant velocity joint

15 Pot joint housing
16 Pot joint boot
17 Shaft
18 Bearing cap
19 Needle bearing

early models

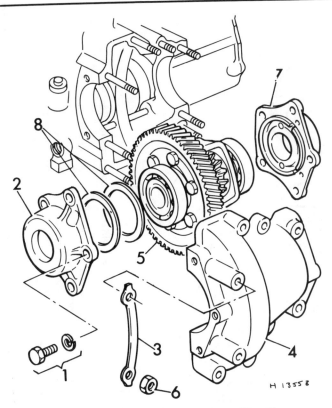

2.4 Removing the differential housing

Fig. 8.2 Drive housing components (Sec 2)

1   Differential side cover
    securing bolt and
    spring washer
2   LH differential side cover
3   Tab washer
4   Differential unit housing

5   Final drive and differential
    unit
6   Differential unit housing
    securing nut
7   RH differential sidecover
8   Adjustment shims

11 Fit a new right-hand cover gasket and then refit the cover. Tighten the five securing bolts and spring washers to the specified torque.
12 Using a soft metal drift located on the outer track of the left-hand bearing, tap the differential to ensure the right-hand bearing is in full contact with the right-hand side cover (Fig. 8.4).
13 Fit the left-hand side cover, leaving out the gasket. Tighten the cover bolts progressively in a diagonal manner to ensure full contact of the cover spigot with the bearing, without applying any pre-load.
14 Using a feeler gauge, accurately determine the gap between the cover flange and the differential housing at not less than three points, to ensure even tightness of the cover bolts.
15 If uneven readings are obtained in the tested positions, adjust the tightness of the bolts until the same reading is ontained. This will eliminate any distortion in the cover flange.
16 Should a condition arise whereby there is no gap between the flange and the casing, remove the cover and add a known thickness of shims between the cover and bearing to produce a clearance. The thickness of shims used, must be included in the calculation of the pre-load shim requirementt.
17 The compressed thickness of the new side cover gasket is 0.008 in (0.203 mm) and the required pre-load is 0.001 to 0.002 in (0.025 to 0.05 mm) The clearance between the cover flange and casing must be adjusted with shims to 0.009 to 0.010 in (0.229 to 0.254 mm).
18 To act as a guide the following sample calculation is given:

Measured clearance	0.007 in (0.178 mm)
Gasket compressed thickness	0.008 in (0.203 mm)
Required pre-load	0.001 to 0.002 in (0.025 to 0.05 mm)
Shim thickness required	0.002 in (0.05 mm)

Note: Shims are available in 0.002 and 0.003 in (0.05 and 0.076 mm) thickness.
19 Tighten the differential housing nuts to the specified torque and lock the nuts, by bending over the lock tabs.

2.5 Removing the differential assembly

3   Differential unit – dismantling and reassembly

1   Using a good quality three legged puller and suitable thrust block, draw each differential carrier bearing from the differential carrier. This is only necessary, of course, if the bearings are worn and require renewal.
2   With a scriber, or file, mark the crownwheel and differential cage so that they can be refitted in their original positions (Fig. 8.3).
3   Release the lockwasher tabs and undo and remove the eight crownwheel securing bolts. Lift away the crownwheel.
4   Using a small diameter pin punch, carefully tap out the two roll pins that retain the differential pinion pin.
5   With a soft metal drift, remove the pinion pin from the differential carrier.
6   Push the differential pinions and concave thrust washers around and remove the case.
7   Ease the two side gears and thrust washers towards the centre of the differential case and lift away through the openings in the case.
8   Clean all the removed parts in paraffin and dry. Examine the gears for wear and chipped or damaged teeth, the thrust washers for wear or cracking and the pinion pin for wear or loose fit in the differential housing.
9   If there was excessive noise in the drive or overrun conditions, this may be caused by excessive backlash between the differential pinions

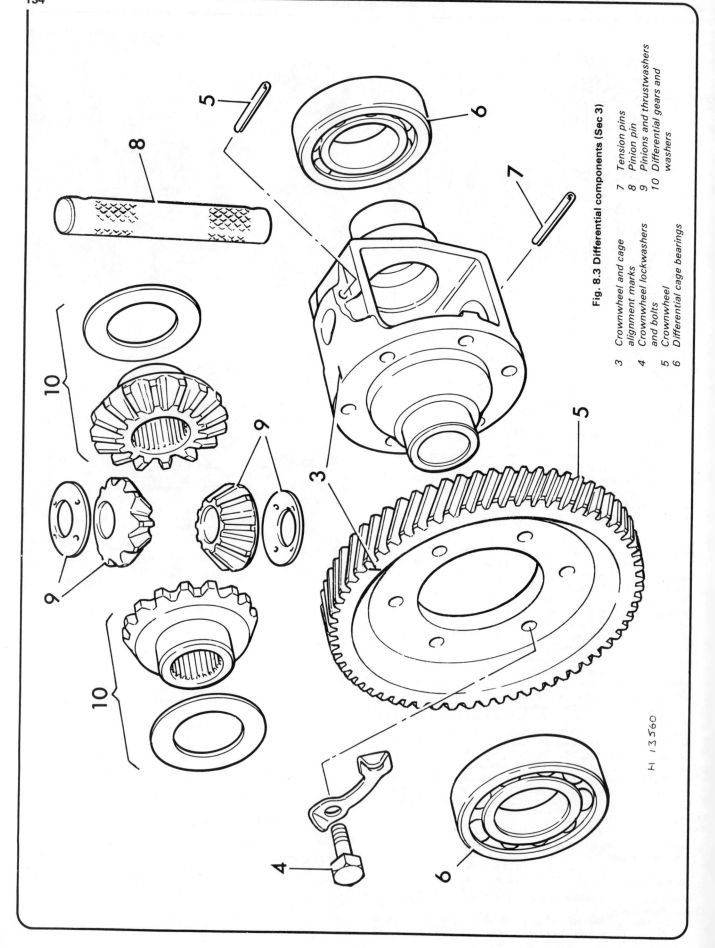

Fig. 8.3 Differential components (Sec 3)

3 Crownwheel and cage alignment marks
4 Crownwheel lockwashers and bolts
5 Crownwheel
6 Differential cage bearings
7 Tension pins
8 Pinion pin
9 Pinions and thrustwashers
10 Differential gears and washers

H 13560

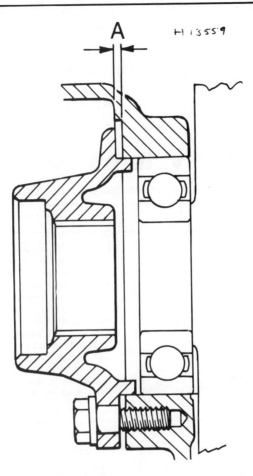

Fig. 8.4 Differential housing to cover gap (Sec 2)

Use feeler gauges to measure dimension A

and differential gears. Fit new pinions and/or differential gear thrust washers.

10 Check the bearings for side play and general wear. Inspect the inner tracks for signs of movement on their mounting, or the outer tracks rotating in their housing, and if either of the conditions exists, fit new parts.

11 If new gears are to be fitted, carefully drift in new circlips using a piece of suitable diameter rod.

12 Reassembly is the reverse sequence to dismantling. It should be noted that the large diameter carrier bearing is fitted to the crownwheel side of the differential assembly, with its 'thrust' marking facing outwards.

Chapter 9 Braking system

For modifications, and information applicable to later models, see Supplement at end of manual

Contents

Specifications

Type

Disc front, drum rear with servo assistance.
Handbrake mechanical to rear wheels

Disc brakes

Disc diameter . . . . 9.68 in (246 mm)
Pad area (total) . . . . 16 in² (103 cm²)
Swept area (total) . . . . 182 in² (1174 cm²)
Minimum pad friction material thickness . . . . 0.06 in (1.6 mm)

Drum brakes

Drum diameter . . . . 8 in (203 mm)
Lining dimensions . . . . 1.5 x 6.25 in (38 x 158.7 mm)
Swept area (total) . . . . 76 in² (490 cm²)
Wheel cylinder diameter . . . . 0.75 in (19 mm)

Vacuum servo unit type

Girling 'Super Vac'

Torque wrench settings

	lbf ft	kgf m
Brake caliper to hub	40 to 50	5.5 to 6.9
Disc to driving flange	38 to 45	5.2 to 6.2
Shield to swivel hub	17 to 25	2.3 to 3.4
Bleed screw	4 to 6	0.5 to 0.8
Brake adjuster nut	4 to 6	0.5 to 0.8
Master cylinder to servo	17	2.3
Tandem master cylinder – tipping valve securing nut	35 to 45	4.8 to 6.2
Pressure reducing valve – end plug	25 to 35	3.5 to 4.8
Pressure reducing valve – piston locknut	3 to 4	0.4 to 0.55
P D W A valve – electrical switch	2 to 2.5	0.28 to 0.35
P D W A valve – manual reset type		
End plugs	20	2.8
Switch	2.5	0.35
P D W A valve – self reset type		
Adaptor	38	5.2
Switch	3	0.5
Roadwheel nuts	46	6.2
Hub nuts (align to next hole)		
Front	200	27.6
Rear	60	8.3

1 General description

Disc brakes are fitted to the front wheels, and drum brakes to the rear. All are operated under servo assistance from the brake pedal, this being connected to the master cylinder and servo assembly mounted on the bulkhead.

The front brakes are of rotating disc and sliding yoke caliper design, whilst the rear brakes are of the internal expanding, single leading shoe type and operated by either the hand or foot brake.

The front brake disc is secured to the driving flange of the hub and the caliper mounted on the steering swivel. On the inner disc face side of the caliper is a single hydraulic cylinder in which are placed two outward facing pistons. One piston is in contact with a friction pad which, in turn, is in contact with one face of the disc and the second piston presses on a yoke which transmits the pressure to a second pad on contact with the outer face of the disc. Hydraulic fluid is able to pass to the cavity between the two pistons.

The rear brakes have one cylinder operating two shoes. Attached to each of the rear wheel operating cylinders is a mechanical expander, operated by the handbrake lever through a cable, which runs from the brake lever to the backplate brake levers. This provides an independent means of rear brake application.

The rear brakes have to be adjusted periodically to compensate for wear in the linings, but the front disc brakes are adjusted automatically. It is not normal to have to adjust the handbrake system, as its efficiency is largely dependent on the condition of the brake linings and the adjustment of the brake shoes. The handbrake can, however, be adjusted separately to the footbrake operated hydraulic system.

The hydraulic brake functions in the following manner: On application of the brake pedal, hydraulic fluid under pressure is pushed from the master cylinder to the brake operating cylinders at each wheel by means of a four-way union, steel pipes and flexible hoses.

A pressure regulating valve, located next to one of the radius arms, is fitted into the pipe line leading to the rear brakes, so that under normal light brake action, the valve does not operate and brake fluid passes freely to the rear brake wheel cylinders. Under heavy braking action, the valve comes into operation and limits the pressure to the rear brakes, so minimizing the possibility of rear wheel lock.

The mechanically operated stop light switch is secured to the pedal mounting plate inside the car and is operated by an extension of the brake pedal arm.

2 Rear brakes – adjustment

1   Jack up the rear of the car and place on firmly based stands. Also chock the front wheels to ensure that the car cannot roll backwards or forwards.

2   Release the handbrake and, working under the car, locate the adjuster. The brakes are adjusted by turning the square headed adjuster (photo). Always use a square headed brake adjuster spanner, as the edges of the adjuster are easily burred if an adjustable wrench or open ended spanner is used.

3   Turn the adjuster in a clockwise direction, when viewed from the centre of the car, until the brake shoes lock the wheel. Turn the adjuster back until the wheel is free to rotate without the shoes rubbing.

4   Spin the wheel and apply the brakes hard to centralise the shoes. Re-check that it is not possible to turn the adjuster screw further, without locking the wheel.

5   A rubbing noise when the wheel is spun is usually due to dust on the brake drum and shoe lining. If there is no obvious slowing down of the wheel due to brake binding, there is no need to slacken off the adjusters until the noise disappears. It is better to remove the drum and clean, taking care not to inhale any dust.

6   Repeat this process for the other brake drum. Apply a little graphite penetrating oil to the adjuster threads to check any possibility of seizure by rusting.

3 Hydraulic system – bleeding

Whenever the brake hydraulic system has been overhauled, a part renewed, or the level in the reservoir becomes too low, air will have

2.2 Adjusting the rear brakes

entered the system necessitating its bleeding. During the operation, the level of hydraulic fluid in the reservoir should not be allowed to fall below half full, otherwise air will be drawn in again.

1   Obtain a clean and dry glass jam jar, plastic tubing at least fifteen inches long and of suitable diameter to fit tightly over the bleed screw, and a supply of the specified brake fluid.

2   Check that on each rear brake backplate the wheel cylinder is free to slide within its locating slot. Ensure that all connections are tight and all bleed screws closed. Chock the wheels and release the handbrake.

3   Fill the master cylinder reservoir and the bottom inch of the jam jar with hydraulic fluid. Take extreme care that no fluid is allowed to come into contact with the paintwork as it acts as a solvent and will damage the finish.

4   The front brake caliper farthest from the master cylinder should be bled first unless a tandem master cylinder is fitted. For a tandem master cylinder with a front/rear split system first bleed the rear RH wheel cylinder. For a tandem system which is split diagonally first bleed the front LH caliper. Unscrew the relevant bleed screw about $\frac{1}{2}$ a turn.

Master cylinder (single)

5   An assistant should now pump the brake pedal by first depressing it one full stroke followed by three short but rapid strokes and allowing the pedal to return of its own accord. Check the fluid level in the reservoir. Carefully watch the flow of fluid into the glass jar and when air bubbles cease to emerge with the fluid during the next down stroke, tighten the bleed screw. Remove the plastic bleed tube and tighten the bleed screw, do not overtighten. Replace the rubber dust cap. Top up the fluid in the reservoir.

6   Repeat operations in paragraphs 4 and 5 for the second front brake caliper as applicable.

7   The rear brakes should be bled in the same manner as the front, except that each brake pedal stroke should be slow with a pause of three or four seconds between each stroke. This is to ensure that the valve fitted into the rear brake line does not operate.

8   Sometimes it may be found that the bleed operation for one or more cylinders is taking a considerable time. The cause is probably air being drawn past the bleed screw threads when the screw is loose. To counteract this condition, it is recommended that at the end of each downward stroke the bleed screw be tightened to stop air being drawn past the threads.

9   If after the bleed operation has been completed, the brake pedal operation still feels spongy, this is an indication that there is still air in the system, or that the master cylinder is faulty.

Master cylinder (tandem)

10 Start bleeding as described in paragraph 4 and continue in the following pattern:

Front/rear split system : LH rear, RH front, LH front
Diagonal split system : RH rear, RH front, LH rear

Operate the brake pedal slowly, using light pressure and allow it to return slowly. Pause between strokes and repeat until all air is expelled. Tighten the bleed screw immediately after the last downward stroke, keeping the pedal depressed until the bleed screw has been tightened.

11 On completion, check the tightness of all the bleed screws and wipe up any spilt fluid.

12 If the ignition is switched on during the bleed operation and the pressure differential warning light is illuminated, bleeding must be continued until the light goes out. Ascertain which brake circuit caused the light to glow and then attach a bleed pipe to a bleed screw in the other circuit. Open the bleed screw, depress the pedal slowly and when the light goes out, release the pedal and tighten the bleed screw.

13 Check and if necessary top up the fluid reservoir, using fresh hydraulic fluid. Never re-use old brake fluid.

4 Rear brake shoes – inspection, removal and refitting

After high mileages, it will be necessary to fit shoes with new linings. Refitting new brake linings to shoes is not considered economic, or possible, without the use of special equipment. However, if the services of a local garage or workshop having brake re-lining equipment are available, there is no reason why the original shoes should not be successfully relined. Ensure that the correct specification linings are fitted to the shoes.

1 Chock the front wheels, jack up the rear of the car and place on firmly based axle stands. Remove the roadwheel.

2 Release the handbrake and back off the brake shoe adjuster by turning in an anti-clockwise direction, when viewed from the centre of the car.

3 Using a wide bladed screwdriver, carefully prise off the hub dust cap, (Fig. 9.1).

4 With a pair of pliers, straighten the ears of the hub nut split pin and then withdraw the split pin.

5 With a suitable sized spanner, undo and remove the hub nut. Note that the left-hand hub has a left-hand thread, and the right-hand hub has a right-hand thread. Lift away the plain spacing washer.

6 It may not be possible to pull the brake drum off by hand and any attempt to hammer them off is likely to damage the drums. A suitable hub puller can be purchased from an accessory shop, or it may be possible to obtain one on hire from a local garage (photo).

7 The brake linings should be renewed if they are so worn that the rivet heads are flush with the surface of the lining. If bonded linings are

fitted, they must be renewed when the lining material has worn down to 0.063 in (1.6 mm), at its thinnest point.

8 Using a pair of pliers, release the trailing brake shoe anti-rattle springs by rotating through 90°. Lift away the steady pin, spring and cup washer (Fig. 9.2).

9 Disengage the trailing shoe from the wheel cylinder abutment and then the abutment link in the adjuster link.

10 Repeat the operation in paragraph 8 for the leading shoe.

11 Carefully remove both brake shoes complete with springs, at the same time easing the handbrake operating lever from the leading shoe. Take care that the links in the adjuster housing do not fall out, and retain them with an elastic band around the adjuster assembly.

12 If the shoes are to be left off for a while, do not depress the brake pedal, otherwise the piston will be ejected from the cylinder causing unnecessary work.

13 Thoroughly clean all traces of dust from the shoes, backplates and brake drums using a stiff brush, but take care not to inhale any of the dust. Brake dust can cause judder or squeal and it is important to clean out as described.

14 Check that the piston is free in iits cylinder, that the rubber dust covers are undamaged and in position and that there are no hydraulic fluid leaks. Ensure the handbrake lever assembly is free and the brake adjuster operates correctly. Lubricate the threads on the adjusting wedge with a graphite based penetrating oil.

15 Prior to reassembly, smear a trace of brake grease to the steady platforms, both ends of the brake shoes and the adjuster links. Do not allow any grease to come into contact with the linings, or rubber parts. Refit the shoes in the reverse sequence to removal, taking care that the adjuster links are correctly positioned in the adjuster housing with the angle of the link registering against the adjuster wedge. The two pull off springs should preferably be renewed every time new shoes are fitted and must be refitted in their original web holes (photo).

16 Back off the adjuster and refit the brake drum and hub assembly. Refit the plain washer and castellated nut tightening the latter to the specified torque. Align to the next split pin hole and lock with a new split pin. Do not pack the dust cap with grease. Refit the roadwheel.

17 Adjust the rear brakes as described in Section 2 and then lower the car to the ground. Check correct adjustment of the handbrake and finally road test.

5 Rear brake cylinder – removal, inspection and overhaul

If hydraulic fluid is leaking from the brake wheel cylinder, it may be necessary to dismantle it and replace the seal. Should brake fluid be found running down the side of the wheel or if it is noticed that a pool of liquid forms alongside one wheel and the level in the master cylinder has dropped, it is indicative of failed seals.

1 Remove the brake drum/hub assembly and brake shoes as described in Section 4. Clean down the rear of the backplate using a

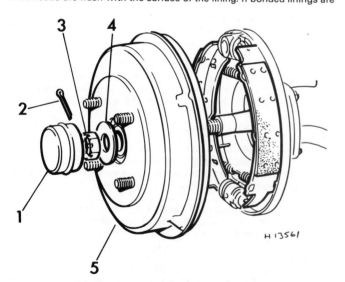

Fig. 9.1 Rear brake drum removal (Sec 4)

1	*Hub cap*	*4*	*Plain washer*
2	*Split pin*	*5*	*Brake drum*
3	*Castellated nut*		

4.6 Removing a rear brake drum

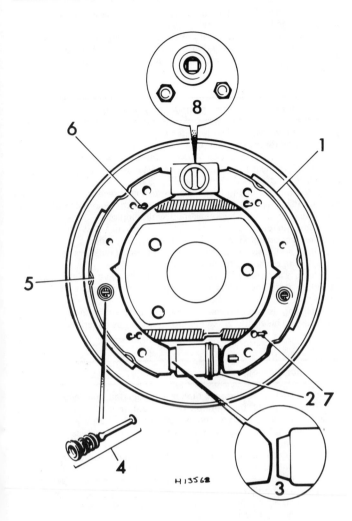

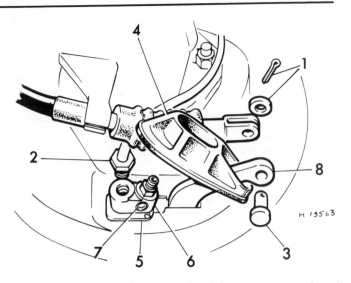

Fig. 9.3 Wheel cylinder attachments (Sec 5)

1	Split pin and washer	5	Retaining plate
2	Brake hydraulic pipe	6	Spring plate
3	Clevis pin	7	Wheel cylinder
4	Rubber boot	8	Handbrake lever

Fig. 9.2 Rear brake components (Sec 4)

1	Leading shoe	5	Trailing shoe
2	Wheel cylinder	6	Return spring (plain)
3	Abutment for trailing shoe	7	Return spring (shaped)
4	Anti-rattle spring assembly	8	Adjuster

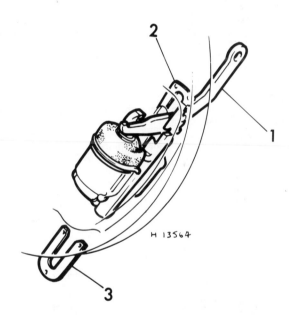

Fig. 9.4 Wheel cylinder fixing (Sec 5)

1	Handbrake lever	3	Retaining plate
2	Spring plate		

4.15 Rear brake shoes and springs

stiff brush. Place a quantity of rag under the backplate to catch any hydraulic fluid that may issue from the open pipe, or wheel cylinder.

2 Wipe the top of the brake master cylinder reservoir and unscrew the cap. Place a piece of thick polythene over the top of the reservoir and refit the cap. This is to stop hydraulic fluid syphoning out.

3 Using an open ended spanner, carefully unscrew the hydraulic pipe connection union to the rear of the wheel cylinder.

4 Extract the split pin and lift away the washer and clevis pin connecting the handbrake cable yoke to the wheel cylinder operating lever (Fig. 9.3).

5 Ease off the rubber boot from the rear of the wheel cylinder.

6 Using a screwdriver, carefully draw off the retaining plate and spring plate from the rear of the wheel cylinder (Fig. 9.4).

7   The wheel cylinder may now be lifted away from the brake back-plate. Detach the handbrake lever from the wheel cylinder.

8   To dismantle the wheel cylinder, first ease off the rubber dust cover retaining ring with a screwdriver and the rubber dust cover itself. Withdraw the piston from the wheel cylinder body and with the fingers, remove the piston seal from the piston noting which way round it is fitted. Do not use a metal screwdriver as this could scratch the piston.

9   Inspect the inside of the cylinder for score marks caused by impurities in the hydraulic fluid. If any are found, the cylinder and piston will require renewal. If the wheel cylinder requires renewal, always ensure that the replacement is exactly similar to the one removed.

10 If the cylinder is sound, thoroughly clean it out with fresh hydraulic fluid.

11 The old rubber seal will probably be swollen and visibly worn. Smear the new rubber seal with hydraulic fluid and reassemble into the cylinder. Fit a new dust seal and retaining clip.

12 Smear the backplate where the wheel cylinder slides with brake grease and refit the handbrake lever on the wheel cylinder, ensuring that it is the correct way round. The spindles of the lever must engage in the recess on the cylinder arms.

13 The handbrake lever may now be fed through the slot in the back-plate until the neck of the wheel cylinder is correctly located in the slot.

14 Slide the spring plate between the wheel cylinder and backplate. The retaining plate may now be inserted between the spring plate and wheel cylinder, taking care the pips of the spring plate engage in the holes of the retaining plate.

15 Refit the rubber boot and reconnect the handbrake cable yoke to the handbrake lever. Insert the clevis pin, head upwards and plain washer. Lock with a new split pin.

16 Reassembling the brake shoes and drum/hub assembly is the reverse of the removal procedure. Finally, bleed the hydraulic system as described in Section 3.

6   Rear brake shoe adjuster – removal and refitting

1   Should it be necessary to remove the brake adjuster, first remove the roadwheel, brake drum/hub assembly and brake shoes, as described in Section 4.

2   Release the two adjuster retaining nuts and lift away, together with the spring washers. The adjuster can now be lifted away from the backplate.

3   Check that the screw can be screwed both in and out to its fullest extent without showing signs of tightness.

4   Lift away the two adjuster links and thoroughly clean the adjuster

assembly. Inspect the adjuster body and two links for signs of excessive wear and fit new parts as necessary.

5   Lightly smear the adjuster links with brake grease and reassemble. Double check correct operation by holding the two links between the fingers and rotating the adjuster screw whereupon the links should move out together.

7   Rear brake backplate – removal and refitting

1   To remove the backplate, refer to Section 4, paragraphs 1 to 6 inclusive and remove the brake/hub assembly.

2   Extract the split pin and lift away the plain washer locking clevis pin, securing the handbrake cable yoke to the wheel cylinder handbrake lever. Lift away the clevis pin (Fig. 9.6).

3   Wipe the top of the brake master cylinder reservoir and unscrew the cap. Place a piece of thick polythene over the reservoir and refit the cap. This is to stop the hydraulic fluid syphoning out.

4   Using an open ended spanner, carefully unscrew the hydraulic pipe connection union to the rear of the wheel cylinder.

5   Undo and remove the three nuts with spring washers securing the hub axle and backplate to the radius arm.

6   Using a tapered soft metal drift, carefully drive the hub axle and backplate from the radius arm and separate the hub axle from the backplate.

7   Refitting is the reverse of the removal procedure. It will be necessary to bleed the brake hydraulic system as described in Section 3.

8   Handbrake – adjustment

1   It is usual when the rear brakes are adjusted, that any excessive free movement of the handbrake will automatically be taken up. However, in time, the handbrake catches will stretch and it will be necessary to take up the free play by shortening the cables at the point where they are attached to the handbrake lever.

2   Never try to adjust the handbrake to compensate for wear on the rear brake linings. It is usually badly worn brake linings that lead to the excessive handbrake travel. If upon inspection the rear brake linings are in good condition, or they have been renewed recently and yet the handbrake reaches the end of its ratchet travel before the brakes operate, adjust the cables as follows:

3   Refer to Section 2 and ensure the rear brakes are correctly adjusted.

4   Release the handbrake lever and then pull it on until the third notch position on the ratchet is reached.

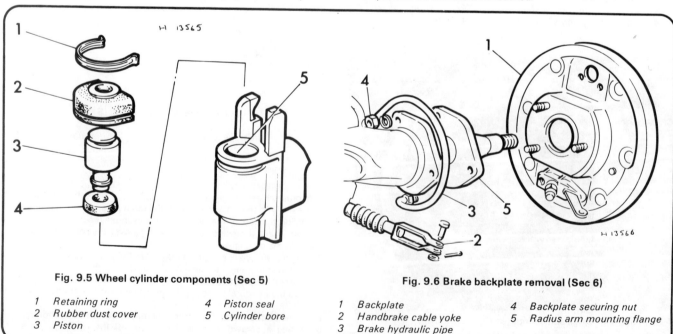

Fig. 9.5 Wheel cylinder components (Sec 5)

1	Retaining ring	4	Piston seal
2	Rubber dust cover	5	Cylinder bore
3	Piston		

Fig. 9.6 Brake backplate removal (Sec 6)

1	Backplate	4	Backplate securing nut
2	Handbrake cable yoke	5	Radius arm mounting flange
3	Brake hydraulic pipe		

5   Adjust the nuts at the handbrake lever end of the two cables until the rear wheels can just be turned by heavy hand pressure.
6   Release the handbrake lever and check that the rear brakes are not binding.

9   Handbrake cable – removal and refitting

1   Chock the front wheels, jack up the rear of the car and support on firmly based axle stands. Remove the passenger seat and on later cars, the seat belt stem bolts.
2   Release the handbrake lever. Undo and remove the respective handbrake cable adjustment nut followed by the outer cable adjustment nut.
3   Detach the inner cable from the handbrake lever and lift away the long spring and plain washer.
4   Release the outer cable to body clips, from the underside of the floor panels.
5   Extract the split pin and lift away the washer and clevis pin connecting the handbrake cable yoke to the wheel cylinder operating yoke.
6   Detach the rubber boot from the outer cable rear abutment and then disengage the outer cable from the radius arm clips.
7   Withdraw the complete handbrake cable assembly rearwards from the large body rubber grommet.
8   Refitting is the reverse of the removal procedure. It will be necessary to adjust the cable, as described in Section 8.

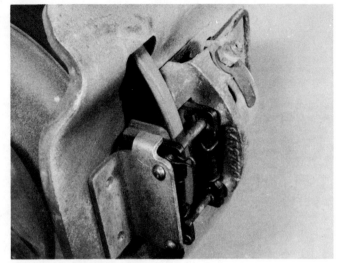

10.2a Withdrawing a locking clip

10   Front disc brake pad – removal, inspection and refitting

1   Apply the handbrake, jack up the front of the car and place on firmly based axle stands. Remove the roadwheel.
2   Using a pair of pliers, withdraw the two pad retaining pin locking wire clips and withdraw the retaining pins. The two pads may now be lifted out of the caliper (photos).
3   Inspect the thickness of the lining material and if it is less than 0.06 in (1.6 mm), it is recommended that the pads be renewed. If one of the pads is slightly more worn than the other, it is permissible to change these round. Always fit new pads of the manufacturer's recommended specification and fit a complete set of four.
4   To refit the pads, it is first necessary to extract a little brake fluid from the system. To do this, fit a plastic bleed tube to the bleed screw and immerse the free end in 1 in (25 mm) of hydraulic fluid in a jar. Slacken off the bleed screw one complete turn and press back the indirect piston. Next, push the yoke towards the disc until the new indirect pad can be inserted. Press back the direct piston into the bore and then tighten the bleed screw. Fit the new direct pad.
5   Insert the retaining pins with their heads furthermost from the caliper pistons and secure with wire clips.
6   Wipe the top of the hydraulic fluid reservoir and remove the cap. Top up and depress the brake pedal several times to settle the pads and then recheck the hydraulic fluid level.

10.2b Withdrawing a pin

11   Front disc brake caliper – removal, overhaul and refitting

1   Chock the rear wheels, apply the handbrake, remove the front wheel trim and slacken the wheel nuts. Jack up the front of the car and support on firmly based stands. Remove the roadwheel.
2   Wipe the top of the brake master cylinder reservoir and unscrew the cap. Place a piece of thick polythene over the top and refit the cap. This is to prevent hydraulic fluid syphoning out.
3   Using an open ended spanner, undo the union nut securing the brake hydraulic pipe to the caliper.
4   Undo and remove the two bolts and spring washers which secure the caliper to the steering swivel assembly and carefully lift away the caliper from the disc.
5   Using a pair of pliers, withdraw the two pad retaining pin wire clips and remove the two retaining pins. Lift away the pads.
6   Place the yoke of the caliper between soft faces in a bench vice and tighten sufficiently to hold the caliper.
7   Using the fingers, press the indirect piston fully into its bore in the caliper and then press the cylinder body down (Fig. 9.7).
8   Make a note of the position of the yoke spring relative to the yoke and then lift away the spring.

10.2c Withdrawing a pad

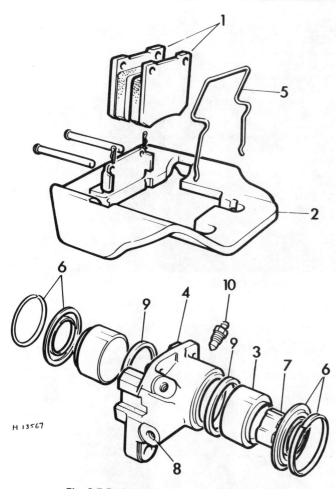

Fig. 9.7 Brake caliper components (Sec 11)

1   Brake pads   cover
2   Yoke   7   Bias spring
3   Indirect piston   8   Hydraulic fluid inlet
4   Cylinder body   9   Piston seal
5   Yoke spring   10 Bleed screw
6   Dust cover retaining ring and

9   Very carefully remove the retaining rings and dust covers from the cylinder, if necessary using a small screwdriver. The bore or piston must not be scratched.
10 Lift out the special bias ring from the indirect piston.
11 Using a compressed air jet, or foot pump, applied to the hydraulic pipe connection bore, eject the two pistons, taking suitable precautions not to allow them to fly out.
12 The seals may be removed from the cylinder using a non-metal rod, or the fingers.
13 Finally remove the bleed screw. It is important that the adjustment screw within the cylinder body is not disturbed.
14 Thoroughly clean the internal parts of the caliper using only clean brake fluid or methylated spirit.
15 Carefully inspect the fine finish of the bore and pistons and if signs of scoring or corrosion are evident, a new caliper assembly must be obtained. Before commencing to reassemble, obtain a new seal set and also a new bias spring.
16 To reassemble the caliper, first fit the new bias spring into the indirect piston in such a manner that the radius end enters the piston first.
17 Apply a little clean hydraulic fluid to the pistons and seals, but not to the cylinder grooves, or sliding edges of the yoke.
18 Very carefully fit the previously wetted seals into the cylinder grooves and then fit the pistons into the cylinder. The indirect piston with the bias ring must be fitted to the opposite end of the cylinder to the pads.
19 Refit the dust cover and retaining rings, making sure that the

widest retaining ring secures the dust cover furthermost from the pads.
20 The yoke spring is next refitted to the yoke and this must be positioned as was noted during dismantling.
21 Fit the cylinder to the yoke, engaging the tongue of the yoke into the slot of the bias ring fitted into the indirect piston.
22 With a small screwdriver, locate the legs of the yoke spring into the sliding grooves on the cylinder. The angled leg of the spring must engage in the groove on the cylinder opposite to the bleed screw. Refit the bleed screw.
23 The pads may now be refitted, this being the reverse of the removal procedure.
24 Refitting the caliper is the reverse of the removal procedure. It will be necessary to bleed the hydraulic system, full details of which may be found in Section 3.

12 Front brake disc – removal, renovation and refitting

1   Chock the rear wheels, apply the handbrake, jack up the front of the car and support on firmly based axle stands. Remove the roadwheel.
2   Using a pair of pliers, bend straight the ears of the hub nut locking split pin and withdraw the split pin (Fig. 9.8).
3   Undo and remove the hub nut using a suitable socket or ring spanner. If the nut is very tight, it may be necessary to fit the roadwheel temporarily and lower the wheel to the ground to prevent the hub from turning.
4   Support the weight of the lower suspension arm with a small jack or suitable packing.
5   Undo and remove the upper swivel balljoint two securing bolts and spring washers. Detach the brake pipe support bracket.
6   Undo and remove the two bolts and spring washers that secure the caliper to the steering swivel. Hang the caliper on wire or string so as not to strain the flexible pipe.
7   Using a universal three legged puller, with the feet located behind the wheel mounting flange (drive plate), and a suitable thrust pad, carefully draw the disc and drive plate assembly from the hub.
8   Mark the relative positions of the disc and drive plate so that they may be refitted in their original positions, and separate the two parts.
9   Thoroughly clean the disc and inspect for signs of deep scoring or excessive corrosion. If these are evident, the disc may be reground, but no more than 0.06 in (1.5 mm) may be removed. It is however, preferable to fit a new disc.

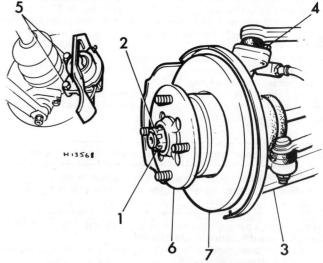

Fig. 9.8 Front brake disc removal (Sec 12)

1   Split pin   securing bolts
2   Hub nut   5   Caliper securing bolts
3   Lower suspension arm   6   Driveplate
4   Upper swivel balljoint   7   Disc

10 Refitting the disc is the reverse of removal. However, to avoid problems with the bearings not seating properly, draw the disc and drive flange onto the driveshaft by temporarily fitting a large plain washer below the hub nut (in place of the split collar) and tightening

the nut. The washer dimensions are 2.56 in (65 mm) diameter, 0.256 in (6.5 mm) thick, 0.98 in (25 mm) hole diameter.

11 Remove the nut and special washer, fit the split collar and retighten the nut to the specified torque. Tighten the nut further if necessary to align a split pin hole, and fit a new split pin.

12 Measure the run out at the outer periphery of the disc by means of feeler gauges positioned between the inside of the caliper and the disc. If the run out of the friction faces exceeds 0.009 in (0.23 mm), remove the disc and reposition it on the drive plate. Should the run-out be really bad, the disc is probably distorted due to overheating and a new one must be fitted.

13 Master cylinder (single) – removal and refitting

1 Apply the handbrake and chock the front wheels. Drain the fluid from the master cylinder reservoir and master cylinder, by attaching a plastic bleed tube to one of the brake bleed screws. Undo the screw one turn and then pump the fluid out into a clean glass container by means of the brake pedal.

2 Wipe the area around the four way hydraulic pipe union and, with an open ended spanner, disconnect the hydraulic pipe to the master cylinder at the four-way union.

3 Undo and remove the two nuts and spring washer securing the brake master cylinder to the rear of the servo unit and lift away the master cylinder and hydraulic pipe.

4 Refitting is the reverse of the removal procedure. Always start the union nut at the end of the short hydraulic pipe before finally tightening the master cylinder retaining nuts. It will be necessary to bleed the hydraulic system and full details will be found in Section 3.

14 Master cylinder (single) – dismantling and reassembly

If a new master cylinder is to be fitted, it will be necessary to lubricate the seals before fitting to the car, as they have a protective coating when originally assembled. Remove the blanking plug from the hydraulic pipe union seating. Ease back and remove the plunger dust cover. Inject clean hydraulic fluid into the master cylinder and operate the piston several times so the fluid will spread over all the internal working surfaces.

If the master cylinder is to be dismantled after removal, proceed as follows:

1 Carefully withdraw the complete plunger assembly from the bore. The assembly is separated by lifting the thimble leaf over the shouldered end of the plunger. The plunger seal may now be eased off using the fingers only (Fig. 9.9).

2 Depress the plunger return spring, allowing the valve stem to slide through the keyhole in the thimble, thus releasing the tension in the spring.

3 Detach the valve spacer, taking care of the spacer spring washer which will be found located under the valve head.

4 Examine the bore of the cylinder carefully for any signs of scores or ridges. If it is found to be smooth all over, new seals can be fitted. If however there is any doubt of the condition of the bore, a new master cylinder must be fitted.

5 If examination of the seals shows them to be apparently oversize, swollen, or very loose in the plunger, suspect oil contamination in the system. Ordinary lubricating oil will swell these rubber seals, and if one is found to be swollen, it is reasonable to assume that all seals in the braking system will need attention.

6 Thoroughly clean all parts in either clean brake fluid, or methylated spirit. Ensure that the bypass ports are clear.

7 All components should be assembled wet by dipping in clean brake fluid. Fit a new valve seal so that the flat side is correctly seating on the valve head (Fig. 9.9). Place the dished washer with the dome against the underside of the valve head. Hold it in position with the valve spacer, ensuring that the legs face towards the valve seal.

8 Refit the plunger return spring centrally on the spacer, insert the thimble into the spring, and depress until the valve stem engages in the keyhole in the thimble.

9 Ensure that the spring is central on the spacer before fitting a new plunger seal onto the plunger, with the flat face of the seal against the

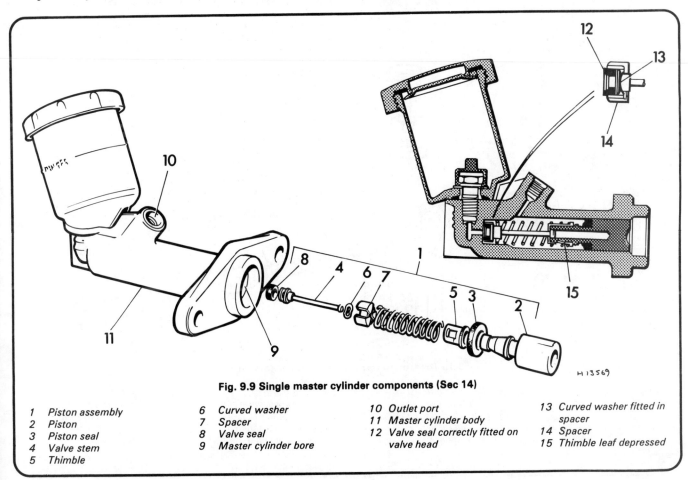

Fig. 9.9 Single master cylinder components (Sec 14)

1 Piston assembly	6 Curved washer	10 Outlet port	13 Curved washer fitted in
2 Piston	7 Spacer	11 Master cylinder body	spacer
3 Piston seal	8 Valve seal	12 Valve seal correctly fitted on	14 Spacer
4 Valve stem	9 Master cylinder bore	valve head	15 Thimble leaf depressed
5 Thimble			

face of the plunger.

10 Insert the reduced end of the plunger into the thimble until the thimble engages under the shoulder of the plunger and press home the thimble leaf.

11 Check that the master cylinder bore is clean and smear with clean brake fluid. With the plunger suitable wetted with brake fluid, carefully insert the assembly into the bore with the valve end first. Ease the lips of the plunger seal carefully into the bore.

12 The master cylinder is now ready for refitting to the car.

15 Master cylinder (tandem) – removal and refitting

1 Drain the tandem master cylinder and reservoir in a similar manner to that described for the single master cylinder. Full information will be found in Section 13.

2 Using an open ended spanner, undo the union connecting the master cylinder fluid pipe from the P D W A valve. This is the union on the top left-hand side when looking at the valve from the front of the car.

3 Undo and remove the two hydraulic pipe union nuts on the side of the tandem master cylinder.

4 Undo and remove the two nuts and spring washers securing the brake master cylinder to the rear of the servo unit and lift away the master cylinder.

5 Refitting is the reverse of the removal procedure. Always start the union nuts before finally tightening the master cylinder retaining nuts. It will be necessary to bleed the hydraulic system and full details will be found in Section 3.

16 Master cylinder (tandem) – dismantling and reassembly

1 Refer to the introduction to Section 14 with regard to new master cylinders.

2 Undo and remove the two screws holding the reservoir to the master cylinder body. Lift away the reservoir. Using a suitable sized Allen key, or wrench, unscrew the tipping valve nut and lift away the seal. Using a suitable diameter rod, push the primary plunger down the bore, this operation enabling the tipping valve to be withdrawn (Fig. 9.10).

3 Using a compressed air jet, very carefully applied to the rear outlet pipe connection, blow out all the master cylinder internal components. Alternatively, shake out the parts. Take care that adequate precautions are taken to ensure all parts are caught as they emerge.

4 Separate the primary and secondary plungers from the intermediate spring. Use the fingers to remove the gland seal from the primary plunger.

5 The secondary plunger assembly should be separated by lifting the thimble leaf over the shouldered end of the plunger. Using the fingers, remove the seal from the secondary plunger.

6 Depress the secondary spring, allowing the valve stem to slide through the keyhole in the thimble, thus releasing the tension on the spring.

7 Detach the valve spacer, taking care of the spring washer which will be found located under the valve head.

8 Examine the bore of the cylinder carefully for any signs of scores or ridges. If it is found to be smooth all over new seals can be fitted. If however there is any doubt of the condition of the bore, a new cylinder

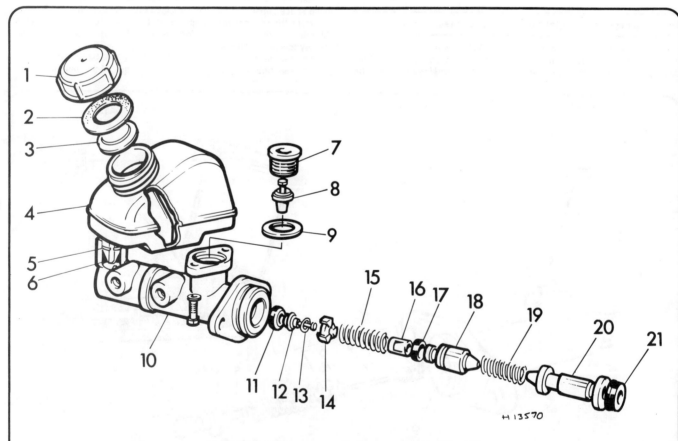

Fig. 9.10 Tandem master cylinder components (Sec 16)

1 Filler cap	7 Securing nut	12 Valve stem	17 Seal
2 Gasket assembly	8 Tipping valve	13 Spring washer – curved	18 Secondary plunger
3 Baffle	9 Face seal	14 Valve spacer	19 Intermediate spring (black)
4 Reservoir – dual	10 Cylinder body	15 Secondary spring	20 Primary plunger
5 Circlip – internal	11 Valve seal	16 Spring retainer	21 Gland seal
6 Seal			

must be fitted.

9 If examination of the seals shows them to be apparently oversize, swollen, or very loose on the plungers, suspect oil contamination in the system. Oil will swell these rubber seals, and if one is found to be swollen, it is reasonable to assume that all seals in the braking system will need attention.

10 Thoroughly clean all parts in either clean brake fluid or methylated spirit. Ensure that the by-pass ports are clear.

11 All components should be assembled wet by dipping in clean brake fluid. Using fingers only, fit new seals to the primary and secondary plungers ensuring that they are the correct way round. Place the dished washer with the dome against the underside of the valve seat. Hold it in position with the valve spacer ensuring that the legs face towards the valve seal.

12 Fit the plunger return spring centrally on the spacer, insert the thimble into the spring and depress until the valve stem engages in the keyhole of the thimble.

13 Insert the reduced end of the plunger into the thimble, until the thimble engages under the shoulder of the plunger, and press home the thimble leaf. Fit the intermediate spring between the primary and secondary plungers.

14 Check that the master cylinder bore is clean and smear with clean brake fluid. With the complete assembly suitably wetted with brake fluid, carefully insert the assembly into the bore. Ease the lips of the plunger seals carefully into the bore. Push the assembly fully home.

15 Refit the tipping valve assembly, and seal, to the cylinder bore and tighten the securing nut to the specified torque. Refit the hydraulic fluid reservoir and tighten the two retaining screws.

16 The master cylinder is now ready for refitting to the servo unit. Bleed the complete hydraulic system and road test the car.

17 Vacuum servo unit – description

A vacuum servo unit is fitted into the brake hydraulic circuit in series with the master cylinder, to provide assistance to the driver when the brake pedal is depressed. This reduces the effort required by the driver to operate the brakes under all braking conditions.

The unit operates by vacuum obtained from the induction manifold and comprises basically a booster diaphragm, control valve, and a non-return valve.

The servo unit and hydraulic master cylinder are connected together so that the servo unit piston rod acts as the master cylinder pushrod. The driver's braking effort is transmitted through another pushrod to the servo unit piston and its built-in control system. The servo unit piston does not fit tightly into the cylinder, but has a strong diaphragm to keep its edges in constant contact with the cylinder wall, so assuring an air tight seal between the two parts. The forward chamber is held under vacuum conditions created in the inlet manifold of the engine and, during periods when the brake pedal is not in use, the controls open a passage to the rear chamber so placing it under vacuum conditions as well. When the brake pedal is depressed, the vacuum passage to the rear chamber is cut off and the chamber opened to atmospheric pressure. The consequent rush of air pushes the servo piston forward in the vacuum chamber and operates the main pushrod to the master cylinder.

The controls are designed so that assistance is given under all conditions and, when the brakes are not required, vacuum in the rear chamber is established when the brake pedal is released. All air from the atmosphere entering the rear chamber is passed through a small air filter.

18 Vacuum servo unit – removal and refitting

1 Wipe the area around the four way connector and then disconnect the hydraulic fluid pipe using an open ended spanner on the union nut.

2 Slacken the clip securing the vacuum hose to the servo unit. Carefully draw the hose from its union.

3 Undo and remove the parcel shelf securing screws and then lift the parcel shelf sufficiently to give access to the brake pedal mountings.

4 Using a pair of pliers, extract the split pin in the end of the brake pedal to pushrod clevis pin. Lift away the plain washer and withdraw the clevis pin.

5 Move the accelerator pedal to give better access to the servo unit securing nuts. Undo and remove the four nuts and spring washers

which hold the servo unit to the bulkhead.

6 The servo unit, complete with master cylinder, can now be lifted away from the engine compartment.

7 Undo and remove the two nuts and spring washers securing the master cylinder to the servo unit and separate the two parts. Take care that the internal parts of the master cylinder do not fall out and also that no hydraulic fluid is spilled from the reservoir.

8 Refitting is the reverse of removal. Make sure that the clevis pin for the pushrod is fitted to the lower of the two holes in the brake pedal arm.

9 Bleed the hydraulic system, as described in Section 3.

19 Vacuum servo unit – servicing

1 The servo unit which must not be dismantled and the domed screw in the end of the output rod should never be disturbed. Service kits are available for the filter, seal and plate assembly and the non-return valve.

2 To renew the filter, pull back the rubber dust cover at the pushrod end, release the end cap and extract the old filter. Cut the new filter as shown in Fig. 9.11, fit it over the pushrod and press the filter into the neck of the servo. Refit the end cap and dust cover.

3 To fit a new non-return valve, first release the clip on the vacuum hose to the valve and detach the valve. Note the angular position of the valve nozzle, then insert a wide bladed screwdriver between the valve and the grommet, prise the valve out and extract the grommet.

4 Fit a new grommet to the servo. Lubricate the ribs of the new valve with rubber grease, position the new valve so that its nozzle is in the same position as the valve which was removed and then press the valve into the grommet until the flange of the valve is in contact with the grommet.

5 Connect the vacuum hose to the valve and tighten the hose clip.

6 There are two different types of seal and plate for the pushrod aperture of the servo. Either type may be used, but the way in which they are fitted is different.

7 Remove the old seal and plate and discard them. Lubricate the new seal and plate with rubber grease and fit them as shown in Fig. 9.12, noting that if the plate is dished it is fitted to the servo before the seal is fitted. If the plate is flat, it is fitted to the servo after the seal has been fitted.

8 Fit the servo unit to the car as described in the previous Section. To test the servo unit for correct operation after overhaul, first start the engine and run for a minimum period of two minutes and then switch off. Wait for ten minutes and apply the footbrake very carefully, listening to hear the rush of air into the servo unit. This will indicate that vacuum was retained and, therefore, operating correctly.

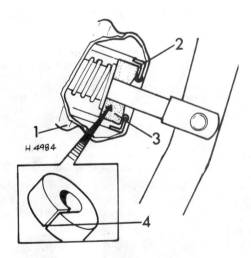

Fig. 9.11 Filter renewal (Sec 19)

1 Dust cover	3 Filter
2 End cap	4 Position of cut

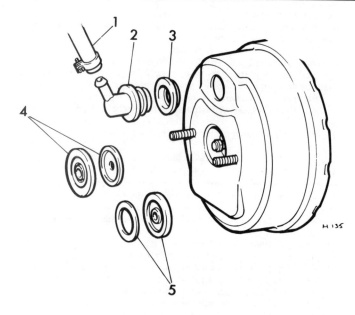

Fig. 9.12 Servo unit (Sec 19)

1 Vacuum hose
2 Non-return valve
3 Grommet
4 Seal and plate (dished plate)
5 Seal and plate (flat plate)

20 Pressure differential warning actuator valve – removal and refitting

1 Wipe the top of the brake hydraulic fluid reservoir and unscrew the cap. Place a piece of polythene over the top and refit the cap. This is to prevent hydraulic fluid syphoning out. For safety reasons disconnect the battery.
2 Detach the cable connector at the top of the pressure differential warning actuator valve (PDWA) switch (photo).
3 Wipe the area around the PDWA valve assembly and using an open ended spanner, unscrew the union nut securing the rear brake fluid pipe to the valve, followed by the master cylinder to valve rear brake pipe, front brake fluid pipe and finally the master cylinder to valve front brake pipe.
4 Undo the PDWA valve securing bolt and lift away the bolt, spring washer and the valve itself.

20.2 PDWA valve and switch

5 Refitting is the reverse of removal and on completion, the hydraulic system will need to be bled as described in Section 3.

21 Pressure reducing valve – removal and refitting

1 Wipe the top of the brake hydraulic fluid reservoir and unscrew the cap. Place a piece of polythene over the top and refit the cap. This is to prevent hydraulic fluid syphoning out.
2 Wipe the area around the valve and using an open ended spanner detach the two brake pipes from the valve.
3 Undo and remove the valve securing bolt and spring washer.
4 Carefully disconnect the flexible hose from the connector on the radius arm as described in Section 22.
5 The valve and flexible hose may now be lifted away from under the car.
6 Under no circumstances should the pressure reducing valve be dismantled. If the operation of the valve is suspect, fit a new unit complete.
7 Refitting the reducing valve is the reverse of removal and on completion, the hydraulic system will need to be bled as described in Section 3.

22 Flexible hoses – inspection, removal and refitting

1 Inspect the condition of the flexible brake pipes and renew any which are cracked, chafed, or swollen.
2 Unscrew the metal pipe union nut from its connection to the flexible hose and then while holding the hexagon on the hose with a spanner, unscrew the attachment nut.
3 Remove the shakeproof washer and withdraw the end of the flexible hose from the mounting bracket.
4 Disconnect the other end of the hose from the wheel cylinder by unscrewing it with a spanner.
5 Refitting is the reverse of removal but when brake hydraulic components are being renewed, make sure that the parts are compatible. Early models have UNF threaded components and later ones are metric. If the thread of a component is in doubt, screw the hydraulic connection or bleed screw fully in with the fingers. If they cannot be screwed right in or if they are unduly slack, the threads may not be compatible. See Chapter 13 for details.

23 Brake pedal – removal and refitting

1 Refer to Section 18 and remove the servo unit and brake master cylinder from the bulkhead.
2 Refer to Chapter 3 and remove the accelerator pedal.
3 Working under the dashboard, release the speedometer cable

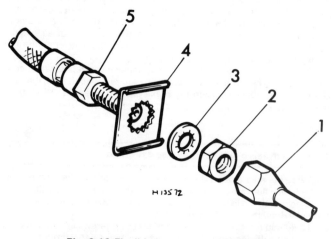

Fig. 9.13 Flexible hose removal (Sec 22)

1 Union nut
2 Flexible hose locknut
3 Shakeproof washer
4 Mounting bracket
5 Flexible hose

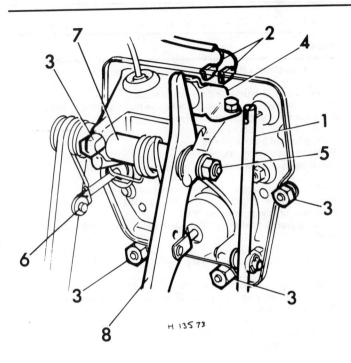

H 13573

Fig. 9.14 Brake pedal removal (first stage) (Sec 23)

1 *Accelerator pedal*	4 *Brake light switch*
2 *Brake light switch Lucar*	5 *Pedal pivot nut*
terminals	6 *Clutch pedal clevis pin*
3 *Pedal mounting bracket*	7 *Pedal pivot*
mounting nuts	8 *Brake pedal*

from the rear of the speedometer head.
4   Detach the two cable connectors to the brake light switch located at the top of the pedal arm (Fig. 9.14).
5   Undo and remove the four nuts and spring washers that secure the pedal mounting bracket to the bulkhead.
6   Slacken the clip securing the servo vacuum hose to the inlet manifold adaptor and remove the vacuum hose (Fig.9.15).
7   Note which way round the clutch lever return spring is fitted and detach the spring (if fitted) from the clutch slave cylinder.
8   Undo and remove the two bolts securing the clutch slave cylinder to the clutch housing. Carefully withdraw the slave cylinder from the pushrod and tie back out of the way.
9   Undo and remove the two top mounting bracket retaining bolts and spring washers.
10 Undo and remove the mounting bracket to the subframe.
11 Release the speedometer cable from the transmission casing.
12 Carefully manipulate the pedal mounting bracket from the body aperture.
13 To release the brake pedal, undo and remove the nut and washer from the pedal pivot shaft.
14 Extract the split pin and remove the plain washer and clevis pin from the clutch pedal to pushrod yoke.
15 Using a suitable diameter soft metal drift, drive the pivot shaft and clutch pedal from the mounting bracket. The brake pedal may now be lifted away.
16 Refitting is the reverse of the removal procedure. Lubricate the clutch, brake and accelerator pedal pivots with a little grease. It will be necessary to bleed the brake hydraulic system and full information will be found in Section 3.

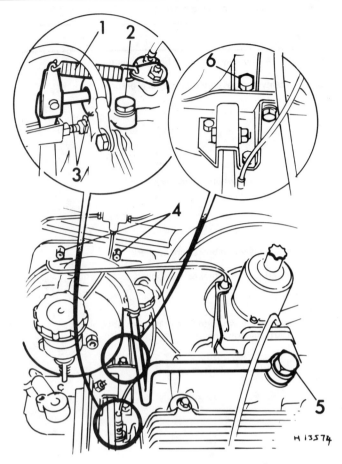

H 13574

Fig. 9.15 Brake pedal removal (second stage) (Sec 23)

1 *Clutch return spring*	4 *Mounting bracket top bolts*
2 *Clutch slave cylinder*	5 *Servo unit vacuum pipe*
securing bolt	*connection to manifold*
3 *Clutch slave cylinder and*	6 *Mounting bracket to*
pushrod	*subframe securing bolt*

24 Brake light switch – removal and refitting

1   For safety reasons disconnect the battery terminals.
2   Disconnect the two cable connectors from the brake light switch located at the top of the brake pedal.
3   Undo and remove the two bolts with spring washers securing the switch mounting bracket to the pedal mounting bracket. Lift away the bracket, complete with switch.
4   To separate the switch from the bracket first, using a pair of pliers, withdraw the long switch locking split pin. Finally unscrew the switch from the bracket.
5   To refit the switch, screw it into the bracket until one complete thread of the switch housing is visible on the pedal side of the mounting bracket. Thereafter, refitting is the reverse of the removal procedure.

See overleaf for 'Fault diagnosis – braking system'

25 Fault diagnosis – braking system

Symptom	Reason(s)
Pedal travels a long way before the brakes operate	Rear brake shoes set too far from the drums
Stopping ability poor, even though pedal pressure is firm	Linings, discs or drums badly worn, or scored One or more wheel hydraulic cylinders seized, resulting in a shoe or pad not pressing against its disc Friction linings contaminated with oil Wrong type of friction linings Shoes or pads fitted incorrectly Servo unit not functioning
Car veers to one side when brakes are applied	Brake pads or linings on one side contaminated with oil Hydraulic wheel cylinders on one side partially, or fully seized A mixture of lining materials fitted Unequal wear between sides caused by partially seized wheel cylinders
Pedal feels spongy when brakes are applied	Air present in the hydraulic system
Pedal feels springy when brakes are applied	Brake linings not bedded after fitting new ones Master cylinder, disc, or brake backplate mountings loose Brake discs not true
Pedal travels right down, with little or no resistance and brakes are virtually non-operative	Severe loss of fluid resulting from leakage Master cylinder failure
Binding, juddering, overheating	Incorrect adjustment of handbrake Incorrect adjustment of rear brakes Brake discs not true Seized wheel cylinder

Chapter 10 Electrical system

For modifications, and information applicable to later models, see Supplement at end of manual

Contents

Specifications

System	12 volt, negative earth
Battery	40, 50 or 60 amp hr at 20 hr rate

Dynamo

Type	Lucas C40/1
Maximum output	22 ± 1 Amp
Minimum brush length	$\frac{1}{4}$ in (6.4 mm)

Alternator

	Lucas 16ACR	**Lucas 17ACR**
Type		
Output at 14V and 6000 alternator rpm	34A	36A
Minimum brush length protruding beyond brush box	0.2 in (5 mm)	0.2 in (5 mm)

Starter motor type

Early cars	Lucas M35G
Later cars	
1500	Lucas M35J
1750	Lucas M35J pre-engaged

Cold countries:
    1500 . . . .   Lucas M35J pre-engaged
    1750 . . . .   Lucas 2M100 pre-engaged

Lucas M35G
Brush spring tension . . . .   15 to 25 oz (425 to 709 gm)
Minimum brush length . . . .   0.32 in (7.9 mm)
Light running:
    Speed . . . .   9500 to 11 000 rpm
    Current . . . .   45 amps
    Voltage . . . .   8.8 to 9.2 volts
    Lock torque . . . .   10 lbf ft (1.38 kgf m)
    Current . . . .   420 to 440 amps
    Voltage . . . .   7.8 to 7.4 volts

Lucas M35J
Brush spring tension . . . .   28 oz (790 gm)
Minimum brush length . . . .   0.38 in (9.5 mm)
Minimum commutator thickness . . . .   0.08 in (2.05 mm)
Lock torque . . . .   7 lbf ft (0.97 kgf m) with 350-375 amps
Torque at 1000 rpm . . . .   4.4 lbf ft (0.61 kgf m) with 260 to 275 amps
Light running current . . . .   65 amps at 8000 to 10 000 rpm

Lucas M35J – pre-engaged
Brush spring tension . . . .   28 oz (790 gm)
Minimum brush length . . . .   0.38 in (9.5 mm)
Minimum commutator thickness . . . .   0.08 in (2.05 mm)
Lock torque . . . .   7 lbf ft (0.97 kgf m) with 350 to 375 amps
Torque at 1000 rpm . . . .   4.4 lbf ft (0.61 kgf m) with 260 to 275 amps
Light running current . . . .   65 amp at 8000 to 10 000 rpm
Maximum armature endfloat . . . .   0.010 in (0.25 mm)
Solenoid:
    Closing (series) winding resistance . . . .   0.21 to 0.025 ohms
    Hold-on (shunt) winding resistance . . . .   0.9 to 1.1 ohms

Lucas 2M100 – pre-engaged
Brush spring tension . . . .   36 oz (1020 gm)
Minimum brush length . . . .   0.38 in (9.5 mm)
Minimum commutator thickness . . . .   0.140 in (3.5 mm)
Lock torque . . . .   14.4 lbf ft (2.02 kgf m) with 463 amps
Torque at 1000 rpm . . . .   7.3 lbf ft (1.02 kgf m) with 300 amps
Light running current . . . .   40 amp at 6000 rpm (approx)
Maximum armature endfloat . . . .   0.010 in (0.25 mm)
Solenoid:
    Closing (series) winding resistance . . . .   0.25 to 0.27 ohms
    Hold-on (shunt) winding resistance . . . .   0.76 to 0.80 ohms

Control unit (dynamo)
System . . . .   Current – voltage control
Type . . . .   Lucas RB 340
Setting at 3000 rpm:
    0 to 25°C (32 to 77°F) . . . .   14.4 to 15.5 volts (open circuit)
    26 to 40°C (78 to 104°F) . . . .   14.25 to 15.25 volts (open circuit)
Cut-in voltage . . . .   12.7 to 13.3 volts
Drop-off voltage . . . .   9.5 to 11.0 volts

Air gap settings:	**Prior to 37563**	**37563 onwards**
Voltage and current regulator	0.054 ± 0.002 in	0.022 ± 0.003 in
	(1.37 ± 0.05 mm)	(0.559 ± 0.08 mm)
Cut-out relay	0.040 ± 0.005 in	0.030 ± 0.005 in
	(1.02 ± 0.13 mm)	(0.76 ± 0.13 mm)

Wiper motor
Type . . . .   Lucas 14W two speed, self switching
Armature endfloat . . . .   0.004 to 0.008 in (0.1 to 0.2 mm)
Running current (light) . . . .   1.5 amps at 13.5 volts
Armature winding resistance . . . .   0.27 to 0.35 ohm at 16°C (60°F)
Brush length (minimum) . . . .   0.19 in (4.8 mm)
Brush spring tension . . . .   5 to 7 oz (150 to 210 gm)
Arm pressure on screen . . . .   11 to 13 oz (310 to 370 gm)

Horns
Type . . . .   Lucas 9H or 6H
Maximum current consumption:
    9H . . . .   4 amps
    6H . . . .   3 amps

Bulbs

	BL part number	Watts
Headlamp LHD – except France and North America	GLB 410	45/40
Headlamp LHD – France – vertical dip – yellow	GLB 411	45/40
Sealed beam headlamp unit (RHD left dip)	GLU 101	60/45
Sidelamp and flasher repeater	GLB 989	6
Direction indicator	GLB 382	21
Direction indicator repeater	GLB 233	4
Tail and stop lamps	GLB 380	6/21
Rear number plate lamp	GLB 207	6
Reverse lamp	GLB 273	21
Interior lamp	GLB 254	6
Panel and warning lamp	GLB 2132	2.2

Torque wrench settings

	lbf ft	kgf m
Alternator/dynamo mounting bolts	18 to 22	2.5 to 3.0
Generator pulley nut	25 to 28	3.5 to 3.9
Starter motor bolts	30	4.1

1   General description

The electrical system is 12 volt, with negative earth. On early models the electrical generator is a dynamo which works in conjunction with a voltage and current regulator and a cut-out. Later models are fitted with an alternator instead of a dynamo and the voltage regulator and provision for an ignition warning light are incorporated within the alternator. Apart from requiring less maintenance than a dynamo, an alternator has a power output which is largely independent of engine speed and there is less need for the battery to supplement the generator output when the engine speed is low and the electrical demand is high.

When fitting electrical accessories such as radios, tape recorders, electronic ignition systems and electrical tachometers, or any other equipment which incorporates semi conductor devices such as transistors, it is important to ensure that the item is suitable for a negative earth system and is connected correctly. Failure to ensure this, will cause the equipment to be damaged.

2   Battery – removal and refitting

1   The battery is in a special carrier fitted on the right-hand wing valance of the engine compartment. It should be removed once every three months for cleaning and testing. Disconnect the negative then the positive leads from the battery terminals by slackening the clamp retaining nuts and bolts or by unscrewing the retaining screws if terminal caps are fitted instead of clamps.
2   Unscrew the clamp bar retaining nuts and lower to the side of the battery. Carefully lift the battery out of its compartment and hold it vertically to ensure that none of the electrolyte is spilled.
3   Refitting is a direct reversal of this procedure. Refit the positive lead before the negative lead and smear the terminals with petroleum jelly, or a proprietary corrosion inhibitor. Never use an ordinary grease.

3   Battery – maintenance and inspection

1   Normal weekly battery maintenance consists of checking the electrolyte level of each cell to ensure that the separators are covered by 0.25 in (6.5 mm) of electrolyte. If the level has fallen, top up the battery using distilled water only. Do not overfill. If the battery is overfilled or any electrolyte spilled, immediately wipe away the excess as electrolyte attacks and corrodes any metal it comes into contact with very rapidly.
2   If the battery is of the Pacemaker design a special topping up procedure is necessary as follows:

(a) The electrolyte levels are visible through the translucent battery case or may be checked by fully raising the vent cover and tilting it to one side. The electrolyte level in each cell must be kept such that the separator plates are just covered. To avoid flooding, the battery must not be topped up within half an hour of it having been charged from any source other than from the generating system fitted to the car
(b) To top up the levels in each cell, raise the vent cover and pour distilled water into the trough until all the rectangular filling slots are full of distilled water and the bottom of the trough is just covered. Wipe the cover seating grooves dry and press the cover firmly into position. The correct quantity of distilled water will automatically be distributed to each cell
(c) The vent must be kept closed at all times except when being topped up

3   As well as keeping the terminals clean and covered with vaseline, the top of the battery and especially the top of the cells should be kept clean and dry. This helps to prevent corrosion and ensures that the battery does not become partially discharged by leakage through dampness and dirt.
4   Once every three months remove the battery and inspect the battery securing nuts, battery clamp, tray and battery leads, for corrosion. (White fluffy deposit on the metal which is brittle to touch). If any corrosion is found, clean off the deposit with ammonia and paint over the clean metal with an anti-rust, anti-acid paint.
5   At the same time inspect the battery case for cracks. If a crack is found, clean and plug it with one of the proprietary compounds made for this purpose. If leakage through the crack has been excessive then it will be necessary to refill the appropriate cell with fresh electrolyte as described below. Cracks are frequently caused at the top of the battery case by pouring in distilled water in the middle of winter, *after* instead of *before* a run. This gives the water no chance to mix with the electrolyte and so the former freezes and splits the battery case.
6   If topping up the battery becomes excessive and the case has been inspected for cracks that could cause leakage, but none are found, the battery is being overcharged and the regulator will have to be checked and reset (dynamo only).
7   With the battery on the bench at the three monthly interval check, measure the specific gravity with a hydrometer to determine the state of charge and condition of the electrolyte. There should be very little variation between the different cells and if a variation in excess of 0.025 is present it will be due to either:

(a) Loss of electrolyte from the battery at some time caused by spilling or a leak, resulting in a drop in the specific gravity of the electrolyte when the deficiency was replaced with distilled water instead of fresh electrolyte
(b) An internal short circuit caused by buckling of the plates or similar malady pointing to the likelihood of total battery failure in the near future

8   The specific gravity of the electrolyte for fully charged conditions at the electrolyte temperatures indicated, is listed in Table A. The specific gravity of a fully discharged battery at different temperatures of the electrolyte is given in Table B.

Table A
Specific Gravity – Battery Fully Charged
1.268 at 100°F or 38°C electrolyte temperature
1.272 at 90°F or 32°C electrolyte temperature
1.276 at 80°F or 27°C electrolyte temperature
1.280 at 70°F or 21°C electrolyte temperature
1.284 at 60°F or 16°C electrolyte temperature
1.288 at 50°F or 10°C electrolyte temperature
1.292 at 40°F or 4°C electrolyte temperature
1.296 at 30°F or –1.1°C electrolyte temperature

Table B

Specific Gravity – Battery Fully Discharged
1.098 at 100°F or 38°C electrolyte temperature
1.102 at 90°F or 32°C electrolyte temperature
1.106 at 80°F or 27°C electrolyte temperature
1.110 at 70°F or 21°C electrolyte temperature
1.114 at 60°F or 16°C electrolyte temperature
1.118 at 50°F or 10°C electrolyte temperature
1.122 at 40°F or 4°C electrolyte temperature
1.126 at 30°F or –1.1°C electrolyte temperature

4 Battery – electrolyte replenishment

1   If the battery is in a fully charged state and one of the cells maintains a specific gravity reading which is 0·025 or more lower than the others and a check of each cell has been made with a special cadmium rod type voltmeter to check for short circuits, then it is likely that electrolyte has been lost from the cell with the low reading at some time.

2   Top up the cell with a solution of 1 part sulphuric acid to 2·5 parts of water. If the cell is already fully topped up draw some electrolyte out with a pipette.

3   When mixing the sulphuric acid and water *never add water to sulphuric acid* –always pour the acid slowly onto the water in a glass container. *If water is added to sulphuric acid there will be a violent reaction.*

4   Continue to top up the cell with the freshly made electrolyte and then recharge the battery and check the hydrometer readings.

5 Battery – charging

1   When heavy demand is placed upon the battery, such as when starting from cold, and much electrical equipment is continually in use, it is a good idea occasionally to have the battery fully charged from an external source at the rate of 3·5 to 4 amps.

2   Continue to charge the battery at this rate until no further rise in specific gravity is noted over a four hour period.

3   Alternatively, a trickle charger, charging at the rate of 1·5 amps can be safely used overnight.

4   Except for topping up, the vent on Pacemaker type batteries must be kept closed. The electrolyte will flood over if the cover is raised while the battery is being trickle or fast charged.

5   Fast charging must only be undertaken in extreme circumstances and must not exceed 40 amps for A9 or AZ9 batteries, or 50 amps for A11, A13 or AZ11 batteries, for a maximum period of one hour.

6   When checking or testing a Pacemaker type battery, a single cell heavy duty discharge tester cannot be used.

7   Whilst charging a battery, the temperature of the electrolyte should never exceed 38°C (100°F).

6 Dynamo – maintenance

1   Routine maintenance consists of checking the tension of the fan belt, and lubricating the dynamo rear bearing once every 6000 miles (9700 km).

2   The fan belt should be tight enough to ensure no slip between the belt and the dynamo pulley. If a shrieking noise comes from the engine when the unit is accelerated rapidly, it is likely that it is the fan belt slipping. On the other hand, the belt must not be too taut or the bearings will wear rapidly and cause dynamo failure or bearing seizure. Ideally 0·5 in (12 mm) of total free movement should be available at the fan belt midway between the fan and the dynamo.

3   To adjust the fan belt tension, slightly slacken the three dynamo retaining bolts, and swing the dynamo on the upper two bolts outwards to increase the tension, and inwards to lower it (Fig. 10.1).

4   It is best to leave the bolts fairly tight so that considerable effort has to be used to move the dynamo, otherwise it is difficult to get the correct setting. If the dynamo is being moved outwards to increase the tension and the bolts have only been slackened a little, a long spanner acting as a lever, placed behind the dynamo with the lower end resting against the block, works very well in moving the dynamo outwards. Tighten the dynamo bolts and check that the dynamo pulley is correctly aligned with the fan belt.

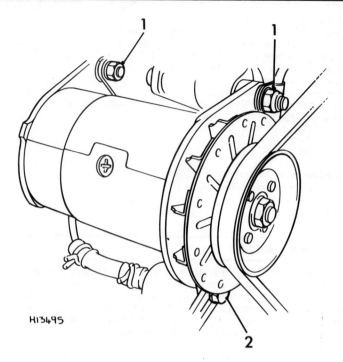

H13495

Fig. 10.1 Dynamo mounting (Sec 6)

1   Upper front and rear mountings   2   Adjustment link securing bolt

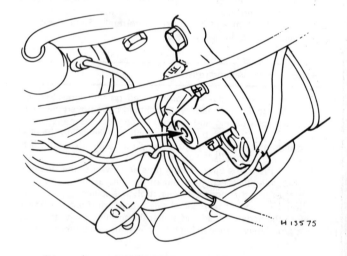

H13575

Fig. 10.2 Dynamo lubrication point (arrowed) (Sec 6)

5   Lubrication on the dynamo consists of inserting three drops of engine oil in the small oil hole in the centre of the commutator end bracket. This lubricates the rear bearing (Fig. 10.2). The front bearing is pre-packed with grease and requires no attention.

7 Dynamo – testing in position

1   If, with the engine running, no charge comes from the dynamo, or the charge is very low, first check that the fan belt is in place and is not slipping. Then check that the leads from the control box to the dynamo are firmly attached and that one has not come loose from its terminal.

2   The lead from the 'D' terminal on the dynamo should be connected to the 'D' terminal on the control box, and similarly the 'F' terminals on the dynamo and control box should also be connected together. Check that this is so and that the leads have not been incorrectly fitted.

3   Make sure none of the electrical equipment such as the lights or radio, is on, and then pull the leads off the dynamo terminals marked 'D' and 'F'. Join the terminals together with a short length of wire.
4   Attach to the centre of this length of wire the positive clip of a 0–20 volts voltmeter and run the other clip to earth on the dynamo yoke. Start the engine and allow it to idle at approximately 750 rpm. At this speed the dynamo should give a reading of about 15 volts on the voltmeter. There is no point in raising the engine speed above a fast idle as the reading will then be inaccurate.
5   If no reading is recorded then check the brushes and brush connections. If a very low reading of approximately 1 volt is obsrved then the field winding may be suspect.
6   If a reading of between 4 to 6 volts is recorded it is likely that the armature winding is at fault.
7   With the Lucas C40-1 windowless yoke dynamo, it must be removed and dismantled before the brushes and commutator can be attended to.
8   If the voltmeter shows a good reading, then with the temporary link still in position, connect both leads from the control box to 'D' and 'F' on the dynamo ('D' to 'D' and 'F' to 'F'). Release the lead from the 'D' terminal at the control box end and clip one lead from the voltmeter to the end of the cable, and the other lead to a good earth. With the engine running at the same speed as previously, an identical voltage to that recorded at the dynamo should be noted on the voltmeter. If no voltage is recorded there is a break in the wire. If the voltage is the same as recorded at the dynamo then check the 'F' lead in a similar fashion. If both readings are the same as at the dynamo then it will be necessary to test the control box.

8   Dynamo – removal and refitting

1   Undo and remove the bolt from the adjustment link and disconnect the electrical leads.
2   Slacken the two mounting bolts and nuts and push the dynamo towards the engine. Lift the fan belt from the pulley.

3   Remove the mounting nuts and bolts and lift away the dynamo.
4   Refitting is a reversal of the removal procedure. Do not finally tighten the retaining bolts and adjustment link bolt until the fan belt has been tensioned correctly.

9   Dynamo – dismantling and inspection

1   Mount the dynamo in a vice and unscrew and remove the two through bolts from the commutator end bracket.
2   Mark the commutator end bracket and the dynamo casing so the end bracket can be refitted in its original position. Pull the end bracket off the armature shaft. Some versions of the dynamo may have a raised pip on the edge of the casing. If so, marking the end bracket and casing is unnecessary. A pip may also be found on the drive end bracket at the opposite end of the casing.
3   Lift the two brush springs and draw the brushes out of the brush holders.
4   Measure the brushes and if worn beyond the specified minimum length, unscrew the screws holding the brush leads to the end bracket. Take off the brushes complete with leads.
5   If no locating pip can be found, mark the drive end bracket and the dynamo casing so that the drive end bracket can be refitted in its original position. Then pull the drive end bracket, complete with armature, out of the casing.
6   Check the condition of the ball bearing in the drive end plate by firmly holding the plate and noting if there is visible side movement of the armature shaft in relation to the end plate. If play is present, the armature assembly must be separated from the end plate. If the bearing is sound there is no need to carry out the work described in the following two paragraphs.
7   Hold the armature in one hand (mount it carefully in a vice if preferred) and undo the nut holding the pulley wheel and fan in place. Pull off the pulley wheel and fan.
8   Next move the Woodruff key from its slot in the armature shaft and also the bearing locating ring.

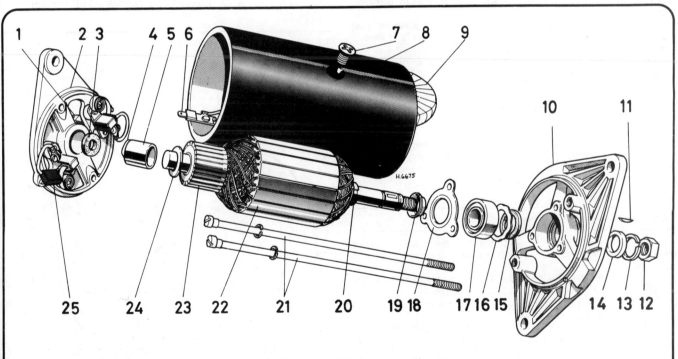

Fig. 10.3 The Lucas C40/1 dynamo (Sec 9)

1 Output terminal 'D'	7 Pole shoe securing screws	13 Lockwasher	19 Shaft collar retaining cup
2 Commutator end bracket	8 Yoke	14 Pulley spacer	20 Shaft collar
3 Felt ring	9 Field coils	15 Felt ring	21 Through-bolts
4 Felt ring retainer	10 Driving end bracket	16 Corrugated washers	22 Armature
5 Bronze bush	11 Shaft key	17 Ball bearing	23 Commutator
6 Field terminal 'F'	12 Shaft nut	18 Bearing retaining plate	24 Thrustwasher
			25 Brush

9   Place the drive end bracket across the open jaws of a vice with the armature downwards and gently tap the armature shaft from the bearing in the end plate with the aid of a suitable drift.

10   Carefully inspect the armature and check it for open or short circuited windings. It is a good indication of an open circuited armature when the commutator segments are burnt. If the armature has short circuited, the commutator segments will be very badly burnt, and the overheated armature windings badly discoloured. If open or short circuits are suspected then test by substituting a new armature for the suspect one.

11   Check the resistance of the field coils. To do this, connect an ohmmeter between the field terminals and the yoke and note the reading on the ohmmeter which should be about 6 ohms. If the ohmmeter reading is infinity this indicates an open circuit in the field winding. If the ohmmeter reading is below 5 ohms this indicates that one of the field coils is faulty and must be renewed.

12   Field coil renewal involves the use of a wheel operated screwdriver, a soldering iron, caulking and riveting. This operation is considered to be beyond the scope of most owners. Therefore, if the field coils are at fault either purchase a rebuilt dynamo, or take the casing to a BL garage or electrical engineering works for new field coils to be fitted.

13   Next check the condition of the commutator. If it is dirty and blackened, clean it with a petrol dampened rag. If the commutator is in good condition the surface will be smooth and quite free from pits or burnt areas, and the insulated segments clearly defined.

14   If, after the commutator has been cleaned, pits and burnt spots are still present, wrap a strip of glass paper round the commutator taking great care to move the commutator $\frac{1}{4}$ of a turn every ten rubs till it is thoroughly clean.

15   In extreme cases of wear, the commutator can be mounted in a lathe and, with the lathe turning at high speed, a very fine cut may be taken off the commutator. Then polish it with glass paper. If it has worn so that the insulators between the segments are level with the top of the segments, then undercut the insulators. The best tool to use for this purpose is half a hacksaw blade ground to a thickness of the insulator, and with the handle end of the blade covered in insulating tape to make it comfortable to hold.

16   Check the bush bearing in the commutator end bracket for wear by noting if the armature spindle rocks when placed in it. If worn it must be renewed.

17   The bush bearing can be removed by a suitable extractor or by screwing a 0.63 in (15.8 mm) tap four or five times into the bush. The tap, complete with bush, is then pulled out of the end bracket.

18   The bush bearing is of the porous bronze type and, before fitting a new one, it is essential that it is allowed to stand in SAE 30 engine oil for at least 24 hours before fitment. In an emergency the bush can be immersed in oil at 100°C (212°F) for 2 hours.

19   Carefully fit the new bush into the end plate, pressing it in until the end of the bearing is flush with the inner side of the end plate. If available, press the bush in with a smooth shouldered mandrel the same diameter as the armature shaft.

10 Dynamo – repair and reassembly

1   To renew the ball bearing fitted to the drive end bracket, drill out the rivets which hold the bearing retainer plate to the end bracket and lift off the plate.

2   Press out the bearing from the end bracket and remove the corrugated and felt washers from the bearing housing.

3   Thoroughly clean the bearing housing and the new bearing, and pack with high melting point grease.

4   Place the felt washer and corrugated washer in that order in the end bracket bearing housing.

5   Fit the new bearing.

6   Gently tap the bearing into place with the aid of a suitable drift.

7   Refit the bearing plate and fit three new rivets.

8   Open up the rivets with the aid of a suitable cold chisel.

9   Finally peen over the open end of the rivets with the aid of a ball hammer.

10   Refit the drive end bracket to the armature shaft. Do not try and force the bracket on but, with the aid of a suitable socket abuting the bearing, tap the bearing on gently, so pulling the end bracket down with it.

11   Slide the spacer up the shaft and refit the Woodruff key.

12   Refit the fan and pulley wheel and then fit the spring washer and nut and tighten the latter. The drive bracket end of the dynamo is now fully assembled.

13   If the brushes are little worn and are to be used again then ensure that they are placed in the same holders from which they were removed. When refitting brushes either new or old, check that they move freely in their holders. If either brush sticks, clean with a petrol moistened rag and if still stiff, lightly polish the sides of the brush with a very fine file until the brush moves quite freely in its holder.

14   Tighten the two retaining screws and washers which hold the wire leads to the brushes in place.

15   It is far easier to slip the end piece with brushes over the commutator, if the brushes are raised in their holders, and held in this position by the pressure of the springs resting against their flanks.

16   Refit the armature to the casing and then the commutator end plate, and screw up the two through bolts.

17   Finally, hook the ends of the two springs off the flanks of the brushes and onto their heads so that brushes are forced down into contact with the armature.

11 Alternator – maintenance

1   The bearings of the alternator are packed with grease on assembly and routine lubrication is not necessary.

2   Regular checking of the drivebelt tension is necessary and this should be done at least every 6000 miles (9700 km).

3   Slacken the alternator hinge bolt and also the bolt on the adjusting link. Move the alternator to the position required to give the correct belt tension, which is when the longest span of the belt can be deflected 0.5 in (13 mm) by moderate thumb pressure.

4   If it is necessary to use leverage on the alternator, use a piece of wood and lever against the drive end bracket only. Leverage against any other part of the alternator may result in damage to it.

5   Do not exceed the recommended belt tension because this will result in excessive wear on the alternator and water pump bearings.

6   After tightening the alternator bolts, recheck the belt tension.

12 Alternator – testing in position

1   Before making the tests, ensure that the alternator drive belt is tensioned correctly, the battery terminals are clean and tight, the

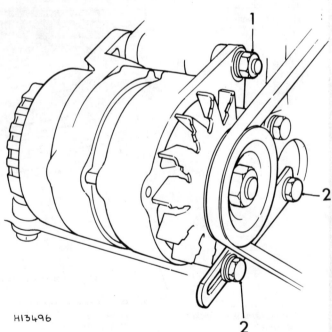

H13496

Fig. 10.4 Alternator mounting (Sec 11)

1   Hinge bolt   *2   Adjusting link bolts*

battery is in good condition and that the cables and connections of the charging circuit are in good condition.

2   Remove the cable connector from the alternator. Connect the negative side of a voltmeter with a range of at least 0 to 12 volts to earth.

3   Switch the ignition ON and connect the positive voltmeter lead to the IND terminal of the cable connector (yellow/brown wire). The meter should indicate battery voltage and if it does not, check the ignition warning light bulb and the warning light circuit for continuity.

4   Transfer the positive lead to the main charging cable connector (thick brown wire). The meter should indicate battery voltage and if it does not, check the continuity of the connections between the battery and the alternator connector.

5   If the tests of paragraphs 3 and 4 are satisfactory, switch the ignition OFF, disconnect the voltmeter and reconnect the cable connector to the alternator. Disconnect the brown cable with an eyelet at its end from its terminal on the starter motor solenoid.

6   Connect an ammeter with a range of at least 10 amps between the end of the brown cable and the terminal from which it was removed. Connect a voltmeter with a range of 15 volts across the battery.

7   Run the engine at about half full speed and note the readings of both the ammeter and the voltmeter.

   (a) If the ammeter reading is zero, the alternator is defective and should be removed for overhaul, or exchange

   (b) If the ammeter reading is less than 10 amps and the voltmeter

reading is between 13.6 and 14.4 volts, the alternator is suspect unless the battery is fully charged. If the alternator is suspect it should be removed and tested on the bench by an auto electrical specialist*

   (c) If the ammeter reading is below 10 amps and the voltage is below 13.6 volts, remove the alternator and fit a new voltage regulator, or an exchange alternator

   (d) If the ammeter reading is above 10 amps and the voltage above 14.4 volts, remove the alternator and fit a new voltage regulator, or an exchange alternator

13 Alternator – removal and refitting

1   Disconnect the battery.

2   Release the ignition shield fixing clips and remove the ignition shield.

3   Release the spring clip retaining the alternator connector and withdraw the connector from the alternator.

4   Remove the two bolts securing the ignition coil to the engine and move the coil away from the engine.

5   Remove the adjusting link bolt.

6   Remove the alternator mounting bolt. Disengage the drivebelt from the alternator pulley and remove the alternator.

7   Refitting is the reverse of removal, but tension the drivebelt correctly after refitting.

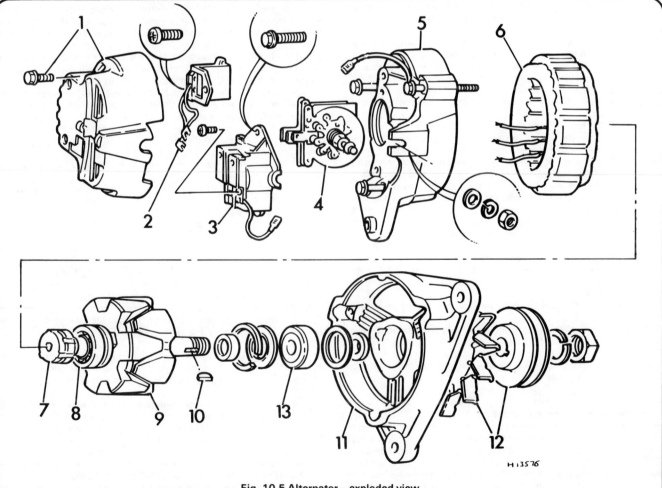

H 13576

Fig. 10.5 Alternator – exploded view

1	Moulded end cover	5	Slip ring end bracket	8	End bearing (slip ring)	11	Drive end bracket
2	Connector	6	Stator winding	9	Pressure ring	12	Fan and pulley
3	Brush box assembly	7	Slip ring moulding	10	Key	13	End bearing (drive end)
4	Rectifier pack						

14 Alternator – dismantling, repair and reassembly

1   The screws on some alternators are sealed and if the screws have been removed, the unit may not be acceptable for exchange.
2   Remove the two screws securing the end cover. These are recessed and it is difficult to remove them without a 4BA box or socket spanner. Remove the cover.
3   Disconnect the cable from the terminal blade on the outer of the three rectifier plates.
4   Make a careful note of the way the wires are connected to the screws securing the brush assemblies, then remove the four screws to release the two brush assemblies from the brush holder
5   Remove the three set screws to release the brush holder and regulator assembly from the slip ring end bracket.
6   Remove the screw securing the regulator assembly to the brush holder and remove the regulator assembly.
7   Remove the bolt securing the rectifier earthing link to the slip ring end bracket.
8   Do not dismantle any further unless you are experienced at soldering electronic equipment and have an instrument soldering iron.
9   Make a note of the way in which the three stator coil wires are connected to the rectifier. Using a pair of pliers as a thermal shunt, so that the diodes are not overheated and damaged, unsolder each of the three cables in turn.
10 Slacken the nut and withdraw the rectifier assembly from the slip ring end bracket.
11 Put mating marks on the drive end bracket, the stator lamination pack and the slip ring end bracket to ensure that they are reassembled correctly and then remove the three through bolts.
12 Withdraw the slip ring end bracket and the stator lamination pack. Remove the O-ring from inside the slip ring end bracket.
13 Remove the nut and spring washer from the end of the rotor and draw the pulley and fan off the shaft.
14 Remove the pulley key and pull the distance piece off the shaft.
15 Press the rotor out of the drive end bracket and withdraw the distance piece from the drive end of the rotor shaft.
16 Remove the circlip from the drive end bracket and remove the bearing cover plate, bearing, O-ring, cover plate and felt washer.
17 Check the bearings for wear and roughness. If necessary repack them with Shell Avania RA grease. If the slip ring end bearing needs renewing, unsolder the two slip ring connections and draw off the bearing and slip ring assembly from the rotor shaft. Do not attempt this unless you have suitable equipment, because you may damage the slip ring assembly. When reassembling, the shielded side of the bearing should face the slip ring assembly and the connections to the slip ring should be made with resin-cored solder of radio quality.
18 Clean the slip rings, using methylated spirit and if there are any signs of burning, remove them using very fine sandpaper.
19 Check that the brushes have not reached their wear limit. If they protrude less than 0·2 in (5 mm) beyond the brush box moulding, new brushes must be fitted.
20 Reassembly is the reverse of dismantling, but the following points should be noted.
21 The inner track of the bearing should be supported when the rotor is pressed into the drive end bracket.
22 When soldering the stator wires to the rectifier pack, use a pair of pliers as a heat shunt, complete the operation as quickly as possible and use resin-cored solder of radio quality.

15 Starter motor – general description

One of four types of starter motor have been fitted to the Maxi depending on the date of the manufacture and the destined market.
All starter motors are interchangeable and engage with a common flywheel starter ring gear. With the inertia type starter motor, the relay is fitted to the rear of the front grille, whereas the pre-engaged type has the solenoid switch on the top of the motor.
The principle of operation of the inertia type starter motor is as follows: When the ignition switch is turned, current flows from the battery to the starter motor relay switch which causes it to become energized. Its internal plunger moves inwards and closes an internal switch so allowing full starting current to flow from the battery to the starter motor. This causes a powerful magnetic field to be induced into the field coils which causes the armature to rotate.

Mounted on helical splines is the drive pinion which, because of the sudden rotation of the armature, is thrown forwards along the armature shaft and so into engagement with the flywheel ring gear. The engine crankshaft will then be rotated until the engine starts to operate on its own and, at this point, the drive pinion is thrown out of mesh with the flywheel ring gear.
The pre-engaged starter motor operates by a slightly different method using end face commutator brushes instead of brushes located on the side of the commutator.
The method of engagement on the pre-engaged starter differs considerably in that the drive pinion is brought into mesh with the starter ring gear before the main starter current is applied.
When the ignition is switched on, current flows from the battery to the solenoid which is mounted on the top of the starter motor body. The plunger in the solenoid moves inwards so causing a centrally pivoted engagement lever to move in such a manner that the forked end pushes the drive pinion into mesh with the starter ring gear. When the solenoid plunger reaches the end of its travel, it closes an internal contact and full starting current flows to the starter field coils. The armature is then able to rotate the crankshaft so starting the engine.
A special one way clutch is fitted to the starter drive pinion so that when the engine just fires and starts to operate on its own, it does not drive the starter motor.

16 Starter motor (M35G) – testing on engine

1   If the starter motor fails to operate, then check the condition of the battery by turning on the headlamps. If they glow brightly for several seconds and then gradually dim, the battery is in an uncharged condition.
2   If the headlamps glow brightly and it is obvious that the battery is in good condition then check the tightness of the battery wiring connections (and in particular the earth lead from the battery terminal to its connection on the bodyframe). Check the tightness of the connections at the relay switch and at the starter motor. Check the wiring with a voltmeter for breaks or shorts.
3   If the wiring is in order then check that the starter motor switch is operating. To do this, press the rubber covered button in the centre of the relay switch under the bonnet. If it is working, the starter motor will be heard to 'click' as it tries to rotate. Alternatively check it with a voltmeter.
4   If the battery is fully charged, the wiring in order, and the switch working but the starter motor fails to operate then it will have to be removed from the car for examination. Before this is done, however, ensure that the starter pinion has not jammed in mesh with the flywheel. Check by turning the square end of the armature shaft with a spanner. This will free the pinion if it is stuck in engagement with the flywheel teeth.

17 Starter motor (M35G) – removal and refitting

1   Disconnect the negative and then the positive terminals from the battery. Also disconnect the starter motor cable from the terminal on the starter motor end cover.
2   Undo and remove the two bolts which secure the starter motor to the clutch and flywheel housing. Lift the starter motor away by manipulating the drivegear out from the ring gear area and then from the engine compartment.
3   Refitting is the reverse procedure to removal. Make sure that the starter motor cable, when secured in position by its terminal, does not touch any part of the body or power unit which could damage the insulation.

18 Starter motor (M35G) – dismantling and reassembly

1   With the starter motor on the bench, loosen the screw on the cover band and slip the cover band off. With a piece of wire bent into the shape of a hook, lift back each of the brush springs in turn and check the movement of the brushes in their holders by pulling on the flexible connectors. If the brushes are so worn that their faces do not rest against the commutator, or if the ends of the brush leads are exposed on their working face, they must be renewed.
2   If any of the brushes tend to stick in their holders then wash them

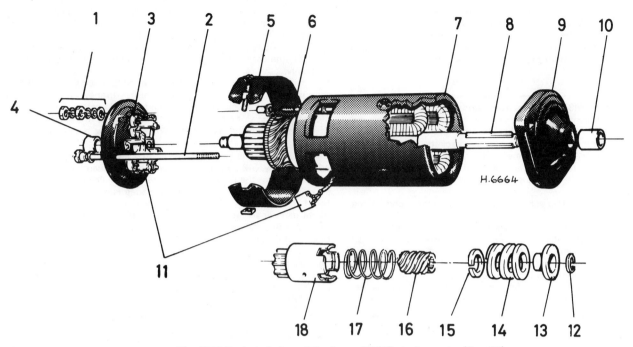

Fig. 10.6 Exploded view of the Lucas M35G starter motor (Sec 18)

1 Terminal nuts and washers	6 Terminal post	11 Brushes	15 Impact washer
2 Through-bolt	7 Yoke	12 Circlip	16 Sleeve
3 Brush spring	8 Armature shaft	13 Locating washer	17 Restraining spring
4 Bearing	9 Driving end bracket	14 Main spring	18 Pinion assembly
5 Band cover	10 Bearing bush		

with a petrol moistened cloth and, if necessary, lightly polish the sides of the brush with a very fine file until the brushes move quite freely in their holders.

3 If the surface of the commutator is dirty or blackened, clean it with a petrol dampened rag. Secure the starter motor in a vice and check it by connecting a heavy gauge cable between the starter motor terminal and a 12 volt battery.

4 Connect the cable from the other battery terminal to earth in the starter motor body. If the motor turns at high speed it is in good order.

5 If the starter motor fails to function or if it is wished to renew the brushes, then it is necessary to further dismantle the motor.

6 Lift the brush springs with the wire hook, and lift all four brushes out of their holders one at a time.

7 Remove the terminal nuts and washers from the terminal post on the commutator end bracket.

8 Unscrew the two through bolts which hold the end plates together and pull off the commutator end bracket. Also remove the driving end bracket which will come away complete with the armature.

9 At this stage, if the brushes are to be renewed, their flexible connectors must be unsoldered and the connectors of new brushes soldered in their place. Check that the new brushes move freely in their holders as detailed above. If cleaning the commutator with petrol fails to remove all the burnt areas and spots, then wrap a piece of glass paper round the commutator and rotate the armature.

10 If the commutator is very badly worn, remove the drive gear as detailed below. Then mount the armature in a lathe and with the lathe turning at high speed, take a very fine cut out of the commutator and finish the surface by polishing with glass paper. *Do not undercut the mica insulators between the commutator segments.*

11 With the starter motor dismantled, test the four field coils for an open circuit. Connect a 12 volt battery with a 12 volt bulb in one of the leads between the field terminal post and the tapping point of the field coils to which the brushes are connected. An open circuit is proved by the bulb not lighting.

12 If the bulb lights, it does not necessarily mean that the field coils are in order, as there is a possibility that one of the coils will be earthed to the starter yoke or pole shoes. To check this, remove the lead from the brush connector and place it against a clean portion of the starter yoke. If the bulb lights, the field coils are earthing. Renewal of the field

coils calls for the use of a wheel operated screwdriver, a soldering iron, caulking and riveting operations and is beyond the scope of the majority of owners. The starter yoke should be taken to a reputable electrical engineering works for new field coils to be fitted. Alternatively, purchase an exchange Lucas starter motor.

13 If the armature is damaged, this will be evident after visual inspection. Look for signs of burning, discolouration, and for conductors that have lifted away from the commutator.

14 With the starter motor stripped down, check the condition of the bushes. They should be renewed when they are sufficiently worn to allow visible side movement of the armature shaft.

15 The old bushes are simply driven out with a suitable drift and the new bushes inserted by the same method. As the bushes are of the phosphor bronze type it is essential that they are allowed to stand in engine oil for at least 24 hours before fitment. Alternatively soak in oil at 100°C (212°F) for 2 hours.

16 To dismantle the starter motor drive, first use a press to push the retainer clear of the circlip which can then be removed. Lift away the retainer and main spring.

17 Slide the remaining parts with a rotary action of the armature shaft.

18 It is most important that the drivegear is completely free from oil, grease and dirt. With the drivegear removed, clean all parts thoroughly in paraffin. *Under no circumstances oil the drive components.* Lubrication of the drive components could easily cause the pinion to stick.

19 Reassembly of the starter motor drive is the reverse sequence to dismantling. Use a press to compress the spring and retainer sufficiently to allow a new circlip to be fitted to its groove on the shaft. Remove the drive from the press.

20 Reassembly of the starter motor is the reverse sequence to dismantling.

19 Starter motor (M35J) – testing on engine

The test procedure for this type of starter motor is basically identical to that for the Lucas M35G and full information will be found in Section 16.

20 Starter motor (M35J) – removal and refitting

The removal and refitting sequence for this type of starter motor is basically identical to that for the Lucas M35G and full information will be found in Section 17.

21 Starter motor (M35J) – dismantling and reassembly

1 With the starter motor on the bench, first mark the relative positions of the starter motor body to the two end brackets.
2 Undo and remove the two screws and spring washers securing the drive end bracket to the body. The drive end bracket, complete with armature ann and drive, may now be drawn forwards from the starter motor body.
3 Lift away the thrust washer from the commutator end of the armature shaft.
4 Undo and remove the two screws securing the commutator end bracket to the starter motor body. The commutator end bracket may now be drawn back about 1 in (25 mm) allowing sufficient access so as to disengage the field bushes from the bracket. Once these are free, the end bracket may now be completely removed.
5 With the motor stripped, the brushes and brush gear may be inspected. To check the brush spring tension, fit a new brush into each holder in turn and, using an accurate spring balance, push the brush on the balance tray until the brush protrudes approximately 0·063 in (1·6 mm) from the holder. Make a note of the reading, which should be approximately 28 oz (790 gm). If the spring pressures vary considerably the commutator end bracket must be renewed as a complete assembly.
6 Inspect the brushes for wear and renew a brush which is nearing the minimum length of 0·38 in (9·5 mm). To renew the end bracket brushes, cut the brush cables from the terminal posts and with a small file or hacksaw, slot the head of the terminal posts to a sufficient depth to accommodate the new leads. Solder the new brush leads to the posts.
7 To renew the field winding brushes, cut the brush leads approximately 0·25 in (6 mm) from the field winding junction and carefully solder the new brush leads to the remaining stumps, making sure that the insulation sleeves provide adequate cover.
8 If the commutator surface is dirty or blackened, clean it with a petrol dampened rag. Carefully examine the commutator for signs of excessive wear, burning or pitting. If evident it may be reconditioned by having it skimmed at the local engineering works or BL dealer who possesses a centre lathe. The thickness of the commutator must not be less than 0·08 in (2 mm). For minor reconditioning, the commutator may be polished with glass paper. *Do not undercut the mica insulators between the commutator segments.*
9 With the starter motor dismantled, test the field coils for open

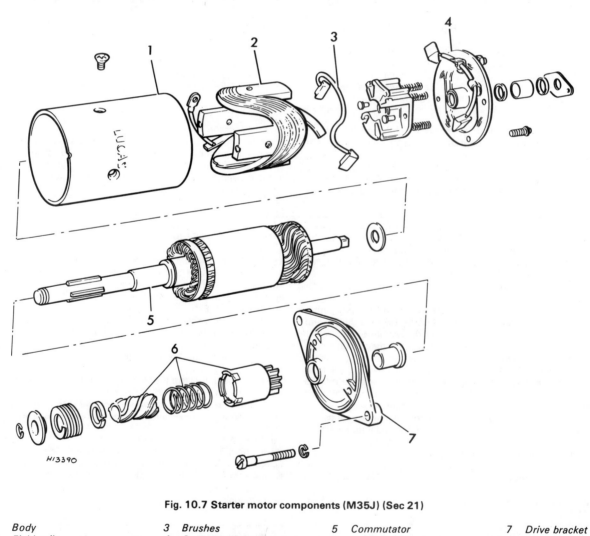

Fig. 10.7 Starter motor components (M35J) (Sec 21)

1 Body	3 Brushes	5 Commutator	7 Drive bracket
2 Field coils	4 Commutator end bracket	6 Drive	

circuit. Connect a 12 volt battery with a 12 volt bulb in one of the leads between each of the field brushes and a clean part of the body. The lamp will light if continuity is satisfactory between the brushes, windings and body connection.

10 Renewal of the field coils calls for the use of a wheel operated screwdriver, a soldering iron, caulking and riveting operations and is beyond the scope of the majority of owners. The starter motor body should be taken to an automobile electrical engineering works for new field coils to be fitted. Alternatively purchase an exchange Lucas starter motor.

11 Check the condition of the bushes and they should be renewed when they are sufficiently worn to allow visible side movement of the armature shaft.

12 To renew the commutator end bracket bush, drill out the rivets securing the brush box moulding and remove the moulding, bearing seal retaining plate and felt washer seal.

13 Screw in a 0·5 in (13 mm) tap and withdraw the bush with the tap.

14 As the bush is of the phosphor bronze type it is essential that it is allowed to stand in engine oil for at least 24 hours before fitment. Alternatively soak in oil at 100°C (212°F) for 2 hours.

15 Using a suitable diameter drift, drive the new bush into position. Do not ream the bush as its self lubricating properties will be impaired.

16 To remove the drive end bracket bush it will be necessary to remove the drivegear as described in paragraphs 18 and 19.

17 Using a suitable diameter drift remove the old bush and fit a new one as described in paragraphs 14 and 15.

18 To dismantle the starter motor drive, first use a press to push the retainer clear of the circlip which can then be removed. Lift away the retainer and main spring.

19 Slide off the remaining parts with a rotary action of the armature shaft.

20 It is most important that the drivegear is completely free from oil, grease and dirt. With the drivegear removed, clean all parts thoroughly in paraffin. *Under no circumstances oil the drive components.* Lubrication of the drive components could easily cause the pinion to stick.

21 Reassembly of the starter motor drive is the reverse sequence to dismantling. Use a press to compress the spring and retainer sufficiently to allow a new circlip to be fitted to its groove on the shaft.

Remove the drive from the press.

22 Reassembly of the starter motor is the reverse sequence to dismantling.

22 Starter motor (M35J pre-engaged) – testing on engine

The testing procedure is basically similar to the M35G starter described in Section 16.

23 Starter motor (M35J pre-engaged) – removal and refitting

1 Disconnect the negative and then the positive terminals from the battery.

2 Make a note of the electrical connections at the rear of the solenoid and disconnect the top heavy duty cable. Also release the Lucar terminals situated below the heavy duty cable. There is no need to undo the lower heavy duty cable at the rear of the solenoid.

3 Undo and remove the two bolts which hold the starter motor in place and lift away upwards.

4 Refitting is a straightforward reversal of the removal sequence. Check that the electrical cable connections are clean and firmly attached to their respective terminals.

24 Starter motor (M35J pre-engaged) – dismantling and reassembly

1 Detach the heavy duty cable, linking the solenoid STA terminal to the starter motor terminal, by undoing and removing the securing nuts and washers (Fig. 10.8).

2 Undo and remove the two nuts and spring washers securing the solenoid to the drive end bracket.

3 Carefully withdraw the solenoid coil unit from the drive end bracket.

4 Lift off the solenoid plunger and return spring from the engagement lever.

5 Remove the rubber sealing block from the drive end bracket.

6 Remove the retaining ring (spire nut) from the engagement lever

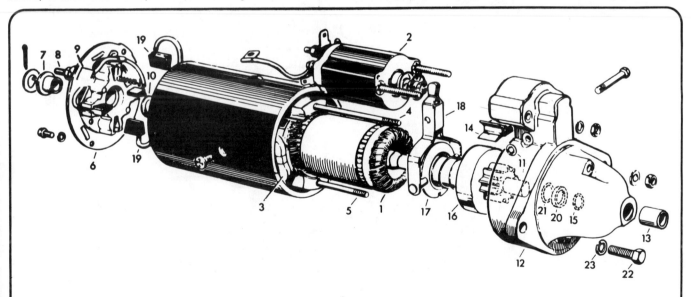

Fig. 10.8 Starter motor components (M35J pre-engaged) (Sec 24)

1	Armature	7	Commutator end bracket bush
2	Solenoid		
3	Field coil	8	Field terminal
4	Pole piece and long stud	9	Terminal insulating bush
5	Pole piece and short stud	10	Thrustplate
6	Commutator end bracket	11	Pivot pin retaining clip

12	Drive end bracket	18	Lever and pivot assembly
13	End bracket bush	19	Brush
14	Grommet	20	Thrust collar
15	Jump ring	21	Shim
16	Roller clutch drive	22	Fixing bolt
17	Bearing bush	23	Lockwasher

pivot pin and withdraw the pin.

7 Unscrew and remove the two drive end bracket securing nuts and spring washers and withdraw the bracket.

8 Lift away the engagement lever from the drive operating plate.

9 Extract the split pin from the end of the armature and remove the shim washers and thrust plate from the commutator end of the armature shaft.

10 Remove the armature, together with its internal thrust washer.

11 Withdraw the thrust washer from the armature.

12 Undo and remove the two screws securing the commutator end bracket to the starter motor body.

13 Carefully detach the end bracket from the yoke, at the same time disengaging the field brushes from the brush gear. Lift away the end bracket.

14 Move the thrust collar clear of the jump ring, and then remove the jump ring. Withdraw the drive assembly from the armature shaft.

15 Inspection and renovation is basically the same as for the Lucas M35G starter motor and full information will be found in Section 18. The following additions necessitated by the fitting of the solenoid coil should be noted:

16 If a bush is worn, so allowing excessive side movement of the armature shaft, the bush must be renewed. Drive out the old bush with a piece of suitable diameter rod, preferably with a shoulder on it to stop the bush collapsing.

17 Soak a new bush in engine oil for 24 hours or if time does not permit, heat in an oil bath at 100°C (212°F) for 2 hours prior to fitting.

18 As new bushes must not be reamed after fitting it must be pressed into position using a small mandrel of the same diameter as the bush and with a shoulder on it. Place the bush on the mandrel and press into position using a bench vice.

19 Use a test light and battery to test the continuity of the coil windings between terminal STA and a good earth point on the solenoid body. If the light fails to come on, the solenoid should be renewed.

20 To test the solenoid contacts for correct opening and closing, connect a 12 volt battery and a 60 watt test light between the main unmarked Lucar terminal and the STA terminal. The light should not come on.

21 Energise the solenoid with a separate 12 volt supply connected to the small unmarked Lucar terminal and a good earth on the solenoid body.

22 As the coil is energised the solenoid should be heard to operate and the test lamp should light with full brilliance.

23 The contacts may only be renewed as a set, ie moving and fixed contacts. The fixed contacts are part of the moulded cover.

24 To fit a new set of contacts, first undo and remove the moulded cover securing screws.

25 Unsolder the coil connections from the cover terminals.

26 Lift away the cover and moving contact assembly.

27 Fit a new cover and moving contact assembly, soldering the connections to the cover terminals.

28 Refit the moulded cover securing screws.

29 Whilst the motor is apart, check the operation of the drive clutch. It must provide instantaneous take up of the drive in one direction and rotate easily and smoothly in the opposite direction.

30 Make sure that the drive moves smoothly on the armature shaft splines without binding or sticking.

31 Reassembly of the starter motor is the reverse sequence to dismantling. The following additional points should be noted.

32 When assembling the drive, always use a new retaining ring (spire nut) to secure the engagement lever pivot pin.

33 Make sure that the internal thrust washer is fitted to the commutator end of the armature shaft before the armature is fitted.

34 Make sure that the thrust washers and plate are assembled in the correct order and are prevented from rotating separately by engaging the collar pin with the locking piece on the thrust plate.

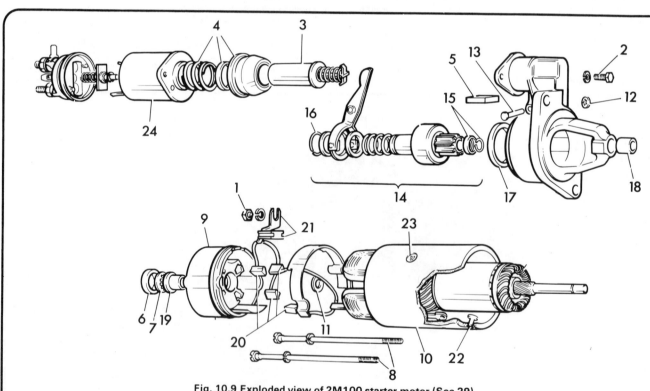

Fig. 10.9 Exploded view of 2M100 starter motor (Sec 29)

1	Connecting link securing nut	6	Armature end cap seal	13	Engagement lever pivot pin	19	Commutator end cover armature shaft bush
2	Solenoid to drive end bracket securing set-screw	7	Armature shaft retaining ring (spire nut)	14	Armature and roller clutch drive assembly	20	Field coil brushes
3	Solenoid plunger	8	Through bolts	15	Thrust collar and jump ring	21	Terminal and rubber grommet
4	Solenoid plunger return spring, spring seat and dust excluder	9	Commutator end cover	16	Spring ring	22	Rivet
5	Rubber grommet	10	Yoke	17	Dirt seal	23	Pole shoe retaining screw
		11	Thrustwasher	18	Drive end bracket armature shaft brush	24	Solenoid
		12	Retaining ring (spire nut)				

25 Starter motor (2M100 pre-engaged) – testing on engine

The test procedure for this type of starter motor is basically identical to that for the Lucas M35J pre-engaged starter motor and the M35G. Full information will be found in Section 12.

26 Starter motor (2M100 pre-engaged) – removal and refitting

The removal and refitting sequence for this type of starter motor is basically identical to that for the Lucas M35J pre-engaged type starter motor. Full information will be found in Section 23.

27 Starter motor (2M100 pre-engaged) – dismantling and reassembly

1 Undo and remove the nut and spring washer that secures the connecting link between the solenoid and starter motor at the solenoid 'STA' terminal. Carefully ease the connecting link out of engagement of the terminal post on the solenoid.
2 Undo and remove the two nuts and spring washers that secure the solenoid to the drive end bracket.
3 Carefully ease the solenoid back from the drive end bracket, lift the solenoid plunger and return spring from the engagement lever, and completely remove the solenoid.
4 Recover the shaped rubber block that is placed between the solenoid and starter motor body.
5 Carefully remove the end cap seal from the commutator end cover.
6 Ease the armature shaft retaining ring (spire nut) from the armature shaft. The retaining ring must *not* be reused, but a new one obtained ready for fitting.
7 Undo and remove the two long through bolts and spring washers.
8 Detach the commutator end cover from the yoke, at the same time disengaging the field brushes from the brush box moulding.
9 Lift away the thrust washer from the armature shaft.
10 The starter motor body may now be lifted from the armature and drive end assembly.
11 Ease the retaining ring (spire nut) from the engagement lever pivot pin. The retaining ring must *not* be reused, but a new one obtained ready for fitting.
12 Using a parallel pin punch of suitable size, remove the pivot pin from the engagement lever and drive end bracket.
13 Carefully move the thrust collar clear of the jump ring, and slide the jump ring from the armature shaft.
14 Slide off the thrust collar, and finally remove the roller clutch drive and engagement lever assembly from the armature shaft.
15 For inspection and servicing information of the brush gear, commutator, and armature refer to Section 21, paragraphs 5 to 8 inclusive.
16 To test the field coils refer to Section 21, paragraphs 9 and 10.
17 Check the condition of the brushes and if they show signs of wear remove the old ones and fit new as described in Section 21, paragraphs 11 to 17. Disregard the reference in paragraph 16 to the removal of the drivegear as this will have already been done.
18 Whilst the motor is apart, check the operation of the drive clutch. It must provide instantaneous take up of the drive in one direction and rotate easily and smoothly in the opposite direction.
19 Make sure that the drive moves smoothly on the armature shaft splines without binding or sticking.
20 Reassembling the starter motor is the reverse sequence to dismantling. The following additional points should be noted:
21 When assembling the drive end bracket always use a new retaining ring (spire nut) to secure the engagement lever pivot pin.
22 Make sure that the internal thrust washer is fitted to the commutator end of the armature shaft before the armature end cover is fitted.
23 Always use a new retaining ring (spire nut) on the armature shaft, to give a maximum clearance of 0·010 in (0·25 mm) between the retaining ring and the bearing bush shoulder. This will be the armature endfloat.

28 Control box – general description

1 The control box is positioned on the right-hand wing valance and

comprises three units; two separate vibrating armature-type single contact regulators and a cut-out relay. One of the regulators is sensitive to change in current and the other to changes in voltage (Fig. 10.10).
2 Adjustments can be made only with a special tool which resembles a screwdriver with a multi-toothed blade. This can be obtained through Lucas agents.
3 The regulators control the output from the dynamo depending on the state of the battery and the demands of the electrical equipment, and ensure that the battery is not overcharged. The cut-out is really an automatic switch and connects the dynamo to the battery when the dynamo is turning fast enough to produce a charge. Similarly it disconnects the battery from the dynamo when the engine is idling or stationary so that the battery does not discharge through the dynamo.

29 Cut-out and regulator contacts – maintenance

1 Every 12 000 miles check the cut-out and regulator contacts. If they are dirty or rough or burnt, first disconnect the battery, then place a piece of fine glass paper (do not use emery paper or carborundum paper) between the cut-out contacts, close them manually and draw the glass paper through several times.
2 Clean the regulator contacts in exactly the same way, but use emery or carborundum paper and not glass paper. Carefully clean sets of contacts from all traces of dust with a rag moistened in methylated spirits.

30 Regulator – adjustment

1 The regulator requires very little attention during its service life, and if there should be any reason to suspect its correct functioning, tests of all circuits should be made to ensure that they are not the reason for the trouble.
2 These checks include the tension of the fan belt, to make sure that it is not slipping and so providing only a very low charge rate. The battery should be carefully checked for possible low charge rate due to a faulty cell, or corroded battery connections.
3 The leads from the generator may have been crossed during fitting, and if this is the case, then the regulator points will have stuck together as soon as the generator starts to charge. Check for loose or broken leads from the generator to the regulator.
4 If, after a thorough check, it is considered advisable to test the regulator, this should be carried out only by an electrician who is well acquainted with the correct method, using test bench equipment.
5 Pull off the Lucar connections from the two adjacent control box terminals 'B'. To start the engine it will now be necessary to join together the ignition and battery leads with a suitable wire.
6 Connect a 0-20 voltmeter between terminal 'D' on the control box and terminal 'WL'. Start the engine and run it at 3000 rpm. The reading on the voltmeter should be steady and lie between the limits detailed in the Specifications.
7 If the reading is unsteady this may be due to dirty contacts. If the reading is outside the specified limits stop the engine and adjust the voltage regulator in the following manner.
8 Take off the control box cover and start and run the engine at 3000 rpm. Using the correct tool, turn the voltage adjustment cam anti-clockwise to lower the setting and clockwise to raise it. To check that the setting is correct, stop the engine, and then start it and run it at 3000 rpm noting the reading. Refit the cover and the connections to the 'WL' and 'D' terminals.

31 Current regulator – adjustment

1 The maximum output from the current regulator should equal the maximum output from the dynamo which is 22 amps. To test this it is necessary to bypass the voltage regulator by holding the contacts together.
2 Remove the cover from the control box and with a bulldog clip hold the voltage regulator contacts together.
3 Pull off the wires from the adjacent terminals 'B' and bridge them together.
4 Connect a 0-40 moving-coil ammeter to the terminals and leads.
5 Turn on all the lights and run the engine at 4500 rpm. The ammeter should give a steady reading between 19 and 22 amps. If the

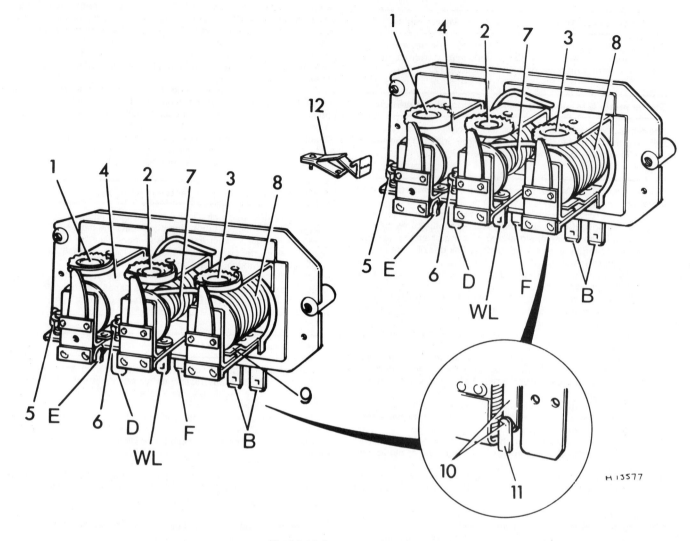

Fig. 10.10 Control box (Sec 28)

1 Adjustment cam – voltage	4 Voltage regulator	7 Current regulator	10 Cut-out contacts
2 Adjustment cam – current	5 Voltage contacts	8 Cut-out relay	11 Fixed contact bracket
3 Adjustment cam – cut-out	6 Current contacts	9 Armature back stop	12 Clip

Early units prior to 37563 identified by flanged adjustment cams

needle flickers it is likely that the points are dirty. If the reading is too low, turn the special Lucas tool clockwise to raise the setting and anti-clockwise to lower it.

32 Cut-out – adjustment

1   Check the voltage required to operate the cut out by connecting a voltmeter between the control box terminals 'D' and 'WL'. Remove the control box cover, start the engine and switch on the headlights, then gradually increase its speed until the cut-out closes. This should occur when the reading is between 12.7 to 13.3 volts.
2   If the reading is outside these limits turn the cut-out adjusting cam by means of the adjusting tool, a fraction at a time clockwise to raise the voltage, and anti-clockwise to lower it.
3   To adjust the drop off voltage, bend the fixed contact blade carefully. To raise the drop off voltage setting, reduce the gap and to lower the setting, increase the gap. The adjustment to the cut-out should be completed within 30 seconds of starting the engine as otherwise heat build-up from the shunt-coil will affect the readings.
4   If the cut-out fails to work, clean the contacts, and if there is still no response, renew the cut-out and regulator unit.

33 Starter motor relay switch – removal and refitting

1   The starter motor relay switch, fitted to models with inertia type starter motors, is located behind the front grille.
2   To remove the switch, first disconnect the negative and then the positive terminals from the battery .
3   Make a note of the electrical cable connections and then detach the two Lucar connectors. Disconnect the two heavy duty cables by undoing and removing their securing nuts.
4   Unscrew and remove the two setscrews holding the relay to the front grille and lift away the relay.
5   Refitting is the reverse of removal.

34 Flasher unit and circuit – fault tracing and rectification

If the flasher unit fails to operate, or works either very slowly or very rapidly, check out the flasher indicator circuit as described below, before assuming there is a fault in the unit itself.

1   Examine the direction indicator bulbs front and rear for broken filaments (see Sections 43 and 44).

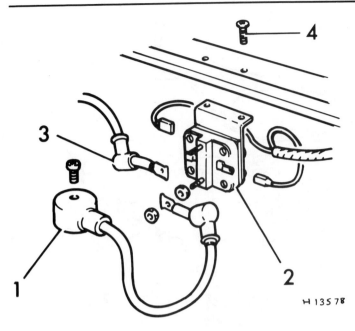

Fig. 10.11 Starter motor relay switch (Sec 33)

1 *Battery terminal*	3 *Heavy duty cable*
2 *Solenoid*	4 *Solenoid bracket screws*

2   If the external flashers are working, but the internal flasher warning lights on one or both sides have ceased to function, check the filaments and renew as necessary.

3   With the aid of the wiring diagram check all the flasher circuit connections if a flasher bulb is sound but does not work.

4   In the event of total indicator failure, check the 7-8 fuse.

5   With the ignition switched on, check that current is reaching the flasher unit by connecting a voltmeter between the 'plus' or 'B' terminal and earth. If this test is positive, connect the 'plus' or 'B' terminal and the 'L' terminal and operate the flasher switch. If the flasher bulb lights up the flasher unit itself is defective and must be renewed as it is not possible to dismantle and repair it.

35 Windscreen wiper arms – removal and refitting

1   Before removing a wiper arm, turn the windscreen switch on and off to ensure the arms are in their normal parked position parallel with the bottom of the windscreen.

2   To remove the arm, pivot the arm back and pull the wiper arm head off the splined drive, at the same time easing back the clip with a screwdriver.

3   When refitting an arm, place it so it is in the correct relative parked position and then press the arm head onto the splined drive till the retaining clip clicks into place.

36 Windscreen wiper mechanism – fault diagnosis and rectification

Should the windscreen wipers fail, or work very slowly then check the terminals for loose connections, and make sure the insulation of the external wiring is not broken or cracked. If this is in order, then check the current the motor is taking by connecting up an ammeter in the circuit and turning on the wiper switch. Consumption should be between 1.5 and 3.4 amps.

If no current is passing, check fuse 5. If the fuse has blown, renew it after having checked the wiring of the motor and other electrical circuits serviced by this fuse for short circuits. If the fuse is in good condition, check the wiper switch.

If the wiper takes a very high current, check the wiper blades for freedom of movement. If this is satisfactory, check the gearbox cover and gear assembly for damage and measure the endfloat which should

be between 0.004 to 0.008 in (0.10 to 0.20 mm).

The endfloat is set by the thrust screw. Check that excessive friction in the cable tubes, caused by too small a curvature, is not the cause of high current consumption and lubricate the gear and spindle with Ragosine Listate 225 grease.

If the motor is suspect, refer to Section 39 for servicing details.

37 Windscreen wiper blades – changing wiper arc

If it is wished to change the area through which the wiper blades move, this is simply done by removing each arm in turn from each splined drive, and then refitting it on the drive in a slightly different position.

38 Windscreen wiper motor – removal and refitting

1   Remove the windscreen wiper arms by lifting the blades and pulling the arms off the splined drive shafts, at the same time easing back the clip with a screwdriver.

2   Disconnect the negative and then the positive terminal from the battery.

3   Release the electric cable terminal block from the connector for the windscreen wiper motor located next to the motor.

4   Undo ther nut which secures the outer cable to the windscreen wiper motor housing.

5   Undo and remove the two screws that secure the motor retaining bracket to the inner wing valance.

6   Carefully draw the wiper motor from the outer cable at the same time the inner cable will be drawn out of the outer cable.

7   Refitting the wiper motor and inner cable is the reverse sequence to removal. Take care in feeding the inner cable through the outer cable and engaging the inner cable with each wiper wheelbox spindle.

39 Windscreen wiper motor – dismantling, inspection and reassembly

1   Refer to Fig. 10.12 and remove the four gearbox cover retaining screws and lift away the cover. Release the circlip and flat washer securing the connecting rod to the crankpin on the shaft and gear. Lift away the connecting rod, followed by the second flat washer.

2   Release the circlip and washer securing the shaft and gear to the gearbox body.

3   De-burr the gear shaft and lift away the gear, making a careful note of the location of the dished washer.

4   Scribe a mark on the yoke assembly and gearbox, to ensure correct reassembly and unscrew the two yoke bolts from the motor yoke assembly. Part the yoke assembly including armature from the gearbox body. As the yoke assembly has residual magnetism, ensure that the yoke is kept well away from metallic dust.

5   Unscrew the two screws securing the brush gear and the terminal and switch assembly and remove both the assemblies.

6   Examine the brushes and renew them if they are worn below the minimum specified length. Check that the brushes move freely in their boxes. If a push type spring gauge is available, check the spring rate which should be between 5 to 7 ounces when the bottom of the brush is level with the bottom of the slot in the brush box. Again, if the spring rate is incorrect, fit a new brush gear assembly.

7   If the armature is suspect take it to an automobile electrician to test for open or short circuiting.

8   Inspect the gearwheel for signs of excessive wear or damage and fit a new one if necessary.

9   Reassembly is the reverse procedure to dismantling but there are several points that require special attention.

10 Use only Ragosine Listate grease to lubricate the gear-wheel teeth and cam, the armature shaft worm gear, connecting rod and its connecting pin, the cross head slide and cable rack and wheelbox gear wheels.

11 Use only Shell Turbo 41 oil to lubricate the bearing bushes, the armature shaft bearing journals (sparingly) the gearwheel shaft and crankpin, the felt washer in the yoke bearing (thoroughly soak) and the wheelbox spindles.

12 When a new armature is to be fitted, slacken the thrust screw to provide endfloat for fitting the yoke.

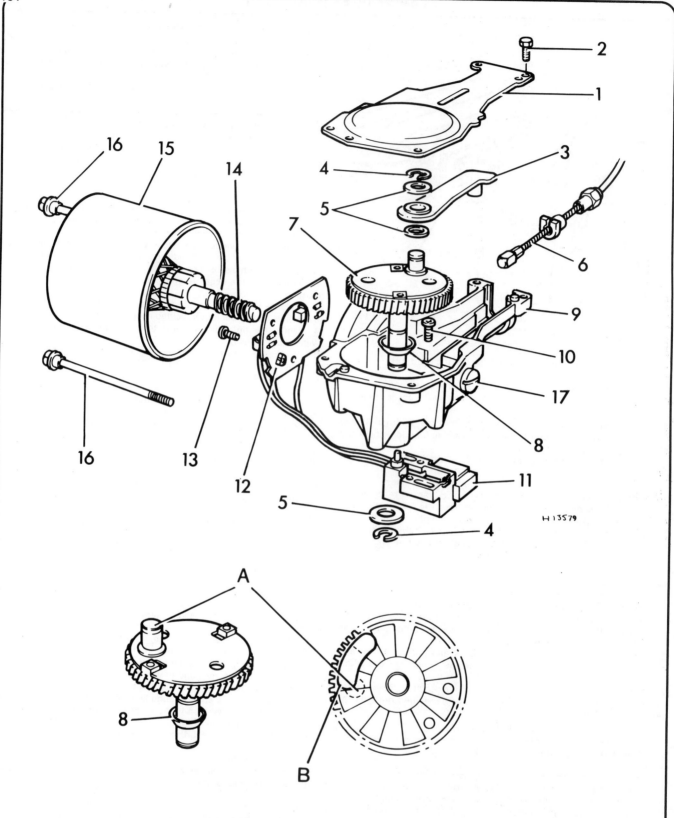

H 13579

Fig. 10.12 Windscreen wiper motor components (Sec 39)

1	Gearbox cover	6	Cross-head screw	11	Limit switch assembly	16	Yoke bolts
2	Screw for cover	7	Shaft and gear	12	Brush gear	17	Armature thrust screw
3	Connecting rod	8	Dished washer	13	Screw for brush gear	A	Crankpin
4	Circlip	9	Gearbox	14	Armature	B	Contact
5	Plain washers	10	Screw for limit switch	15	Yoke assembly		

13 The thrust disc inside the yoke bearing should be fitted with the concave side towards the endface of the bearing. The dished washer fitted beneath the gearwheel should have its concave side towards the gearwheel. If a new gearwheel is being fitted, make sure that crankpin A is correctly aligned with the contact B, for parking the wiper blades with the rack extended (Fig. 10.12).

14 The larger of the two flat washers is fitted underneath the connecting rod and the smaller one on top, under the retaining circlip.

15 To adjust the armature endfloat, tighten the thrust screw and then turn it back one quarter of a turn to give an endfloat of between 0.004 and 0.008 in (0.102 and 0.203 mm). The gap should be measured under the head of the thrust screw. Fit a shim of suitable size beneath the head and tighten the screw.

40 Horns – fault tracing and rectification

1 If a horn works badly or fails completely, first check the wiring leading to it for short circuits and loose connections. Also check that the horn is firmly secured and that there is nothing lying on the horn body.

2 The horn should never be dismantled, but it is possible to adjust it. This adjustment is to compensate for wear of the moving parts only and will not affect the tone.

3 On either the Lucas 9H or 6H models there is a small adjustment screw on the broad rim of the horn nearly opposite the two terminals. Do not confuse this with the large screw in the centre.

4 Turn the adjustmernt screw anti-clockwise until the horn just fails to sound. Then turn the screw a quarter of a turn clockwise which is the optimum setting.

5 It is recommended that if the horn has to be reset in the car, the fuse 2 should be removed and replaced with a piece of wire, otherwise the fuse will continually blow due to the continuous high current required for the horn in continual operation.

6 With twin horns, the horn which is not being adjusted should be disconnected while adjustment of the other takes place.

41 Headlight units – removal and refitting

1 Sealed beam, or renewable bulb light units are fitted depending on the market for which the car was originally destined.

2 The method of gaining access to the light unit for replacement is identical for all types of light units and bulbs.

3 Undo and remove the screw securing the rim and carefully lift off the rim (photo).

4 Undo and remove the three screws securing the light unit retaining plate to the light assembly body. Lift away the retaining plate.

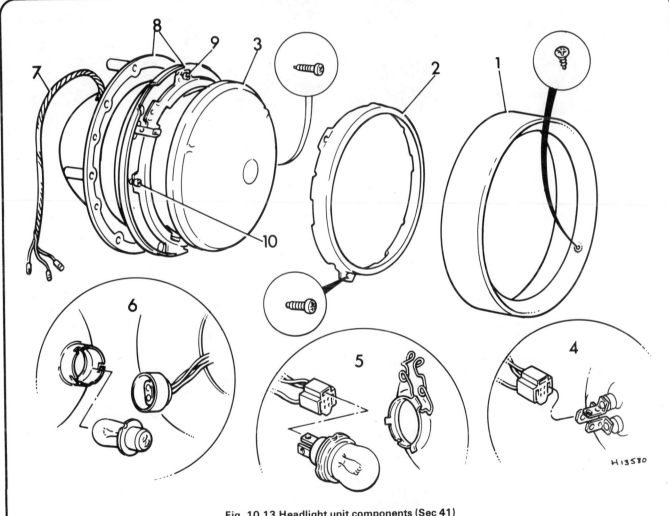

Fig. 10.13 Headlight unit components (Sec 41)

1	Outer rim		connector
2	Light unit retaining rim	5	Spring clip type bulb holder
3	Light unit		and connector
4	Sealed beam light unit		

6 Cap type bulb holder
7 Wiring to rear of light unit assembly

8 Back shell
9 Vertical adjustment screw
10 Horizontal adjustment screw

41.3 Removing the headlight rim

41.5 Removing the headlight assembly

43.1 Side light and front flasher bulbs

43.3 Side flasher bulb

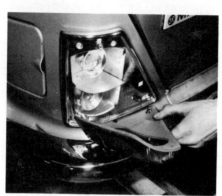
44.1 Stop, tail and rear flasher bulbs

45.1 Number plate and reversing light bulbs

5   Draw the light unit forwards away from the light assembly body (photo).

6   To remove the sealed beam unit, detach the three pin connector from the reflector and lift away the light unit.

7   On spring clip type bulb holders, detach the three pin connector and disengage the spring clip from the reflector lugs. The bulb may now be lifted away.

8   When a cap type bulb holder is fitted, press and turn the cap in an anti-clockwise direction. Lift off the cap and then the bulb.

9   Refitting the sealed beam unit is the reverse sequence to removal.

10   When fitting a bulb in a spring clip type bulb holder, make sure that the pip on the bulb flange engages in the slot in the reflector. Refit the spring clip, ensuring that the coils in the clip are resting on the base of the bulb and that the legs of the clip are fully engaged under the reflector lugs.

11   With the cap type bulb holder, make sure that the notch in the bulb flange locates on the ridge in the reflector. Engage the cap lugs in the reflector slots. Press in and turn the cap in a clockwise direction.

12   Place the three lugs on the outer edge of the light unit in the slots formed in the lamp body. Refit the retaining plate and secure with the three screws.

13   Finally refit the outer rim and secure with the one retaining screw.

42   Headlight – beam adjustment

The headlights may be adjusted for both vertical and horizontal beam position by two screws, these being shown in Fig. 10.13. For vertical movement screw 9 should be used and horizontal movement screw 10.

They should be set so that on full or high beam, the beams are set slightly below parallel with a level road surface. Do not forget that the beam position is affected by how the car is normally loaded for night driving, and set the beams loaded to this position.

Although this adjustment can be approximately set at home, it is recommended that this be left to the local garage who will have the necessary equipment to do the job more accurately.

43   Side and front flasher bulbs – removal and refitting

1   Undo and remove the two screws securing the lamp lens to the lamp body and lift away the lens taking care not to damage the seal (photo).

2   Either bulb is retained by a bayonet fixing, so to remove a bulb push in slightly and rotate in an anti-clockwise direction.

3   To gain access to a direction indicator side repeater bulb, remove the screw securing the lens and lift away the lens. A single filament bayonet cap bulb is fitted (photo).

44   Stop, tail and rear flasher bulbs – removal and refitting

1   Undo and remove the three screws securing the lamp lens to the lamp body and lift away the lens taking care not to damage the seal (photo).

2   Two bulbs are used, the lower one being of the double filament type, and are retained in position by a bayonet fixing. To remove a bulb, push in slightly and rotate in an anti-clockwise direction.

3   The lower, double filament bulb has offset pins on the bayonet fixing, so it is not possible to fit it the wrong way round.

45   Number plate and reverse light bulbs – removal and refitting

1   Undo and remove the two set screws securing the cover to the lamp body and lift away the cover (photo).

2   Lift away the relevant lens and remove the bulb by pushing in slightly and rotating in an anti-clockwise direction.

3   Refitting is the reverse sequence to removal.

46 Instrument operation – testing

Special test equipment is necessary when checking correct operation of the voltage stabilizer, fuel gauge and temperature gauge so, if a fault is suspect, the car must be taken to the local BL garage who will have this equipment.

There are, however, several initial checks that can be carried out without this equipment.

1   Connect a 0 – 20 voltmeter across the 2 terminal (bottom fuse) of the fuse block and a good earth on the car body.

2   Switch on the ignition and note the reading on the meter. It should be approximately 12 volts.

3   Start the engine and run at a fast idle speed of between 1000 to 1100 rpm. The ignition warning light should be out and the meter registering between 12 and 14 volts.

4   Next make sure that the instrument panel wiring multi-connector plug is correctly fitted to the back of the panel.

5   Finally the wiring harness to the multi-connector plug should be checked for continuity and all instrument earth connections checked for tightness.

6   Should the cause of the trouble not have been found, further tests will have to be carried out by the local BL dealer.

47 Instrument panel and printed circuit (cable gear change models) – removal and refitting

1   Disconnect the negative and then the positive terminals from the battery.

2   Working beneath the instrument panel undo and remove the three screws and plain washers securing the instrument panel to the facia (Fig. 10.14).

3   Release the speedometer cable from the rear of the instrument.

4   Withdraw the multi-pin wiring plug from the instrument panel.

5   The instrument panel may now be removed by moving it downwards slightly to disengage the upper mounting lugs and lifting away the complete instrument panel.

6   If it is necessary to remove the instrument panel printed circuit refer to Section 49 and remove the fuel and temperature gauges.

7   Refer to Section 51 and remove the voltage stabilizer.

8   The three voltage stabilizer terminals should next be removed, these being held by small self-tapping screws (Fig. 10.15).

9   Remove the seven bulb holders from the printed circuit board.

10   Using a knife, thin screwdriver or pliers, very carefully remove the four pins that secure the printed circuit board to the rear of the instrument panel.

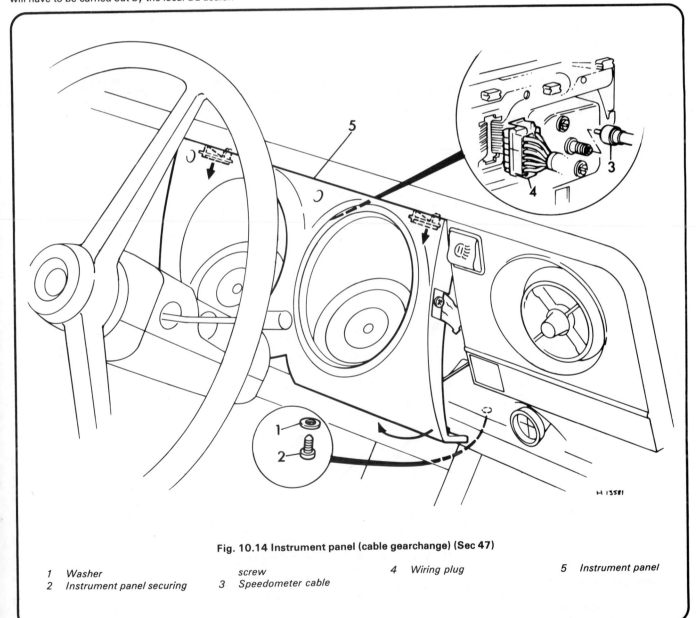

Fig. 10.14 Instrument panel (cable gearchange) (Sec 47)

1 Washer	screw	4 Wiring plug	5 Instrument panel
2 Instrument panel securing	3 Speedometer cable		

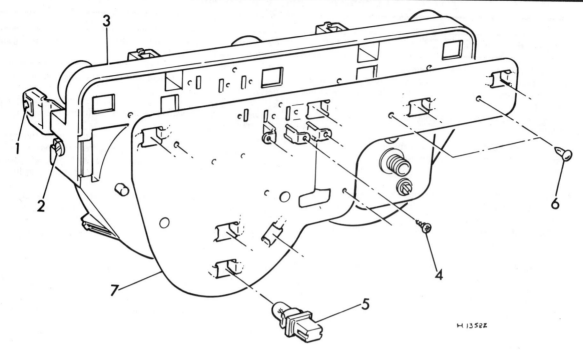

Fig. 10.15 Printed circuit components (Sec 47)

1 Instrument panel securing clip	fixing screw	4 Voltage stabilizer terminals	6 Printed circuit retaining pins
2 Instrument panel bracket	3 Instrument panel	5 Bulb holder	7 Printed circuit

H 1358Z

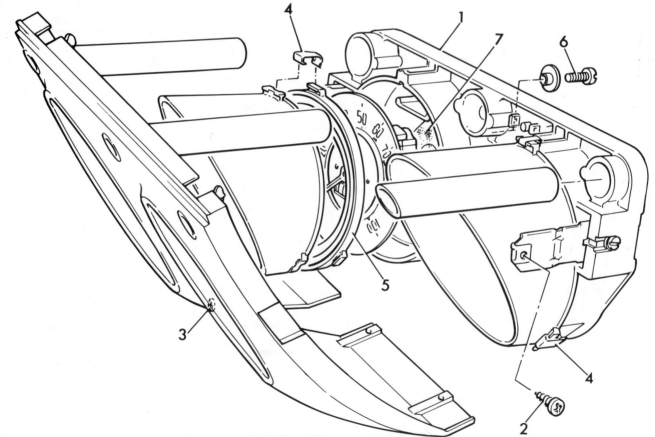

Fig. 10.16 Speedometer head removal (cable gearchange)
(Sec 48)

H 13583

1 Instrument panel	3 Centre retaining screw	6 Speedometer head retaining screw and washers	7 Speedometer mounting rubber
2 Side screws retaining instrument moulding	4 Cowl assembly retaining clips		
	5 Seat slip ring		

11 The printed circuit board may now be removed from the rear of the instrument panel.

12 Refitting the printed circuit and instrument panel is the reverse sequence to removal.

48 Speedometer head and cable (cable gear change models) – removal and refitting

1 Refer to Section 47 paragraphs 1 to 5 and remove the instrument panel.

2 Locate and then remove the two self tapping screws that retain the instrument moulding to the facia panel (Fig. 10.16).

3 Slacken the centre retaining screw and remove the instrument moulding together with the tubes for the warning lights.

4 Release the three clips and carefully withdraw the instrument cowl assembly.

5 Remove the seat slip ring mask assembly.

6 Undo and remove the two screws with shaped plain washers and lift away the speedometer head. It is not necessary to remove the speedometer mounting rubber.

7 Refitting the speedometer head is the reverse sequence to removal.

8 Should it be necessary to remove the speedometer cable, it should first be released from the rear of the speedometer head and then from the transmission unit connection. Next, release the rubber clip retaining the speedometer cable to the air cleaner intake tube. The speedometer cable may now be withdrawn from the car.

9 Refitting the speedometer cable is the reverse sequence to removal but the following additional points should be noted:

(a) *Well lubricate the inner cable by withdrawing it and lightly greasing it except for 8 in (200 mm) at the speedometer end. Refit the inner cable and wipe away excess grease*

(b) *It is important that there is approximately 0.4 in (10 mm) of inner cable projecting from the outer cable at the speedometer end*

(c) *The positioning of the cable is important, so that there are no sharp bends at any point and no bend at all near either end of the cable*

(d) *The cable retaining clips must not be overtightened*

(e) *Do not overtighten the connections at the ends of the cables. These should not be more than finger tight*

49 Fuel and temperature gauge (cable gear change models) – removal and refitting

1 Refer to Section 47 paragraphs 1 to 5 and remove the instrument panel.

2 Locate and then remove the two self tapping screws that retain the instrument moulding to the facia panel (Fig. 10.17).

3 Slacken the centre retaining screw and remove the instrument moulding together with the tubes for the warning lights.

4 Release the three clips and carefully withdraw the instrument cowl assembly.

5 Remove the seat slip ring/mask assembly.

6 Undo and remove the nuts and plain washers that secure the two gauges, and lift away the fuel and temperature gauges. Take extreme care not to touch the needles as these are fragile and easily bent.

7 Refitting is the reverse sequence to removal.

50 Instrument panel and printed circuit (rod gear change models) – removal and refitting

1 Refer to Chapter 12 and remove the facia panel.

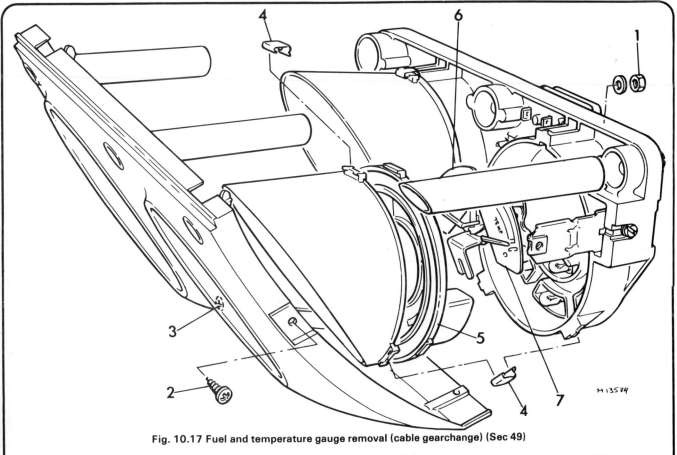

Fig. 10.17 Fuel and temperature gauge removal (cable gearchange) (Sec 49)

1 Gauge securing nuts	3 Centre retaining screw	*clips*	6 Fuel gauge
2 Side screws retaining instrument moulding	4 Cowl assembly retaining	5 Mask assembly	7 Temperature gauge

2   Undo and remove the three retaining nuts and carefully withdraw the instrument panel together with the tubes for the warning lights.
3   To detach the printed circuit from the instrument panel is basically identical to that for cable gear change models. Full information will be found in Section 47, paragraphs 6 to 11 inclusive.
4   Refitting the printed circuit and instrument panel is the reverse sequence to removal.

51 Speedometer head and cable (rod gear change models) – removal and refitting

1   Refer to Section 50 and remove the instrument panel.
2   Using a screwdriver or a knife, carefully ease up the glass rim retaining clips and lift away the glass rim assembly (Fig. 10.18).
3   Undo and remove the two screws and shaped plain washers which secure the speedometer head and lift it away. It is not necessary to remove the speedometer mounting rubber.
4   Refitting is the reverse sequence to removal.
5   Removal and refitting of the speedometer drive cable is basically identical to the cable gear change models and full information will be found in Section 48 paragraphs 8 and 9.

52 Fuel and temperature gauge (rod gear change models) – removal and refitting

1   Refer to Chapter 12 and remove the facia panel.
2   Undo and remove the three retaining nuts and carefully withdraw the instrument panel together with the tubes for the warning lights (Fig. 10.19).
3   Using a knife or screwdriver, carefully ease up the glass rim retaining clips and lift away the glass rim assembly.
4   Undo and remove the nuts and plain washers that secure the two gauges and lift away the fuel and temperature gauges. Take extreme care not to touch the needles as these are fragile and easily bent.
5   Refitting is the reverse sequence to removal.

53 Voltage stabilizer – removal and refitting

1   The voltage stabilizer is a push fit into the rear of the instrument panel printed circuit board.
2   Before removal, as a safety precaution disconnect the negative and then the positive terminals from the battery.
3   Carefully pull the voltage stabilizer from the rear of the printed circuit.
4   Refitting is the reverse sequence to removal. Note that the terminals of the stabilizer are offset, so it cannot be fitted the wrong way round.

54 Fuses

Early models

All fuses are mounted in block form and located on the right-hand side panel between the facia panel and the parcel shelf. There are four fuses in the electrical circuit and a further two spares in the cover. The layout is shown in Fig. 10.20.
Fuse 1 (1-2) This has a 35 amp rating and protects the equipment which operates independent of the ignition switch. These include the horn, interior light and headlamp flasher circuit.
Fuse 2 (3-4) This has a 15 amp rating and protects the right-hand panel side and tail lamps.
Fuse 3 (5-6) This has a 15 amp rating and protects the left-hand panel, side and tail lamps.
Fuse 4 (7-8) This has a 35 amp rating and protects the circuits which operate only when the ignition switch is on. These include the windscreen wipers, direction indicators, brake lights, heater booster fan, heated backlight and cigar lighter (when fitted).
    If any of the fuses blow due to a short circuit, or similar trouble, trace the source of trouble and rectify before fitting a new fuse.

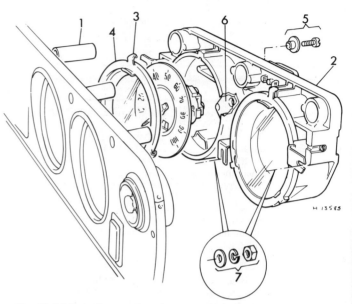

Fig. 10.18 Speedometer head removal (rod gearchange) (Sec 51)

1   *Warning light tube*
2   *Instrument panel*
3   *Glass rim retaining clips*
4   *Glass rim assembly*
5   *Speedometer head retaining*

screws and washers
6   *Speedometer mounting rubber*
7   *Instrument panel securing nuts and washers*

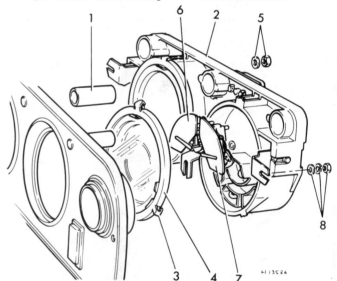

Fig. 10.19 Fuel and temperature gauge removal (rod gearchange) (Sec 52)

1   *Warning light tube*
2   *Instrument panel*
3   *Glass rim retaining clips*
4   *Glass rim assembly*
5   *Gauge securing nuts*

6   *Fuel gauge*
7   *Temperature gauge*
8   *Instrument panel securing nuts and washers*

Later models

The layout for later models is identical to the early models although the fuse rating is different and two in-line fuses have been added. The fuses are numbered 1 to 4 from the top on the later models.
    Fuse 1. This has an 8 amp rating and protects the left-hand side and tail lamps, left-hand number plate lamp, instrument panel lamps, and light switch warning and illumination lamps.
    Fuse 2. This has an 8 amp rating and protects the wiper motor, washer motor, and direction indicators.

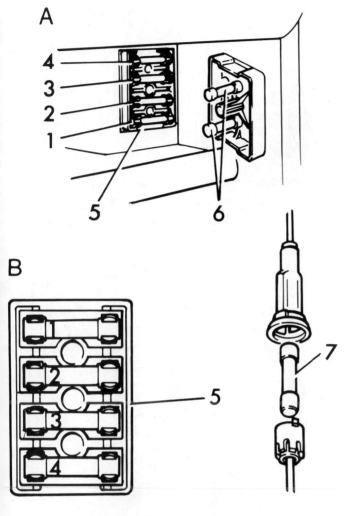

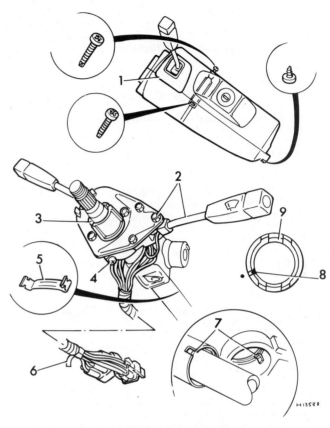

Fig. 10.21 Direction indicator, main beam and horn control switch
for models 1979 on (Sec 55)

1	Control arm finisher	6	Wiper/wash switch lead
2	Wiper/washer switch	7	Locating lug and slot
3	Cancelling ring	8	Alignment marks
4	Clamp screw	9	Cancelling ring slot
5	Harness clip		

H13587

Fig. 10.20 Fuse box layout (Sec 54)

A	Early type	4	Fuse
B	Late type	5	Fuse box
1	Fuse	6	Spare fuses
2	Fuse	7	Line fuse
3	Fuse		

Fuse 3. This has a 17 amp rating and protects the stop lamps, heated rear window and warning light, reverse lamp, and automatic gearbox selector lamp (where fitted).

Fuse 4. This has a 17 amp rating and protects the horns, interior lamp, headlamp flasher switch, brake failure lamp, and lighter.

An 8 amp in-line fuse protects the heater motor.

A further 8 amp in-line fuse protects the hazard warning system, right-hand side and tail lamp, and the right-hand number plate lamp.

If any of the fuses blow due to a short circuit, or similar trouble, trace the source of trouble and rectify before fitting a new fuse.

---

55 Direction indicator, horn and headlamp flasher switch – removal and refitting

Cable gear change models

1   Refer to Chapter 11, and remove the steering wheel.

2   For safety reasons disconnect the battery negative and then positive terminals.

3   Undo and remove the screw securing the top half of the switch

cowl and lift away the cowl half.

4   Undo and remove the two screws securing the bottom half of the switch cowl and lift away the cowl half.

5   Disconnect the wiring loom multi-pin plug from the socket which is located beneath the facia panel.

6   Undo and remove the switch bracket clamp screw and release the bracket. Lift away the switch complete with wiring.

7   Refitting is the reverse sequence to removal.

Rod gear change models 1971 to 1978

8   The sequence for removal of the switch combination is basically identical to that for the cable gear change models with the exception that the instructions given in paragraphs 3 and 4 should be reversed.

Rod gear change models 1979 on

9   This switch also incorporates the windscreen wiper/wash switch. First disconnect the battery.

10   Prise out the control arm finishers on either side of the steering column, remove the screw and withdraw the upper cowl.

11   Remove the two screws and withdraw the lower cowl.

12   Remove the steering wheel as described in Chapter 11.

13   Extract the clip securing the wiring harness and disconnect the multi-plug blocks.

14   Loosen the clamp screw and withdraw the switch assembly over the steering column.

15   To remove the wiper/wash switch unwind the insulating tape, detach the electrical lead, and remove the three retaining screws.

16   Refitting is a reversal of removal but make sure that the cancelling ring rotates freely, the switch lug locates in the steering column slot, and the arrowed flange aligns with the hole in the cover.

56 Switches – removal and refitting

Panel switch (Cable gear change models)
1   Using a screwdriver, ease one side of the switch away from the panel. It will be necessary to pack the other side of the switch while lifting under the flange (Fig. 10.23).
2   Push and lift under the flange on the other side of the switch and withdraw from the panel.
3   Note the electrical cable connections and remove the switch complete with bezel.
4   Using screwdrivers ease the bezel retaining clips and separate the switch from the bezel.
5   Refitting is the reverse sequence to removal.

Panel switch (Rod gear change models – 1971 to 1978)
6   Remove the facia board (see Chapter 12).
7   Depress the spring leaves at each end of the switch to remove the retaining plate.
8   Draw the switch out of the panel. Before disconnecting any of the leads, note where each one is fitted.
9   Depress the spring leaves at each end of the switch to remove the switch bezel.
10 Refitting is the reverse sequence to removal.

Panel switch (Rod gear change models 1979 on)
11 Disconnect the battery then disconnect the wire and plug from the rear of the switch.
12 Depress the two springs on the top and bottom of the switch and eject the switch from the panel.
13 Refitting is a reversal of removal.

57 Lighter – removal and refitting

1   Disconnect the battery and pull out the lighter unit.
2   From behind the facia disconnect the wiring and loosen the back-shell from the case.
3   Hold the back-shell and unscrew the case from the front of the facia. Remove the back-shell.
4   Refitting is a reversal of removal.

58 Radios and tape players – fitting (general)

A radio or tape player is an expensive item to buy and will only give its best performance if fitted properly. It is useless to expect concert hall performance from a unit that is suspended from the dash panel on string with its speaker resting on the back seat or parcel shelf! If you do not wish to do the installation yourself there are many in-car entertainment specialists who can do the fitting for you.

Make sure the unit purchased is of the same polarity as the car, and ensure that units with adjustable polarity are correctly set before commencing installation.

It is difficult to give specific information with regard to fitting, as final positioning of the radio/tape player, speakers and aerial is entirely a matter of personal preference. However, the following paragraphs give guidelines to follow, which are relevent to all installations.

Radios
Most radios are a standardised size of 7 inches wide, by 2 inches deep – this ensures that they will fit into the radio aperture provided in most cars. If your car does not have such an aperture, then the radio must be fitted in a suitable position either in, or beneath the dashpanel. Alternatively, a special console can be purchased which will fit between the dashpanel and the floor, or on the transmission tunnel. These consoles can also be used for additional switches and instrumentation if required. Where no radio aperture is provided, the following points should be borne in mind before deciding exactly where to fit the unit:

(a) The unit must be within easy reach of the driver wearing a seat belt
(b) The unit must not be mounted in close proximity to an

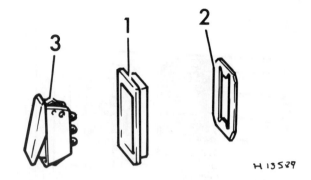

Fig. 10.22 Panel switches (rod gearchange) (Sec 56)

1	Bezel	3	Switch
2	Retaining plate		

Fig. 10.23 Panel switches (Cable gearchange) (Sec 56)

electric tachometer, the ignition switch and its wiring, or the flasher unit and associated wiring
(c) The unit must be mounted within reach of the aerial lead, and in such a place that the aerial lead will not have to be routed near the components detailed in the preceding paragraph 'b'
(d) The unit should be not positioned in a place where it might cause injury to the car occupants in an accident; for instance, under the dashpanel above the driver's or passengers' legs
(e) The unit must be fitted really securely

Some radios will have mounting brackets provided together with instructions; others will need to be fitted using drilled and slotted metal strips, bent to form mounting brackets – these strips are available from most accessory shops. The unit must be properly earthed, by fitting a separate earthing lead between the casing of the radio and the vehicle frame.

Use the radio manufacturers' instructions when wiring the radio into the vehicle's electrical system. If no instructions are available refer to the relevant wiring diagram to find the location of the radio 'feed' connection in the vehicle's wiring circuit. A 1-2 amp 'in-line' fuse must be fitted in the radio's 'feed' wire – a choke may also be necessary (see next Section).

The type of aerial used, and its fitted position is a matter of personal preference. In general the taller the aerial, the better the reception. It is best to fit a fully retractable aerial – especially, if a mechanical car-wash is used or if you live in an area where cars tend to be vandalised. In this respect electric aerials which are raised and lowered automatically when switching the radio on or off are convenient, but are more likely to give trouble than the manual type.

When choosing a site for the aerial the following points should be considered:

(a) *The aerial lead should be as short as possible – this means that the aerial should be mounted at the front of the car*

(b) *The aerial must be mounted as far away from the distributor and HT leads as possible*

(c) *The part of the aerial which protrudes beneath the mounting point must not foul the roadwheels, or anything else*

(c) *If possible the aerial should be positioned so that the coaxial lead does not have to be routed through the engine compartment*

(e) *The plane of the panel on which the aerial is mounted should not be so steeply angled that the aerial cannot be mounted vertically (in relation to the 'end-on' aspect of the car). Most aerials have a small amount of adjustment available*

Having decided on a mounting position, a relatively large hole will have to be made in the panel. The exact size of the hole will depend upon the specific aerial being fitted, although, generally, the hole required is of ¾ inch (19 mm) diameter. On metal bodied cars, a 'tank-cutter' of the relevant diameter is the best tool to use for making the hole. This tool needs a small diameter pilot hole drilled through the panel, through which the tool clamping bolt is inserted. When the hole has been made the raw edges should be de-burred with a file and then painted, to prevent corrosion.

Fit the aerial according to the manufacturer's instructions. If the aerial is very tall, or if it protrudes beneath the mounting panel for a considerable distance it is a good idea to fit a stay between the aerial and the vehicle frame. This stay can be manufactured from the slotted and drilled metal strips previously mentioned. The stay should be securely screwed or bolted in place. For best reception it is advisable to fit an earth lead between the aerial and the vehicle frame.

It will probably be necessary to drill one or two holes through bodywork panels in order to feed the aerial lead into the interior of the car. Where this is the case ensure that the holes are fitted with rubber grommets to protect the cable, and to stop possible entry of water.

Positioning and fitting of the speaker depends mainly on its type. Generally, the speaker is designed to fit directly into the aperture already provided in the car (usually in the shelf beneath the rear seats, or in the top of the dashpanel). Where this is the case, fitting the speaker is just a matter of removing the protective grille from the aperture and screwing or bolting the speaker in place. Take great care not to damage the speaker diaphragm whilst doing this. It is a good idea to fit a 'gasket' between the speaker frame and the mounting panel, in order to prevent vibration – some speakers will already have such a gasket fitted.

If a 'pod' type speaker was supplied with the radio, the best acoustic results will normally be obtained by mounting it on the shelf behind the rear seat. The pod can be secured to the mounting panel with self-tapping screws.

When connecting a rear mounted speaker to the radio, the wires should be routed through the vehicle beneath the carpets or floor mats – preferably the middle, or along the side of the floorpan, where they will not be trodden on by passengers. Make the relevant connections as directed by the radio manufacturer.

By now you will have several yards of additional wiring in the car; use PVC tape to secure this wiring out of harm's way. Do not leave electrical leads dangling. Ensure that all new electrical connections are properly made (wires twisted together will not do) and completely secure.

The radio should now be working, but before you pack away your tools it will be necessary to 'trim' the radio to the aerial. If specific instructions are not provided by the radio manufacturer, proceed as follows. Find a station with a low signal strength on the medium-wave band; slowly turn the trim screw of the radio in, or out, until the loudest reception of the selected station is obtained – the set is then trimmed to the aerial.

Tape players

Fitting instructions for both cartridge and cassette stereo tape players are the same and in general the same rules apply as when fitting a radio. Tape players are not usually prone to electrical interference like radio – although it can occur – so positioning is not so critical. If possible the player should be mounted on an 'even-keel'. Also, it must be possible for a driver wearing a seat belt to reach the unit in order to change or turn over tapes.

For the best results from speakers designed to be recessed into a panel, mount them so that the back of the speaker protrudes into an enclosed chamber within the car (eg door interiors or the boot cavity).

To fit recessed type speakers in the front doors first check that there is sufficient room to mount the speakers in each door without fouling the latch or window winding mechanism. Hold the speaker against the skin of the door, and draw a line around the periphery of the speaker. With the speaker removed draw a second 'cutting' line, within the first, to allow enough room for the entry of the speaker back, but at the same time providing a broad seat for the speaker flange. When you are sure that the 'cutting-line' is correct, drill a series of holes around its periphery. Pass a hacksaw blade through one of the holes and then cut through the metal between the holes until the centre section of the panel falls out.

De-burr the edges of the hole and then paint the raw metal to prevent corrosion. Cut a corresponding hole in the door trim panel – ensuring that it will be completely covered by the speaker grille. Now drill a hole in the door edge and a corresponding hole in the door surround. These holes are to feed the speaker leads through – so fit grommets. Pass the speaker leads through the door trim, door skin and out through the holes in the side of the door and door surround. Refit the door trim panel and then secure the speaker to the door using self-tapping screws. If the speaker is fitted with a shield to prevent water dripping on it, ensure that this shield is at the top.

Pod type speakers can be fastened to the shelf behind the rear seat, or anywhere else offering a corresponding mounting point on each side of the car. If the pod speakers are mounted on each side of the shelf behind the rear seat, it is a good idea to drill several large diameter holes through to the boot cavity beneath each speaker – this will improve the sound reproduction. Pod speakers sometimes offer a better reproduction quality if they face the rear window – which then acts as a reflector – so it is worthwhile to do a little experimenting before finally fixing the speaker.

59 Radios and tape players – suppression of interference (general)

To eliminate buzzes and other unwanted noises, costs very little and is not as difficult as sometimes thought. With a modicum of common sense and patience and following the instructions in the following paragraphs, interference can be virtually eliminated.

The first cause for concern is the generator. The noise this makes over the radio is like an electric mixer and the noise speeds up when you rev up (if you wish to prove the point, you can remove the drivebelt and try it). The remedy for this is simple; connect a 1.0 uf-3.0 uf capacitor between earth, probably the bolt that holds down the generator base, and the *large* terminal on the dynamo or alternator. This is most important for if you connect it to the small terminal, you will probably damage the generator permanently (see Fig. 10.24).

A second common cause of electrical interference is the ignition system. Here a 1.0 ohm capacitor must be connected between earth and the 'SW' or '+' terminal on the coil (see Fig. 10.25). This may stop the tick-tick-tick sound that comes over the speaker. Next comes the spark itself.

There are several ways of curing interference from the ignition HT system. One is to use carbon film HT leads but these have a tendency to 'snap' inside and you don't know then, why you are firing on only half your cylinders. So the second, and more successful mthod is to use resistive spark plug caps (see Fig. 10.26) of about 10 000 ohm to 15 000 ohm resistance. If, due to lack of room, these cannot be used, an alternative is to use 'in-line' suppressors (Fig. 10.26) – if the interference is not too bad, you may get away with only one suppressor in the coil to distributor line. If the interference does continue (a 'clacking' noise) then doctor all HT leads.

At this stage it is advisable to check that the radio is well earthed, also the aerial, and to see that the aerial plug is pushed well into the seat and that the radio is properly trimmed (see preceding Section). In addition, check that the wire which supplies the power to the set is as short as possible and does not wander all over the car. At this stage it is a good idea to check that the fuse is of the correct rating. For most sets this will be about 1 to 2 amps.

At this point the more usual causes of interference have been suppressed. If the problem still exists, a look at the cause of interference may help to pinpoint the component generating the stray electrical discharges.

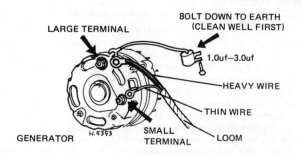

Fig. 10.24 The corrct way to connect a capacitor to the generator

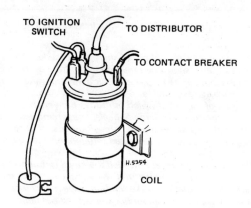

Fig. 10.25 The capacitor must be connected to the ignition switch side of the coil

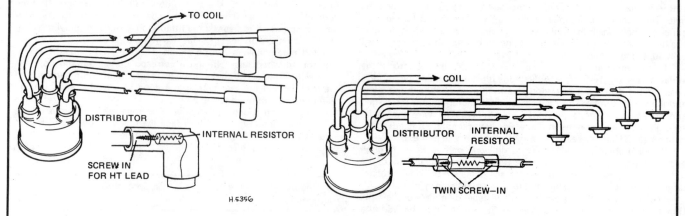

Fig. 10.26 Ignition HT lead suppressors

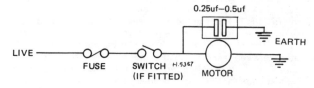

Fig. 10.27 Correct method of suppressing electric motors

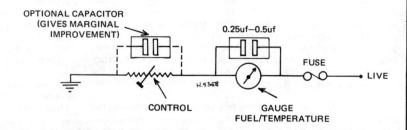

Fig. 10.28 Method of suppressing gauges and their control units

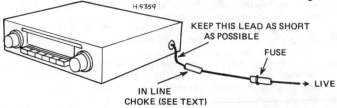

Fig. 10.29 An 'in-line' choke should be fitted into the live supply head as close to the unit as possible

The radio picks up electromagnetic waves in the air; now some are made by radio stations and other broadcasters and some, not wanted, are made by the car. The home made signals are produced by stray electrical discharges floating around the car. Common producers of these signals are electric motors; ie, the windshield wipers, electric screen washers, electric window winders, heater fan or an electric aerial if fitted. Other sources of interference are electric fuel pumps, flashing turn signals, and instruments. The remedy for these cases is shown in Fig. 10.27 for an electric motor whose interference is not too bad and Fig. 10.28 for instrument suppression. Turn signals are not normally suppressed. In recent years, radio manufacturers have included in the line (live) of the radio, in addition to the fuse, an 'in-line' choke. If your installation lacks one of these, put one in as shown in Fig. 10.29.

All the foregoing components are available from radio shops or accessory shops. For a transistor radio, a 2A choke should be adequate. If you have an electric clock fitted this should be suppressed by connecting a 0.5 uf capacitor directly across it as shown for a motor in Fig. 10.27.

If after all this, you are still experiencing radio interference, first assess how bad it is, for the human ear can filter out unobtrusive unwanted noise quite easily. But if you are still adamant about eradicating noise, then continue.

As a first step, a few 'experts' seem to favour a screen between the radio and the engine. This is O.K. as far as it goes, literally! – for the whole set is screened and if interference can get past that then a small piece of aluminium is not going to stop it.

A more sensible way of screening is to discover if interference is coming down the wires. First, take the live lead; interference can get between the set and the choke (hence the reason for keeping the wires short). One remedy here is to screen the wire and this is done by buying screened wire and fitting that. The loudspeaker lead could be screened also to prevent 'pick-up' getting back to the radio – although this is unlikely.

Without doubt, the worst source of radio interference comes from the ignition HT leads, even if they have been suppressed. The ideal way of suppressing these is to slide screening tubes over the leads themselves. As this is impractical, we can place an aluminium shield over the majority of the lead areas. In a vee – or twin-cam engine, this is relatively easy but for a straight engine the results are not particularly good.

Now for the really impossible cases, here are a few tips to try out. Where metal comes into contact with metal, an electrical disturbance is caused which is why good clean connections are essential. To remove interference due to overlapping or butting panels you must bridge the join with a wide braided earth strap (like that from the frame to the engine/transmission). The most common moving parts that could create noise and should be strapped are, in order of importance:

(a) *Silencer to frame*
(b) *Exhaust pipe to engine block and frame*
(c) *Air cleaner to frame*
(d) *Front and rear bumpers to frame*
(e) *Steering column to frame*
(f) *Bonnet and boot lids to frame*
(g) *Hood frame to frame on soft tops*

These faults are most pronounced when (1) the engine is idling, (2) labouring under load. Although the moving parts are already connected with nuts, bolts, etc, these do tend to rust and corrode, thus creating a high resistance interference source.

If you have a 'ragged' sounding pulse when mobile, this could be wheel or tyre static. This can be cured by buying some anti-static powder and sprinkling it liberally inside the tyres.

If the interference takes the shape of a high pitched screeching noise that changes its note when the car is in motion and only comes now and then, this could be related to the aerial, especially if it is of the telescopic or whip type. This source can be cured quite simply by pushing a small rubber ball on top of the aerial (yes, really!) as this breaks the electric field before it can form; but it would be much better to buy yourself a new aerial of a reputable brand. If, on the other hand, you are getting a loud rushing sound every time you brake, then this is brake static. This effect is most prominent on hot dry days and is cured only by fitting a special kit, which is quite expensive.

In conclusion, it is pointed out that it is relatively easy, and therefore cheap, to eliminate 95 per cent of all noises, but to eliminate the final 5 per cent is time and money consuming. It is up to the individual to decide if it is worth it. Please remember also that you will not get concert hall performance from a cheap radio.

Finally at the beginning of this Section are mentioned tape players; these are not usually affected by interference but in a very bad case, the best remedies are the first three suggestions plus using a 3-5 amp choke in the 'live' line and in incurable cases screen the live and speaker wires.

Note: *If your car is fitted with electronic ignition, then it is not recommended that neither the spark plug resistors nor the ignition coil capacitor be fitted as these may damage the system. Most electronic ignition units have built-in suppression and should, therefore, not cause interference.*

See overleaf for 'Fault diagnosis – electrical system

Chapter 10 Electrical system

59 Fault diagnosis – electrical system

Symptom	Reason(s)
Starter motor	
Fails to turn engine	Battery discharged, or defective
	Battery terminal loose, or dirty
	Starter motor solenoid, or relay faulty
	Starter motor defective
	Starter motor lead, or earthing strap loose
Turns engine slowly	Battery discharged, or defective
	Battery terminal loose, or dirty
	Starter motor solenoid, or relay faulty
	Starter motor lead, or earthing strap loose
Spins, but does not turn engine	Starter motor clutch, or Bendix defective
Noisy on engagement	Worn starter ring, or starter motor pinion
	Loose mounting bolts
Battery	
Does not hold charge	Battery defective
	Electrolyte level low
	Fan belt slipping
	Generator, or regulator defective
Ignition light stays on	Broken fan belt
	Generator defective
	Cut-out defective
Horn	
Operates all the time	Horn push stuck, or horn cable is earthed
Fails to operate	Blown fuse
	Wiring fault
	Defective horn
	Defective horn switch
Sounds intermittently	Intermittent connection in wiring, or dirty horn switch contacts
Lights	
Give poor illumination	Regulator voltage low
	Dirty contact, or corroded earth connection
Wipers	
Motor fails to work	Blown fuse
	Switch, or wiring fault
	Worn brushes
Works slowly, or erratically	Excessive load caused by worn linkage, or lack of lubrication
	Worn, or dirty brushes

Key to wiring diagram on pages 178, 179, 180, 181, 182 and 183

1   Alternator or dynamo
2   Control box
3   Battery
4   Starter solenoid
5   Starter motor
6   Light switch
7   Headlamp dip switch
8   Headlamp (dipped beam)
9   Headlamp (main beam)
10   Main beam warning lamp
11   RH sidelamp
12   LH sidelamp
14   Panel lamps
15   Number plate lamps
16   Stop lamps
17   RH tail lamp
18   Stop lamp switch
19   Fuse block
20   Interior lamp
21   Door switch
22   LH tail lamp
23   Horn
24   Horn push
25   Flasher unit
26   Direction indicator switch
27   Direction indicator warning lamp(s)
28   RH front flasher lamp
29   LH front flasher lamp
30   RH rear flasher lamp
31   LH rear flasher lamp
32   Heater blower switch
33   Blower motor
34   Fuel gauge
35   Tank unit
36   Windscreen wiper switch
37   Windscreen wiper motor
38   Ignition/starter switch
39   Ignition coil
40   Distributor
42   Oil pressure switch
43   Oil pressure warning lamp
44   Ignition warning lamp
45   Headlamp flasher switch

46   Water temperature gauge
47   Water temperature transmitter
49   Reverse lamp switch
50   Reverse lamp
57   Cigar lighter
60   Radio *
64   Voltage stabilizer
67   Line fuse *
75   Automatic transmission starter inhibitor switch *
76   Automatic transmission indicator lamp*
77   Windscreen washer
78   Windscreen washer switch
82   Switch illumination lamp
83   Induction heater and thermostat *
84   Carburettor suction chamber heater *
110 Repeater flasher(s)
111 LH repeater flasher
115 Rear window demist switch
116 Rear window demist unit
118 Combined wash/wipe switch
139 Alternative connections when alternator is fitted
150 Rear window demist warning lamp
152 Hazard lamp
153 Hazard switch
154 Hazard flasher unit
158 Instrument panel (printed circuit)
159 Brake pressure warning lamp and pushbutton
160 Brake pressure differential warning switch
164 Ballast resistor *
208 Lighter illumination
266 Headlamp wiper motor *
267 Headlamp wiper motor *
268 Headlamp wash/wipe switch *
289 Blocking diode (direction indicator warning lamp)
297 Brake failure warning lamp

* Optional or special marked fitment

Colour code

N	Brown	P	Purple	W	White
U	Blue	G	Green	Y	Yellow
R	Red	LG	Light Green	B	Black
		O	Orange	K	Pink

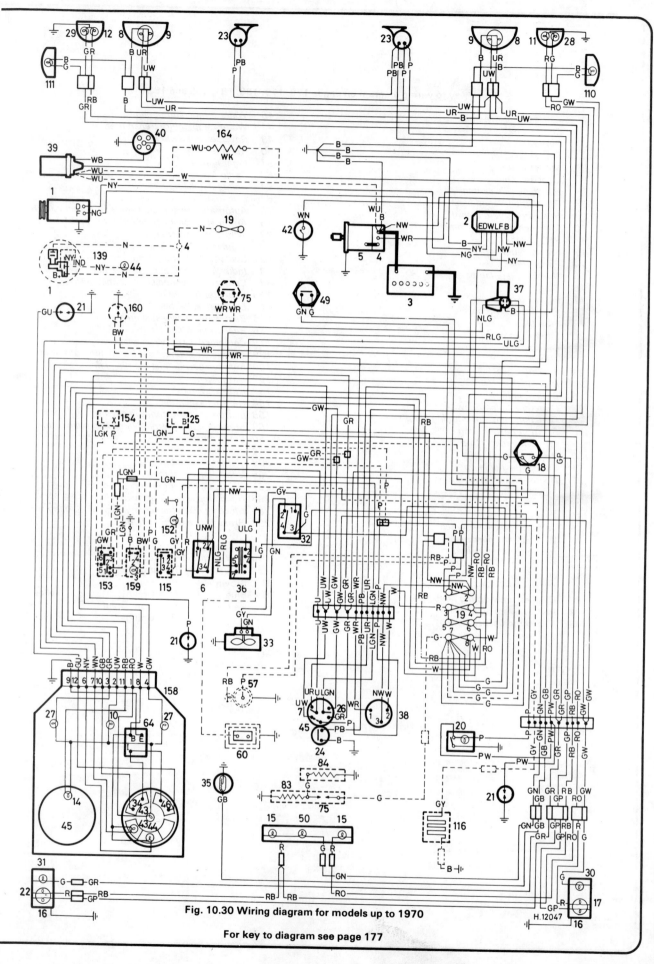

Fig. 10.30 Wiring diagram for models up to 1970

For key to diagram see page 177

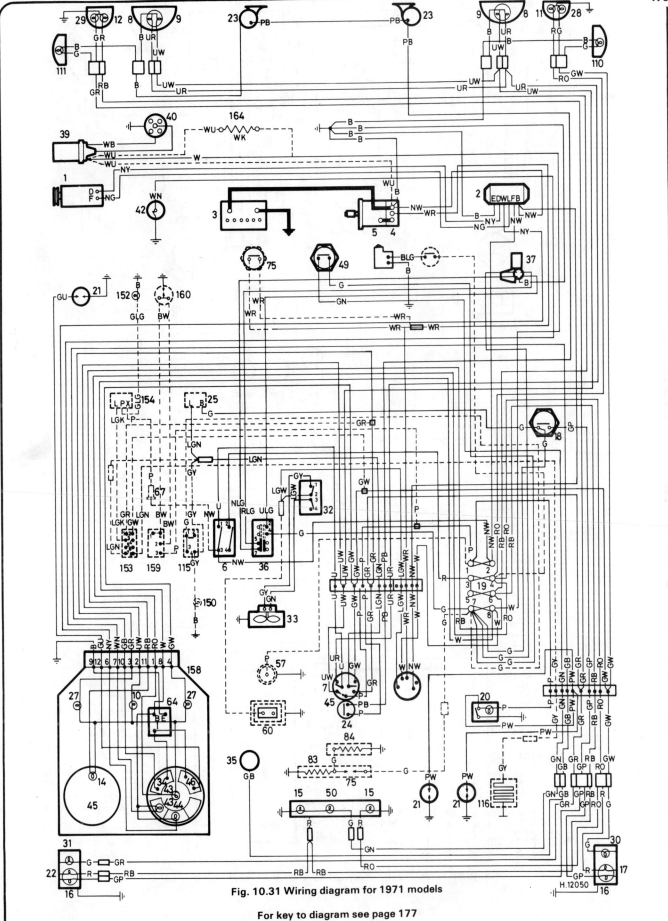

Fig. 10.31 Wiring diagram for 1971 models

For key to diagram see page 177

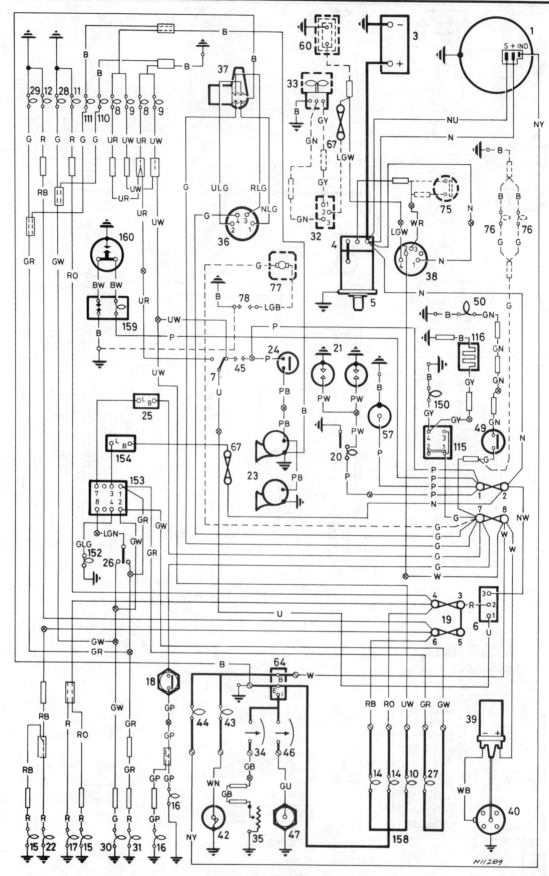

Fig. 10.32 Wiring diagram for right-hand drive models from 1972 to 1978

For key to diagram see page 177

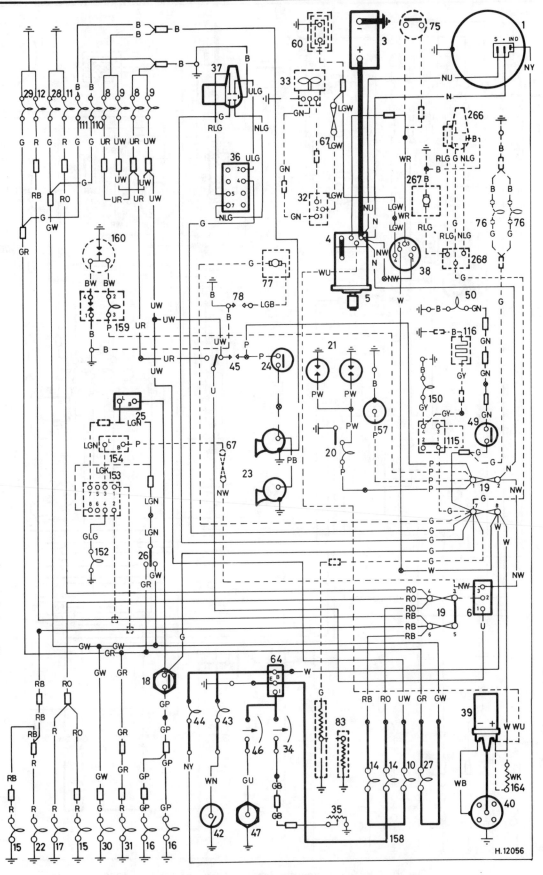

Fig. 10.33 Wiring diagram for left-hand drive models from 1972 to 1978

For key to diagram see page 177

182

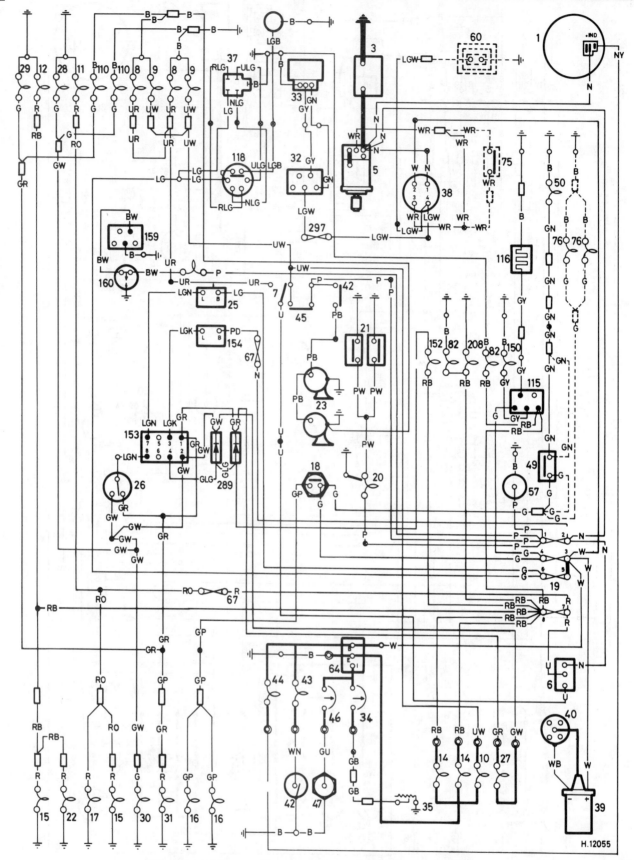

Fig. 10.34 Wiring diagram for right-hand drive models from 1979 to 1980

For key to diagram see page 177

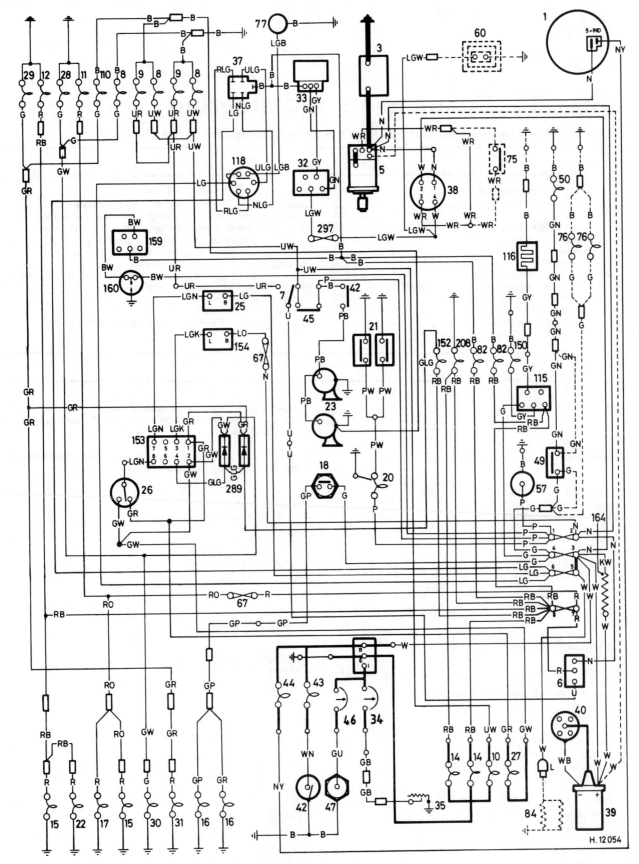

Fig. 10.35 Wiring diagram for left-hand drive models from 1979 to 1980

For key to diagram see page 177

183

Chapter 11 Suspension and steering

For modifications, and information applicable to later models, see Supplement at end of manual

Contents

Specifications

Front suspension .... Independent. Hydrolastic, or Hydragas displacers interconnected front and rear and mounted crosswise in subframe. Swivel axles balljointed to upper and lower arms

Rear suspension .... Independent with trailing radius arms, rubber and balljoint mounted to horizontally mounted Hydrolastic, or Hydragas displacers

Suspension trim (unladen)
Front wheel arch to hub centre .... 14.13 ± 0.38 in (358 ± 9.5 mm)
Trim height variation (transverse) .... 0.38 in (9.5 mm) maximum

Suspension pressures (approximate)
Model year up to 1970 .... 245 lbf/in² (17.2 kgf/cm²)
Model year 1971 to 1977 .... 225 lbf/in² (15.8 kgf/cm²)
Model year 1978 on .... 340 lbf/in² (23.9 kgf/cm²)
The pressure must be adjusted to give the correct trim

Steering
Type .... Rack and pinion

Steering wheel diameter
Cable gear change .... 16.25 in (413 mm)
Rod gear change .... 15 in (381 mm)

Steering wheel turns – lock to lock
Cable gear change 3.9
Rod gear change 4.2

Front suspension data (unladen)
Toe-in:
  Cable gear change .... $\frac{1}{16}$ in (1.6 mm)
  Rod gear change .... 0 to $\frac{1}{8}$ in (0 to 3.8 mm)
Swivel hub inclination .... 12°
Camber angle:
  Cable gear change .... 1° positive
  Rod gear change .... $1\frac{1}{2}° \pm \frac{3}{4}°$ positive
Castor angle:
  Cable gear change .... 4° positive
  Rod gear change .... $2° \pm 1°$ positive

Rear suspension data (unladen)
Toe-in:
  Cable gear change .... 0 to $\frac{1}{16}$ in (0 to 1.6 mm)
  Rod gear change .... $\frac{3}{16} \pm \frac{1}{8}$ in (4.76 ± 3.18 mm)

Camber angle:
Cable gear change . . . . 0° ± 1°
Rod gear change . . . . 0° ± 1°

Wheels and tyres
Wheels . . . . 4½C x 13
Tyres:
HL and HLS models . . . . 165–13 radial ply, tubeless
All models except HL and HLS . . . . 155–13 radial ply, tubeless
Tyre pressure (all conditions):
Front . . . . 26 lbf/in² (1.8 kgf/cm²)
Rear . . . . 24 lbf/in² (1.7 kgf/cm²)

Torque wrench settings

	lbf ft	kgf m
Front suspension		
Upper and lower balljoint assembly	45	6.2
Lower arm to body	15	2.1
Lower arm pivot nuts	50	6.9
Subframe to body	15	2.1
Subframe to dash lower panel	15	2.1
Hub nut (align to next hole)	200	27.6
Balljoint assembly to swivel hub	38 to 45	5.2 to 6.2
Mud shield to swivel hub	17 to 25	2.35 to 3.46
Driving flange to brake disc	38 to 45	5.3 to 6.22
Caliper nut to swivel hub bolts	40 to 50	5.53 to 6.91
Suspension upper arm pivot pin nut		
Aerotight	60	8.3
Philidas	75	10.4
Roadwheel nuts	46	6.2
Rear suspension		
Support brackets to body	25	3.4
Pivot joint to housing and body	65	9
Rear arch springs to body	15	2.1
Outer bearing retaining bolts	60	8.3
Outer bearing to body fixing bolts	30	4.1
Hub nut (align to next hole)	60	8.3
Pivot joint to reaction lever	70 to 80	9.7 to 11
Cap nut – ball joints	70 to 80	9.7 to 11
Roadwheel nuts	46	6.2
Steering		
Steering wheel nut	32 to 37	4.4 to 5.1
Column coupling to pinion	15	2.1
Balljoint to steering arms	25	3.4
Rack cover plate	12 to 18	1.7 to 2.5
Balljoint locking ring	33 to 37	4.6 to 5.1
Ball end locknuts	35 to 40	4.8 to 5.5

1 General description

The suspension system makes use of a special shock absorbing displacer on each wheel. The absorbers are fluid filled and the front and rear displacers on each side are connected to each other.

On early models the suspension is Hydrolastic and the units consist of an upper and lower housing, a nylon-reinforced diaphragm and a compressed rubber conical spring. The fluid filling is an alcohol/water mixture with corrosion inhibitors.

The Hydragas system on later models is similar in principle except that the one chamber of the displacer units is filled with compressed nitrogen.

The front displacer units are mounted horizontally in the cross tube which is formed in the front subframe. The displacer units react against upper wishbones with lower arms providing a fore and aft location. The swivel axles are ball-jointed top and bottom. The upper wishbones are fitted with Simplex bonded rubber bushes, whilst the lower arms are mounted at the front end in Silentbloc rubber bushes, and at the rear in Metalastic bonded rubber bushes.

The rear displacers are mounted centrally at the rear and react against short balljoint-mounted levers coupled to the trailing arms. Torsional type trim bars are fitted which react against the trailing arms. The trailing arms are mounted at their outer end in Metalastic bonded rubber bushes.

Rack and pinion steering is fitted to models covered by this manual. Positioned at each end of the rack is a balljoint which is

attached to the inner end of the tie-rod. The balljoint, and part of the tie-rod, is enclosed in a rubber gaiter which is held in position by a clip at each end. It protects the balljoint and rack, preventing road dust and dirt entering and causing premature wear.

The outer end of the tie-rod is threaded for adjustment, and is adjusted by shims between the end cover and pinion housing, whilst backlash between the pinion and rack is controlled by shims between the cover plate yoke and the pinion housing.

2 Front hubs – removal and refitting

1 Remove the brake disc assembly (Chapter 9).
2 Undo and remove the nut securing the steering arm swivel balljoint and, using a universal balljoint separator, release the balljoint from the steering arm.
3 Undo and remove the two bolts and spring washers securing the lower suspension arm balljoint to the swivel flange.
4 Using a universal three legged puller and suitable thrust block, carefully draw the hub assembly from the driveshaft.
5 Should the inner track of the hub bearing be retained on the driveshaft, it will be necessary to remove it using the universal puller, and binding the legs together with wire to stop them springing off the inner track when the puller centre bolt is screwed in.
6 To dismantle the swivel hub for overhaul, unscrew the six bolts securing the bearing housing to the swivel flange and withdraw the bearing housing from the swivel flange.

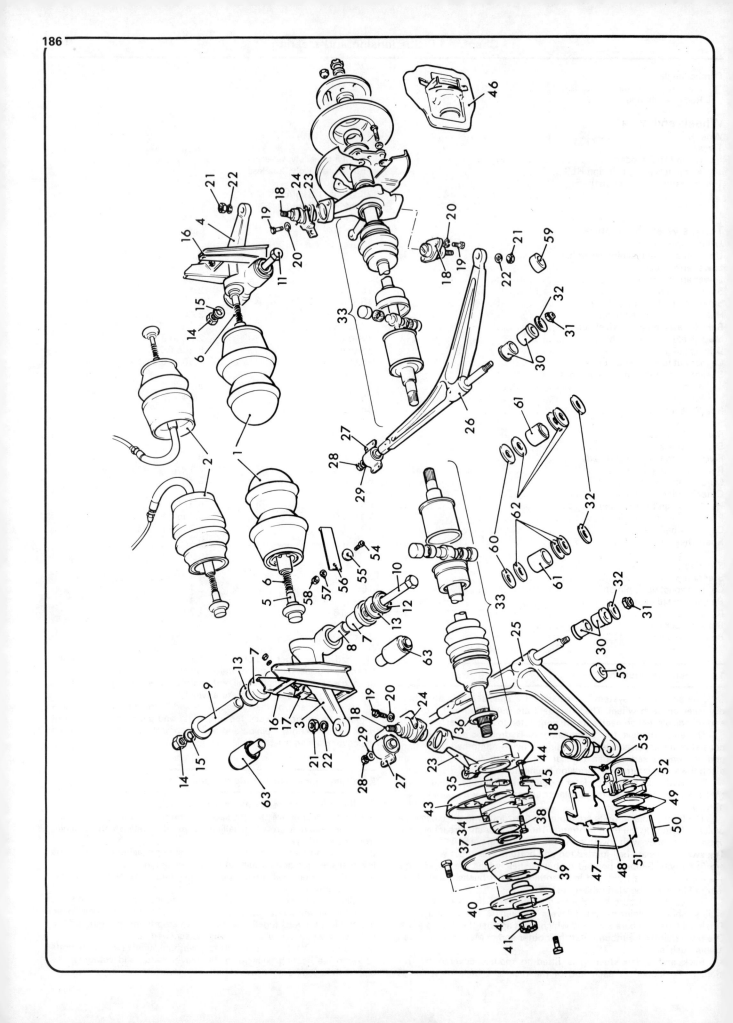

Fig. 11.1 Front suspension components (Sec 1)

1 Displacer units – Hydragas (model year 1978 on)
2 Displacer units – Hydrolastic (model year up to 1977)
3 Upper suspension arm – RH
4 Upper suspension arm – LH
5 Knuckle joint
6 Spring
7 Bearing bush (rubber) } model year up to 1970
8 Sleeve for bush
9 Pivot tube
10 Pivot bolt – RH
11 Pivot bolt – LH
12 Bearing end cap } model year up to 1970
13 Washer for bearing
14 Nut for pivot bolt
15 Washer for nut
16 Bump and rebound bracket

17 Rebound rubber
18 Balljoint
19 Bolt for balljoint
20 Washer for bolt
21 Nut for balljoint
22 Washer for nut
23 Swivel flange and steering lever
24 Bracket for brake pipe
25 Lower suspension arm – RH
26 Lower suspension arm – LH
27 Bearing for suspension arm – rear
28 Nut for bearing
29 Washer for nut
30 Bearing for suspension arm (model year up to 1970)
31 Nut for bearing

32 Washer for nut
33 Driveshaft
34 Hub bearing housing
35 Hub bearing
36 Oil seal – inner
37 Oil seal – outer
38 Bolt for bearing housing
39 Brake disc
40 Drive flange
41 Nut for hub
42 Spacer for nut
43 Mud shield
44 Bolt for mud shield
45 Washer for bolt
46 Brake calliper assembly
47 Yoke
48 Spring for yoke
49 Friction pads

50 Retaining pins for pads
51 Clip for pins
52 Piston assembly
53 Bleed screw
54 Bolt for retaining bracket
55 Washer for bolt
56 Retaining bracket for displacer unit
57 Washer for nut
58 Nut for bolt
59 Nylon bush – when fitted (model year up to 1970)
60 Washer for lower suspension arm pivot } model year 1971 on
61 Bush for sub-frame housing
62 Buffer washers
63 Upper suspension arm bush

7 Lift away the brake disc shield from the swivel flange.

8 Using a screwdriver, ease the oil seal from the swivel flange and also from the bearing housing. New oil seals will be required for refitting.

9 Using a vice and suitable diameter tube to locate on the outer track of the bearing, press the bearing from the housing.

10 Thoroughly wash all parts, except for the oil seals which must be renewed, and carefully examine the bearing housing and swivel flange for signs of wear, damage and cracks. Obtain new parts as necessary.

11 Inspect the bearing for wear, by reassembling if the inner track has parted from the assembly and holding the inner track. Rotate the outer track and feel for signs of roughness or excessive movement. Look for pit marks or signs of overheating due to lack of lubricant. If the bearing assembly is suspect always obtain a new assembly.

12 To reassemble, first pack the bearing assembly with grease and place the two oil seals in the clean oil. Allow to soak for a few minutes.

13 Using a suitable diameter piece of metal tube, carefully drift the oil seal into the swivel flange. The lip of the oil seal must face inwards.

14 With the vice and packing, press the bearing assembly into the housing.

15 In a similar manner to that described in paragraph 13, fit the second disc shield to the swivel flange followed by the bearing housing, and secure with the six bolts.

16 Refit the brake disc shield to the swivel flange followed by the bearing housing, and secure with the six bolts.

17 Refitting the swivel flange assembly is now the reverse sequence to removal but it will be necessary to make up a tool like the one shown in Fig. 7.5 (Chapter 7) to enable the assembly to be drawn onto the driveshaft.

3 Rear hubs – removal and refitting

1 Remove the rear brake drum and hub assembly (Chapter 9).

2 Should the inner track of the inside bearing still be in position on the rear hub axle, it will be necessary to draw it off using a universal puller and binding the legs together with wire to stop them springing off the inner track when the puller centre bolt is screwed in.

3 Using a screwdriver, ease the oil seal from the centre of the drum/hub assembly noting which way round the seal is fitted.

4 Using a soft metal drift, drive out the inner track of the inner bearing. Lift out the distance piece, noting that the reduced internal diameter or internally shouldered end is fitted next to the outer bearing.

5 The soft metal drift is now used again to drive out the inner track of the outer bearing.

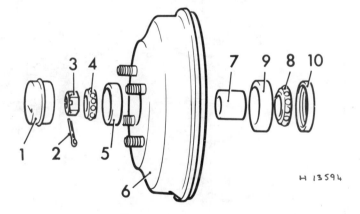

H 13594

Fig. 11.2 Rear hub components (Sec 3)

1 Dust cap
2 Split pin
3 Castellated nut
4 Race and inner track (outer bearing)
5 Outer track (outer bearing)
6 Brake drum
7 Spacer
8 Race and inner track (inner bearing)
9 Outer track (inner bearing)
10 Oil seal

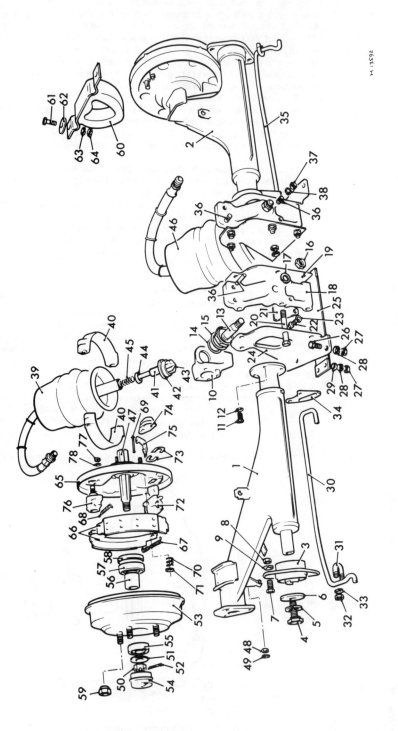

Fig. 11.3 Rear suspension components (cable gearchange) (Sec 1)

1   Radius arm – RH
2   Radius arm – LH
3   Rubber bearing for radius arm
4   Bolt for radius arm
5   Spring washer
6   Locking washer
7   Bolt for bearing
8   Nut
9   Spring washer for bolt
10 Reaction lever
11 Bolt – arm to lever
12 Spring washer for bolt
13 Pivot joint
14 Shim for pivot joint
15 Lockwasher for pivot joint

16 Nut for pivot joint
17 Spring washer for nut
18 Support for pivot joint
19 Support housing – LH
20 Bolt for support
21 Rebound buffer
22 Bolt for buffer
23 Spring washer
24 Support housing – RH
25 Support plate
26 Bolt for supports
27 Nut
28 Spring washer
29 Spacer
30 Trim bar – RH
31 U-bolt for trim bar

32 Nut
33 Spring washer
34 Reaction plate for trim bar
35 Trim bar – LH
36 Stud for support
37 Nut
38 Spring washer
39 Displacer unit – RH
40 Support for displacer unit
41 Displacer strut
42 Rubber boot for strut
43 Nylon cap for strut
44 Spacer for strut
45 Spring for strut
46 Displacer unit – LH
47 Stub axle

48 Nut for axle
49 Spring washer for nut
50 Nut for hub
51 Washer
52 Split pin
53 Hub and brake drum assembly
54 Cap for hub
55 Bearing for hub – outer
56 Spacer
57 Bearing for hub – inner
58 Oil seal
59 Nut for roadwheel
60 Arch spring assembly
61 Bolt for arch spring
62 Washer

63 Spring washer
64 Nut
65 Brake backplate
66 Brake shoes
67 Pull-off spring – cylinder side
68 Pull-off spring – adjuster side
69 Brake shoe retainer
70 Spring for retainer
71 Cup for retainer
72 Wheel cylinder
73 Retainer for cylinder
74 Rubber boot for cylinder
75 Handbrake lever
76 Brake shoe adjuster
77 Nut for adjuster
78 Washer

6   Finally drift out the outer tracks of both the inner and outer bearings.

7   Thoroughly wash all parts, except for the oil seal which must be renewed, and carefully examine the hub and shaft for wear, damage and cracks. Obtain new parts as necessary.

8   Inspect the bearings for wear by reassembling and holding the inner track. Rotate the outer track and feel for signs of roughness or excessive movement. Look for pit marks or signs of overheating due to lack of lubricant. If a bearing assembly is suspect, always obtain a new assembly.

9   To reassemble, first pack the bearing assembly with grease. Place the new oil seal in clean oil and allow to soak for a few minutes.

10   Reassembly is now the reverse sequence to dismantling with the exceptions mentioned in the following paragraphs:

11   The bearing spacer must be fitted with its reduced internal diameter or internally shouldered end next to the outer bearing.

12   When refitting the new oil seal, the lip must face inwards and the outer edge be flush with its housing.

13   The hub dust caps must not be filled with grease, but fitted dry.

5.2 Swivel joint and flange

---

4   Rear hub axle – removal and refitting

1   Remove the rear brake and hub assembly (Chapter 9).

2   Extract the split pin, and lift away the plain washer locking the clevis pin securing the handbrake cable yoke to the wheel cylinder handbrake lever. Lift away the clevis pin.

3   Wipe the top of the brake master cylinder reservoir and unscrew the cap. Place a piece of thick polythene over the reservoir and refit the cap. This is to stop the hydraulic fluid syphoning out.

4   Using an open ended spanner, carefully unscrew the hydraulic pipe connection unit to the rear of the wheel cylinder.

5   Undo and remove the three nuts with spring washers securing the hub axle and backplate to the radius arm.

6   Using a tapered soft metal drift, carefully drive the hub axle and backplate from the radius arm and separate the hub axle from the backplate.

7   Refitting is the reverse sequence to removal. It will be necessary to bleed the brake hydraulic system as described in Chapter 9.

---

5   Lower suspension arm (front) – removal and refitting

1   Apply the handbrake and chock the rear wheels. Jack up the front of the car and place on firmly based stands. Remove the roadwheel.

2   Undo and remove the two bolts with spring washers that secure the lower swivel balljoint to the swivel flange (photo).

3   Undo and remove the large nut and special plain washer from the suspension arm front bearing shaft (photo).

4   **Cable gear change models.** Carefully ease out the rubber bush from the subframe housing, exposed when the nut and washer were removed as in the previous paragraph.

5   **Rod gear change models.** Lift away the rubber buffer washers from the subframe housing, exposed when the nut and washer were removed as in paragraph 3.

6   Undo and remove the four bolts with spring washers securing the suspension arm rear bearing housing to the body.

7   The lower suspension arm assembly may now be lifted away from the subframe housing.

8   **Rod gear change models.** Remove the rubber buffer washer and large washer from the suspension arm.

9   **Cable gear change models.** Remove the nylon bush (if fitted), or the rubber bush, from the suspension arm.

10   Undo and remove the nut and spring washer securing the swivel balljoint to the suspension arm.

11   Using a universal balljoint separator, part the balljoint from the suspension arm.

12   Undo and remove the rear bearing retaining nut and ease off the rear bearing.

13   Inspect all bushes for signs of wear or oil contamination and, if either is evident, obtain new parts.

14   To reassemble, first refit the rear bearing and retaining nut but do not tighten fully yet.

15   Refit the swivel balljoint and secure with the retaining nut and spring washers.

16   **Cable gear change models.** Refit the rubber bush or nylon bush

5.3 Suspension arm front bearing nut and washer

as was originally fitted.

17   **Rod gear change models.** Fit the large washer, making sure the chamfer is facing towards the rear of the suspension arm, and then the rubber buffer washer.

18   Refitting the suspension arm assembly is the reverse sequence to removal. It is very important that all fixings are finally tightened to the specified torque with the car on the ground in the normal unladen condition.

19   The front wheel alignment must be checked and further information will be found in Section 23.

---

6   Upper suspension arm (front) – removal and refitting

1   Before commencing work, refer to Section 13 where information will be found on depressurisation of the suspension. Unless the equipment is close at hand at a BL garage it is recommended that the work in this Section should not be attempted, but entrusted to a garage.

2   Reference in this Section is made to the left-hand side or right-hand side of the car. This is relevant to which side the upper suspension arm is fitted and not to the driver's position.

3   **Left-hand side.** Working in the engine compartment undo and remove the two bolts, plain and rubber washers that secure the radiator top mounting bracket to the cowling (Fig. 11.5).

4   Chock the rear wheels and apply the handbrake. Jack up the front

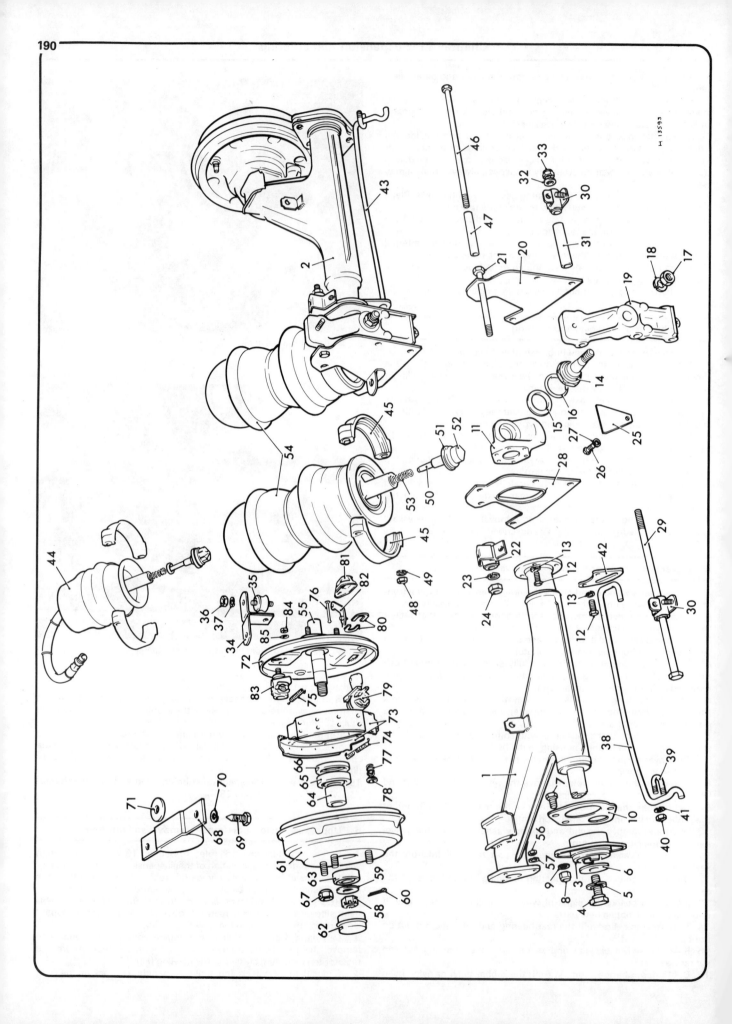

H 13593

Fig. 11.4 Rear suspension components (rod gearchange) (Sec 1)

1 Radius arm – RH
2 Radius arm – LH
3 Rubber bearing for radius arm
4 Bolt for radius bolt
5 Spring washer for bolt
6 Locking washer
7 Bolt for bearing
8 Nut for bolt
9 Spring washer for bolt
10 Lashing plate
11 Reaction lever
12 Bolt – arm to lever
13 Spring washer for bolt
14 Pivot joint
15 Shim for pivot joint
16 Lockwasher for pivot joint
17 Nut for pivot joint
18 Spring washer for nut

19 Support for pivot joint
20 Support housing – LH
21 Upper bolt for support
22 Upper mounting bracket
23 Spring washer
24 Nut for support bolt
25 Rebound buffer
26 Bolt for buffer
27 Spring washer for bolt
28 Support housing – RH
29 Lower bolt for support
30 Lower mounting bracket
31 Distance tube for support bolt
32 Flat washer
33 Nut for support bolt
34 Exhaust pipe mounting bracket
35 Rubber mounting

36 Nut for rubber mounting
37 Spring washer
38 Trim bar – RH mounting
39 U-bolt for trim bar
40 Nut for bolt
41 Spring washer for bolt
42 Reaction plate for trim bar
43 Trim bar – LH
44 Displacer unit – Hydrolastic (model year up to 1977)
45 Support for displacer unit
46 Bolt for displacer unit
47 Distance tube for support bolt
48 Nut for displacer support bolt
49 Spring washer
50 Displacer unit strut
51 Rubber boot for strut

52 Nylon cap for strut
53 Spring for stud
54 Displacer unit – Hydragas (model year 1978 on)
55 Stub axle
56 Nut for axle
57 Spring washer for nut
58 Nut for hub
59 Washer for nut
60 Split pin for nut
61 Hub and brake drum assembly
62 Cap for hub
63 Bearing for hub – outer
64 Spacer for bearings
65 Bearing for hub – inner
66 Oil seal
67 Nut for roadwheel

68 Arch spring assembly
69 Bolt for arch spring
70 Spring washer for bolt
71 Washer for bolt
72 Brake backplate
73 Brake shoes
74 Pull-off spring – cylinder side
75 Pull-off spring – adjuster side
76 Brake shoe retainer
77 Spring for retainer
78 Cup for retainer
79 Wheel cylinder
80 Retainer for cylinder
81 Rubber boot for cylinder
82 Handbrake lever
83 Brake shoe adjuster
84 Nut for adjuster
85 Washer for nut

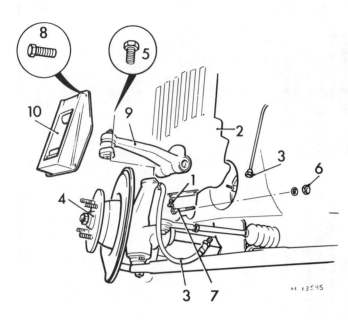

Fig. 11.5 Front upper suspension arm (Sec 6)

1 *Engine to radiator lower bracket bolts*	6 *Suspension arm pivot bolt nut*
2 *Radiator*	7 *Pivot bolt*
3 *Brake pipe*	8 *Bump stop and rebound plate securing bolts*
4 *Hub assembly*	9 *Suspension arm*
5 *Upper swivel balljoint securing bolt*	10 *Bump and rebound plate*

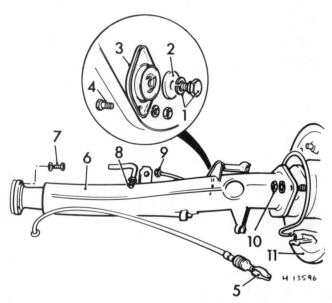

Fig. 11.6 Rear radius arm (Sec 7)

1 *Radius arm to bearing retaining bolt*	6 *Radius arm assembly*
2 *Locating washer*	7 *Radius arm to reaction lever securing bolts*
3 *Bearing and housing assembly*	8 *Flexible brake hose*
4 *Lashing plate securing bolts*	9 *Flexible brake hose*
5 *Handbrake cable*	10 *Hub shaft securing nuts*
	11 *Hub and shaft assembly*

of the car and place on firmly based axle stands. Remove the roadwheel.

5 The suspension may now be depressurised. For this it is usually necessary to use special equipment, but it may be done by unscrewing the valve cap and, using a large jam jar to catch the fluid, very carefully depressing the centre of the valve. Do not depress it fully as the hydrolastic suspension is pressurized to approximately 245 lbf/sq in and the hydragas to 340 lbf/sq in.

6 **Left-hand side.** Undo and remove the two bolts with plain and rubber washers that secure the radiator lower mounting bracket to the radiator. Carefully move the radiator sufficiently for the upper suspension arm pivot bolt to be removed later on.

7 Wipe the top of the brake master cylinder reservoir and unscrew the cap. Place some thick polythene over the top of the reservoir and refit the cap. This is to stop hydraulic fluid syphoning out when the brake pipe is disconnected.

8 Using an open ended spanner, disconnect the brakepipe at its connection with the flexible hose.

9 With a small garage jack, or suitable packing, support the weight of the hub assembly.

10 Undo and remove the two bolts and spring washers that secure the upper swivel balljoint to the swivel.

11 Undo and remove the nut and spring washer from the upper suspension arm pivot and then withdraw the pivot bolt.

12 Undo and remove the four bolts that secure the bump stop and rebound plate.

13 Carefully lower the hub assembly and lift away the bump stop and rebound plate.

14 The upper suspension arm may now be lifted from the front suspension subframe.

15 If the bearing fitted into the inner end of the suspension arm requires renewal, this is a job best left to the local BL garage who will have the necessary tools and equipment to do the job in a satisfactory manner.

16 Refitting is the reverse sequence to removal but the following additional points should be noted:

17 Before refitting the suspension arm, make sure that the displacer unit spring is positioned correctly.

18 The knuckle joint assembly and suspension arm bearing surfaces must be lubricated with PBC (Polybutylcuprysil) or Duckhams LBM 10 Grease.

19 Provided the BL garage is only a short distance away, the suspension may be completely assembled, the brakes bled and then the car driven very slowly to have the suspension pressurised again.

---

7 Radius arm (rear) – removal and refitting

When removing the left-hand radius arm, disconnect the exhaust system from its rear mountings. Remove the spare wheel when removing the right-hand radius arm.

1 Refer to Section 10 and remove the trim bar.

2 Extract the split pin locking the handbrake cable yoke clevis pin at the handbrake lever on the brake/backplate. Lift away the plain washer and withdraw the clevis pin. Note that the head of the clevis pin is uppermost (Fig. 11.6).

3 Wipe the top of the brake master cylinder reservoir and unscrew the cap. Place some thick polythene over the top of the reservoir and refit the cap. This is to stop hydraulic fluid syphoning out when the brakepipe is disconnected.

4 Using an open ended spanner, disconnect the brake pipe at its connection with the flexible hose located at the centre of the radius arm.

5 Undo and remove the radius arm to bearing retaining bolt, spring washer and bearing locating washer from the outer bearing.

6 Undo and remove the bolt that secures the lashing plate. (Rod gear change model only).

7 The two bolts securing the outer bearing may now be removed and then, using a suitable drift, drive the bearing and housing assembly outwards from the body.

8 Undo and remove the four bolts and spring washers that secure the radius arm to the reaction lever.

9 The complete radius arm and hub assembly may now be lifted away from under the car.

10 Release the brake pipe from the clip on the radius arm.

11 Undo and remove the three nuts and spring washers that secure the hub shaft to the radius arm and, using a suitable diameter drift, drive the hub and shaft assembly from the radius arm.
12 Refitting the rear radius arm is the reverse sequence to removal. It is important that the retaining boss of the radius arm aligns with the lugs of the outer bearing before fitting the locating washer and bolt.

8 Reaction lever assembly – removal and refitting

Rod gear change models
1   Refer to Section 7 and remove the rear radius arm.
2   Refer to Section 12 and remove the two rear displacer units.
3   Using a garage jack, support the reaction lever assembly.
4   Raise the rear seat cushion and undo and remove the two nuts with spring and plain washers. Also remove the six bolts with spring and plain washers, all these fixings securing the reaction lever assembly to the underside of the body.
5   Lift away the reaction lever assembly from under the car.
6   Refitting is the reverse sequence to removal. Note that the two uppermost bolts have the largest diameter plain washers under their heads.

Cable gear change models
7   Follow the previous sequence for removal, paragraphs 1 to 3 inclusive.
8   Undo and remove the two nuts and spring washers from the outer support plate securing bolts.
9   Raise the rear seat cushion and undo and remove the six nuts with washers securing the reaction lever assembly to the underside of the body.
10 Lift away the reaction lever assembly from under the car.
11 Refitting is the reverse sequence to removal.

9 Reaction lever assembly – dismantling and reassembly

Rod gear change models
1   Undo and remove the two upper bolts that secure the side support plates to the reaction lever assembly (Fig. 11.7).
2   Undo and remove the long bolt and spacer that holds the two side support plates together.
3   Undo and remove the large diameter nut and spring washer that secures the reaction pivot. Carefully push the reaction lever and pivot assembly from the housing support.
4   Lift away the spring from the pivot joint.
5   Unlock and remove the pivot joint housing, complete with ball pin and top socket, using a long box spanner. Lift away the lock washers and shims.
6   The reaction lever assembly is now completely dismantled and should be washed and wiped dry ready for inspection.
7   Check the components of the ballpin and socket assembly for signs of wear. If evident, a new assembly must be obtained. Generally inspect the side support plates and reaction lever for evidence of strain, elongation of bolt holes, and bent long through bolts. Obtain new parts as necessary.
8   To reassemble, lubricate the ball pin and sockets with Dextragrease Super GP, then fit the ball pin, top socket and housing, leaving out the lock washer and shims.
9   Hold the threaded end of the ball pin and make sure it can be rotated about its axis. Then measure the gap between the housing and reaction lever with feeler gauges.
10 Remove the ball pin and housing assembly and fit a new lock washer, shims to the thickness of the measured gap less 0.036 in (0.914 mm) for the thickness of the lock washer and 0.009 to 0.013 in (0.229 to 0.33 mm) for the required preload.
11 Refit and tighten the housing assembly to the specified torque, using either a long socket, or a box spanner with socket on the end to give the required connection to the torque wrench.
12 Reassembly is the reverse sequence to removal.

Cable gear change models
13 Follow the dismantling sequence for rod gear change models with the exception of paragraph 2 and the first half of paragraph 3.

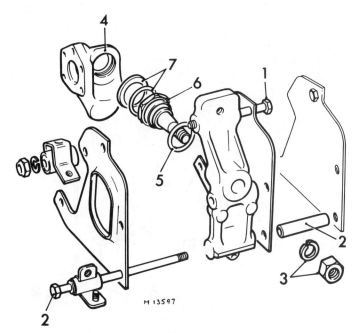

Fig. 11.7 Reaction lever components (rod gearchange) (Sec 9)

1   Side support plates to reaction lever securing upper bolts
2   Side support plates to reaction lever securing lower bolt and spacer
3   Reaction lever pivot retaining nut and washer
4   Reaction lever pivot assembly
5   Spring
6   Ballpin and socket assembly
7   Lockwashers and shims

14 When the ball pin and top socket has been removed, the bottom socket in the reaction lever may be removed (Fig. 11.8).
15 Inspection and reassembly is the same procedure as for rod gear change models except for the difference in dismantling as noted in the first paragraph of this sub-section.

10 Trim bar – removal and refitting

1   Before commencing work refer to Section 6, paragraphs 1 and 13, where information will be found on depressurisation of the suspension.
2   Chock the front wheels. Jack up the rear of the car and support on firmly based stands. Remove the roadwheel.
3   Depressurise the system.
4   Using a small jack, raise the hub until the radius arm compresses the rear wheel arch stop.
5   Undo and remove the two nuts and spring washers from the U-bolt that secures the trim bar to the body (Fig. 11.9).
6   Undo and remove the two bolts and spring washers that secure the reaction plate to the radius arm.
7   The trim bar and reaction plate may now be lifted away from under the car.
8   Refitting is the reverse sequence to removal. Provided a BL garage is only a short distance away, the suspension may be left deflated and the car driven very slowly to the garage to have the suspension pressurised again.

11 Displacer unit (front) – removal and refitting

1   Refer to Section 6 and remove the upper suspension arm.
2   Working in a similar manner to the removal of a brake or clutch flexible hose, disconnect the displacer hose from the steel suspension pipe.
3   Undo and remove the clip nut, bolt and spring washer securing the outer end of the displacer hose to the body.
4   Undo and remove the nut, bolt, plain and spring washer securing

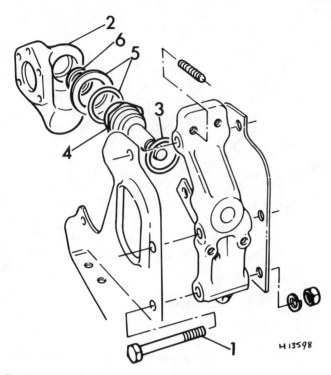

Fig. 11.8 Reaction lever components (cable gearchange) (Sec 9)

1 Side support plates to   3 Spring
   reaction lever securing   4 Ball-pin and socket assembly
   bolts   5 Lockwasher and shims
2 Reaction lever pivot   6 Bottom socket
   assembly

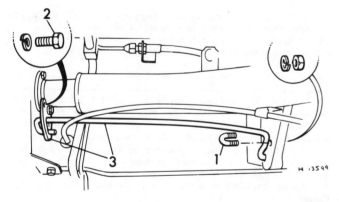

Fig. 11.9 Trim bar (Sec 10)

1 U-bolt   to radius arm
2 Bolts securing reaction plate 3 Trim bar and reaction plate

the displacer unit retaining bracket (hydrolastic models) and lift away
the displacer unit.
5   Refitting is the reverse sequence to removal. It is important that
the bearing surfaces of the knuckle joint assembly and upper suspension arm are lubricated with PBC (Polybutylcuprysil) or Duckhams
LBM 10 grease.

12 Displacer unit (rear) – removal and refitting

Rod gear change

1   Before commencing work refer to Section 6, paragraphs 1 and 13
where information will be found on depressurisation of the hydrolastic
system.

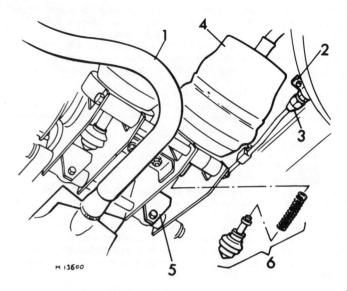

Fig. 11.10 Rear displacer unit removal (rod gearchange) (Sec 12)

1 Exhaust system   pipe
2 Displacer hose clip   4 Displacer unit
3 Displacer unit hose   5 Rebound rubber
   connection to suspension   6 Knuckle joint assembly

2   Depressurise the system. Remove the spare wheel when working
on the right-hand displacer unit on models fitted with hydragas
suspension.
3   Chock the front wheels. Jack up the rear of the car and support on
firmly-based stands. Remove the road wheels.
4   **Left-hand side.** For safety reasons disconnect the battery. Refer
to Chapter 3 and remove the fuel tank; also completely remove the
exhaust system from the car (hydrolastic models). On hydragas models
it is only necessary to disconnect the exhaust system centre bracket.
5   Undo and remove the clip nut, bolt, plain and spring washer securing the outer end of the displacer hose to the body (Fig. 11.10).
6   Working in a similar manner to the removal of a brake flexible
hose, disconnect the displacer hose from the steel suspension pipe.
7   Undo and remove the two bolts that secure the displacer unit
supports, making a note that distance tubes are fitted on the bolts
between the support plates.
8   The displacer may now be lifted away from the underside of the
car.
9   Finally remove the spring, knuckle joint assembly and nylon cap.
10   Refitting is the reverse sequence to removal but the following
additional points should be noted:

(a) It is important that the bearing surfaces of the knuckle joint
     assembly and reaction lever are lubricated with PBC
     (Polybutylcuprysil) or Duckhams LBM 10 grease
(b) When reassembling the knuckle joint, the rubber boot of the
     knuckle joint must be fitted to the nylon cap before refitting
     into the reaction lever
(c) The displacer supports must be fitted with their flat faces
     towards the rear of the car
(d) When removing the displacer unit support clamp of hydragas
     units, do not disturb the ones which locate on the short
     threaded ends of the studs on the right-hand side. When
     reassembling, always enter the studs from the right-hand side

Cable gear change

11   Refer to the instructions above for the rod gear change paragraphs
1 and 3.
12   Undo and remove the two long through bolts, nuts and spring
washers securing the displacer unit supports (Fig. 11.11).
13   Undo and remove the four nuts, bolts, spring and plain washers
securing the tie plate and lift away the tie plate. Note which way round
it is fitted.
14   Remove the knuckle joint assembly, spacers, nylon cap and spring.

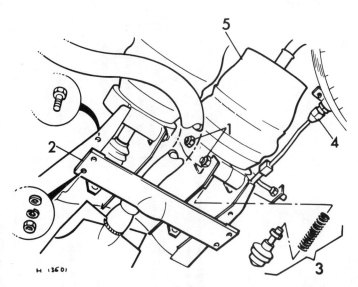

**Fig. 11.11 Rear displacer unit removal (cable gearchange)
(Sec 12)**

1   *Displacer unit support
    securing bolts*
2   *Tie-plate*
3   *Knuckle joint assembly*

4   *Displacer unit hose
    connection to suspension
    pipe*
5   *Displacer unit*

15 Undo and remove the clip nut, bolt, plain and spring washer, securing the outer end of the displacer hose to the body.
16 Working in a similar manner to the removal of a brake flexible hose, disconnect the displacer hose from the steel suspension pipe.
17 The displacer may now be lifted away from the underside of the car.
18 Refitting is the reverse sequence to removal but the additional points noted for the rod gear change are also applicable. (See paragraph 10 of the previous sub section).

13 Trim height – adjustment

1   Should it be necessary to adjust the suspension height or carry out work on the suspension which entails depressurisation or repressurisation of the suspension system, it is advisable to ensure that there is a BL garage nearby who can repressurise the system once the work has been completed. When the need arises to depressurise the system one method is given using a screwdriver to depress the valve core and catch the fluid in a large jam jar (see Section 6, paragraph 5), but it cannot be over emphasised that care must be taken because of the high pressure involved.
2   The car must be driven very slowly with the suspension system in the deflated condition as the suspension will be up against the bump rubbers. This is also the case when the car has suffered accidental damage and the system has lost the special fluid.
3   The trim height of the car may be checked and adjusted by altering the pressure within the system, the latter work being carried out by the local BL garage. To check trim height proceed as follows:
4   Remove any excess luggage from the car so that it is in its normal unladen condition, and drive it onto a flat hard area.
5   Check and adjust the tyre pressures.
6   Bounce the car several times at the front and rear to allow the suspension to be in its normal ride condition.
7   Using a rule or tape, check the trim height and compare the results with those figures fiven in the Specifications at the beginning of this Chapter.
8   The pressure may be increased to raise, or decreased to lower, the trim height. Should the trim height be difficult to obtain, further investigation will be necessary. The cause of the trouble is usually found to be a faulty displacer or flexible hose.

14 Steering – special maintenance

1   Lubrication of the rack and pinion during normal servicing is unnecessary as the lubricant is retained in the assembly by the rubber gaiters. However, should a loss occur due to a leak from the rack housing or rubber gaiters, then the correct amount of oil should be inserted using an oil can. Obviously before replenishing is carried out, the source of the leak must be found and rectified.
2   To top up the oil in the rack and pinion steering assembly, remove the clip from the rubber gaiter on the right-hand end of the steering rack housing and rotate the steering wheel until the rack is in the normal straight ahead position. Allow any remaining oil to seep out, so that it is not overfilled. Using an oil can, insert the nozzle into the end of the rack housing and refill with not more than $\frac{2}{3}$ pint of the recommended grade of oil.
3   Reposition the gaiter and tighten the clip quickly to ensure minimum loss of oil, and then move the steering wheel from lock to lock very slowly to distribute the oil in the housing.
4   If at any time the car is raised and the front wheels are clear of the ground, do not use any excessive force or rapid movement when moving the wheels, especially from one lock to the other, otherwise damage could occur to the steering mechanism.

15 Steering wheel – removal and refitting

1   **Cable gear change models.** Ease the motif from the centre of the steering wheel hub.
2   **Rod gear change models.** Using a knife ease the steering wheel pad from the steering wheel spokes by releasing the eight clips positioned in pairs along the length of the pad.
3   With a pencil or scriber mark the relative positions of the steering wheel hub and column so that they may be correctly aligned upon reassembly.
4   Using a socket or box spanner, unscrew the steering wheel retaining nut. Lift away the nut and shakeproof washer.
5   Undo and remove the screw that retains the top half of the switch cowl.
6   Lift the top half of the switch cowl from the column.
7   Undo and remove the screws that retain the lower half of the switch cowl and lift away the bottom half of the switch cowl.
8   Remove the steering wheel by thumping the rear of the rim adjacent to the spokes with the palms of the hands which should loosen the hub splines from the column splines. Lift away the steering wheel.
9   Refitting is the reverse procedure to removal. Align the two marks previously made to ensure the spokes are in the correct position. Refit the shakeproof washer and nut and tighten to the specified torque.

16 Steering lock and ignition/starter switch – removal and refitting

1   Refer to Section 18 or 19, as applicable, and remove the steering column.
2   Refer to Chapter 10 and remove the direction indicator switch assembly.
3   Using an Easy Out or other suitable means, undo and remove the three special shear retaining screws. If a tool is not available, they can be drilled out very carefully.
4   The housing and lock assembly may now be lifted away from the column.
5   Refitting the housing and lock assembly is the reverse sequence to removal. New shear screws must be used and tightened until the heads shear at the waisted point.

17 Steering column top bush – removal and refitting

1   Refer to Chapter 10 and remove the direction indicator and headlamp flasher switch.
2   With a pencil or scriber, mark the exact position of the direction indicator switch trip relative to the inner column.
3   Using a small screwdriver, undo and remove the trip grub screw and slide off the trip ring.

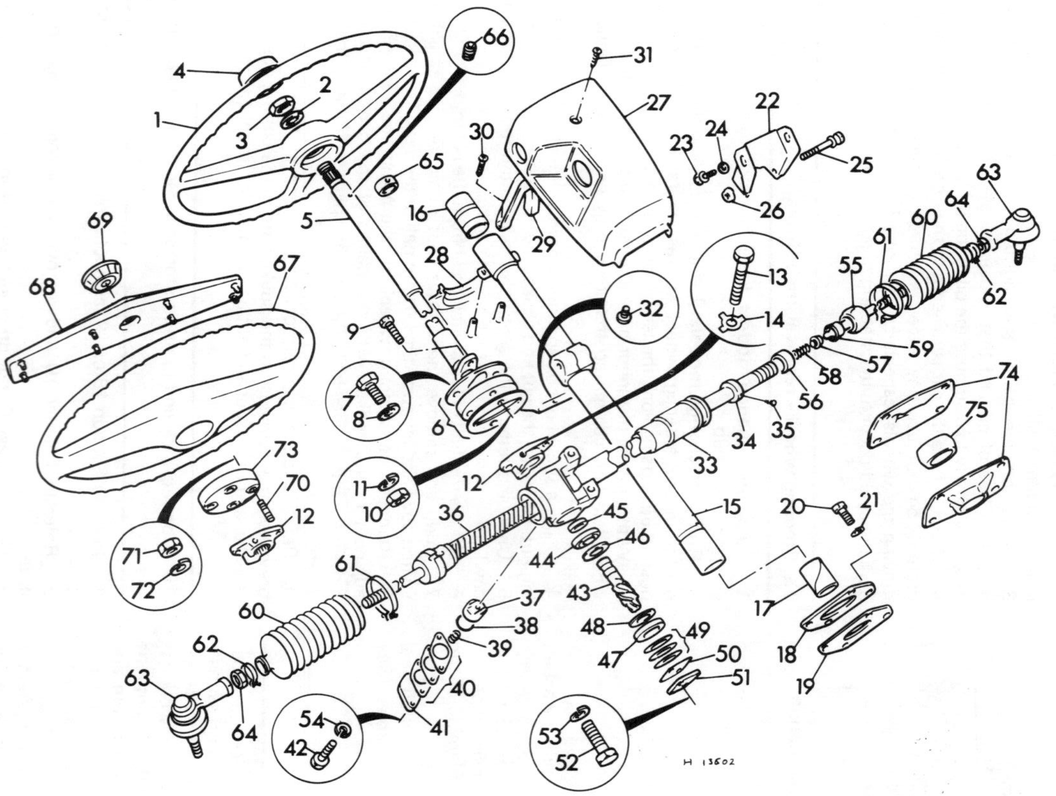

Fig. 11.12 Steering gear components (Sec 22)

1 Steering wheel – cable gearchange
2 Steering wheel nut
3 Washer
4 Steering wheel motif – cable gearchange
5 Inner steering column
6 Coupling } cable gear change
7 Bolt – coupling to pinion flange } cable gear change
8 Spring washer for bolt } cable gear change
9 Bolt – column flange to coupling
10 Nut
11 Washer
12 Pinion flange
13 Pinch bolt
14 Lockwasher
15 Steering column – outer
16 Bush for column (plastic)
17 Bush for column
18 Toe-plate
19 Gasket
20 Bolt
21 Washer
22 Bracket for column
23 Bolt for bracket (shear)
24 Washer
25 Bolt for column (shear)
26 Nut for bolt (captive)
27 Cowl for column – upper
28 Cowl for column – lower
29 Bracket for cowl
30 Screw for bracket
31 Screw for cowl
32 Screw for cowl
33 Rack housing
34 Bush for housing
35 Screw for bush
36 Rack
37 Damper yoke
38 O-ring for yoke
39 Damper spring
40 Shims
41 Cover for damper
42 Bolt
43 Pinion
44 Bearing for pinion – upper
45 Oil seal
46 Thrustwasher
47 Bearing for pinion – lower
48 Thrustwasher
49 Shims
50 Gasket
51 Cover for pinion housing
52 Bolt
53 Washer
54 Washer
55 Ballhousing
56 Locking ring
57 Seat
58 Spring for seat
59 Tie-rod
60 Gaiter
61 Clip for gaiter – large
62 Clip for gaiter – small
63 Ball end assembly
64 Locknut
65 Trip for direction indicator switch
66 Screw for trip } rod gear change
67 Steering wheel } rod gear change
68 Steering wheel pad } rod gear change
69 Steering wheel motif } rod gear change
70 Stud – coupling to pinion flange } rod gear change
71 Nut } rod gear change
72 Spring washer } rod gear change
73 Flexible coupling } rod gear change
74 Clamp plates } rod gear change
75 Bush for clamp plates } rod gear change

4   Completely remove the direction indicator switch.
5   With a small centre punch or a hook made from thin sheet steel, carefully draw out the old top bush.
6   Refitting the new bush is the reverse sequence to removal, but the following additional points should be noted:

   (a) The new bush should be fitted with the chamfered end of the bush entering the outer column first
   (b) Make sure the depression in the outer column engages with the slot in the bush

18 Steering column (rod gear change) – removal and refitting

1   For safety, disconnect the battery.
2   Disconnect the column switch wiring loom at the multi-pin connector located below the facia.
3   Refer to Section 15 and remove the steering wheel.
4   Undo and remove the four bolts, nuts and spring washers that secure the toe plates. Carefully ease the two toe plates and the rubber grommet, which is between the two plates, up the steering column.
5   Undo and remove the two nuts and spring washers that secure the steering column coupling to the pinion flange.
6   Using a small hacksaw blade, cut a screwdriver slot in the head of the shear bolt that secures the column to the mounting bracket. With a screwdriver unscrew the shear bolt. The shear bolt nut is locked to the bracket so do not try to turn it.
7   The complete steering column assembly may now be lifted away from inside the car. Take care not to touch the headlining with the steering wheel end of the column.
8   To refit the column, first make sure the wheels are in the straight ahead position.
9   Turn the inner column until it is in the straight ahead position and place it in its approximate fitted position.
10 Using a new shear bolt, attach the steering column to its mounting bracket but do not fully tighten it yet.
11 Refit the steering wheel in its original marked position and make sure that the column, gear and steering wheel are all in the straight ahead position.
12 Refit the two nuts with spring washers that secure the column coupling to the pinion flange, and fully tighten.
13 Ease the two toe plates and rubber grommet down the steering column and refit the four nuts, bolts and spring washers.
14 Carefully tighten the steering column to mounting shear bolt, until the hexagon head shears at the waisted joint.
15 Refit the steering wheel shakeproof washer and securing nut and tighten to the specified torque.
16 Reconnect the steering column switch wiring loom multi-pin connector and finally the two battery terminals.

19 Steering column (cable gear change) – removal and refitting

1   Undo and remove the two bolts that secure the steering pinion flange to the coupling.
2   For safety, disconnect the battery.
3   Disconnect the column switch wiring loom at the multi-pin connector located below the facia.
4   Undo and remove the four bolts, nuts and spring washers that secure the toe plates. Carefully ease the two toe plates and rubber grommet, which is located between the two plates, up the steering column.
5   Refer to Section 15 and remove the steering wheel.
6   Undo and remove the screw that retains the top half of the switch cowl.
7   Lift the top of the switch cowl from the column.
8   Undo and remove the screws that retain the lower half of the switch cowl and lift away the lower half.
9   Using a small hacksaw blade, cut a screwdriver slot in the head of the shear bolt that secures the column to the mounting bracket. With a screwdriver unscrew the shear bolt. The shear bolt is locked to the bracket so do not try to turn it.
10 The complete steering column assembly may now be lifted away from inside the car. Take care not to touch the headlining with the steering wheel end of the column.
11 To refit the column first make sure the wheels are in the straight

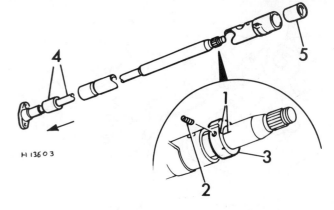

H 13603

Fig. 11.13 Steering column components (Sec 20)

1	*Alignment marks*	*4*	*Lower column and felt bush*
2	*Grub screw*	*5*	*Upper felt bush*
3	*Trip ring*		

ahead position.
12 Turn the inner column until it is in the straight ahead position and place it in its approximate fitted position.
13 Using a new shear bolt, attach the steering column to its mounting bracket but do not fully tighten it yet.
14 Refit the steering wheel in its original marked position and make sure that the column, gear and steering wheel are all in the straight ahead position.
15 Carefully tighten the steering column to mounting shear bolt until the hexagon head shears at the waisted joint.
16 Refitting is now the reverse procedure to removal. The steering wheel nut must be tightened to the specified torque.

20 Steering column – dismantling, overhaul and reassembly

1   Refer to Chapter 10 and remove the combined direction indicator switch.
2   Refer to Section 16 of this Chapter and remove the steering lock and ignition/starter switch.
3   With a pencil or scriber, mark the exact position of the direction indicator switch trip relative to the inner column (Fig. 11.13).
4   Using a small screwdriver, undo and remove the trip grub screw and slide off the trip ring.
5   The inner column may now be drawn downwards from the outer column. Recover the lower felt bush should it come away from the outer column.
6   If the upper plastic bush has worn, it may be removed by drifting it out using a long metal drift.
7   Undo and remove the two bolts that secure the flexible coupling to the inner column should it have deteriorated.
8   The two toe plates and rubber grommet may now be slid from the outer column.
9   Inspect the rubber grommet between the two toe plates and if it has worn or distorted, a new grommet should be obtained.
10 Reassembly is the reverse sequence to removal. The inner column should be entered into the outer column and positioned so that about 3 in (76 mm) of the inner column slender portion is still visible. Fit the felt bush round the slender portion and into its housing. Press the felt inner bush and inner column fully home.

21 Steering gear – removal and refitting

1   Apply the handbrake, chock the rear wheels, jack up the front of the car and support on firmly based stands.
2   Turn the steering wheel until it is in the straight ahead position.
3   Using a scriber or file, mark the pinion housing, coupling and column flange so that they may be correctly refitted (Fig. 11.14).
4   Undo and remove the two nuts, bolts and spring washers from the steering column coupling flange.
5   Undo and remove the nut on each of the two steering arm balljoints and, using a universal balljoint separator, release the balljoints

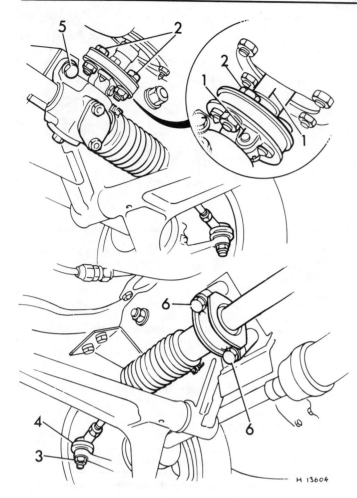

Fig. 11.14 Steering gear removal (Sec 21)

1   Alignment marks
2   Steering column coupling securing bolts
3   Steering arm swivel balljoint nut
4   Balljoint
5   Pinion housing to body securing bolts
6   Steering gear clamp securing bolts

from the steering arms (photo).

6   Undo and remove the two bolts and spring washers that secure the pinion housing to the body.

7   Undo and remove the two bolts and spring washers that secure the steering gear clamp.

8   Carefully move the steering gear assembly to the left sufficiently to disengage it from between the right-hand lower suspension arm and subframe.

9   The steering gear may now be withdrawn from below the right-hand side of the body.

10 Refitting the steering gear is the reverse sequence to removal.

22 Steering gear – dismantling, overhaul and reassembly

It is not possible to make any adjustments to the rack and pinion steering gear unless it is removed from the car. With it removed, it is recommended that it be dismantled and the whole unit examined before making any adjustments. This will save having to remove the unit again later because of initial non-detection of wear. If wear is bad, it is best to fit an exchange reconditioned unit

1   Hold the rack at the pinion body between the soft faces fitted to the jaws of a vice.

2   Ease back the tabs on the pinion flange securing bolt lock washer and unscrew the securing bolt (Fig. 11.12).

3   Turn the pinion until the rack is in the straight ahead position. Note the relative position of the pinion marking (this being either a slot or an arrow should point downwards) the marking on the pinion flange, and their relative positions to a longitudinal centre line of the steering gear. Withdraw the flange.

4   Slacken the ball end locknuts and unscrew the two ball ends from the tie-rods.

5   Unscrew the rubber gaiter securing clips to the housing and tie-rods and completely remove the clips.

6   Ease the tie-rod end of one of the gaiters from contact with the tie-rod and allow the oil to drain out – approximate capacity $\frac{1}{3}$ pint (0.2 litre).

7   The two rubber gaiters may now be removed.

8   Remove the two damper housing cover plate securing bolts and spring washers (photo) and lift away the cover plate, joint washer and packing shims. Place these shims to one side so that they can be refitted as a set upon reassembly. Lift out the damper spring and finally the damper.

9   Remove the bolts and spring washers securing the pinion end cover and lift away the end cover, joint washer and shims. Also lift out the lower thrust washer, bearing and bearing race. The pinion may now be withdrawn from the pinion housing.

10 Lift away the upper bearing race, bearing and thrust washer.

11 Using a screwdriver, ease out the pinion shaft oil seal. This should be discarded and a new one obtained.

12 With a pin punch, open the indentations in the locknut clear of the

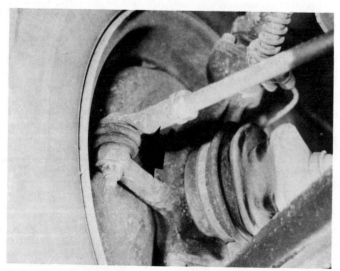

21.5 Steering arm balljoint

22.8 Steering damper cover plate

milled slots in the balljoint housing. For this operation use a C spanner of suitable size. This will release the tie-rod, ball seat and seat tension spring. Repeat this operation for the other end of the rack.

13 Very carefully, withdraw the rack from the pinion end of the housing, so preventing the teeth damaging the bush in the other end of the housing.

14 Remove the bush retaining screw and extract the bush and its housing from the rack housing.

15 Thoroughly clean all parts with paraffin. Carefully inspect the teeth on the rack and also the pinion for chipping, roughness, uneven wear, hollows or fractures.

16 Carefully inspect the component parts of the inner balljoints for wear or ridging and renew as necessary.

17 The outer track-rod joints cannot be dismantled and, if worn, must be renewed as a complete assembly. Examine the component parts of the damper and renew any parts that show signs of wear. Pay particular attention to the oil seals and as a precautionary measure it is always best to renew them.

18 As it is difficult to refill the rack and pinion assembly with oil once it is fitted to the car, make sure that the rubber gaiters are sound before refitting them. If they are in the least bit torn or perished complete loss of oil could occur later and they would then have to be renewed.

19 To reassemble, first fit a new bush into the housing so that the flats of the bush are offset to the bush retaining screw hole in the housing.

20 Insert a metal rod into the bush so that it acts as a support preventing the bush distorting and drill a hole 0.119 in (3 mm) diameter through the existing hole in the housing and then through the bush. Coat the threaded portion, and under the head of the screw, with a thick non-setting oil resistant sealer and fit it so securing the bush in the rack housing. Check that the screw does not protrude into the bore of the bush.

21 Carefully position the top pinion housing bearing race, bearing and thrust washer into the pinion housing.

22 The rack may now be inserted into the housing, but care must be taken not to allow the teeth to score the bushes. Move the rack into the straight ahead position.

23 Insert the pinion so that the mark (a slot, or an arrow) on the splined end, is pointing down towards the damper.

24 Refit the lower washer, bearing race and the bearing.

25 Position some shims on the lower bearing, to provide a gap of approximately 0.010 in (0.25 mm) between the face of the housing and the housing cover.

26 Refit the housing cover and tighten the securing bolts evenly until the cover is held firmly. Use feeler gauges to measure the clearance between the housing and the end cover.

27 Remove the cover and adjust the thickness of the shims to give a clearance of 0.007 to 0.009 in. (0.178 to 0.229 mm). Allow 0.006 in (0.15 mm) for the compressed thickness of the cover gasket. This clearance will give a bearing preload of 0.001 to 0.003 in (0.025 to 0.076 mm).

28 Assemble the shim pack so that a 0.060 in (1.52 mm) shim is on the top of the pack and then place it against the cover.

29 Refit the cover and new gasket, and secure with the two bolts and spring washers. It is important that the bolt which is fitted nearest to the damper cover has its threads coated with a sealing compound. Tighten the two bolts to the specified torque.

30 Screw a new ballhousing locking ring onto the rack to the limits of the thread.

31 Refit the seat spring, seat, tie-rod and ballhousing. Tighten the ballhousing until the tie-rod is just nipped.

32 Screw the locking ring back to the ballhousing and check that the tie-rod is still pinched. Now slacken the ballhousing back one eighth of a turn so as to allow full movement of the tie-rod.

33 Tighten the locking ring onto the housing to the specified torque, making sure that the housing does not turn.

34 Lock the ballhousing and locking ring by using a small chisel and driving the clips of the locking ring into the slots in the housing.

35 Fit the damper yoke, damper cover and cover gasket, leaving out the damper spring, O-ring and shims.

36 Refit the cover securing bolts and spring washers, and slowly tighten whilst at the same time turning the pinion backwards and forwards through 180 degrees until the point is reached where it is just possible to rotate the pinion with it held between the fingers.

37 Using feeler gauges, measure the clearance between the cover and its seating on the cover.

38 Remove the cover and fit the O-ring, damper spring and shims to the thickness of the feeler gauge plus 0.002 to 0.005 in (0.051 to 0.0127 mm). Refit the damper cover and tighten the bolts to the specified torque.

39 Using a tube of suitable diameter, fit a new pinion seal to the housing.

40 Refit the two gaiters and secure the housing end clips. Also tighten the clip to the tie-rod furthest from the pinion.

41 Using a squirt type oil can with the nozzle under the free end of the rubber gaiter insert $\frac{1}{3}$ pint of the recommended oil and tighten the remaining gaiter securing clip.

42 Move the rack until it is in its central position and mark the pinion for correct reconnection when refitting to the car. The total rack travel is 6.36 in (161.6 mm) and to the mid position is 3.18 in (80.8 mm). There are 3.9 turns of the pinion from one full lock to the other on early models, 4.2 on later models.

43 Refit the ball ends and locknuts. Screw on both ball ends an equal distance onto each tie-rod. Tighten the locknuts just sufficiently to prevent the ball ends turning, before the rack and pinion assembly is reconnected.

44 The assembly is now ready for refitting to the car.

23 Front wheel alignment

1   The front wheels are correctly aligned when they are turning in at the front by the amount given in the Specifications. It is important that this measurement is taken on a centre line drawn horizontally and parallel to the ground through the centre line of the hub. The exact point should be in the centre of the sidewall of the tyre and not on the wheel rim which could be distorted and give inaccurate readings.

2   The adjustment is effected by loosening the locknut on each tie-rod balljoint and also slackening the rubber gaiter clip holding it to the tie-rod, and turning both tie-rods equally until the adjustment is correct.

3   This is a job best left to your local BL garage as accurate alignment requires the use of special equipment. If the wheels are not in alignment, tyre wear will be heavy and uneven and the steering will be stiff and unresponsive.

See overleaf for 'Fault diagnosis – suspension and steering'

24 Fault diagnosis – suspension and steering

Symptom	Reason(s)
Steering does not feel positive and car tends to wander	Tyre pressures uneven Suspension units defective Steering balljoints badly worn Suspension geometry incorrect Suspension unit fixings loose
Steering stiff and heavy	Tyre pressures too low Steering gear short of lubrication Front wheel toe-in incorrect Steering adjusted too tight
Wheel wobble and vibration	Wheel nuts loose Front wheels and tyres out of balance Driveshaft joints worn Steering balljoints worn Hub bearings worn

Chapter 12 Bodywork and fittings

For modifications, and information applicable to later models, see Supplement at end of manual

Contents

1 General description

The combined body and underframe is of welded steel construction. This makes a very strong and torsionally rigid shell. There are four forward-hinged doors and one full-height tailgate at the rear. The windscreen is slightly curved and is of toughened safety glass. The front seats recline fully whilst the rear seat folds flat to provide a van-type load area.

The instruments are contained in two dials located above the steering column and are supplemented with a range of easy-access controls. A full-flow heating and ventilation system is fitted with outlet ducts at instrument panel level.

2 Maintenance – bodywork and underframe

1   The general condition of a car's bodywork is the one thing that significantly affects its value. Maintenance is easy but needs to be regular. Neglect, particularly after minor damage, can lead quickly to further deterioration and costly repair bills. It is important also to keep watch on those parts of the car not immediately visible, for instance the underside, inside all the wheel arches and the lower part of the engine compartment.

2   The basic maintenance routine for the bodywork is washing – preferably with a lot of water, from a hose. This will remove all the loose solids which may have stuck to the car. It is important to flush these off in such a way as to prevent grit from scratching the finish. The wheel arches and underbody need washing in the same way to remove any accumulated mud which will retain moisture and tend to encourage rust. Paradoxically enough, the best time to clean the underbody and wheel arches is in wet weather when the mud is thoroughly wet and soft. In very wet weather the underbody is usually cleaned of large accumulations automatically and this is a good time for inspection.

3   Periodically it is a good idea to have the whole of the underside of the car steam cleaned, engine compartment included, so that a thorough inspection can be carried out to see what minor repairs and renovations are necessary. Steam cleaning is available at many garages, and is necessary for removal of the accumulation of oily grime which sometimes is allowed to cake thick in certain areas near the engine and gearbox. If steam cleaning facilities are not available, there are one or two excellent water-soluble grease solvents available which can be brush-applied. The dirt can then be simply hosed off.

4   After washing paintwork, wipe off with a chamois leather to give an unspotted clear finish. A coat of clear protective wax polish will give added protection against chemical pollutants in the air. If the paintwork sheen has dulled or oxidised, use a cleaner/polisher combination to restore the brilliance of the shine. This requires a little effort, but is usually necessary where regular washing has been neglected. Always check that the door and ventilator opening drain holes and pipes are completely clear so that water can drain out. Brightwork should be treated the same way as paintwork. Windscreens and windows can be kept clear of the smeary film which often appears if a little ammonia is added to the water. If they are scratched, a good rub with a proprietary metal polish will often clear them. Never use any form of body or chromium polish on glass.

3 Maintenance – upholstery and carpets

Mats and carpets should be brushed or vacuum cleaned regularly to keep them free of grit. If they are badly stained, remove them from the car for scrubbing or sponging and make quite sure they are dry before refitting. Seats and interior trim panels can be kept clean by a wipe over with a damp cloth. If they do become stained (which can be more apparent on light coloured upholstery), use a little liquid detergent and a soft nail brush to scour the grime out of the grain of the material. Do not forget to keep the headlining clean in the same way as the upholstery. When using liquid cleaners inside the car do not over-wet the surfaces being cleaned. Excessive moisture could get into the seams and padded interior causing stains, offensive odours or even rot. If the inside of the car gets wet accidentally it is worthwhile taking some trouble to dry it out properly, particularly where carpets are involved. **Do not leave oil or electric heaters inside the car for this purpose.**

4 Minor body damage – repair

The photographic sequences on pages 206 and 207 illustrate the operations detailed in the following sub-sections.

Repair of minor scratches in the car's bodywork

If the scratch is very superficial, and does not penetrate to the metal of the bodywork, repair is very simple. Lightly rub the area of the scratch with a paintwork renovator, or a very fine cutting paste, to remove loose paint from the scratch and to clear the surrounding bodywork of wax polish. Rinse the area with clean water.

Apply touch-up paint to the scratch using a thin paintbrush; continue to apply thin layers of paint until the surface of the paint in the scratch is level with the surrounding paintwork. Allow the new paint at least two weeks to harden; then blend it into the surrounding paintwork by rubbing the paintwork, in the scratch area with a paintwork renovator or a very fine cutting paste. Finally, apply wax polish.

Where the scratch has penetrated right through to the metal of the bodywork, causing the metal to rust, a different repair technique is required. Remove any loose rust from the bottom of the scratch with a penknife, then apply rust inhibiting paint to prevent the forrnation of rust in the future. Using a rubber or nylon applicator fill the scratch with bodystopper paste. If required, this paste can be mixed with cellulose thinners to provide a very thin paste which is ideal for filling narrow scratches. Before the stopper paste in the scratch hardens, wrap a piece of smooth cotton rag around the top of a finger. Dip the finger in cellulose thinners and then quickly sweep it across the surface of the stopper-paste in the scratch; this will ensure that the surface of the stopper-paste is slightly hollowed. The scratch can now be painted over as described earlier in this Section.

Repair of dents in the car's bodywork

When deep denting of the car's bodywork has taken place, the first task is to pull the dent out, until the affected bodywork almost attains its original shape. There is little point in trying to restore the original shape completely, as the metal in the damaged area will have stretched on impact and cannot be reshaped fully to its original contour. It is better to bring the level of the dent up to a point which is about $\frac{1}{8}$ in (3 mm) below the level of the surrounding bodywork. In cases where the dent is very shallow anyway, it is not worth trying to pull it out at all. If the underside of the dent is accessible, it can be hammered out gently from behind, using a mallet with a wooden or plastic head. Whilst doing this, hold a suitable block of wood firmly against the impact from the hammer blows and thus prevent a large area of the bodywork from being 'belled-out'.

Should the dent be in a section of the bodywork which has double skin or some other factor making it inaccessible from behind, a different technique is called for. Drill several small holes through the metal inside the area — particularly in the deeper section. Then screw long self-tapping screws into the holes just sufficiently for them to gain a good purchase in the metal. Now the dent can be pulled out by pulling on the protruding heads of the screws with a pair of pliers.

The next stage of the repair is the removal of the paint from the damaged area, and from an inch or so of the surrounding 'sound' bodywork. This is accomplished most easily by using a wire brush or abrasive pad on a power drill, although it can be done just as effectively by hand using sheets of abrasive paper. To complete the preparation for filling, score the surface of the bare metal with a screwdriver or the tang of a file, or alternatively, drill small holes in the affected area. This will provide a really good 'key' for the filler paste.

To complete the repair see the Section on filling and respraying.

Repair of rust holes or gashes in the car's bodywork

Remove all paint from the affected area and from an inch or so of the surrounding 'sound' bodywork, using an abrasive pad or a wire brush on a power drill. If these are not available a few sheets of abrasive paper will do the job just as effectively. With the paint removed you will be able to gauge the severity of the corrosion and therefore decide whether to renew the whole panel (if this is possible) or to repair the affected area. New body panels are not as expensive as most people think and it is often quicker and more satisfactory to fit a new panel than to attempt to repair large areas of corrosion.

Remove all fittings from the affected area except those which will act as a guide to the original shape of the damaged bodywork (eg headlamp shells etc). Then, using tin snips or a hacksaw blade, remove all loose metal and any other metal badly affected by corrosion. Hammer the edges of the hole inwards in order to create a slight depression for the filler paste.

Wire brush the affected area to remove the powdery rust from the surface of the remaining metal. Paint the affected area with rust inhibiting paint; if the back of the rusted area is accessible treat this also.

Before filling can take place it will be necessary to block the hole in some way. This can be achieved by the use of one of the following materials: Zinc gauze, Aluminium tape or Polyurethane foam.

Zinc gauze is probably the best material to use for a large hole. Cut a piece to the approximate size and shape of the hole to be filled, then position it in the hole so that its edges are below the level of the surrounding bodywork. It can be retained in position by several blobs of filler paste around its periphery.

Aluminium tape should be used for small or very narrow holes. Pull a piece off the roll and trim it to the approximate size and shape required, then pull off the backing paper (if used) and stick the tape over the hole; it can be overlapped if the thickness of one piece is insufficient. Burnish down the edges of the tape with the handle of a screwdriver or similar, to ensure that the tape is securely attached to the metal underneath.

Polyurethane foam is best used where the hole is situated in a section of bodywork of complex shape, backed by a small box section (eg where the sill panel meets the rear wheel arch — most cars). The usual mixing procedure for this foam is as follows: put equal amounts of fluid from each of the two cans provided in the kit, into one container. Stir until the mixture begins to thicken, then quickly pour this mixture into the hole, and hold a piece of cardboard over the larger apertures. Almost immediately the polyurethane will begin to expand, gushing out of any small holes left unblocked. When the foam hardens it can be cut back to just below the level of the surrounding bodywork with a hacksaw blade.

Bodywork repairs — filling and respraying

Before using this Section, see the Sections on dent, deep scratch, rust holes and gash repairs.

Many types of bodyfiller are available, but generally speaking those proprietary kits which contain a tin of filler paste and a tube of resin hardener are best for this type of repair. A wide, flexible plastic or nylon applicator will be found invaluable for imparting a smooth and well contoured finish to the surface of the filler.

Mix up a little filler on a clean piece of card or board — use the hardener sparingly (follow the maker's instructions on the packet) otherwise the filler will set very rapidly.

Using the applicator apply the filler paste to the prepared area: draw the applicator across the surface of the filler to achieve the correct contour and to level the filler surface. As soon as a contour that approximates the correct one is achieved, stop working the paste — if you carry on too long the paste will become sticky and begin to 'pick up' on the applicator. Continue to add thin layers of filler paste at twenty-minute intervals until the level of the filler is just proud of the surrounding bodywork.

Once the filler has hardened, excess can be removed using a Surform plane or Dreadnought file. From then on, progressively finer grades of abrasive paper should be used, starting with a 40 grade production paper and finishing with 400 grade wet-and-dry paper. Always wrap the abrasive paper around a flat rubber, cork, or wooden block — otherwise the surface of the filler will not be completely flat. During the smoothing of the filler surface the wet-and-dry paper should be periodically rinsed in water. This will ensure that a very smooth finish is imparted to the filler at the final stage.

At this stage the 'dent' should be surrounded by a ring of bare metal, which in turn should be encircled by the finely 'feathered' edge of the good paintwork. Rinse the repair area with clean water, until all of the dust produced by the rubbing-down operation has gone.

Spray the whole repair area with a light coat of primer — this will show up any imperfections in the surface of the filler. Repair these imperfections with fresh filler paste or bodystopper, and once more smooth the surface with abrasive paper. If bodystopper is used, it can be mixed with cellulose thinners to form a really thin paste which is ideal for filling small holes. Repeat this spray and repair procedure until you are satisfied that the surface of the filler, and the feathered edge of the paintwork are perfect. Clean the repair area with clean water and allow to dry fully.

The repair area is now ready for final spraying. Paint spraying must be carried out in a warm, dry, windless and dust free atmosphere. This condition can be created artificially if you have access to a large indoor working area, but if you are forced to work in the open, you will have to pick your day very carefully. If you are working indoors, dousing the floor in the work area with water will help settle the dust which would otherwise be in the atmosphere. If the repair area is confined to one body panel, mask off the surrounding panels; this will help to minimise the effects of a slight mis-match in paint colours. Bodywork fittings (eg chrome strips, door handles etc) will also need to be masked off. Use genuine masking tape and several thicknesses of newspaper for the masking operations.

Before commencing to spray, agitate the aerosol can thoroughly, then spray a test area (an old tin, or similar) until the technique is mastered. Cover the repair area with a thick coat of primer; the thickness should be built up using several thin layers of paint rather than one thick one. Using 400 grade wet-and-dry paper, rub down the surface of the primer until it is really smooth. While doing this, the work area should be thoroughly doused with water, and the wet-and-dry paper periodically rinsed in water. Allow to dry before spraying on more paint.

Spray on the top coat, again building up the thickness by using several thin layers of paint. Start spraying in the centre of the repair area and then using a circular motion, work outwards until the whole repair area and about 2 inches of the surrounding original paintwork is covered. Remove all masking material 10 to 15 minutes after spraying on the final coat of paint.

Allow the new paint at least two weeks to harden, then, using a paintwork renovator or a very fine cutting paste, blend the edges of the paint into the existing paintwork. Finally, apply wax polish.

5 Major body damage – repair

Where serious damage has occurred or large areas need renewal due to neglect, it means certainly that completely new sections of panels will need welding in and this is best left to professionals. If the damage is due to impact it will also be necessary to completely check the alignment of the bodyshell structure. Due to the principle of construction the strength and shape of the whole can be affected by damage to a part. In such instances the services of a BL dealer with specialist checking jigs are essential. If a body is left misaligned it is first of all dangerous as the car will not handle properly and secondly uneven stresses will be imposed on the steering, engine and transmission, causing abnormal wear or complete failure. Tyre wear may also be excessive.

6 Front door – dismantling and reassembly

Interior door handle and trim

1   Make sure the window is fully closed, then undo and remove the screw and washer that secure the window regulator handle. Lift away the handle and its escutcheon (Fig. 12.1).
2   Carefully, using a screwdriver, ease the two halves of the plastic bezel from the control unit, moving the top half upwards and the bottom half downwards (photo).
3   Undo and remove the two screws that secure the armrest to the door. Lift away the armrest.
4   Insert a screwdriver blade between the lower edge of the trim panel and the door, and very carefully lever the pad retaining clips from the door panel plugs. Lift away the trim panel.
5   Remove the four screws securing the latch to the door panel (photo). Detach the latch release rod from its plastic clip and the lock control rod from the locking lever bush.
6   Refitting the trim panel and interior handle is the reverse sequence

to removal. Note that the locating dowel on the window handle escutcheon must be at the bottom.

Door glass

7   Remove the interior handle and door trim panel as described in paragraphs 1 to 4.
8   Unscrew the trim panel finisher securing screws, and lift away the finisher and door capping (Fig. 12.3).
9   Carefully peel back the plastic cover from the door inner panel.
10 Undo and remove the two screws that secure the glass stop to the lower part of the door inner panel. Lift away the glass stop.
11 Carefully wind the glass down fully (refit the handle for this operation) and disengage the window regulator from the channel.
12 Tilt the glass inwards and lift it up so as to clear the top of the door. Lift away the glass from the door.
13 Refitting is the reverse sequence to removal.

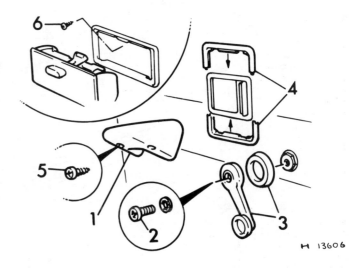

Fig. 12.1 Door interior handle and trim (Sec 6)

1   Armrest
2   Window regulator handle retaining screw
3   Window regulator handle and escutcheon
4   Door lock remote control plastic bezel
5   Armrest retaining screws
6   Ashtray and retaining screws

6.2 Removing the door latch bezel

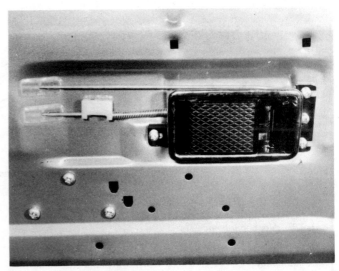

6.5 Door latch attachment screws

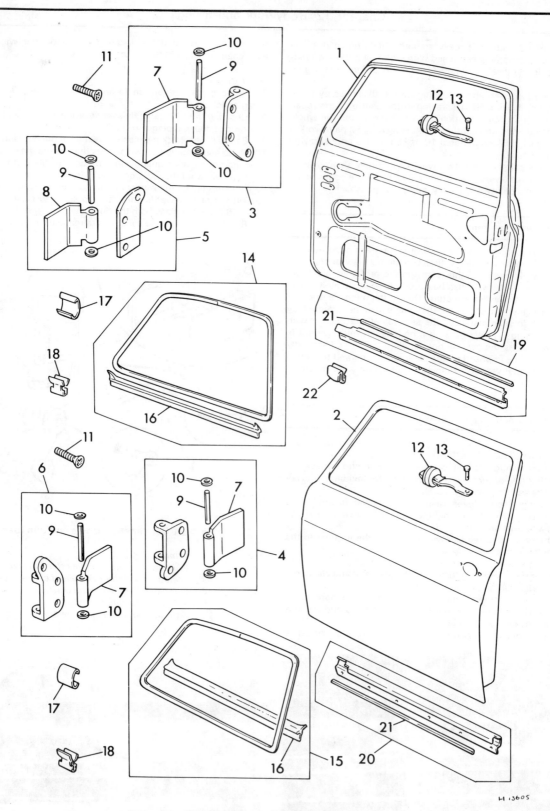

Fig. 12.2 Door components (Sec 6)

1	RH door shell	assembly	18 Clip
2	LH door shell	6 LH door lower hinge	19 RH inner waist capping
3	RH door upper hinge	assembly	assembly
	assembly	7 Hinge leaf	20 LH inner waist capping
4	LH door upper hinge	8 Hinge leaf	21 Weatherstrip
	assembly	9 Hinge pin	22 Clip
5	RH door lower hinge	10 Brass washer	

11 Screw
12 Door check arm
13 Clevis pin
14 RH outer moulding assembly
15 LH outer moulding assembly
16 Weatherstrip
17 Moulding capping

H 13605

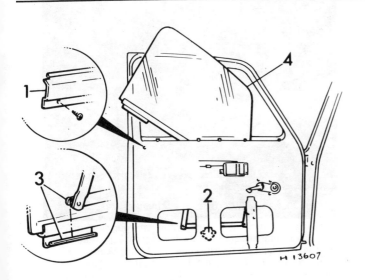

Fig. 12.3 Door glass removal (Sec 6)

1   Trim pad finisher
2   Glass stop retaining screws
3   Regulator disengaged from channel
4   Door glass

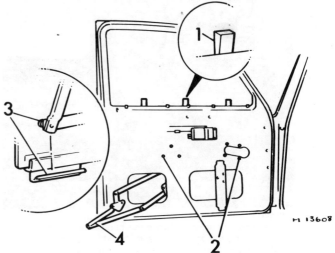

Fig. 12.4 Door glass regulator removal (Sec 6)

1   Tapered wedge
2   Regulator retaining screws
3   Regulator disengaged from channel
4   Regulator assembly contracted

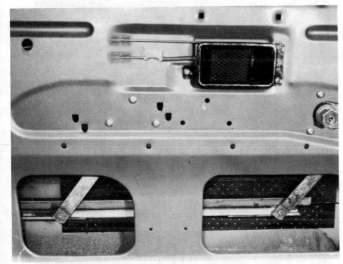

6.19 Window regulator link and channel

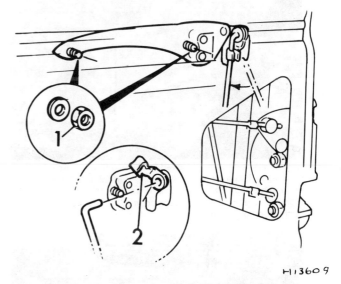

Fig. 12.5 Exterior door handle removal (Sec 6)

1   Handle securing nuts
2   Disengagement of link from pushbutton arm

Door glass regulator

14 Remove the interior handle and door trim panel as described in paragraphs 1 to 4.
15 Temporarily refit the window regulator handle and check that the glass is in the fully raised position.
16 Retain the glass in the raised position by using tapered rubber or wooden wedges between the inner panel and the glass (Fig. 12.4).
17 Carefully peel back the plastic cover from the door inner panel.
18 Undo and remove the seven screws that secure the window regulator to the door inner panel.
19 Working inside the door, disengage the regulator from the glass channel (photo).
20 Contract the window regulator assembly and withdraw it from the lower rear cut out in the door inner panel.
21 Refitting the window regulator assembly is the reverse sequence to removal. Well lubricate all moving parts with oil.

Exterior door handle

22 Remove the interior handle and door trim panel as described in paragraphs 1 to 4.
23 Carefully peel back the plastic cover from the door inner panel.
24 Undo and remove the two nuts and plain washers securing the exterior door handle to the door outer panel (Fig. 12.5).
25 Carefully disengage the link from the pushbutton arm.
26 The exterior door handle may now be lifted away from the door.
27 To refit, first position the handle on the outer door panel then press the end of the link into the pushbutton arm bush and secure it with the clip.
28 Refit the two plain washers and securing nuts.
29 Move the latch to the fully latched position and check the operation of the pushbutton. A little free movement of the button must be felt before the sliding contactor begins to lift, and the latch must release from the striker before the pushbutton is fully depressed.
30 To adjust the pushbutton plunger screw, disconnect the

This sequence of photographs deals with the repair of the dent and paintwork damage shown in this photo. The procedure will be similar for the repair of a hole. It should be noted that the procedures given here are simplified — more explicit instructions will be found in the text

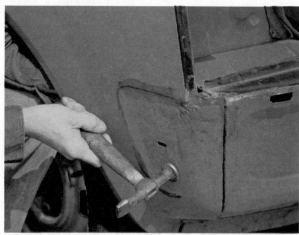

In the case of a dent the first job — after removing surrounding trim — is to hammer out the dent where access is possible. This will minimise filling. Here, the large dent having been hammered out, the damaged area is being made slightly concave

Now all paint must be removed from the damaged area, by rubbing with coarse abrasive paper. Alternatively, a wire brush or abrasive pad can be used in a power drill. Where the repair area meets good paintwork, the edge of the paintwork should be 'feathered', using a finer grade of abrasive paper

In the case of a hole caused by rusting, all damaged sheet-metal should be cut away before proceeding to this stage. Here, the damaged area is being treated with rust remover and inhibitor before being filled

Mix the body filler according to its manufacturer's instructions. In the case of corrosion damage, it will be necessary to block off any large holes before filling — this can be done with aluminium or plastic mesh, or aluminium tape. Make sure the area is absolutely clean before ...

... applying the filler. Filler should be applied with a flexible applicator, as shown, for best results; the wooden spatula being used for confined areas. Apply thin layers of filler at 20-minute intervals, until the surface of the filler is slightly proud of the surrounding bodywork

Initial shaping can be done with a Surform plane or Dreadnought file. Then, using progressively finer grades of wet-and-dry paper, wrapped around a sanding block, and copious amounts of clean water, rub down the filler until really smooth and flat. Again, feather the edges of adjoining paintwork

The whole repair area can now be sprayed or brush-painted with primer. If spraying, ensure adjoining areas are protected from over-spray. Note that at least one inch of the surrounding sound paintwork should be coated with primer. Primer has a 'thick' consistency, so will find small imperfections

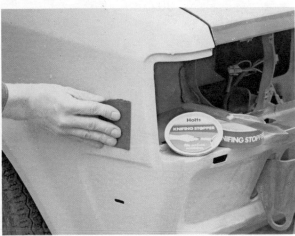

Again, using plenty of water, rub down the primer with a fine grade wet-and-dry paper (400 grade is probably best) until it is really smooth and well blended into the surrounding paintwork. Any remaining imperfections can now be filled by carefully applied knifing stopper paste

When the stopper has hardened, rub down the repair area again before applying the final coat of primer. Before rubbing down this last coat of primer, ensure the repair area is blemish-free — use more stopper if necessary. To ensure that the surface of the primer is really smooth use some finishing compound

The top coat can now be applied. When working out of doors, pick a dry, warm and wind-free day. Ensure surrounding areas are protected from over-spray. Agitate the aerosol thoroughly, then spray the centre of the repair area, working outwards with a circular motion. Apply the paint as several thin coats

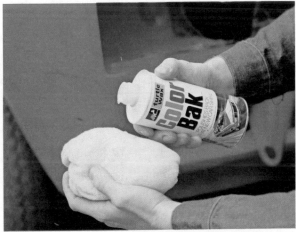

After a period of about two weeks, which the paint needs to harden fully, the surface of the repaired area can be 'cut' with a mild cutting compound prior to wax polishing. When carrying out bodywork repairs, remember that the quality of the finished job is proportional to the time and effort expended

208

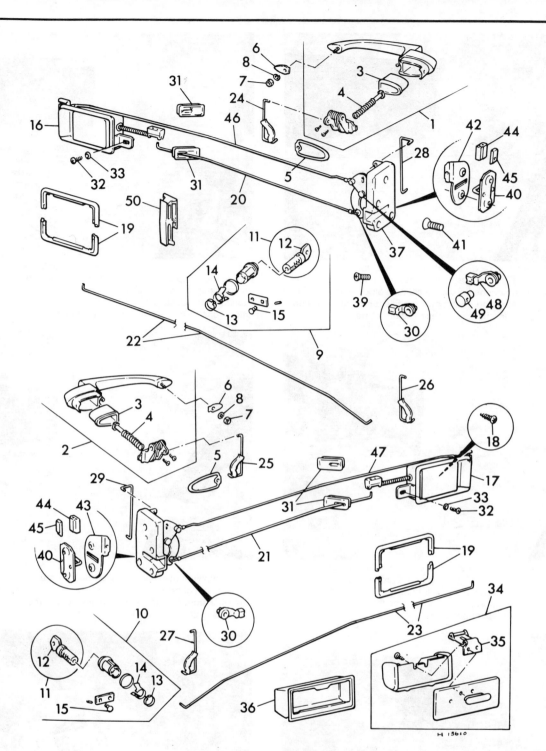

Fig. 12.6 Door lock components (Sec 6)

1 Door handle assembly	14 Retaining clip	27 Handle pushbutton rod	39 Screw
2 Door handle assembly	15 Operating stud	28 Private lockrod	40 Striker
3 Pushbutton	16 Remote control	29 Private lockrod	41 Screw
4 Spring	17 Remote control	30 Clip	42 Striker plate
5 Washer	18 Screw	31 Grommet	43 Striker plate
6 Washer	19 Bezel	32 Screw	44 Seal
7 Nut	20 Remote control rod	33 Shakeproof washer	45 Retainer
8 Spring washer	21 Remote control rod	34 Ashtray assembly	46 Lock operating rod
9 Door lock assembly	22 Remote control rod	35 Spring	47 Lock operating rod
10 Door lock assembly	23 Remote control rod	36 Ashtray case	48 Clip
11 Barrel assembly	24 Handle pushbutton rod	37 Door lock	49 Adjustment pin
12 Key	25 Handle pushbutton rod	38 Door lock	50 Guide link
13 Spring clip	26 Handle pushbutton rod		

pushbutton link and lift the cranked pushbutton arm. Turn the plunger screw in the required direction.
31 Reassembly is now the reverse sequence to dismantling.

Door lock

32 Before the locking mechanism is considered to be defective, refer to Section 9 and make sure that the striker plate is adjusted correctly.
33 Remove the interior handle and door trim panel as described in paragraphs 1 to 4.
34 Carefully peel back the plastic cover from the door inner panel.
35 Detach the latch release rod from its plastic clip.
36 Disconnect the lock control rod from the locking lever bush.
37 Undo and remove the three screws with shakeproof and plain washers securing the remote control to the door inner panel. Lift away the remote control assembly from the door.
38 Release the clip, and detach the latch release rod from the release lever bush.
39 Detach the clip and withdraw the lock control rod from the locking quadrant bush.
40 Carefully ease the window channel from the door channel and move it to one side. Note that this channel is retained in position with adhesive.
41 Release the clip and detach the pushbutton link from the contactor slide bush.
42 Next release the clip, and detach the key-operated link from the latch locking lever bush (photo).
43 Undo the four latch securing screws and lift away the latch assembly.
44 Release the two-legged spring collar and withdraw the lock complete with link from outside the door. It is not necessary to disturb the self-adhesive washer under the lock head.
45 To remove the striker, first remove the seat belt anchor bolt and ease away the door post trim panel with a screwdriver.
46 Unscrew the two striker retaining screws and lift away the cover plate.
47 To reassemble, if the striker and cover plate have been removed these should first be refitted. Lightly tighten the two securing screws and replace the door post trim panel and seat belt anchor bolt.
48 Make sure that the plastic bush is correctly fitted in the operating arm of the key operated lock. The bush must be inserted towards the keyslot end with the link retaining clip fitted under its head.
49 It should be noted that the locks are handed. When fitted, the operating arm must be inclined towards the door shut face with the key slot inverted.
50 Carefully press the lock link into the plastic bush towards the key slot end and retain in position with the clip.
51 Make sure that the self-adhesive washer is fitted to the lock and then fit the spring collar.
52 Insert the lock assembly into the door aperture and press it firmly home.
53 Fit the plastic bushes into the locking lever and latch release lever, towards the latch, with the spring clips fitted under the heads of the bushes.
54 Fit the bush into the slide contactor, away from the latch, so that the spring clip is fitted on the tail end of the bush.
55 Insert the bush into the latch locking lever towards the latch, with the clip fitted under the head of the bush.
56 Pass the latch operating levers, latch release lever first, through the aperture in the door shut face.
57 Secure the latch in position with the four retaining screws.
58 Move the latch disc to the fully latched position.
59 Push the key-operated link inwards into the latch locking lever bush and retain with the clip.
60 Push the pushbutton link outwards into the sliding contactor bush and retain with the clip.
61 Check the operation of the pushbutton and adjust the plunger screw in the required direction until there is a little free movement of the button before the sliding contactor begins to lift.
62 Press the end of the latch release rod upwards into its plastic clip.
63 Next press the end of the lock control rod into its bush in the locking lever.
64 Locate the control rods in their respective guides.
65 Position the remote control unit on the door inner panel and hold it in position with the three bolts, shakeproof and plain washers. Do not tighten fully yet.
66 Press the latch release rod into the bush in the latch release lever.

6.42 Lock and latch release rods

67 Move the control unit towards the latch, without compressing the rod spring, until the latch release lever is up against its stop. Should control unit movement be restricted by the screw slot, enlarge the slot using a round file.
68 Move the latch disc to the closed position.
69 Check the operation of the latch release lever. It should release the striker before the full range of its movement is reached.
70 Move the latch disc to the closed position.
71 Adjust the screwed end pivot on the lock control rod until it fits freely into its bush in the locking quadrant.
72 Press the pivot into its bush and secure the rod with the clip.
73 Check the operation of the safety locking lever and the key. Lubricate all moving parts with oil.
74 Refit the door interior panel plastic cover, door trim panel and interior handle which is the reverse sequence to that previously described.

7 Rear door – dismantling and reassembly

The sequence for dismantling and reassembling the rear door is identical to that for the front door. Full information will be found in the previous Section.

8 Front and rear doors – removal and refitting

1   Disconnect the door check strap by extracting the split pin and withdrawing the clevis pin. Note that its head is positioned uppermost. Take care that the door is not opened too far with the check strap disconnected, otherwise the wing or door panel could be dented.
2   Using a pencil, accurately mark the outline of the hinge relative to the door, to assist refitting. It is desirable to have an assistant to take the weight of the door once the two hinges have been released.
3   Undo and remove the three screws that secure each hinge to the door and lift away the complete door assembly.
4   For storage, it is best to stand the door on an old blanket and allow it to lean against a wall also suitably padded at the top to stop scratching.
5   Refitting the door is the reverse sequence to removal. If, after fitting, adjustment is necessary, it should be done at the hinges to give correct alignment, or the striker reset if the door either moves up or down on final closing.

9 Striker plate – adjustment

1   It is important that before attempting to close the door after a lock has been refitted, the latch disc is in the open position. Operate the push button several times and then pull a screwdriver through the

latch opening.

2   Whilst adjustments are being made, it is not necessary to slam the door as zero-torque locks are fitted.

3   If the striker plate has been removed, tighten the screws just sufficiently to allow the door to close and latch.

4   Firmly press the door inwards, or pull it outwards without depressing the pushbutton, until it lines up with the general contour of the body.

5   Open the door and, with a soft pencil, mark the outline of the striker plate to establish its new horizontal position.

6   Note that the over-travel stop tends to twist the striker during adjustment, so this must be corrected making the loop at right angles to the door hinge axis.

7   Retighten the striker screws.

8   Using the method of trial and error, position the striker accurately until the door can be closed easily, without rattling, and with no apparent lifting or dropping.

9   Close the door and check the adjustment by pressing on the door to see that the striker has not been set too far in. A fractional movement should be possible as the seals are compressed.

10 Door rattles – tracing and rectification

1   The commonest cause of door rattles is a misaligned, loose or worn striker plate, but other causes can be:

(a) Loose door handles, window winder handles, or door hinges
(b) Loose, worn or misaligned door lock components
(c) Loose or worn remote control mechanism

2   It is quite possible for door rattles to be the result of a combination of the above faults, so a careful examination must be made to determine the causes.

3   If the loop of the striker plate is worn, and as a result the door rattles, renew it and adjust as described in Section 9.

4   Should the hinges be worn, they must be renewed and then adjusted as described in Section 3.

11 Windscreen and rear glass – removal and refitting

1   Windscreen replacement is no easy task. Leave this to the specialist if possible. Instructions are given below however.

2   Refer to Chapter 10 and remove the windscreen wiper arms.

3   Using a screwdriver, carefully prise up the end of the moulding finisher strip and withdraw it from its slot in the moulding.

4   If the glass is unbroken, the assistance of a second person to catch the glass when it is released from the aperture will be required.

5   Working inside the car, commencing at one top corner, press the glass and ease it from the rubber moulding.

6   Remove the rubber moulding from the windscreen aperture.

7   If the windscreen has shattered, remove all the fragments of glass. Use a vacuum cleaner to extract as much as possible. Switch on the heater boost motor and adjust the controls to Screen Defrost but watch out for flying pieces of glass which might be blown out of the ducting.

8   Carefully inspect the rubber moulding for signs of splitting or deterioration. Clean all traces of sealing compound from the rubber moulding and windscreen aperture flange.

9   To refit the glass, first place the rubber seal onto the aperture flange.

10   Lubricate the channel in the seal with a concentrated soap and water solution, or with washing-up liquid.

11   Place the lower edge of the glass in the channel and, using a piece of plastic or tapered wood, ease the rubber lip over the glass.

12   The finisher strip must next be fitted to the moulding and for this a special tool is required. An illustration of this tool is shown in Fig. 12.7 and a handyman should be able to make up an equivalent using netting wire and a wooden file handle.

13   Fit the eye of the tool into the groove and feed in the finisher strip.

14   Push the tool around the complete length of the moulding, feeding the finisher into the channel as the eyelet opens it. The back half beds the finisher into the moulding.

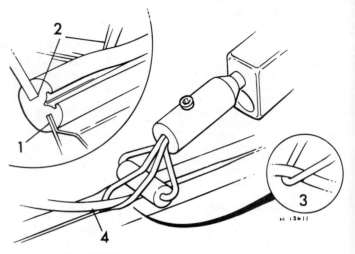

Fig. 12.7 Finisher strip refitting tool (Sec 11)

1   Windscreen glass aperture flange
2   Easing rubber lip over glass
3   Finisher strip threaded through wire loop
4   Eye of tool inserted in finisher groove

12 Facia board (rod gear change) – removal and refitting

Models up to 1979

1   For safety, disconnect the terminal from the battery.

2   Release the choke control cable from the carburettor choke linkage.

3   Refer to Section 24 and remove the glovebox.

4   Refer to Section 21 and remove the heater controls as described in paragraphs 5 to 8 inclusive.

5   Undo and remove the four screws and cup washers that secure the facia to the body. Note that the longest of the four screws is located at the top centre position (Fig. 12.8).

6   Draw the facia forwards by about three inches and detach the fresh air pipes from the facia ventilators.

7   Detach the two tubes from the windscreen washer pump. Note which way round they are fitted.

8   Unscrew the knurled nut securing the speedometer outer cable to the rear of the instrument.

9   Note the electrical cable connections to the rear of the switches and release these connections from their terminals.

10   Detach the multi-pin plug from the rear of the instrument panel.

11   Remove the facia board from its location, whilst at the same time drawing the choke control cable through its rubber grommet.

12   Refitting is the reverse sequence to removal. The choke cable should be fed through the grommet in the engine bulkhead as the facia board is refitted.

1979 on models

13   Disconnect the battery.

14   Remove the top nacelle and the heater control knobs.

15   Release the choke cable from the carburettor.

16   Prise off the heater masking plate and remove the two heater control retaining screws.

17   Remove the two screws retaining the glovebox to the facia board and disengage the glovebox lid stay.

18   Follow the previous paragraphs 5 to 12 omitting paragraph 7.

13 Facia panel (cable gearchange) – removal and refitting

1   For safety, disconnect the terminals from the battery.

2   Release the choke control cable from the carburettor choke linkage.

3   Disconnect the control cable from the heater valve.

4   Refer to Chapter 11 and remove the steering column.

5   Refer to Chapter 10 and remove the instrument panel.

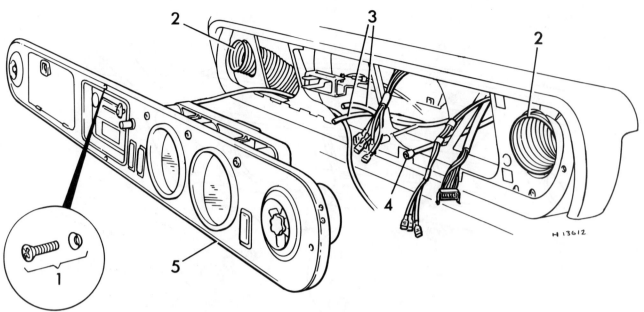

Fig. 12.8 Facia board – pre-1979 (rod gearchange) (Sec 12)

1   Retaining screws
2   Fresh air pipes

3   Windscreen washer pump
    pipes

4   Speedometer cable

5   Facia board

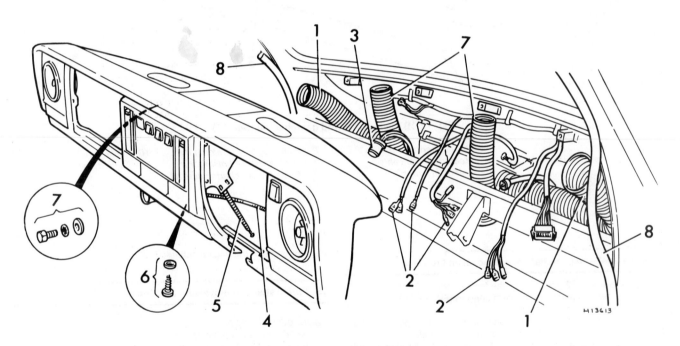

Fig. 12.9 Facia panel (cable gearchange) (Sec 13)

1   Fresh air pipes
2   Electric cables

3   Speedometer cable
4   Heater valve control cable

5   Heater control cable
6   Facia lower retaining screw

7   Facia upper retaining screw
8   Door aperture finisher trim

6   Refer to Section 24 of this Chapter and remove the glovebox.
7   Disconnect the demister tubes from the facia ducts.
8   Disconnect the fresh air pipe from the facia ventilators (Fig. 12.9).
9   Note the electrical cable connections to the rear of the switches and release these connections from their terminals.
10 Unscrew the windscreen washers pump from its push.
11 Disconnect the heater control cables from the heater unit.
12 Unscrew and remove the self-tapping screws and plain washers that secure the lower edge of the facia panel.

13 Unscrew and remove the bolts with shakeproof and plain spring washers that secure the upper half of the facia panel.
14 Very carefully release the finisher trim from the body flange on each door aperture in the vicinity of the facia panel.
15 Draw the facia panel from the body and lift away from the inside of the car.
16 Refitting is the reverse sequence to removal. As the facia panel is being finally positioned, feed the choke and heater valve control cables through the engine bulkhead grommets.

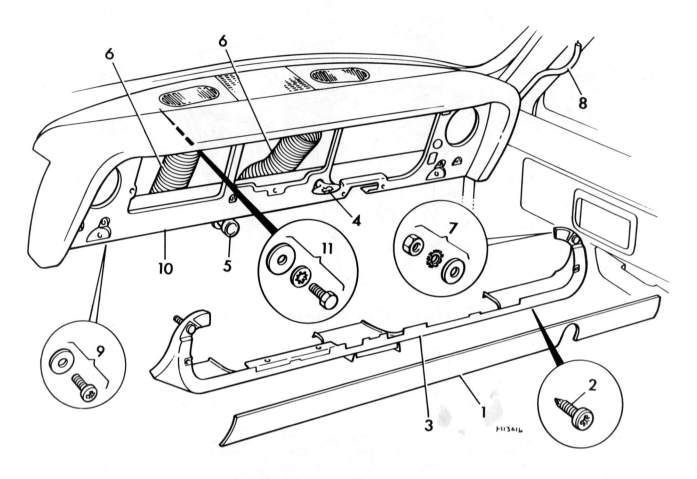

Fig. 12.10 Facia panel (rod gearchange) (Sec 14)

1 Trim pad	4 Bonnet control cable	7 Facia support retaining nut	10 Facia panel
2 Facia support lower securing screws	5 Heater control cable	8 Door aperture finisher trim	11 Facia panel upper securing screws
3 Facia support	6 Demister tubes	9 Facia lower securing screws	

14 Facia panel (rod gearchange) – removal and refitting

1   Refer to Section 12 and remove the facia board.
2   Remove the trim pad from the facia support (Fig. 12.10).
3   Completely remove the ashtray.
4   Undo and remove the nut, shakeproof washer and plain washer securing the facia support to each end of the facia panel.
5   Undo and remove the facia support lower securing screws and carefully draw away the facia support.
6   Disconnect the bonnet control cable from the bonnet lock, then release the control cable from its support clips on the inner wing valance.
7   Disconnect the heater control cable from the heater valve.
8   Detach the demister tubes from the facia ducts.
9   Undo and remove the facia panel lower securing screws and plain washers located at each end of the facia panel.
10 Undo and remove the facia panel upper securing bolts with shakeproof and plain washers.
11 Carefully release the finisher trim from the body flange on each door aperture in the area of the facia panel.
12 The facia panel may now be drawn rearwards and lifted away from inside the car.
13 Refitting is the reverse sequence to removal. As it is being finally positioned, feed the bonnet and heater valve control cables through the grommets in the engine bulkhead.

15 Parcel shelf – removal and refitting

Cable gearchange

1   Undo and remove the four screws that secure the parcel shelf to the body (Fig. 12.11). Remove the heater shroud, if fitted.
2   Undo and remove the two screws and plain washers that secure the fuse box located on the right hand side of the parcel shelf.
3   Carefully draw the parcel shelf rearwards and lift away from inside the car.
4   Refitting is the reverse sequence to removal.

Rod gearchange

5   Using a hacksaw, cut a screwdriver slot in the head of the shear bolt that secures the steering column to the mounting bracket.
6   Unscrew and remove the shear bolt. It should be noted that the nut of the shear bolt is locked to the bracket and cannot be turned.
7   Follow the instructions given in paragraphs 1 to 4 inclusive for cable gearchange models.
8   Refitting is the reverse sequence to removal. A new shear bolt attaching the steering column to the mounting bracket must be used and tightened until the hexagon head shears at the waisted point.

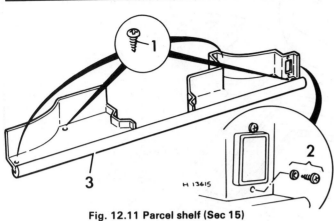

Fig. 12.11 Parcel shelf (Sec 15)

1 *Parcel shelf securing screws*
2 *Fusebox retaining screws*
3 *Parcel shelf*

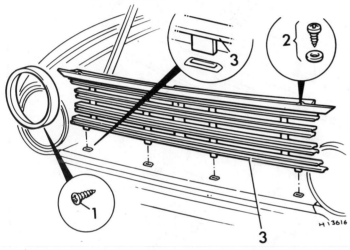

Fig. 12.12 Radiator grille attachment (Sec 16)

1 *Headlamp rim securing*
    screw
2 *Radiator grille securing*
    screws and plain
    washers
3 *Grille legs*

16 Radiator grille (rod gearchange) – removal and refitting

1 Unscrew the self-tapping screw securing each headlamp rim and, with a screwdriver, ease each rim from the light unit body.
2 Undo and remove the four self-tapping screws and plain washers securing the top of the radiator grille to the body.
3 Carefully lift the grille upwards, so releasing the four legs from their rubber inserts in the front valance.
4 Refitting the radiator grille is the reverse sequence to removal.

17 Tailgate – removal and refitting

1 Using a screwdriver, carefully remove the two outer hinge finishers. On later models, remove the trim and peel back the roof lining.
2 The help of an assistant should be obtained to take the weight of the tailgate.
3 Undo and remove the two bolts, nuts and washers that secure each ram to the body and tailgate. Note which way round the rams are fitted as they must not, under any circumstances, be fitted the wrong way round.
4 Undo and remove the two nuts from each pair of hinge studs exposed as described in paragraph 1.

5 Carefully remove the tailgate from the rear of the car.
6 Refitting the tailgate is the reverse sequence to removal.
7 Do not attempt to dismantle the rams, and keep them away from sources of heat.

18 Tailgate lock (cable gearchange) – removal and refitting

Pushbutton lock
1 Undo and remove the self-tapping screws that secure the tailgate trim pad, then carefully lever the trim pad from the tailgate with a wide-bladed screwdriver.
2 Recover the plastic retaining pegs as they are released when the trim pad is removed.
3 Disengage the latch operating rods from the operating bracket.
4 Unscrew the lock retaining ring and remove the operating bracket. For this, a blunt chisel can be used to start movement of the lock retaining ring.
5 Lift away the pushbutton lock assembly.
6 Using a pair of circlip pliers, remove the circlip and withdraw the spring seat and spring from the pushbutton assembly.
7 The pushbutton lock barrel may now be withdrawn.
8 Refitting is the reverse sequence to removal. Make sure that the operating rod bushes are pressed into the lock operating bracket towards its spring with the retaining clips fitted between the heads of the bushes and the bracket. Lubricate all moving parts with a little oil.

Latch-type lock
9 Undo and remove the self-tapping screws that secure the tailgate trim pad, then carefully lever the trim pad from the tailgate with a wide-bladed screwdriver.
10 Recover the plastic retaining pegs as they are released when the trim pad is removed.
11 Disengage the latch operating rods from the operating bracket.
12 Undo and remove the latch unit securing screws for each latch unit, then withdraw each latch unit complete with operating rod.
13 Finally detach the rod from each latch unit.
14 To refit, first check that the bushes for the operating rods are fitted into the latch lever of each latch unit from the spring side of the lever with the clip fitted on the tail end of the bush.
15 Press the control rods into their bushes from the tailgate side and retain each with its clip.
16 Refit the latch units to the tailgate.
17 Each latch should now be manually set to the closed position.
18 Adjust the pegs on the operating rods until they correctly align in their respective bushes. Press the pegs into the bushes and retain the rods with the clips.
19 Depress the pushbutton and make sure that the two latches release at the same time. Lubricate all moving parts,

Adjustment
20 Move the latch disc to the closed position and then depress the pushbutton. Make sure that there is a definitive free movement of the pushbutton before the sliding contactor begins to rise and also that the latch is released from the striker before the pushbutton is fully depressed.
21 To adjust the pushbutton plunger, it is first necessary to disconnect the pushbutton link. Next lift the cranked pushbutton arm and turn the plunger screw in the required direction.
22 Slacken the dovetail alignment guide securing screws and close the tailgate. Check its alignment with the body.
23 Adjust the positions of the strikers until the tailgate closes under the pressure applied to the centre of the tailgate and the latch(es) engages in the striker(s).
24 Check that the striker(s) is (are) not set too far in by applying pressure to the tailgate and checking that slight movement is possible as the seals are compressed.
25 Finally tighten the alignment guide securing screws.

19 Tailgate lock (rod gearchange) – removal and refitting

Turnbutton lock
1 Using a wide-bladed screwdriver, carefully lever the trim pad from

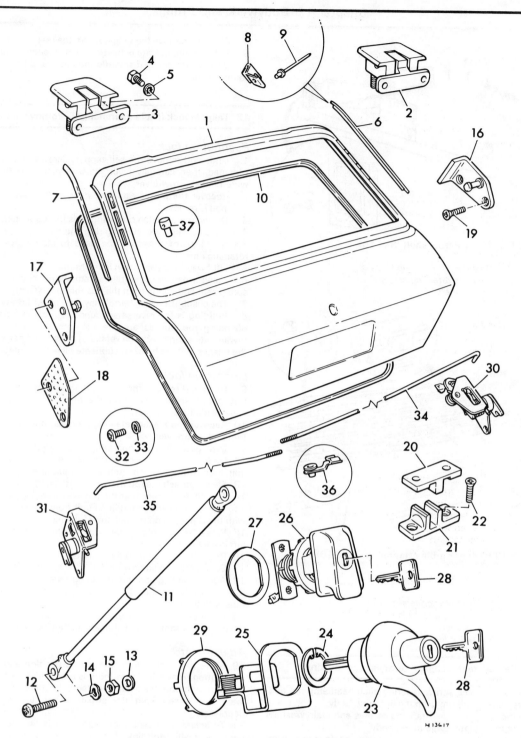

Fig. 12.13 Tailgate components (Secs 18 and 19)

1 Tailgate panel	gearchange)	26 Tailgate turn button
2 RH hinge	15 Nut	assembly } rod gearchange
3 LH hinge	16 RH striker	27 Sealing washer
4 Screw	17 LH striker	28 Key
5 Shakeproof washer	18 Shim	29 Pushbutton locknut
6 RH moulding	19 Screw	30 RH latch
7 LH moulding	20 Upper dovetail	31 LH latch
8 Clip	21 Lower dovetail	32 Screw
9 Rivet	22 Screw	33 Shakeproof washer
10 Seal	23 Tailgate push button	34 RH link rod
11 Ram	assembly } cable gearchange	35 LH link rod
12 Screw	24 Circlip	36 Clip
13 Plain washer	25 Centre plate	37 Adjustment pin
14 Anti-rattle washer (cable		

H 13617

the tailgate.

2 Recover the plastic retaining pegs as they are released when the trim pad is removed.

3 Disengage the latch operating rods from the operating plate.

4 Unscrew and remove the screw that retains the operating plate to the turnbutton lock and withdraw the plate.

5 Unscrew the lock retaining ring. For this, a blunt chisel can be used to start movement of the lock retaining ring.

6 Lift away the turnbutton lock assembly.

7 Using a small screwdriver, ease the small circlip from the lock assembly. Lift away the spring.

8 Insert the key into the lock barrel and turn the key in a clockwise direction.

9 Slide off the threaded sleeve from the lock assembly.

10 Using a small diameter parallel pin punch, carefully drive out the retaining pin from the lock assembly and withdraw the turnbutton lock barrel.

11 Refitting the lock is the reverse sequence to removal. Make sure that the ends of the spring are engaged in the slot in the threaded sleeve and the groove in the lock barrel housing. Lubricate all moving parts.

Latch-type lock

12 Using a wide-bladed screwdriver, carefully lever the trim pad from the tailgate.

13 Recover the plastic retaining pegs as they are released when the trim pad is removed.

14 Disengage the latch operating rods from the operating plate.

15 Unscrew and remove the screws and shakeproof washers that secure the end latch unit. Lift away each latch unit complete with operating rod.

16 Detach the rod from each latch unit.

17 To refit, first make sure that the operating rod bushes are pressed into the lock operating plate towards the lock assembly spring, with the retaining clips fitted between the heads of the bushes and the operating plate.

18 Make sure also that the bushes for the operating rods are fitted into the latch of each latch unit from the spring side of the lever, with the clip fitted on the tail end of the bush.

19 Next press the control rods into their bushes in the latch units from the tailgate side, and retain each with its clips.

20 Refit the latch units to the tailgate.

21 Each latch should now be manually set to the closed position.

22 Adjust the pegs on the operating rods until they align with their respective bushes. Press the pegs into the bushes and retain the rods with the clips.

23 Move the turnbutton anti-clockwise and check that both latches release at the same time. Lubricate all moving parts with oil.

Adjustment

24 For full information refer to Section 18.

20 Bonnet – removal and refitting

1 Using a soft pencil, mark the outline position of both the hinges at the bonnet to act as a datum for refitting.

2 With the help of an assistant to take the weight of the bonnet, undo and remove the two lower stay retaining screws.

3 Undo and remove the hinges–to–bonnet securing bolts with plain and spring washers. There are two bolts to each hinge.

4 Lift away the bonnet and put in a safe place so that it will not be scratched.

5 Refitting the bonnet is the reverse sequence to removal.

21 Bonnet lock and control cable (rod gearchange) – removal and refitting

1 Disconnect the terminals from the battery.

2 Slacken the locknut and detach the cable from the trunnion at the lock lever (Fig. 12.14).

3 Detach the outer cable from the clip on the bonnet lock and from the clips on the right-hand wing valance.

4 Undo and remove the screws that secure the glovebox lid support.

5 Undo and remove the two screws and plain washer that secure

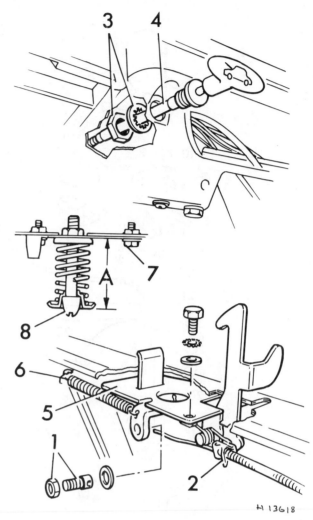

Fig. 12.14 Bonnet lock and control assembly (Sec 21)

1 Lock lever
  trunnion-to-cable
  connection
	4 Cable assembly

	5 Bonnet lock assembly
2 Cable retaining clip	6 Lock return spring

3 Cable securing nut and
  shakeproof washer
	7 Locking pin assembly
	  retaining screws

	8 Locking pin

For dimension A see text

the glovebox lid striker.

6 Undo and remove the glovebox side and lower end retaining screws and draw the glovebox rearwards.

7 Unscrew the nut and shakeproof washer that secures the outer cable to the facia panel.

8 The inner and outer cable can now be withdrawn from the large body grommet.

9 Detach the bonnet lock return spring from the bonnet lock platform.

10 Undo and remove the bolts, shakeproof and plain washers that secure the lock to the front cross panel. Lift away the bonnet lock assembly.

11 Should it be necessary to remove the locking pin assembly on the underside of the bonnet, undo and remove the two retaining bolts, shakeproof and plain washers. Lift away the locking pin assembly.

12 Refitting is the reverse sequence to removal but the following additional points should be noted:

(a) If the locking pin assembly has been removed, it should be set so that there is a distance of 2 in (50 mm) between the outer edge of the thimble and the bonnet panel.

(b) The bonnet lock cable must be threaded through the same body grommet as the choke cable.

(c) Lubricate all moving parts with oil

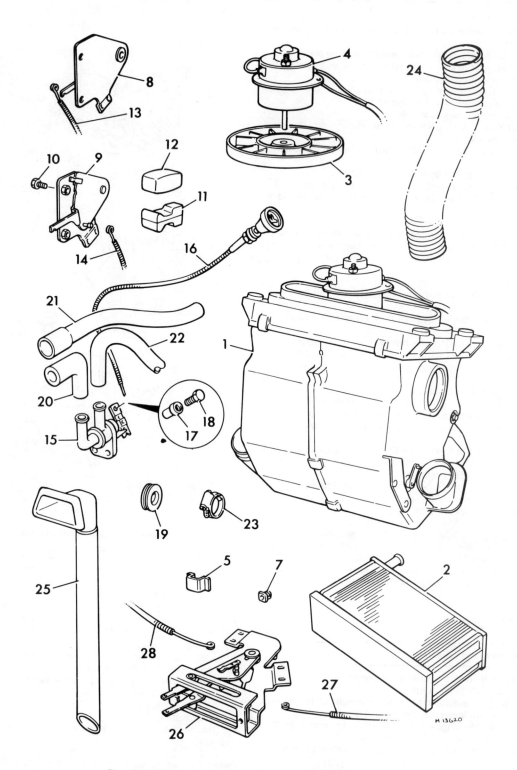

Fig. 12.15 Heater components (cable gearchange) (Sec 23)

1 Heater assembly
2 Heater matrix
3 Fan
4 Motor
5 Clip
6 Clip
7 Locknut
8 Temperature control lever } Cable
9 Demister control lever   } gearchange
10 Screw

11 Knob
12 Knob (rod gearchange)
13 Temperature control cable } Cable
14 Demister control cable   } gearchange
15 Water control valve
16 Water control valve cable
17 Trunnion for cable
18 Screw
19 Grommet

20 Heater-to-water control valve hose
21 Hose
22 Control valve-to-water pump hose
23 Hose clip
24 Demister hose
25 Heater intake duct drain tube
26 Temperature and demister control
27 Temperature control cable } Rod
28 Demister control cable   } gearchange

22 Heater unit – removal and refitting

Cable gearchange

1 Disconnect the terminals from the battery.
2 Refer to Chapter 2 and drain the complete cooling system.
3 Slacken the clips securing the small bore water hoses to the heater unit on the engine side of the bulkhead. Detach the hoses (Fig. 12.16).
4 Refer to Section 15 and remove the parcel shelf.
5 Refer to Chapter 10 and remove the instrument panel.
6 Refer to Section 24 and remove the glovebox.
7 Detach the demister and fresh air flexible hoses from the heater unit.
8 Disconnect the temperature control cable from the heater flap, and detach the cable from its retaining clip.
9 Disconnect the air control cable from the heater flap and detach the cable from its retaining clip.
10 Make a note of the electrical cable connections at the blower control switch and detach the two connectors.
11 Unscrew and remove the heater unit lower retaining screw and plain washer from beneath the heater unit.
12 Unscrew and remove the four nuts and washers that secure the heater unit. Note that there is an earth cable located under the right-hand rear nut.
13 Place some polythene sheeting over the carpeting so any water left in the heater matrix does not stain the carpeting. Very carefully lift away the heater unit.

14 Refitting the heater unit is the reverse sequence to removal.

Rod gearchange

15 Disconnect the terminals from the battery.
16 Refer to Chapter 2 and drain the complete cooling system.
17 Slacken the clips securing the small bore water hoses to the heater unit on the engine side of the bulkhead. Detach the hoses (Fig. 12.17).
18 Refer to Section 24 and remove the glovebox.
19 Using a small screwdriver, unscrew the grub screws that secure the control knobs to the heater controls. Remove the two knobs.
20 With a knife carefully prise away the heater control masking plate.
21 Undo and remove the two bolts and shakeproof washers that secure the heater controls to the facia board.
22 Disconnect the temperature and air control cables from the heater. Detach the cables from the retaining clips.
23 Refer to Section 15 and remove the parcel shelf.
24 Detach the demister hoses from the heater unit.
25 Make a note of the electrical cable connections at the blower control switch and detach the two Lucar connectors.
26 Removal is now identical to that for the cable gearchange (paragraphs 11 to 13 inclusive).
27 Refitting the heater unit is the reverse sequence to removal.

23 Heater unit – dismantling and reassembly

1 Release the spring from the heater flap.
2 *Rod gear change models only:* Disconnect the control cables from

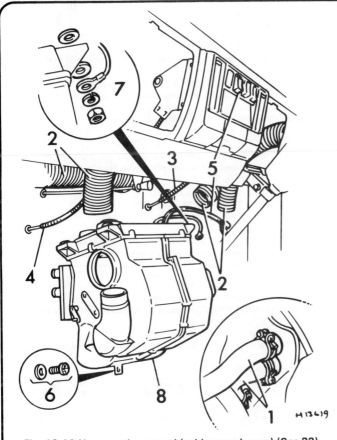

Fig. 12.16 Heater unit removal (cable gearchange) (Sec 22)

1 Heater pipe connections
2 Demister and fresh air flexible hoses
3 Temperature control cable
4 Air control cable
5 Blower control switch
6 Heater lower retaining screw
7 Heater securing nut and earth cable
8 Heater assembly

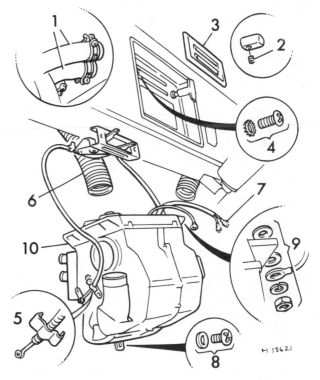

Fig. 12.17 Heater unit removal (rod gearchange) (Sec 22)

1 Heater pipe
2 Heater control knob
3 Heater control masking plate
4 Heater control-to-facia board securing screws
5 Heater control cables securing clips
6 Heater demist hoses
7 Blower control switch connections
8 Heater lower retaining screw
9 Heater securing nut and earth cable
10 Heater assembly

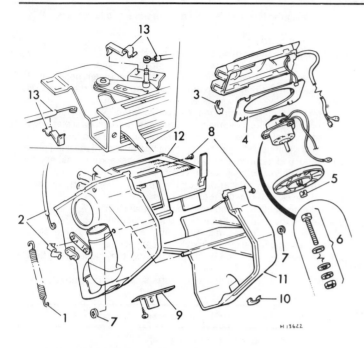

Fig. 12.18 Heater components (rod gearchange) (Sec 23)

1 Flap control spring	spindle)
2 Control cables and securing	8 Backing plate securing screw
clips	9 Lower mounting bracket
3 Clip (booster fan motor	10 Casing clips
mounting plate)	11 Casing half
4 Fan mounting baffle plate	12 Heater matrix
5 Clip (fan to motor spindle)	13 Control cable
6 Motor securing bolts	attachment to
7 Clip (control flap mounting	control levers

the heater and detach the cables from the retaining clips.

3   Release the six clips that secure the booster fan motor mounting plate. Lift away the plate complete with fan, motor and electric cables.

4   Lift up the fan mounting plate and, with a soldering iron, unsolder the booster fan motor cables from the resistance.

5   Release the spring clip that secures the fan to the motor spindle. Withdraw the fan.

6   Undo and remove the three long bolts, plain washers and nut that secure the motor. Lift away the motor.

7   Release the clips from the ends of the control flap mounting spindles.

8   Unscrew and remove the screws that secure the backing plate.

9   Remove the lower mounting bracket.

10   Release the clips retaining the two halves of the casing.

11   Carefully part the casing halves and lift away the matrix.

12   Disconnect the control cables from the control levers, and detach the cables from the retaining clips.

13   Reassembly of the heater unit is the reverse sequence to dismantling.

24 Glovebox – removal and refitting

Cable gearchange

1   Unscrew and remove the screw and plain washer that secures the

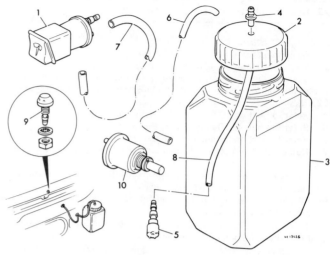

Fig. 12.19 Windscreen washer components (manual pump) (Sec 25)

1 Windscreen washer pump	6 Reservoir-to-pump tube
(cable gearchange)	7 Pump-to-jet tube
2 Reservoir cap	8 Pick-up tube
3 Reservoir	9 Jet
4 Connector	10 Windscreen washer pump
5 Non-return valve	(rod gearchange)

lid support to the lid.

2   Unscrew and remove the three hinge screws and plain washers and lift away the lid.

3   Undo and remove the three glovebox retaining screws, two plain washers and lid striker. Note which way round the striker is fitted.

4   Carefully draw the glovebox compartment rearwards.

5   Refitting is the reverse sequence to removal.

Rod gearchange

6   Undo and remove the screws that secure the glovebox lid support.

7   Undo and remove the two screws and plain washers that secure the glovebox lid striker.

8   Undo and remove the glovebox side and lower end retaining screws, and draw the glovebox compartment rearwards.

9   Refitting is the reverse sequence to removal.

25 Windscreen washer control – removal and refitting

Cable gearchange

1   Remove the glovebox (see previous Section).

2   Disconnect the pipes from the pump then unscrew the pump from the rear of the pushbutton.

3   Ease the pushbutton from the facia.

4   Installation is the reverse of the removal procedure.

Rod gearchange

5   Remove the glovebox (see previous Section)– early models only.

6   Remove the heater controls from the facia (see Section 22) – early models only.

7   Disconnect the pipes from the pump then unscrew the pump bezel.

8   Ease the pump from the facia panel.

9   Installation is the reverse of the removal procedure.

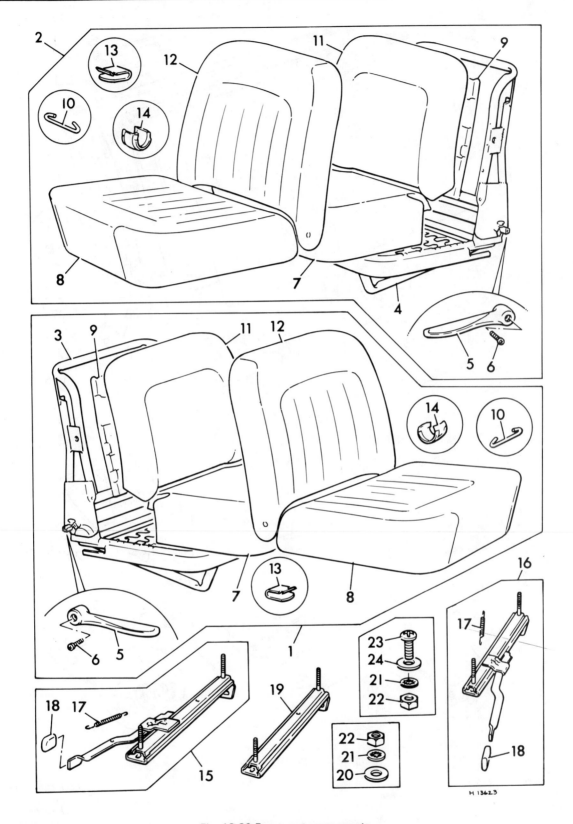

Fig. 12.20 Front seat components

H 13623

1	RH seat assembly	7	Cushion pad	13	Clip	19 Slide
2	LH seat assembly	8	Cushion cover	14	Clip	20 Plain washer
3	RH seat frame	9	Squab diaphragm	15	Locking slide assembly	21 Shakeproof washer
4	LH seat frame	10	Diaphragm hook	16	Locking slide assembly	22 Nut
5	Handle	11	Squab pad	17	Spring	23 Screw
6	Screw	12	Squab cover	18	Knob	24 Plain washer

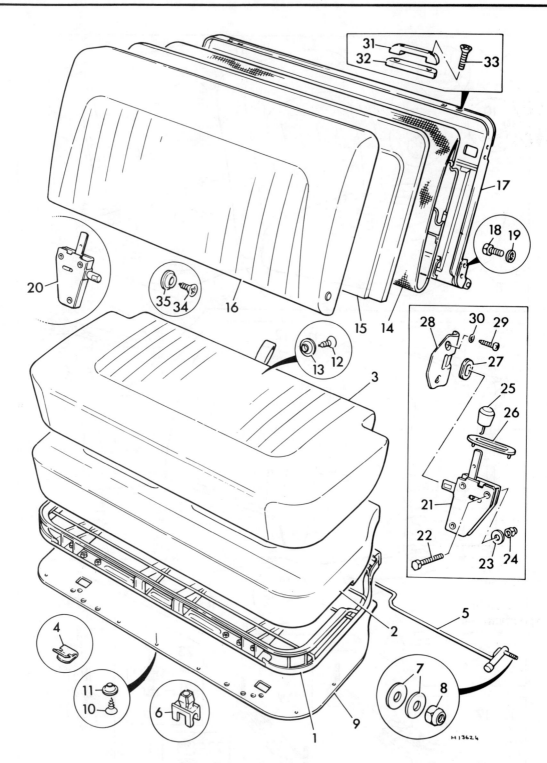

Fig. 12.21 Rear seat components

H 13624

1	Rear cushion frame	10	Screw
2	Rear cushion pad	11	Cup washer
3	Rear cushion cover	12	Screw
4	Clip	13	Cup washer
5	Rear cushion support	14	Rear squab spring case
6	Clip	15	Rear squab pad
7	Plain washer	16	Rear squab pad cover
8	Locknut	17	Squab panel
9	Rear cushion bottom liner	18	Screw

19	Lockwasher	28	Lock striker plate
20	RH squab lock	29	Screw
21	LH squab lock	30	Lockwasher
22	Screw	31	Squab support hasp
23	Plain washer	32	Squab hasp backing plate
24	Locknut	33	Screw
25	Knob	34	Screw
26	Lock escutcheon	35	Cup washer
27	Grommet		

Chapter 13 Supplement:
Revisions and information on later models

Contents

1 Introduction

This Chapter deals mainly with the modifications made to the Maxi range with the introduction of the Series 2 models. In addition, details of component and procedure changes affecting earlier models

have been included.

To use this Chapter to the best advantage, it is suggested that it is referred to *before* the main Chapters in the manual. Any relevant information can then be noted, and the procedure given in the main Chapter modified accordingly. Where no change is indicated for later models, the existing procedures or data should be followed.

2 Specifications

The Specifications listed here are revisions of, or supplementary to, the main Specifications at the beginning of each Chapter. Where no difference is shown, use the relevant data applicable to earlier models.

Fuel and exhaust systems
Carburettor specifications
Late 1500 models:
Carburettor specification number	FZX 1076, FZX 1178
Capstat colour	Natural
Needle	BAS

Late 1750 single carburettor models, 1.7L and HL models:
Carburettor specification number	FZX 1077, FZX 1087, FZX 1207, FZX 1209
Capstat colour	Natural
Needle	BDE

Late 1750 twin carburettor models and 1.7 HLS models:
Carburettor specification number	FZX 1078, FZX 1211
Capstat colour	White (1750) or Natural (1.7)
Needle	BBR

Exhaust emission
CO content at idle (all models)	3% ± 1%

Ignition system
Distributor (1.7 models)
Dwell angle:
Lucas 45D4 distributor	57° ± 5°
Ducellier distributor	57°

Ignition coil (1.7 models)
Make and type	Lucas 15C6 or AC Delco 9977230
Primary resistance at 68°F (20°C)	1.2 to 1.5 ohms
Ballast resistance	1.3 to 1.5 ohms

3   Engine

Engine steady lower bush

1   In 1979 a modified lower bush was fitted to the engine steady lower mounting. The modified bush does not contain an inner steel sleeve; it should be used in conjunction with a shouldered bolt, to prevent the bracket collapsing.

2   Do not mistake the greater movement allowed by the sleeveless bush for a sign that the bush has failed. If a modified bush is used to replace the old sleeved type, make sure that the new type shouldered bolt is used as well.

Oil filter head gasket

3   To improve the sealing between the transmission case and the oil filter head, a modified gasket was introduced from engine Nos 17H 946AK 5541 and 17H 948AL 966. The new gasket can be recognised by a tag which protrudes from its outer edge.

4   When fitting such a gasket to a Maxi with automatic transmission, the tag must be cut off, to avoid fouling the head of one of the oil pump bolts.

Crankshaft thrust washer orientation

5   A few engines were assembled with the crankshaft thrust washers fitted back to front, ie with the oil grooves facing inwards.

6   Regardless of what you may find when dismantling the engine, the correct orientation of the thrust washers is with the oil grooves facing *outwards.*

4   Cooling system

Water pump squeaking

1   If the water pump squeaks in operation, this does not necessarily mean that it is defective or about to fail.

2   Various proprietary compounds are available which when added to the coolant will stop the water pump squeaking. Jaguar-Daimler radiator inhibitor compound (Part No 12953) is recommended by the makers.

Later type pulley and pump

3   The two-piece water pump pulley shown in Chapter 2 has been superseded by a one-piece pulley. The two types are interchangeable.

4   Later type water pumps are longer than early units. If a later type pump is fitted to an early vehicle, different pulleys and a fan spacer must also be fitted to maintain correct fanbelt alignment.

5   Fuel and exhaust systems

Tamperproofed carburettors

1   Later model carburettors may have the idle adjusting screw and/or the jet adjusting nut 'tamperproofed' by means of seals (Fig. 13.1).

2   The purpose of these seals is to prevent adjustment of the carburettor by unqualified or unauthorised persons. At the time of writing, no regulations exist in the UK concerning the removal of such seals by the vehicle owner. Satisfy yourself, however, that you are not breaking any national or local regulations if you intend to remove the seals.

3   With the seals removed, adjustment is carried out as described in Chapter 3. Fit new seals on completion where this is required by law.

Capstat jet assembly

4   All carburettors with specification numbers beginning 'FZX' are fitted with a Capstat jet assembly.

5   The function of the Capstat is to vary the height of the jet in proportion to fuel temperature, thus compensating for variations in mixture strength which would otherwise occur.

Fuel gauge sender unit

6   From vehicle No 130 900 a modified fuel gauge sender unit is installed. The modified unit has an insulated wire connecting the terminal on the retaining plate to the sender unit; previous units used a brass strip, which was sometimes the source of false readings.

7   The new and old type units are interchangeable.

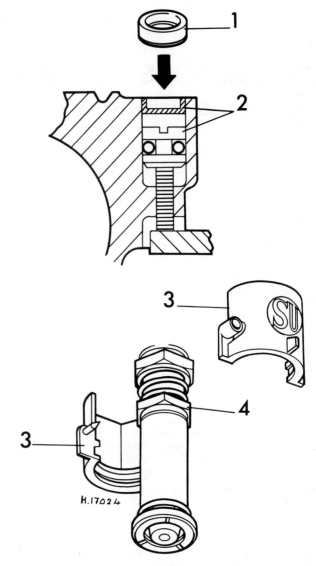

H.17024

Fig. 13.1 The tamperproof caps fitted to the later type sealed carburettors (Sec 5)

1 Throttle adjusting screw cap	*showing cap in position*
2 Throttle adjusting screw	3 Jet adjusting nut seals
	4 Jet adjusting nut

Choke control with warning light

8   Series 2 models are fitted with a 'choke on' warning light. This light is operated by a switch located behind the choke control (Fig. 13.2).

9   Removal is as described in Chapter 3, but disconnect the wiring plug and remove the switch from the cable before withdrawing the cable.

10   On refitting, position the switch with the offset plunger nearest the control knob. The plunger locates in the central hole, and the locating pegs engage in the other two holes.

6   Ignition system

Ballasted ignition system

1   Later models are fitted with an ignition coil designed to operate with only 6 volts across the LT winding. The other 6 volts are lost in a resistor built into the wiring harness, known as the ballast resistor. The coil receives current via the ballast resistor except when the starter motor is operating, when the resistor is bypassed and full battery voltage reaches the coil. This gives a stronger spark for cold

starting, and compensates for the reduction in battery voltage caused by the operation of the starter motor.

2   It is important if renewing the coil or the LT wiring to note whether a ballasted system is used. A normal 12 volt coil will only give a very weak spark if used with a ballast resistor; a 6 volt coil will burn out if it is used on a non-ballasted system.

LT lead fracture
3   If problems are experienced with the LT lead fracturing at the distributor, make sure when repairing that there is adequate slack in the lead. Avoid further trouble by securing the cable to the ignition shield bracket and to the underside of the starter motor solenoid.

Ignition timing using a stroboscopic light
4   Dynamic ignition timing, using a stroboscopic light, is quicker and more accurate than the static timing procedure described in Chapter 4. The procedure is as follows.
5   Highlight the timing marks (on the flywheel or crankshaft pulley – see Chapter 4) with quick-drying white paint. Typist's correcting fluid is ideal for this purpose.
6   Connect a stroboscopic timing light to the engine in accordance with the maker's instructions – usually to No 1 spark plug lead. Some lights require further connections to the battery or to a mains power supply. Ideally, a tachometer should also be connected.
7   Disconnect and plug the vacuum line at the distributor.
8   Start the engine and run it at the speed specified for checking the timing (see Chapter 4). Shine the timing light onto the timing marks, taking care not to get the leads tangled up in any moving parts. The timing marks will appear stationary and (if the timing is correct) in alignment.

9   If the marks are not aligned, slacken the distributor clamp bolt and rotate the distributor body slightly in one direction or the other to bring the timing marks into alignment. Tighten the clamp bolt when adjustment is correct. On early models, fine adjustment may be made using the vernier adjustment on the distributor.
10 If the timing marks appear to flutter or jerk about, this may be due to wear in the distributor or its drive components, or to sticking advance weights in the distributor.
11 A rough check of the centrifugal advance mechanism may be made by increasing the engine speed and observing that the timing marks appear to move away from each other in the direction of advance. Failure to move, or jerky movement, should be investigated.
12 On completion, disconnect the timing light and reconnect the carburettor vacuum pipe.

Ignition timing using LED equipment
13 Series 2 models have provision for the ignition timing to be checked using LED (light emitting diode) equipment. This equipment is unlikely to be possessed by the home mechanic.
14 The system relies on a timing disc fitted to the crankshaft at the pulley end. Take care not to damage this disc, or difficulty may be experienced if a BL dealer wishes to use the LED equipment at a later date.

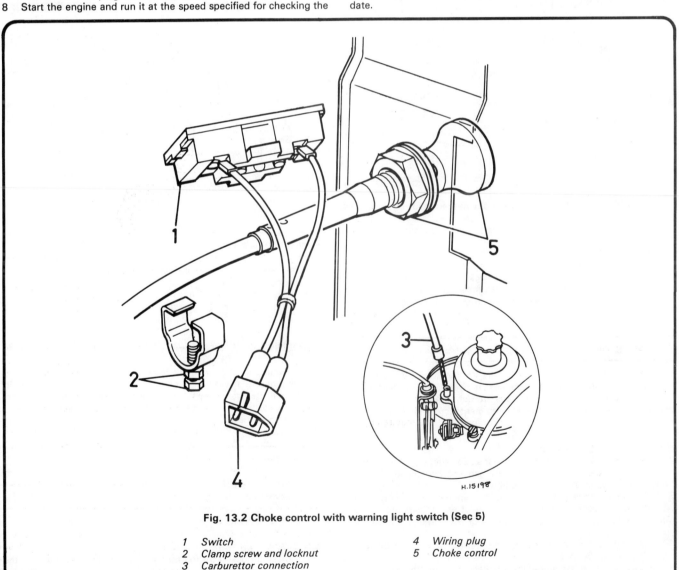

Fig. 13.2 Choke control with warning light switch (Sec 5)

1   Switch
2   Clamp screw and locknut
3   Carburettor connection
4   Wiring plug
5   Choke control

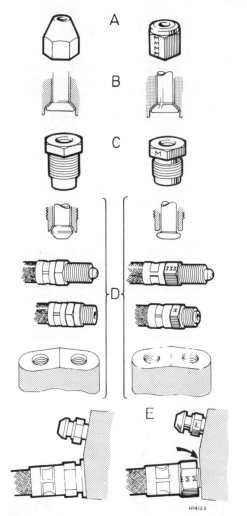

Fig. 13.3 Unified (UNF) and metric brake hydraulic fittings (Sec 7)

A   Metric pipe nuts, unions etc are coloured gold and usually
     carry the letter M
B   UNF (left) and metric (right) flares are different
C   Metric hose end (right) is coloured black or gold
D   UNF (left) and metric (right) fittings
E   Metric hose (right) seals against the bottom of the port,
     leaving a gap (arrowed) at the bottom of the hexagon

---

7   Braking system

Difference between metric and UNF hydraulic fittings

1   Fig. 13.3 shows the differences between metric and UNF
hydraulic fittings. The different threads are **not** compatible. If in doubt
when fitting a new hose or brake component, screw the fitting in by
hand; if this cannot be done, thread incompatibility may be the cause.

Rigid brake pipe renewal

2   The rigid brake pipes should be inspected regularly for corrosion
and damage, especially where they are exposed underneath the car.
Renew any suspect sections immediately.
3   Renewal is simple provided the pipes are purchased already made
up with the necessary bends and the correct end fittings and flares.
Make sure that you know whether metric or UNF fittings are used on
your car.
4   The procedure for disconnecting the flexible hoses from the rigid
pipes is given in Chapter 9.
5   Renew the pipe securing clips if necessary. Bend the tongues of
the securing clips to stop the pipe vibrating.
6   Bleed the brake hydraulic system on completion.

Handbrake warning light switch

7   Series 2 models are equipped with a 'handbrake on' warning light.
The light is operated by a switch mounted on the handbrake lever.
8   Removal and refitting of the switch are self-explanatory. Disconnect the battery before removal, and check for correct operation on
completion.

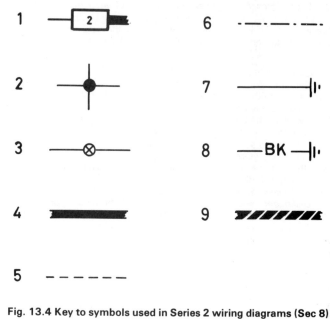

Fig. 13.4 Key to symbols used in Series 2 wiring diagrams (Sec 8)

1   Printed circuit connector   7   Component earthed by
2   Sealed joint   mounting
3   Multi-way connector   8   Component earthed by
4   Printed circuit wiring   cable
5   Optional equipment   9   Battery cable
6   Automatic transmission
     circuit

---

8   Electrical system

Lighting switch removal and refitting (Series 2)

1   Disconnect the battery.
2   Pull the lighting switch from its housing.
3   Disconnect the wiring plug from the rear of the switch.
4   Refitting is a reversal of the removal procedure.

Windscreen wiper delay unit removal and refitting (Series 2)

5   Disconnect the battery earth lead.
6   Disconnect the two wiring plugs from the rear of the delay unit.
7   Remove the screws securing the unit to the facia rail. Note that
there is an earth connection under one of the screw heads.
8   Refitting is the reverse of the removal procedure.

---

9   Suspension and steering

Protection of front displacer units

1   Rubber gaiters are fitted to the front Hydragas units from car No
124 417, to protect the units from stone damage.
2   These gaiters can be fitted to earlier vehicles if desired.

Knock from rear suspension

3   A knocking noise from the rear suspension can be caused by the
trim bar reaction plate striking the bolt or captive nut which secures
the lower mounting bracket. Refer to Chapter 11, Fig. 11.4, to identify
these components (items 42 and 30).

Key to Figs. 13.5 and 13.6. Not all items are fitted to all models

1	Battery	50	Instrument voltage stabiliser
2	Starter solenoid	51	Panel lamps
3	Starter motor	52	Printed circuit
4	Fuse box	53	Fuel gauge
5	Line fuse – RH side and tail lamps	54	Fuel gauge sender
6	Line fuse – rear foglamp	55	Oil pressure warning lamp
7	Line fuse – induction heater	56	Oil pressure switch
8	Line fuse – heater blower motor	57	Coolant temperature gauge
9	Line fuse – radio	58	Coolant temperature gauge sender
10	Ignition/starter switch	59	Automatic transmission selector lamps
11	Ignition coil	60	Automatic transmission starter inhibitor switch
12	Ignition (no charge) warning lamp	61	Windscreen wiper motor
13	Distributor	62	Wiper/washer switch
14	Alternator	63	Wiper delay unit
15	Horn	64	Windscreen washer motor
16	Horn push	65	Heated rear window switch
17	Ballast resistor cable	66	Heated rear window warning lamp
18	Lighting switch	67	Heated rear window element
19	Headlamps (main beam)	68	Heater blower switch
20	Main beam warning lamp	69	Heater blower motor
21	Headlamps (dipped beam)	70	Heater switch illumination lamp
22	Dipswitch	71	Choke warning lamp
23	Headlamp flasher switch	72	Choke warning lamp switch
24	RH sidelamp	73	Induction heater
25	LH sidelamp	74	Suction chamber heater
26	RH tail lamp	75	Handbrake switch
27	LH tail lamp	76	Blocking diode
28	RH number plate lamp	77	Brake failure warning lamp
29	LH number plate lamp	78	Brake pressure differential switch
30	Stop-lamps	79	Handbrake warning lamp
31	Stop-lamp switch	80	Interior lamp
32	Direction indicator flasher unit	81	Interior lamp switches
33	Direction indicator switch	82	Radio
34	Direction indicator warning lamp	83	Cigar lighter
35	Blocking diodes	84	Cigar lighter illumination
36	RH front direction indicator lamp		
37	LH front direction indicator lamp		**Cable colour code**
38	RH side repeater lamp		
39	LH side repeater lamp	BK	Black
40	RH rear direction indicator lamp	BL	Blue
41	LH rear direction indicator lamp	BR	Brown
42	Hazard warning flasher unit	GN	Green
43	Hazard warning switch	LGN	Light green
44	Hazard warning pilot lamp	OR	Orange
45	Reversing lamp	PI	Pink
46	Reversing lamp switch	PU	Purple
47	Rear foglamp switch	RD	Red
48	Rear foglamp	WH	White
49	Rear foglamp warning lamp	YW	Yellow

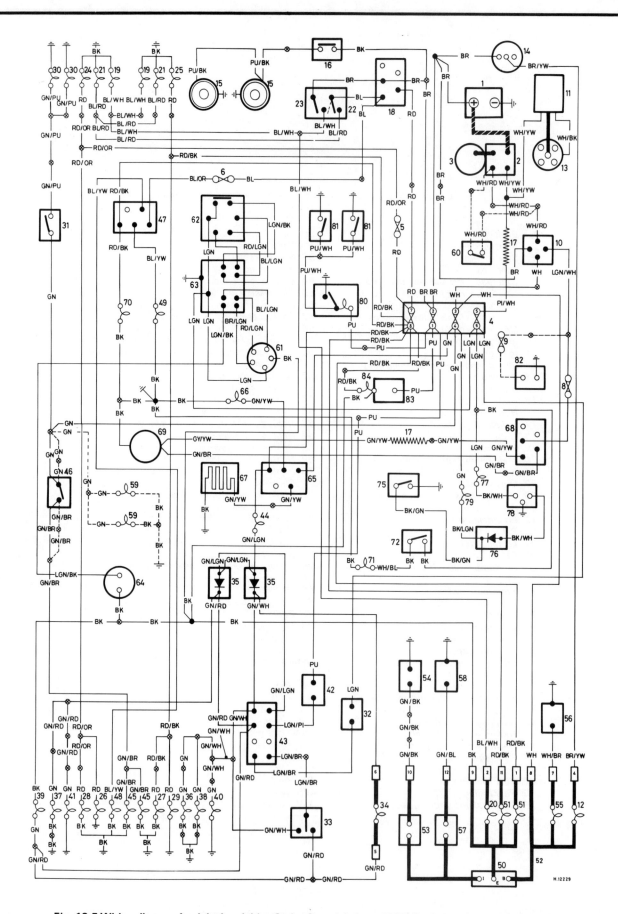

Fig. 13.5 Wiring diagram for right-hand drive Series 2 models from 1980. For key see page 225 (Sec 8)

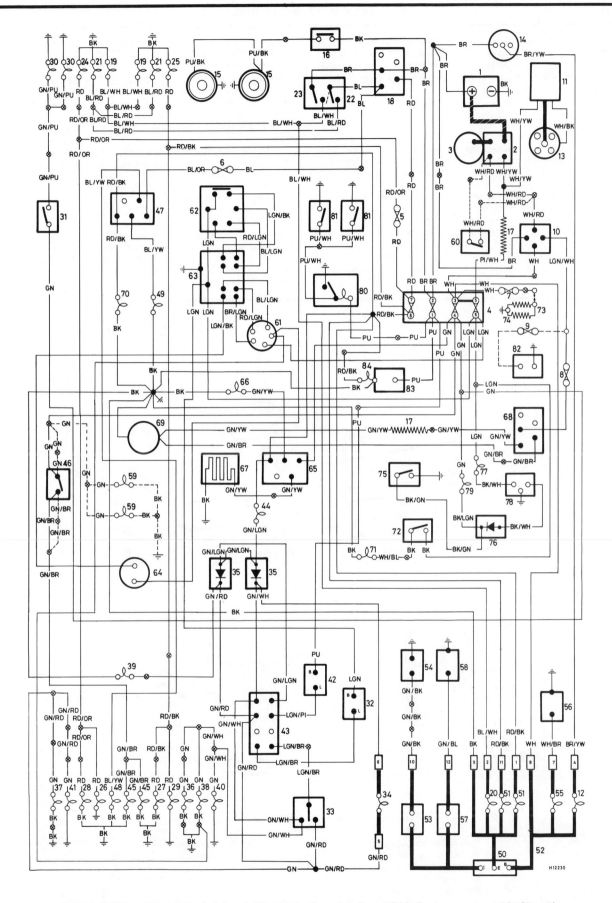

Fig. 13.6 Wiring diagram for left-hand drive Series 2 models from 1980. For key see page 225 (Sec 8)

4   A cure may be effected by shortening the bolt and/or removing metal from the side of the captive nut. Alternatively, the reaction plate and the captive nut may be replaced with later type components, whose dimensions have been altered to avoid this problem.

Excessive rear tyre wear

5   Excessive wear on the outer edges of the rear tyres may be due to excessive rear wheel toe-in. (Excessive toe-in in this case is defined as being greater than 0° 30' per side, with the car unladen and the trim heights correct).

6   Since rear wheel toe-in is set during production and is not adjustable, the problem is corrected by fitting special rear wheel bearings, the centre holes of which are offset.

7   If you suspect that your vehicle would benefit from the fitting of such bearings, consult your local BL dealer or steering specialist. Measurement of the rear wheel alignment with sufficient accuracy will require the use of optical equipment which is unlikely to be possessed by the home mechanic.

10 Bodywork and fittings

Bumpers – removal and refitting (Series 2)

1   Remove the bolt, spring and plain washers and mounting rubber from each side fitting.

2   Remove the nuts and washers which secure the bumper to its mounting brackets. Use a releasing fluid on these nuts if they are very tight.

3   On the front bumper, remove the indicator lamps. On the rear bumper, remove the rear fog lamp(s), the reversing lamp(s) and the number plate lamps. There is no need to disconnect the lamps; if care is taken, they can be fed back through the bumper after removal of their fittings and allowed to hang.

4   Remove the bumper from the vehicle.

5   If wished, the inserts and end cappings can be removed after removing or slackening the securing nuts.

6   Refitting is the reverse of the removal procedure. On the rear bumper, note that the number plate lamp lens is fitted with its chamfer to the rear. Engage the number plate retaining lugs before pushing the lamps into place.

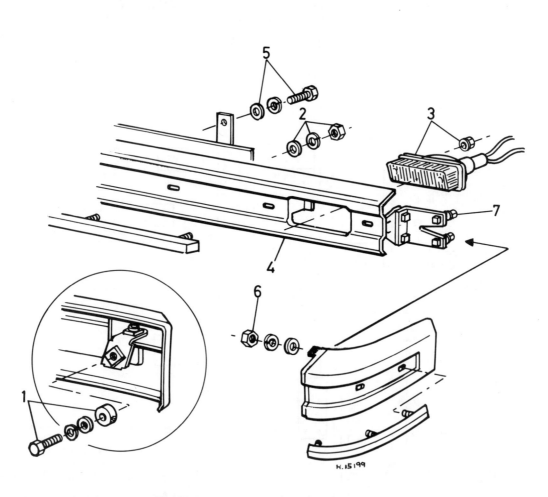

H.15199

Fig. 13.7 Front bumper fitting details (Sec 10)

1   Side fixing components
2   Bracket fixing components
3   Indicator lamp and
    securing nut
4   Bumper main section

5   Number plate fixing
    components
6   Insert fixing components
7   End capping securing nut

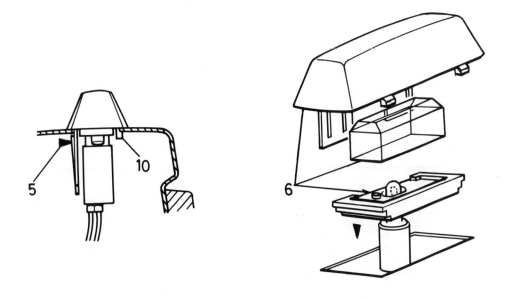

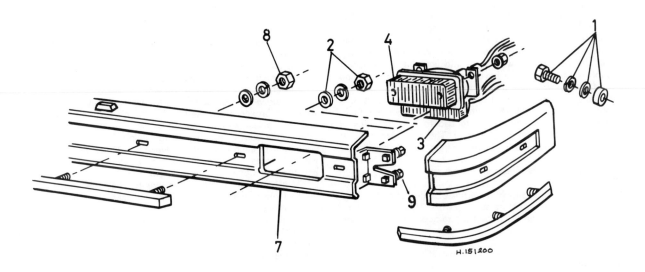

H.151200

Fig. 13.8 Rear bumper fitting details (Sec 10)

1   Side fixing components
2   Bracket fixing components
3   Rear fog lamp

4   Reversing lamp
5   Number plate lamp
    retaining clip

6   Number plate lamp
    components
7   Bumper main section

8   Insert retaining nut
9   End capping securing
    nut
10 Retaining lug

Fault diagnosis

Introduction

The vehicle owner who does his or her own maintenance according to the recommended schedules should not have to use this section of the manual very often. Modern component reliability is such that, provided those items subject to wear or deterioration are inspected or renewed at the specified intervals, sudden failure is comparatively rare. Faults do not usually just happen as a result of sudden failure, but develop over a period of time. Major mechanical failures in particular are usually preceded by characteristic symptoms over hundreds or even thousands of miles. Those components which do occasionally fail without warning are often small and easily carried in the vehicle.

With any fault finding, the first step is to decide where to begin investigations. Sometimes this is obvious, but on other occasions a little detective work will be necessary. The owner who makes half a dozen haphazard adjustments or replacements may be successful in curing a fault (or its symptoms), but he will be none the wiser if the fault recurs and he may well have spent more time and money than was necessary. A calm and logical approach will be found to be more satisfactory in the long run. Always take into account any warning signs or abnormalities that may have been noticed in the period preceding the fault – power loss, high or low gauge readings, unusual noises or smells, etc – and remember that failure of components such as fuses or spark plugs may only be pointers to some underlying fault.

The pages which follow here are intended to help in cases of failure to start or breakdown on the road. There is also a Fault Diagnosis Section at the end of each Chapter which should be consulted if the preliminary checks prove unfruitful. Whatever the fault, certain basic principles apply. These are as follows:

Verify the fault. This is simply a matter of being sure that you know what the symptoms are before starting work. This is particularly important if you are investigating a fault for someone else who may not have described it very accurately.

Don't overlook the obvious. For example, if the vehicle won't start, is there petrol in the tank? (Don't take anyone else's word on this particular point, and don't trust the fuel gauge either!) If an electrical fault is indicated, look for loose or broken wires before digging out the test gear.

Cure the disease, not the symptom. Substituting a flat battery with a fully charged one will get you off the hard shoulder, but if the underlying cause is not attended to, the new battery will go the same way. Similarly, changing oil-fouled spark plugs for a new set will get you moving again, but remember that the reason for the fouling (if it wasn't simply an incorrect grade of plug) will have to be established and corrected.

Don't take anything for granted. Particularly, don't forget that a 'new' component may itself be defective (especially if it's been rattling round in the boot for months), and don't leave components out of a fault diagnosis sequence just because they are new or recently fitted. When you do finally diagnose a difficult fault, you'll probably realise that all the evidence was there from the start.

Electrical faults

Electrical faults can be more puzzling than straightforward mechanical failures, but they are no less susceptible to logical analysis if the basic principles of operation are understood. Vehicle electrical wiring exists in extremely unfavourable conditions – heat, vibration and chemical attack – and the first things to look for are loose or corroded connections and broken or chafed wires, especially where the wires pass through holes in the bodywork or are subject to vibration.

All metal-bodied vehicles in current production have one pole of the battery 'earthed', ie connected to the vehicle bodywork, and in nearly all modern vehicles it is the negative (–) terminal. The various electrical components – motors, bulb holders etc – are also connected to earth, either by means of a lead or directly by their mountings. Electric current flows through the component and then back to the battery via the bodywork. If the component mounting is loose or corroded, or if a good path back to the battery is not available, the circuit will be incomplete and malfunction will result. The engine and/or gearbox are also earthed by means of flexible metal straps to the body or subframe; if these straps are loose or missing, starter motor, generator and ignition trouble may result.

Assuming the earth return to be satisfactory, electrical faults will be due either to component malfunction or to defects in the current supply. Individual components are dealt with in Chapter 10. If supply wires are broken or cracked internally this results in an open-circuit, and the easiest way to check for this is to bypass the suspect wire temporarily with a length of wire having a crocodile clip or suitable connector at each end. Alternatively, a 12V test lamp can be used to verify the presence of supply voltage at various points along the wire and the break can be thus isolated.

If a bare portion of a live wire touches the bodywork or other earthed metal part, the electricity will take the low-resistance path thus formed back to the battery: this is known as a short-circuit. Hopefully a short-circuit will blow a fuse, but otherwise it may cause burning of the insulation (and possibly further short-circuits) or even a fire. This is why it is inadvisable to bypass persistently blowing fuses with silver foil or wire.

Spares and tool kit

Most vehicles are supplied only with sufficient tools for wheel changing; the *Maintenance and minor repair* tool kit detailed in *Tools and working facilities,* with the addition of a hammer, is probably sufficient for those repairs that most motorists would consider attempting at the roadside. In addition a few items which can be fitted without too much trouble in the event of a breakdown should be carried. Experience and available space will modify the list below, but the following may save having to call on professional assistance:

Spark plugs, clean and correctly gapped
HT lead and plug cap – long enough to reach the plug furthest from the distributor
Distributor rotor, condenser and contact breaker points
Drivebelt(s) – emergency type may suffice
Spare fuses
Set of principal light bulbs
Tin of radiator sealer and hose bandage

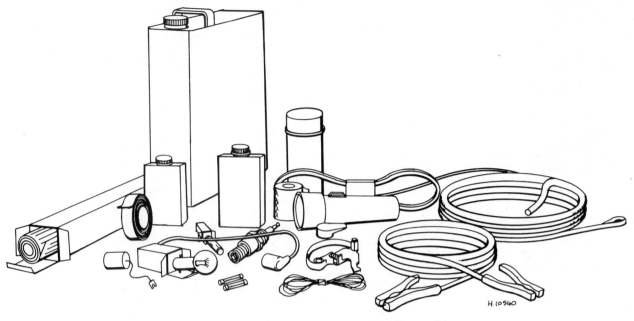

Carrying a few spares can save you a long walk!

Exhaust bandage
Roll of insulating tape
Length of soft iron wire
Length of electrical flex
Torch or inspection lamp (can double as test lamp)
Battery jump leads
Tow-rope
Ignition waterproofing aerosol
Litre of engine oil
Sealed can of hydraulic fluid
Emergency windscreen
'Jubilee' clips
Tube of filler paste

If spare fuel is carried, a can designed for the purpose should be used to minimise risks of leakage and collision damage. A first aid kit and a warning triangle, whilst not at present compulsory in the UK, are obviously sensible items to carry in addition to the above.

When touring abroad it may be advisable to carry additional spares which, even if you cannot fit them yourself, could save having to wait while parts are obtained. The items below may be worth considering:

Throttle cable
Cylinder head gasket
Dynamo or alternator brushes
Fuel pump repair kit
Tyre valve core

One of the motoring organisations will be able to advise on availability of fuel etc in foreign countries.

Engine will not start

Engine fails to turn when starter operated

Flat battery (recharge, use jump leads, or push start)
Battery terminals loose or corroded
Battery earth to body defective
Engine earth strap loose or broken
Starter motor (or solenoid) wiring loose or broken
Automatic transmission selector in wrong position, or inhibitor switch faulty
Ignition/starter switch faulty
Major mechanical failure (seizure)
Starter or solenoid internal fault (see Chapter 10)

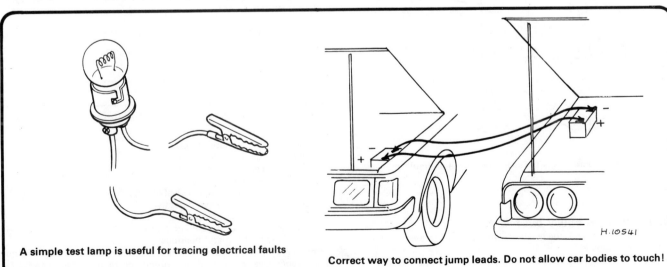

A simple test lamp is useful for tracing electrical faults

Correct way to connect jump leads. Do not allow car bodies to touch!

Starter motor turns engine slowly

Partially discharged battery (recharge, use jump leads, or push start)
Battery terminals loose or corroded
Battery earth to body defective
Engine earth strap loose
Starter motor (or solenoid) wiring loose
Starter motor internal fault (see Chapter 10)

Starter motor spins without turning engine

Flat battery
Starter motor pinion sticking on sleeve
Flywheel gear teeth damaged or worn
Starter motor mounting bolts loose

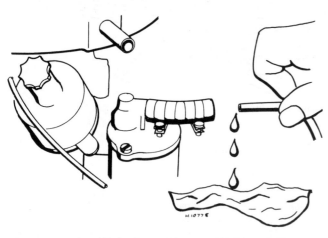

Remove fuel pipe from carburettor and check for fuel delivery

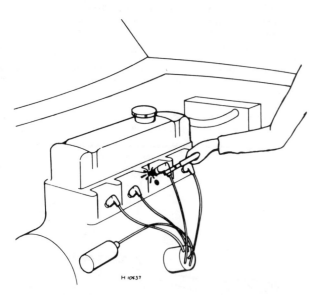

Crank engine and check for spark. Note use of insulated tool

Engine turns normally but fails to start

Damp or dirty HT leads and distributor cap (crank engine and check for spark)
Dirty or incorrectly gapped contact breaker points
No fuel in tank (check for delivery at carburettor)
Excessive choke (hot engine) or insufficient choke (cold engine)

Fouled or incorrectly gapped spark plugs (remove, clean and regap)
Other ignition system fault (see Chapter 4)
Other fuel system fault (see Chapter 3)
Poor compression (see Chapter 1)
Major mechanical failure (eg camshaft drive)

Engine fires but will not run

Insufficient choke (cold engine)
Air leaks at carburettor or inlet manifold
Fuel starvation (see Chapter 3)
Ballast resistor defective, or other ignition fault (see Chapter 4)

Engine cuts out and will not restart

Engine cuts out suddenly – ignition fault

Loose or disconnected LT wires
Wet HT leads or distributor cap (after traversing water splash)
Coil or condenser failure (check for spark)
Other ignition fault (see Chapter 4)

Engine misfires before cutting out – fuel fault

Fuel tank empty
Fuel pump defective or filter blocked (check for delivery)
Fuel tank filler vent blocked (suction will be evident on releasing cap)
Carburettor needle valve sticking
Carburettor jets blocked (fuel contaminated)
Other fuel system fault (see Chapter 3)

Engine cuts out – other causes

Serious overheating
Major mechanical failure (eg camshaft drive)

Engine overheats

Ignition (no-charge) warning light illuminated

Slack or broken drivebelt – retension or renew (Chapter 2)

Ignition warning light not illuminated

Coolant loss due to internal or external leakage (see Chapter 2)
Thermostat defective
Low oil level
Brakes binding
Radiator clogged externally or internally
Engine waterways clogged
Ignition timing incorrect or automatic advance malfunctioning
Mixture too weak

Note: *Do not add cold water to an overheated engine or damage may result*

Low engine oil pressure

Gauge reads low or warning light illuminated with engine running

Oil level low or incorrect grade
Defective gauge or sender unit
Wire to sender unit earthed
Engine overheating
Oil filter clogged or bypass valve defective
Oil pressure relief valve defective
Oil pick-up strainer clogged
Oil pump worn or mountings loose
Worn main or big-end bearings

Note: *Low oil pressure in a high-mileage engine at tickover is not necessarily a cause for concern. Sudden pressure loss at speed is far more significant. In any event, check the gauge or warning light sender before condemning the engine.*

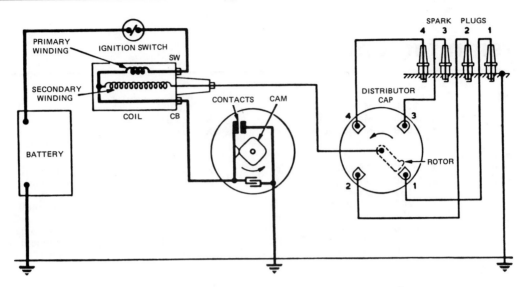

Ignition circuit diagram (models without ballast resistor)

Engine noises

Pre-ignition (pinking) on acceleration

Incorrect grade of fuel
Ignition timing incorrect
Distributor faulty or worn
Worn or maladjusted carburettor
Excessive carbon build-up in engine

Whistling or wheezing noises

Leaking vacuum hose
Leaking carburettor or manifold gasket
Blowing head gasket

Tapping or rattling

Incorrect valve clearances
Worn valve gear
Worn timing chain
Broken piston ring (ticking noise)

Knocking or thumping

Unintentional mechanical contact (eg fan blades)
Worn fanbelt
Peripheral component fault (generator, water pump etc)
Worn big-end bearings (regular heavy knocking, perhaps less under load)
Worn main bearings (rumbling and knocking, perhaps worsening under load)
Piston slap (most noticeable when cold)

Conversion factors

Length (distance)

Inches (in)	X	25.4	= Millimetres (mm)	X	0.0394	= Inches (in)
Feet (ft)	X	0.305	= Metres (m)	X	3.281	= Feet (ft)
Miles	X	1.609	= Kilometres (km)	X	0.621	= Miles

Volume (capacity)

Cubic inches (cu in; in³)	X	16.387	= Cubic centimetres (cc; cm³)	X	0.061	= Cubic inches (cu in; in³)
Imperial pints (Imp pt)	X	0.568	= Litres (l)	X	1.76	= Imperial pints (Imp pt)
Imperial quarts (Imp qt)	X	1.137	= Litres (l)	X	0.88	= Imperial quarts (Imp qt)
Imperial quarts (Imp qt)	X	1.201	= US quarts (US qt)	X	0.833	= Imperial quarts (Imp qt)
US quarts (US qt)	X	0.946	= Litres (l)	X	1.057	= US quarts (US qt)
Imperial gallons (Imp gal)	X	4.546	= Litres (l)	X	0.22	= Imperial gallons (Imp gal)
Imperial gallons (Imp gal)	X	1.201	= US gallons (US gal)	X	0.833	= Imperial gallons (Imp gal)
US gallons (US gal)	X	3.785	= Litres (l)	X	0.264	= US gallons (US gal)

Mass (weight)

Ounces (oz)	X	28.35	= Grams (g)	X	0.035	= Ounces (oz)
Pounds (lb)	X	0.454	= Kilograms (kg)	X	2.205	= Pounds (lb)

Force

Ounces-force (ozf; oz)	X	0.278	= Newtons (N)	X	3.6	= Ounces-force (ozf; oz)
Pounds-force (lbf; lb)	X	4.448	= Newtons (N)	X	0.225	= Pounds-force (lbf; lb)
Newtons (N)	X	0.1	= Kilograms-force (kgf; kg)	X	9.81	= Newtons (N)

Pressure

Pounds-force per square inch (psi; lbf/in²; lb/in²)	X	0.070	= Kilograms-force per square centimetre (kgf/cm²; kg/cm²)	X	14.223	= Pounds-force per square inch (psi; lbf/in²; lb/in²)
Pounds-force per square inch (psi; lbf/in²; lb/in²)	X	0.068	= Atmospheres (atm)	X	14.696	= Pounds-force per square inch (psi; lbf/in²; lb/in²)
Pounds-force per square inch (psi; lbf/in²; lb/in²)	X	0.069	= Bars	X	14.5	= Pounds-force per square inch (psi; lbf/in²; lb/in²)
Pounds-force per square inch (psi; lbf/in²; lb/in²)	X	6.895	= Kilopascals (kPa)	X	0.145	= Pounds-force per square inch (psi; lbf/in²; lb/in²)
Kilopascals (kPa)	X	0.01	= Kilograms-force per square centimetre (kgf/cm²; kg/cm²)	X	98.1	= Kilopascals (kPa)

Torque (moment of force)

Pounds-force inches (lbf in; lb in)	X	1.152	= Kilograms-force centimetre (kgf cm; kg cm)	X	0.868	= Pounds-force inches (lbf in; lb in)
Pounds-force inches (lbf in; lb in)	X	0.113	= Newton metres (Nm)	X	8.85	= Pounds-force inches (lbf in; lb in)
Pounds-force inches (lbf in; lb in)	X	0.083	= Pounds-force feet (lbf ft; lb ft)	X	12	= Pounds-force inches (lbf in; lb in)
Pounds-force feet (lbf ft; lb ft)	X	0.138	= Kilograms-force metres (kgf m; kg m)	X	7.233	= Pounds-force feet (lbf ft; lb ft)
Pounds-force feet (lbf ft; lb ft)	X	1.356	= Newton metres (Nm)	X	0.738	= Pounds-force feet (lbf ft; lb ft)
Newton metres (Nm)	X	0.102	= Kilograms-force metres (kgf m; kg m)	X	9.804	= Newton metres (Nm)

Power

Horsepower (hp)	X	745.7	= Watts (W)	X	0.0013	= Horsepower (hp)

Velocity (speed)

Miles per hour (miles/hr; mph)	X	1.609	= Kilometres per hour (km/hr; kph)	X	0.621	= Miles per hour (miles/hr; mph)

Fuel consumption*

Miles per gallon, Imperial (mpg)	X	0.354	= Kilometres per litre (km/l)	X	2.825	= Miles per gallon, Imperial (mpg)
Miles per gallon, US (mpg)	X	0.425	= Kilometres per litre (km/l)	X	2.352	= Miles per gallon, US (mpg)

Temperature

Degrees Fahrenheit = (°C x 1.8) + 32

Degrees Celsius (Degrees Centigrade; °C) = (°F - 32) x 0.56

*It is common practice to convert from miles per gallon (mpg) to litres/100 kilometres (l/100km), where mpg (Imperial) x l/100 km = 282 and mpg (US) x l/100 km = 235

Index

Suspension
  description – 185
  fault diagnosis – 200
  front
    displacer unit – 193, 194
  lower arm – 189
  upper arm – 189
  rear
    knocking noises – 224
    radius arm – 192
    reaction lever assembly – 193
  specifications – 184
  torque wrench settings – 185
  trim bar – 193
  trim height adjustment – 195
Switches *see under respective headings (starter motor etc)*

T

Tailgate – 213
Tamperproofed carburettors – 222
Tape players – 173
Tappets
  adjustment – 43
  refitting – 43
  removal – 27
  renovation – 37
Thermostat – 51
Thermostat housing – 52
Throttle cable – 64
Timing chain and sprockets
  refitting – 41
  removal – 29
  renovation – 38
Timing chain guides, removal – 30
Timing chain tensioner
  dismantling – 36
  refitting – 41
  removal – 30
Tools – 8
Towing – 10
Transmission
  automatic
    description – 121
    fault diagnosis – 126
    kickdown linkage – 124
    removal and refitting – 122
    reversing light switch – 122
    selector cables – 122
    selector lever mechanism – 125
    selector mechanism – 125
    specifications – 85
    starter inhibitor switch – 122
    torque wrench settings – 85

  manual gearbox
    component renovation – 98
    crankshaft primary gear endfloat – 85
    crankshaft primary gear oil seal – 87
    description – 85
    dismantling cable gearchange – 88
    dismantling rod gearchange – 95
    fault diagnosis – 121
    reassembly cable gearchange – 99
    reassembly rod gearchange – 108
    refitting to engine – 114
    remote control, adjustment (rod gearchange) – 121
    remote control, change speed cables – 118
    remote control, dismantling and reassembly – 118
    remote control, removal and refitting – 115
    remote control, selector shaft (rod gearchange) – 118
    reversing light switch – 121
    separation from engine – 88
    specifications – 84
    torque wrench settings – 84
Tyres
  excessive wear – 228
  pressures – 185
  type – 185

U

Underframe, maintenance – 201
Universal joints
  description – 127
  overhaul (ball type) – 127
  overhaul (roller type) – 129
  type – 127
Upholstery maintenance – 201

V

Valves
  reassembly – 43
  removal – 27
  renovation – 37
Vehicle identification numbers – 7
Ventilation air filter – 34
Voltage stabilizer – 170

W

Water pump – 52, 222
Weights – 6
Wheels – 185
Windscreen and rear glass – 210
Windscreen washer control – 218
Windscreen wiper – 163, 224
Wiring diagrams – 177 to 183, 225 to 227
Working facilities – 8

Printed by
Haynes Publishing Group
Sparkford Yeovil Somerset
England